Multivocali

Multivocality

*Singing on the Borders
of Identity*

KATHERINE MEIZEL

UNIVERSITY PRESS

Oxford University Press is a department of the University of Oxford. It furthers
the University's objective of excellence in research, scholarship, and education
by publishing worldwide. Oxford is a registered trade mark of Oxford University
Press in the UK and certain other countries.

Published in the United States of America by Oxford University Press
198 Madison Avenue, New York, NY 10016, United States of America.

© Oxford University Press 2020

All rights reserved. No part of this publication may be reproduced, stored in
a retrieval system, or transmitted, in any form or by any means, without the
prior permission in writing of Oxford University Press, or as expressly permitted
by law, by license, or under terms agreed with the appropriate reproduction
rights organization. Inquiries concerning reproduction outside the scope of the
above should be sent to the Rights Department, Oxford University Press, at the
address above.

You must not circulate this work in any other form
and you must impose this same condition on any acquirer.

CIP data is on file at the Library of Congress
ISBN 978-0-19-062147-6 (pbk.)
ISBN 978-0-19-062146-9 (hbk.)

1 3 5 7 9 8 6 4 2

Paperback printed by Marquis, Canada
Hardback printed by Bridgeport National Bindery, Inc., United States of America

To Wren Reeve and all mutable, un-mute-able voices.

Figure 0.1 Edvard Eriksen's statue of the Little Mermaid, Copenhagen Harbor. Photo by author.

My body is a body of songs,

and voices to sing them.

I'm Lucinda Williams under my breath along the cacophony of a music-school corridor, when a choral rehearsal washes over me. I can find no card for the piece in the catalog of me, but without permission, my prodigal soprano escapes of its own accord outside the hall. It knows the score, and it strains to sound and not be heard.

This voice remembers me. I recognize it like a second spine I'd forgotten, holding me up all my life silenced and embedded in in my flesh. It will take me an hour to think of Bruckner. The choir falls silent and I carry the song, in my portmanteau voice, home.

Contents

Acknowledgments ix

   Introduction 1

1. Finding a Voice 25
2. Vox Populi, Vox Divo: Voicing Genre Politics in Classical Crossover 49
3. Voice and Disjuncture in Celebrity Impersonation 71
4. Two Voices: Singers in the Hearing/Deaf Borderlands 91
5. Spiritual Multivocality 115
6. The Journey: Voice and Identity in Gender Transition 137
7. Voice Control 159
8. Lost Voices 177
9. Final Reflections: Hear Our Voice 197

Works Cited 217
Index 239

Acknowledgments

I am immensely indebted to all those who shared their experiences with me, and constantly humbled by their generosity in doing so. Each of them has been vital and integral to my study, and everything I've learned has been because of these talented singers. I congratulate them all on their brilliant work and their successes, and thank them for the kindness they have showed me. And my remarkable voice-major colleagues of long ago, and those who came after us, have made me so proud.

To fellow Oberlin Conservatory alumni Rhiannon Giddens, David Miller, Lilah Greendale Shapiro, Limmie Pulliam, Kati Roberts, and Ellen Wolf—

To fellow San Francisco Conservatory alumni Branden James, Daniel Montenegro, Breanna Sinclairé, Gary Ruschman, Jimmy Kansau, Melissa Canaday, Lara Bisserier, Heather Sung, and Kathryn Miller—

To fellow UCSB alumni Nichole Dechaine, Charlene Chi Kim, and Kristin Williams Baugher—

To other marvelous artists (and their managers), scholars, and friends who have taught me how to truly listen to voice—Véronic DiCaire and Rémon Boulerice, Larry Gawatz, TL Forsberg, Mandy Harvey, Janine Roebuck, Michelle Spurlock, Joshua Klipp, Simon DeVoil, Lucia Lucas, Anthony Russell, Lubana al-Quntar, Connie Lim, Lois Najarian, Marion Caffey, Áine Uí Cheallaigh, Joel Derfner, Adrian Dunn, Kaeley Pruitt-Hamm, Naomi Less, Sharon Azrieli-Perez, Wesla Whitfield, Jennifer Goode Cooper, Sean Cooper, Jennifer Grout, Cesar Ouatu, Jeff McNeal, Sheri Wells-Jensen, Adam O'Dell, Susanne Vanderhoef, Polina Proutskova, Nadia Chana, Sandy Cummings, Heather Stroschein, Kyle Fackrell and his class, Aeva Soler, Jerramiah Jean-Baptiste, Ashlyn Flamer, Christopher Doleman, Tyler Suarez, Tyler Jenkins, Saida Dahir, Ben Soto, Amalia Fleming, Madison Yearsley, Sawyer Garrity, Andrea Peña, Nina Lee, two singers who wished to remain anonymous, and two singers who withdrew from this research due to changes in their religious and celebrity statuses respectively. —

I thank you all from the depths of my heart for letting me listen to your voices. I hope you all write books, too.

One of the joys of this project has been an adjacent collaboration with Ron Scherer in Bowling Green State University's Department of Speech and Hearing Disorders, on our preliminary spectrographic study of singing impersonation. Sincerest thanks to Ron, and also to Stephan Pennington, Nadia Chana, Lee Tyson, and Holly Patch for sharing their work in progress, to my dear friend and voice-studies colleague Eve McPherson for the Herculean task of reading through the entire first-draft manuscript, to my friends and colleagues at BGSU Jeremy Wallach, Esther Clinton, Sidra Lawrence, and Mary Natvig for their suggestions and support, to Naomi André and Sarah Gerk for their feedback on the Introduction and chapter 2, and Jeannette DiBernardo Jones for her notes on chapter 4. Additionally, my co-editing work with ultimate voice scholar Nina Eidsheim, as well as inspiring and informative conversations with Nina Fales, Elyse Marrero, Chris Nickell, Arne Spohr, Alisha Jones, Shana Goldin-Perschbacher, Juniper Hill, with Martin Daughtry and Clara Latham at their voice symposium, with Elías Krell, Matt Rahaim, Denise Gill, Jim Grippo, and Caitlin Torres, have been immeasurably important to this book. I thank Will Cheng as well, for his groundbreaking and beautifully realized willingness to write about his own experience with disability. Finally, I've learned much from the work of graduate students both inside and outside of music studies whom I've advised on topics in voice—particularly Xinxin Jiang, Stephanie Salerno, Jeff Klein, and Alec Norkey—and they have left me optimistic and excited about where the transdisciplinary study of voice is going.

Special thanks to my family, 2,000 miles away, whose voices on the phone sustain me. And thank you to Suzanne Ryan, for her patience and advice throughout the book's long process.

Introduction

(I am large, I contain multitudes.)
—Walt Whitman, "Song of Myself"

On a foggy San Francisco day in 2004, I sat in an empty hallway with a fellow conservatory alumna, passing time until auditions began for the fourth season of *American Idol*. We belted out Appalachian ballads and traded tunes sharing her fiddle, against a sonic background of nervous would-be pop stars warming up. Though our paths had crossed in college, I hadn't met her until a mutual friend invited her to join us at the auditions—I was tagging along for my dissertation research, taking notes while they sang hurried, cattle-call covers in front of a judging panel. After we left the stadium, she gave me an autographed copy of her just-completed demo album, which she had titled *Many Voices*. The name referenced the album's collection of heterogeneous sounds and stories sung across western classical, blues, pop, and Scottish traditional styles, and the high lonesome timbres of American old-time music. A lifelong penchant for trying on and trying out different voices had made her, she later told me, "the supreme imitator," and by the time she finished her studies in opera, her musical flexibility had left her struggling with the question, "What *is* my voice?" *Many Voices*, she said later in retrospect, was her way of turning what could have been an identity crisis into an advantage in the music industry (Interview, November 3, 2012). And it did turn out to be an advantage. *American Idol*'s judges turned her away from the pop competition's 2005 season, but only a few years later Rhiannon Giddens became a founding member of the now Grammy Award-winning string band the Carolina Chocolate Drops,[1] then a celebrated solo artist, an actress with a recurring role on the CMT series *Nashville*, was tapped to star in a Broadway show, and in 2018 was the recipient of a MacArthur fellowship and host of an

---

[1] By 2018, she had released her first two solo albums, performed on tours that included *The Late Show with David Letterman*, was nominated for two solo Grammy awards, performed on *Austin City Limits*, and among other awards, won the Steve Martin Prize for Excellence in Banjo and Bluegrass. In 2016 she was hired to replace Audra McDonald in *Shuffle Along* on Broadway when McDonald left for maternity leave, but the show closed instead. She portrayed a recurring character on *Nashville*'s final seasons, which aired on CMT. In 2019, she released *Songs of Our Native Daughters* with Leyla McCalla, Amythyst Kiah, and Allison Russell, as well as *There is No Other* with Francesco Turrisi.

Multivocality. Katherine Meizel, Oxford University Press (2020). © Oxford University Press.
DOI: 10.1093/oso/ 9780190621469.003.0001

acclaimed podcast from the Metropolitan Opera and New York's WQXR. She has brought extensive public attention to the African origins of the banjo, to what Yunina Barbour-Payne has called, after Frank X Walker, the significance of Affrilachian music (Walker 2008, cited in Barbour-Payne 2016), and the history of Black and white shared traditions in the rural South. Her first solo album, *Tomorrow Is My Turn*, like *Many Voices*, contained blues, string band songs, and country music.

Each track on *Many Voices* featured singing generated by the same physiological apparatus in the same body, shaped and adjusted according to the aesthetics of each musical genre and style. But if a singular materiality constituting "Rhiannon Giddens's voice" remained the vehicle across all of these, how might the plurality declared in the title be accounted for? In western discourse, a singer's voice is often described as if it were a static possession, as if it were suited to only one fixed repertory or context ("she has an operatic voice" or "she has a country voice") while the realities of singing in the post-postcolonial, continuously globalizing, continuously commodifying 21st century may allow for—even require—movement and the plasticity to cross boundaries.

Those boundaries of genre and identity are complicated in Ms. Giddens's life, as they are in the lives of many Americans. With a white father, a mother of African American and Ocaneechi Native American heritage, with her own Welsh-derived name, the cultural influences of her youth in North Carolina, her classical vocal training, and her classically trained father's love for 1960s folk revival repertoire, Ms. Giddens has balanced a complex web of cultural relationships with interlocking systems of oppression. Her parents' marriage occurred only shortly after the 1967 *Loving v. Virginia* case ended anti-miscegenation laws, though her father was disinherited for his decision (John 2018). They divorced and Ms. Giddens grew up "spending equal time" (Davidson 2017) between her parents and their respective white and Black identities. And though she does not present herself as Native American, in high school she did also explore the music of that heritage as part of a powwow drum. Then, for the years she studied opera, as was typical at our school in the 1990s, she was not permitted to venture outside of western classical music. But after college she became serious about old-time and Celtic traditional music (Scottish and Irish), and blues. Her explorations were not without conflict. She has said that before she began to learn from Black fiddler Joe Thompson, and before the Carolina Chocolate Drops was formed, she "felt like I was 'sneaking' into this music that wasn't my own." The persistent cultural discourse that has segregated string band music as white and blues as Black "led to me feeling like an alien in what I find out is my own cultural tradition" (Giddens 2017). She has dedicated years to rediscovering and sharing that tradition. Today, Ms. Giddens is one of the world's foremost performers and historians of Black string band, vocal, banjo, and fiddle traditions.

Gathering the multiple strands of her cultural roots and interests, she has been able to firmly locate her identity in *place*. "Where I found my identity was when I realized that I'm from North Carolina" (Jones 2015). And the varied voices of North Carolina constitute her heritage. She has said:

> I'm a good ol' mixed-race North Carolinian. . . . There's an area in North Carolina where there are a lot of Blacks and Indians, and of course, a lot of mixing. I wouldn't be able to say exactly what percentages I am of this, that, or whatever, but we know, you know what I mean? I know history and I know family lore and the way we look. It's not like I would ever put myself forward as an Indian woman, but I'm always interested in finding out musically about these different pieces. I don't know if I have Celtic roots, but it doesn't matter to me, because the music of North Carolina has Celtic roots; that's all I need to know. (Murg 2015)

Additionally, in her recent solo work (such as her 2017 album *Freedom Highway*), first amid the rise of the Black Lives Matter movement and then the surge in public white supremacist activity since the 2016 election, she has focused on singing for those whose voices have been silenced. In particular, she has created original songs from slave narratives of the 19th century. When pressed about these songs at a concert in Greensboro, NC, she told her audience, "Someone asked me why I'm here. It's not to be on *Nashville*—though that's fun. And it's not to play with [country musician] Eric Church—though that's fun. It's to get these voices out" (Harrison 2017). She not only sings with the many material voices of her own body but also becomes a voice telling the story of her cultural history—"*my* history," she says, "where *I* come from" (interview, November 3, 2012)—and is an agent of voices silenced by enslavement, violence, marginalization, and the passage of time. This process of singing plurally, and of singing in a body that through its very existence implies the crossing of imposed boundaries, has not simply passively shaped her identity; it has also become a part of Ms. Giddens's strategy of self, narrated through multiple vocal subjectivities in ways that have become especially pervasive and especially crucial in the 21st century.

A Crisis of Voice

"We are experiencing a contemporary *crisis* of voice" in the West, critical sociologist Nick Couldry wrote in 2010, "across political, economic, and cultural domains, that has been growing for at least three decades" (Couldry 2010: 1–2; emphasis in original). For Couldry, this crisis is rooted in the hegemony of neoliberal doctrine, which in its market-centered framework rhetorically offers voice—in the sense of political, economic, and cultural agency—but in reality does not bestow it (2) and, in fact, works against the full practice of democracy.[2] Neoliberalism, at its core a revival of 19th-century free trade, has been assigned many definitions in the contexts of ideology, discourse, political economy, and governance (Türken et al. 2015). For geographer and anthropologist David Harvey, it is a political-economic theory that holds up "the maximization of entrepreneurial freedoms" as the ultimate vehicle for human well-being (Harvey 2007: 22) and impacts all aspects of a society. Attractive in the 1980s for its hypothetical potential to restore global capital accumulation after the recession and discontent of the 1970s, neoliberalism argues for institutional decentralization, privatization, and the individualization of entrepreneurship and consumerism. It is, as Luigi Esposito and Lauren Finley term it, the "dominant political-economic paradigm of our time" (Esposito and Finley 2014: 76).[3] And Harvey remarks that it has become globally naturalized partly because its rhetoric positions it as a solution to perceived threats against individual freedoms (Harvey 2007)—perceived threats not only from foreign political forces but also from any state policies favoring collective over individual judgement (24), or favoring the communal well-being of citizens over the integrity of financial institutions (31). Harvey suggests that the application of neoliberalism, instead of solving the global capital crisis, has, despite rhetoric promising fair competition, only served to revitalize the dominance of the upper classes (29). And as economic inequality is entangled with other ideologies of dominance, particularly the colonial legacy and white supremacy, neoliberalism also reinforces the marginalization of racialized, gendered, and disabled identities.

In order to comprehend and disrupt the suppression of voice sustained by neoliberalism, Couldry argues, voice itself is best understood as both a *process* and a *value*. At its core, voice as a process comprises "the act of giving an account of oneself [after Butler 2005], and the immediate conditions and qualities of that process" (Couldry 2010: 3): a kind of reflexive agency. The idea of voice as a value is one that *supports* this practice of giving account (8). Valuing voice recognizes every person as a "narratable self" (Cavarero 2000: 34, cited in Couldry 2010: 99), and defends "the potential of voices anywhere to matter" (Couldry 2010: 9). Failing consideration of voice as a value, the only voices allowed to matter are those embedded in the bodies allowed to matter, in the selves and that are deemed acceptably narratable, and in the gazes that determine

---

[2] As Marnie Holborow writes, "[w]hat neoliberalism says and what it does constantly diverge" (Holborow 2015: 9).
[3] Robert McChesney, in his foreword to Noam Chomsky's *Profit over People: Neoliberalism and Global Order*, similarly writes, "Neoliberalism is the defining political economic paradigm of our time" (McChesney 1999: 7).

such acceptability. The inequalities perpetuated in a neoliberal rationality—racialized, gendered, ability-based, and intertwined with economic disparities—are entangled in a market system in which what matters is what sells and what sells is what matters. Couldry cautions against ostensible offers of voice that in fact support the market system rather than true agency, providing nothing more than "opportunity to compete as a commodity" (13). Twenty-first-century televised singing competitions like *American Idol* have demonstrated this over and over again, seemingly giving all young artists and a national audience an equal, democratic opportunity to be heard, but ultimately simply shaping them into profitable products and desirable consumers (Meizel 2011b. For more on the ways *Idol* illuminates the tensions between economic liberalism and democracy, see Stahl 2013).

In this book, I argue that singing with "many voices" may be seen as a practice *at once produced by and resistant to these neoliberal expectations*. On the one hand, the ideal neoliberal subject is not only a self-regulating and perpetually developing, saleable commodity but also an entire solo enterprise in itself. As Dale Chapman writes, such a subject is expected to be "a kind of multitasking virtuoso, whose acquisition of multiple skill sets enables her to remain an agent, rather than object, of volatile market conditions" (Chapman 2013: 452). Chapman understands the contemporary "one-man band," or live solo multi-instrumentalist, as a musical subject whose mode of practice fulfills this requirement. Singing with many voices might serve a similar purpose for the solo singer seeking, and creating, their[4] own space in the music industry. Additionally, the entanglement of neoliberalism, cultural imperialism, globalization, and multiculturalism, further enabled by continually improving, technology-driven access to an immeasurable range of musics, has fostered a widespread, often appropriative musical eclecticism that can mirror the superficial essentialisms of multiculturalist diversity discourse. In the United States, for example, listeners and singers alike may participate in music cultures inside and outside of their own cultural backgrounds, in the name of an American nationalism that prematurely celebrates victory over white supremacy. Jodi Melamed writes of early 21st-century U.S. neoliberal multiculturalism that:

> Today neoliberal multiculturalism incorporates a supra-nationalism into racial formation that privileges the [white] multicultural American citizen as a subject more universal and legitimate than even the multicultural world citizen. Correspondingly, it stigmatizes some forms of personhood seen to conflict with

---

[4] In the interest of inclusivity and acknowledgment of nonbinary gender identities, in this book I use singular they/them/their pronouns, rather than "he or she," when referring to a non-specific person.

neoliberal subjectivity as "monocultural" and therefore lesser. Multicultural reference sustains both sides of the new privilege/stigma dichotomy. (Melamed 2006: 18)

Musical performance that reflects an eclectic, superficial multiculturalism—such as a white singer's adoption and appropriation of multiple music cultures and vocal practices—can reinforce this dichotomy.

On the other hand, singers, especially artists of color like Ms. Giddens, may use multiple ways of singing to create otherwise-denied spaces where their self-narrations can sound. Though such narrations are always unique to each person, they are also always intersubjective. Couldry observes that, due to its inherently relational nature, voice as a value *cannot* be individualist (2010: 9). And because a neoliberal society tends to celebrate above all a competitive (hyper-)individualism that denies the intersubjective complexity of self and identity, I suggest that singing with many voices can also become a form of resistance: a way to narrate oneself that *values* the intersubjective process of voice, therefore functioning as a counter-rational tactic against neoliberalism.

Furthermore, it can work to bolster democratic principles against what Couldry calls the "fiction of 'neoliberal democracy'" (Couldry 2010: 47). Adriana Cavarero points to vocal *plurality*, which she names "pluriphony," as a foundation of democracy—rather than the discursively persistent idea of the masses sounding in unison. In the age of "post-truth," she argues, it isn't the voice of the people but, rather, *the voices of people* that generate the "soundscape of democracy-in-the-making" (Cavarero et al. 2018: 84). Thus, the sounding of any person's multiple, intersubjective voices might be heard as democratic, as well. And when singers like Ms. Giddens raise their voices for those who have been silenced by death, time, and history, that soundscape of democracy in progress is both broadened and more clearly defined.

Given the work it does, singing in any voice may be considered a social practice of being-in-the-world (Heidegger 1962) and of acting in the world. In 1966, avant-garde composer and singer Cathy Berberian associated this function with the concept of *vocality*, encouraging classical singers to explore diverse ways of singing—using a fuller range of vocal aspects and capabilities—as "'ways of being' for the voice and to develop a "New Vocality" (Berberian 2014[1966]: 47). Vocality also forms a crucial part of Steven Feld's notion of *acoustemology*, which constitutes an emplaced, "sonic way of knowing and being in the world" (Feld and Brenneis 2004: 462). For many singers, vocality as epistemology and ontology encompasses not only the discrete sets of linguistic and vocal practices and sounds embedded in the various music cultures they invoke, but also the many points of view and the many stories that have informed their personal experiences of identity.

This book centers on singers like Ms. Giddens, whose many voices are perhaps best understood as multiple vocalities: multiple ways of being and acting in the world through voice, and of applying the intersubjectivity and interstitiality of voice to navigate the in-betweens and border crossings of 21st-century identities. My research has sought intersections of the material and the metaphorical, culture and consciousness in the vocal negotiation of identity. In studying vocalities as vocal ways of being, I locate sounds, practices, techniques, and meanings in the context of singers'[5] experiential truths, and in the complex epistemologies of voice that reflect and shape self and culture. Furthermore, when singers habitually perform across stylistic, genre, cultural, and historical borders, I suggest that not only are they performing in multiple vocalities but, more critically, they are *performing multivocality*—that is, negotiating their narratable selves by singing with many voices.

Brief History of Vocality

Vocality, in its most common usage, simply denotes the presence and/or use of voice, usually having emanated from a human body.[6] However, as Berberian notes, its corporeality, its materiality, makes up only half the story. A brief cross-disciplinary reexamination of the term's readings past and present highlights ways of singing as vocal ways of being, and as sites where the production of sound intersects with colonial structures of power.

Vocality seems to have entered the academic musical lexicon toward the beginning of the twentieth century, with the earliest iterations I have found occurring in two divergent contexts. Scholars of psychoacoustics in the 1910s and 1920s (e.g., Modell and Rich 1915; Weiss 1920) hypothesized a structural correlation between tuning-fork tones and vowels, a vocality of acoustic configuration, or a *vowel-ness*, a human sound perceived within the "pure tone" of the tuning fork's sinusoidal wave. But later that empirical definition was replaced with a performative one that suggests ways of singing as sites of power relations. When a group of musicologists (Bairstow et al. 1929) broached the idea of vocality in *Music and Letters*, they were inquiring how one might determine whether a piece of music was suitable for singing—a question of its *vocality* or *unvocality*. In the printed conversation, British scholar Edward J. Dent raised issues of status and appropriative practices as important factors in such judgments. Taking up the question

---

[5] In this study, I am working with a definition of *singer* that includes those who generally self-identify as singers and also those who have self-identified that way within the framework of any specific musical context. Though many of my consultants have sung professionally, not all of them have.

[6] Some text in this section was previously published in "A Powerful Voice: Studying Vocality and Identity" (Meizel 2011a: 267–273). Used with permission. www.tandfonline.com

of why folk song seemed "vocal enough but difficult to sing well" (Bairstow et al. 1929: 235), Dent, instead of merely citing aesthetics, pointed to class relations. He wrote that:

> People may possibly have come by now to accept folksongs as national possessions, but for a long time it was as much a matter of pretence [sic] as Marie Antoinette's dairymaiding. Cultivated singers had ... to acquire a style which suggested the manner of the imaginary peasants ... and at the same time to sing their songs sufficiently well ... to make them a success in the concert-room.... The difficulty of singing folksongs is mainly a matter of self-consciousness, vanity and snobbery. (Bairstow et al. 1929: 240–241)

For Dent, the appropriateness of folk songs to the voice was never itself in question; instead, he argued, the trouble classically trained singers had in performing them was due to both an inevitable unawareness of lower-class cultural practices and a *hyper*-awareness of economic distinctions. "Folk" and "concert-room" ways of singing, he believed, involved irreconcilable differences of class and practice and, critically, power.

Feld et al. have examined ways in which voice is constructed as a "metaphor for difference" and as a "key representational trope for identity, power, conflict, social position, and agency," a framework that positions vocality as a social practice "understood as an implicit index of authority, evidence, and experiential truth" (Feld et al. 2004: 341). Ontological and epistemological discourse about vocality has indeed long been tied up in discourses of power, within a set of interlaced histories, of European modernity, colonialism, and the institutionalized study of humanity. Documents from the early years of Europe's colonial project show that voices were heard even then as markers of cultural identity and difference. In the 16th century, for example, the voice became a locus for Calvinist missionary Jean de Léry's experience of difference in Portuguese Brazil, as he watched Tupinambá ritual participants dancing and singing, and heard voices shifting from what he called "tuneable" and "pleasing" to "muttering," "trembling," and "howl[ing]," signaling to de Léry what he believed must be possession by the Devil (de Léry 1578)—a vocalized and embodied difference, essentially, of the soul.

By the time European colonial expansion peaked in the second half of the 19th century, the inscription of voices with difference had become an ideological instrument of domination. And it has remained so. In 1992, invoking the legacy of 19th-century geopolitics, voice coach Patsy Rodenburg cautioned performers against what she called "vocal imperialism," or the belief in "one right voice" (Rodenburg 1992: 105)—a hegemony similar to what John Potter identifies as "vocal authority" (Potter 2006 [1998]). This imperialism is not metaphorical but, rather, a literality. Ana María Ochoa Gautier, in her groundbreaking study of the intertwined production and hearing of voice in 19th-century Colombia, positions colonized vocality as "untamed" in the eyes of European colonizers, part of an orality she understands as a "historical mode of *audibility* of the voice" strategically controlled by state aurality (Ochoa Gautier 2014). And considering musicologist Nina Sun Eidsheim's argument that voice is created by the listener as much as by the singer (2019: 157), state aurality and the listening gaze of colonizing powers become paramount in the discussion of vocality. For example, during the period when the British Empire was staking its most expansive geographical claims, the voice came to be treated there explicitly as a site of difference among the world's peoples. Ideas about nation and race were tangled then, but to some, the racialized body, including its vocality as constructed by the British aural gaze, was indicative of national or regional character. In 1869, laryngologist Sir G. Duncan Gibb delivered a paper on the voice to the Anthropological Society of London (published in 1870). He spoke his position plainly, identifying Europe as "the cradle of song" and the European voice as superior to the "Asiatic and African" (Gibb 1870: 258). Some voices he deemed to be "powerful"—German and Tartar (Tatar)[7] voices, both male and female—and some to be "weak"—Chinese, Japanese, and perhaps most significantly the colonized Indian voice. He guessed that the cause of such weakness, and the differences he associated with various ways of singing, might lie in the structure of the larynx (see also Meizel 2011b for further discussion of Gibb's paper). Gibb's views, based largely on anecdotal sources and unsystematic observations, and delivered to an audience with a polygenesist agenda, are untenable in the 21st century, particularly because no scientific evidence has ever been found of any morphological laryngeal or skeletal characteristics indicative of race. Musicologist Nina Eidsheim has explained that, instead, any racialized differences listeners hear are "based on the flexibility and possibility of the instrument, and the choices made" as to the vocal qualities emphasized (Eidsheim 2008: 33). In other words, racializations of vocality, like race itself, are perhaps best considered as social constructs.

Some have also suggested that the sonic characteristics of different languages might shape distinct vocalities, creating disparate ways of singing among cultures. At the height of the Enlightenment, as cultural tensions strained the relations between France and Italy, and as the seeds were planted for the rise of the nation-state, Jean-Jacques Rousseau famously found proto-national identity in the voice as shaped by language. He suggested in his *Dictionnaire de Musique* that dissimilarities between spoken French and Italian led directly to different

---

[7] Turkic peoples then largely inhabiting a swath of central and northern Asia, including today's Russia and neighboring states, and Manchuria in China. (While sometimes European sources conflate the Turkic and Mongol peoples of the region, Gibb does separate them in his assessment.) It is worth noting also that Gibb was praising the power of German voices on the eve of German unification (1871) and the establishment of the German Empire.

modes of singing (Rousseau 1975[1779]). This is a possibility that Sally Sanford also raised twenty years ago in the service of historical performance practice, proposing that the two languages' characteristic patterns of airflow (she offered the Italian phrase "mamma mia" to demonstrate a variable airflow, and the French "ma mère" to demonstrate a continuous one) led to discrete, lasting French and Italian "schools of breathing" and singing techniques in the 17th century (Sanford 1995).

In the later 20th century, as language became a central focus of epistemological inquiry, raising questions about the written and the spoken, literary theorist Paul Zumthor (1987) proposed vocality (*vocalité*) as an intermediate or intermediary point between orality and literacy, in order to circumvent the binary and allow for the possibility of their intersection. His argument, motivated by a neglect of the human voice in the study of poetics, was followed shortly by Ursula Schaefer's (Schaefer1992, Schaefer 1993), in which the field she called *Vokalität* provided a way to acknowledge the continued significance of the voice—here referring to the oral—in the context of literacy (Schaefer 1993: 205). In light of Edward Dent's assessment of folk song in the hands (or throats) of classically trained singers, and other musics that traverse the space between oral and written culture, this updated definition may be especially appropriate.

Musicologists Leslie Dunn and Nancy Jones provided one of the most thorough discussions of vocality in the introduction to their 1994 book *Embodied Voices*, arguing for its interpretation as a cultural construct. They distinguished the concept of vocality from that of *voice* as a "shift from a concern with the phenomenological roots of voice to a conception of vocality as a cultural construct" and as a site where "non-verbal meanings" are made. They acknowledged that voices "inhabit an intersubjective acoustic space," suggesting that a study of vocal meaning must include the "contexts of their hearing" (Dunn and Jones 1994: 2). Drawing on French poststructuralist thinking, they described *vocality* as "all of the voice's manifestations"—speaking, singing, crying, laughing—including and beyond linguistic content. This kind of vocality encompasses both the *pheno-song* and *geno-song* that Roland Barthes introduced: the verbal, linguistic text juxtaposed with the nonverbal, embodied meanings that he famously heard as the "grain of the voice" (Barthes 1977). Barthes, in his *Image, Music, Text*, was also exploring the ties among different forms of human communication, and found in his "grain" something like the middle ground between orality and literacy that Zumthor would locate in vocality—"The sung writing of language," Barthes expounded (185). Barthes's grain, though, linked the oral and the written not simply with the voice but also explicitly with the *body*. For Barthes, the "grain" is "the body in the voice as it sings . . . the hand as it writes, the limb as it performs" (188). And significantly, the burden of embodiment does not fall only on the singer; it is borne by the listener as well. "If I perceive the 'grain'. . . "

Barthes wrote, "I am determined to listen to my *relation with* the body of the man or woman singing" (188; my emphasis). That relationship between the singer and the listener is another crucial theme in the study of vocality. In an application of linguistic anthropology that recalls Rousseau's language divide, Steven Feld et al. chart vocality as a site where music and language meet, serving among the body's primary technologies of difference—where human beings first learn to hear distinct individualities, to aurally separate our own voices from others' (Feld et al. 2004).

Psycholinguist Marie-Cécile Bertau and philosopher Volker Schürmann, in a set of 2008 call-and-response essays, debate the relative significance of both material and abstract conceptions of vocality in the construction of self. Bertau recalls psychologist Lev Vygotsky's assertion that "Through others, we become ourselves" (Vygotsky 1998: 170), and that one must "go *through*" others—must be mediated by others—to reach a sense of self (Bertau 2008b: 124). In other words, vocality (as Eidsheim observes) must be received and interpreted by others in order to impact identity. Schürmann reasons that the idea of vocality as "principle," as an abstraction or as a metaphor, is vital because if it were *only* material, then given "the constitutive effect of the uttered and listened to voice on a self" (Bertau 2008b: 125), people who live and communicate non-vocally or nonverbally—he gives the example of the Deaf community—would have no self, an idea that is clearly patently false (Schürmann 2008). This is, of course, also an idea that has been a heavy force in the oppression of d/Deaf and disabled people, including non-speaking Autistic people and people with neurological or other disabilities whose voices are sometimes out of voluntary control. Audible speech perceived as intelligible has long been, problematically, associated with cognitive and agentive competence.

Perhaps most significantly for the purposes of this book, Holly Patch and Tomke König (2018) emphasize vocality as *lived experience*. Framing the voices of transgender singers within Karen Barad's model of the phenomenon as "*the ontological inseparability/entanglement of intra-acting 'agencies'*" (Barad 2007: 139; emphasis in original), they explain vocality as "the phenomenon that encompasses yet is irreducible to the following (non-exhaustive) intra-acting aspects of the vocal: physical, physiological, biological, representational, constructed, embodied, performative, and lived" (Patch and König 2018: 32).

Given all these interlaced frameworks, in this book I interpret vocality as both an embodied act and a constructive process—as a way of singing inscribed and reinscribed with the lived experience of vocal sounds (linguistic and extralinguistic), practices, techniques, and meanings that factor into the making of culture and identity, and in the negotiation of power. *Multivocality*, then, denotes the performance of many such ways of singing, and highlights the breadth and depth of vocal intersubjectivity.

Multivocality

Multivocality is an idea most strongly associated with Victor Turner's studies of ritual and with studies of Mikhail Bakhtin's literary theory.[8] For Turner, it describes a symbol with diverse or ambiguous meanings and transformative power; the singing voice itself is nothing, if not this. Though the precise term *multivocality* does not appear in a complete English-language translation of Bakhtin's writing, it has nevertheless become, through later scholars' analyses, a popular way of referring to his understanding of intersubjectivity in Dostoevsky's novels. For Bakhtin, voice comprises not only the linguistic and sonic aspects of speech utterance but also its embedded ideologies (Park-Fuller 1986): it is "the speaking personality, the speaking consciousness. A voice always has a will or desire behind it, its own timbre and overtones" (Bakhtin 1981: 434). In his framework, all utterances contain traces of multiple languages (heteroglossia) and multiple voices (polyphony). A Dostoyevsky novel, Bakhtin argues, is characterized by a collective, dialogical authorial voice that highlights the ability of a person's utterance to embody another's while nevertheless remaining itself, creating a dialogic relationship between the two voices (Park-Fuller 1986). Bakhtin locates in Dostoyevsky's work "[a] *plurality of independent and unmerged voices and consciousnesses, a genuine polyphony of fully valid voices*" (1984: 6; emphasis in original). Bakhtin's concept has been translated, as in the quote here, as *polyphony*, but also as *polyvocality* and *multi-voicedness* (Belova et al. 2008: 494)—or, as in Jacob Mey's influential analysis, as *multivocality* (Mey 1998)—all referring to the management of the many voices inherent in dialogic speech.

Mey emphasizes that among the "multiplicity of social voices" (Bakhtin 1981: 263; Mey 1998: 154) in Bakhtin, each is autonomous, and they *do not blend together* to make a cohesive whole, though they may be "orchestrated" by an author to create his novel's narrative text (Mey 1998: 154) and achieve a "unity of a higher order than in homophony" (Bakhtin 1984: 21). Bakhtin understands that amid the heteroglot voices in this text, the writer's "own voice must also sound; these voices create the background necessary" for this to happen, and cannot be truly heard without them (Bakhtin 1981: 278).

Voice itself, to Bakhtin, is "the speaking personality, the speaking consciousness. A voice always has a will or desire behind it, its own timbre and overtones" (Bakhtin 1981: 434). His notions of multi-voicedness and of polyphony in Dostoevsky's novels *never indicate any kind of singular unity* but, rather, always a dialogue, with different voices independently working "as a communion of unmerged souls" (Bakhtin 1984: 26). Nevertheless, many have sought to translate this model to the

---

[8] A small portion of the text in this section is drawn from my chapter "Find Your Voice: Narratives of Women's Voice Loss in American Popular Culture," (Meizel 2019).

text of the individual postmodern experience, and to the construction of personal identity. For Julie Choi, in her work on writing the autoethnography of her own transnational identity, Bakhtin's voices encompass "the realities, value systems, and beliefs of the characters (Choi 2013: 161). By "timbres and overtones," she believes, Bakhtin implies that a voice has its own role, "a distinct character . . . shaped by particular histories, practices, desires and so on" (108). In Choi's narrative of self, she chooses the term *multivocality* to describe the multiplicity of voices that constitute her Korean American identity, preferring it over *multilinguality*. After Makoni and Pennycook (2007), she notes that replacing *multilinguality* with *multivocality* signals "a break away from the enumerative strategy of counting languages and fixed ideas of language as formal systems or undifferentiated wholes with rigid boundaries" (Choi 2013: 30). Makoni and Pennycook worry that the use of multilingualism as a way to talk about diversity only rehearses the "tropes of colonial invention, overlooking the contested history of language inventions, and ignoring the . . . [damage] that their embedded notions of language may be perpetrating" (Makoni and Pennycook 2007: 16; also cited in Choi 2013: 27). Additionally, reifying bilinguality and multilinguality reinforces the idea that monolinguality is natural, despite the historical and present situation to the globalized contrary (Bailey 2007: 262; cited in Choi 2013: 27).

For these reasons, as well as the extralingual components indicated in my definition of vocality, to me multivocality in singing is precisely analogous neither to multilinguality nor to the related concept of *code-switching*. Code-switching, as defined by Kathryn A. Woolard, refers generally to "an individual's use of two or more language varieties in the same speech event or exchange" (2004: 73–74); it may involve the speaking of multiple languages, styles of one language, multiple dialects, or multiple registers. But similarly to Choi's argument for multivocality over multilinguality, Vershawn Ashanti Young points out that the pervasive dominant-language model of code-switching fallaciously "persuades us to imagine" that there is a uniformly standard English language spoken by white Americans, that this standard language is superior to the minoritized dialects relegated to non-public (non-white) spaces, and that in order to be economically successful—a socially mobile neoliberal subject—it is necessary to communicate using this standard English in public (white) spaces (Young 2009: 68–69).[9] To address such problems, Rampton, in the 1990s, proposed another framework for studying these processes: code *crossing*, or communicative movement across ethnic, racial, and community boundaries (Rampton 1995[10])—in other words,

---

[9] For a cinematic treatment of code-switching, see the surreal 2018 film *Sorry to Bother You*, in which a Black telemarketer discovers the importance of sounding white on the phone, illustrating what writer A. T. McWilliams calls the "power and potential peril" of code-switching, and the "tragedy of assimilation" (McWilliams 2018).
[10] See also Rampton 2014 [2005].

vocolinguistic border crossing. (Rampton cites Bakhtin's *double-voicedness* as a parallel. Young draws on W. E. B. Du Bois's concept of double consciousness [Du Bois 1903[11]].)

Multivocality, in this book, constitutes such border crossings within the context of singing. Multivocal singers are often those who must continuously identify and cross borders in their everyday lives—singers of color, singers who are immigrants, or singers navigating gender, ethnic, even religious boundaries. But even singers fitting a hegemonic profile must confront, although certainly with less at stake, the vocal borders of identity.

Navigating Borderscapes Through Multivocality

Martha Feldman observes that voices tend to exist "in the interstices of encounters, the spaces of transition, the spaces in between" (Feldman 2015: 658). At once delineating and mitigating the internal–external borders of the body as it sounds, and working similarly across the geographical and ideological borders of cultural spaces, voices make exquisitely valuable instruments of de-bordering and re-bordering, of border-dwelling and border-crossing. They do not merely exist in interstitial spaces; they help to create, re-create, and reshape the spaces in which they resonate—intertwined with the construction of bodies, identities, relationships. And the need to voice border experiences can generate singers. Living in "a state of psychic unrest" in the ideological and psychological space of a Borderland,[12] Gloria Anzaldúa wrote, "is what makes poets write and artists create" (Anzaldúa 1987: 73). Of her own creativity, translating from the Náhuatl in *Cantares Mexicanos*,[13] she continued:

> My flowers shall not cease to live;
> My songs shall never end:
> I, a singer, intone them;
> They become scattered, they are spread about. (73)

---

[11] Though *The Souls of Black Folk* (1903) is cited most often, Du Bois first presented this concept in an 1897 essay, "The Strivings of the Negro People," published in *The Atlantic Monthly*, August, pp. 194–197.

[12] Through capitalization of the initial *b*, Anzaldúa distinguishes between geographical borderlands and psychic/ideological Borderlands. For the sake of simplicity, I have not capitalized it in my own usage.

[13] The *Cantares Mexicanos* is a collection of Náhuatl-language songs, or *cuicatl*, transliterated into Roman alphabet at some point in the 16th century. It is noteworthy also that for scholars of "Aztec" culture (the term applied by colonial scholarship to the Triple Alliance of Nahua peoples led by the Mexica who flourished from 1428 until Hernán Cortés's arrival in 1521), the Náhuatl expression *in xochitl in cuicatl*, typically translated as "flower and song," has come to be interpreted as a reference to poetry (Tomlinson 1995: 364).

As, despite growing white supremacist and other hegemonic opposition, an increasing number of individuals understand their identities as intersectional, identify as multiracial (Saulny 2011), live across multiple cultures, move between religions (Green 2017), and identify as non-binary, gender-fluid, and transgender, borderland voices are sounding more and more urgently. And the sounding of voices across perceived borders—and the capacity of voice, the *need* for voice, to simultaneously claim space for marginalized identities and erode boundaries in resistance to systems of oppression—has been thrown into new relief.

Marie-Cécile Bertau, summarizing Hubert J. M. Hermans, observes that "The spatialization of self . . . allows for simultaneously different positions, and for movement between these positions. The *I* moves in this space, having the capacity to 'endow each position with a voice' (Hermans 1996), thus establishing dialogical relationships between positions" (Bertau 2007: 96). This movement among subject positions—called voices—Bertau writes, tends to be interpreted as extremely changeable or extremely rigid, the two notions always at once in conflict and complementary (133).

In the process of multivocal movement between positions or voices, borders come into play. In the 2015 colloquy titled "Why Voice Now?," in the *Journal of the American Musicological Society*, convener Martha Feldman discusses Emily Wilbourne's contribution, summarizing her reminder that voice operates at various borders, most significantly "*the border of the human*" (Feldman 2015: 658; emphasis in original). Suzanne Cusick, in 1999, wrote that "All voices, but especially singing voices, perform the borders of the body" (Cusick 1999: 29, also cited in Krell 2015). Elías Krell writes about voices in the context of sonic borderlands, which they define as "a theoretical and experiential marker for identities and bodies that occupy geographic and discursive borderlands" (Krell 2015: 95). Voices separate the humanly internal from the external; they contain and divide bodily spaces, and are used to contain and divide bodies. Vocalities function as sociopolitical spaces at the borders of the human body. They partition discourses of genre, gender, race, class, religion, and in doing so become contested spaces—sites where laryngeal structures intersect with power structures and where identities are negotiated. Thus, in this book, in addition to approaching multivocality as a navigational instrument in the borderlands of identity, I examine voice as a *borderscape* in itself.

The idea of the borderscape became popular in the first decade of the 21st century across several disciplines, and itself is a multivocal concept. For social geographer Anke Strüver, it builds upon Arjun Appadurai's inscription of the *-scape* suffix with implications of flow—cultural flow, information flow, the flow of capital and ideas, and significantly, the flow of populations through tourism, labor, and both voluntary and forced migrations (Appadurai 1990). A borderscape is not a physical place for Strüver but, rather, a site that highlights a confluence of processes. The mapping of borders, Strüver writes, "*'takes place'* through representations, through performative acts, through acts of narration, visualisation, and imagination, including their interpretations—and can be conceived as *borderscaping*," which she defines as the application of "practices through which the imagined border is established and experienced as real" (Strüver 2005: 170; emphasis in original).

In a 2007 book titled *Borderscapes: Hidden Geographies and Politics at Territory's Edge*, geographers Prem Kumar Rajaram and Carl Grundy-Warr examine the concept of borderscape, reminding readers that geographical "[b]order spaces are zones of specific social interactions that give a particular meaning" (Rajaram and Grundy-Warr 2007: xxix). Their understanding of the term *borderscape*[14] highlights "the inherent contestability of the meaning of the border between belonging and non-belonging" (xxviii), and thus its continuous generation of resistances (xxix). A borderscape is even *identifiable*, not geographically but in those very conflicts that arise to negotiate inclusion and exclusion (xxviii). And it is fluid, they write, and never static, "because it is a zone of multiple actors and multiple bodies each calling on different histories [and] solidarities" and invoking "experiences, economies, and politics that are concealed" (xxix). In my framework, voice as borderscape works in these precise ways. Voice is a zone of meaning-making social interaction; a battleground of inclusion and exclusion involving multiple actors, bodies, histories, and solidarities; and the sounding of concealed politics.

Geographer Chiara Brambilla (2015) proposes that a renewed emphasis on borderscapes, studied through the three axes of epistemology, ontology, and methodology, will push critical border studies "towards a new *politics of becoming* based on a *pluritopical* and *plurivocal* interpretation of borders" (29; emphasis in original). In *Multivocality*, I take that directive literally, to study *how singers navigate borderscapes through multiple vocal ways of being*. Border-studies methodology, Brambilla asserts, should be (after Crampton 2009) "*performative, participatory, political*" (Brambilla 2015: 28; emphasis in original); research should attend to the performativity of border-making, the researcher's approach should work to empower the political agencies and subjectivities of those who cross borders, and the work must advance:

> a knowledge capable of throwing light on a space of negotiating actors, experiences, and representations articulated at the intersection of competing and even conflicting tensions revealing the border also as "a site of struggle." By

---

[14] They reference one of the book's authors, Suvendrini Perera, in this discussion; see Perera 2007.

highlighting the role of borders as sites of struggle where *the right to become* can be expressed, the borderscapes method opens a new space of political possibilities, a space within which new kinds of political subjectivities become possible. (29; emphasis in original)

If voice can be a borderscape, then vocalities offer multiple, often compound paths to navigate it. *Multivocality* explores singing voices as sites of struggle and becoming, negotiating material and sonic borders between musical genres, between ideologies, between cultures. Examining the border experiences of singers, the book aims to illuminate the role of voice in multiple types of social epistemologies and ontological processes.

It is also crucial to recognize that for many singers, including Ms. Giddens, multivocality—as the enactment of multiple vocal ways of being—can figure as a sonic negotiation of intersectionality, a strategic intervention that supports the political use of voice against multiple, intertwined systems of oppression. As I suggested earlier in this introduction, multivocality can be a form of resistance.

Recently, some writers on voice have concentrated their work on the relationship between singing and listening practices, or on the perception/reception of vocal sound. In particular, Nina Eidsheim elucidates both the act of singing and the act of listening as cultivated, cultured vibratory practices (Eidsheim 2015) and highlights the contribution of listening to the collective voice (Eidsheim 2019: 53). In this book, though listeners are often present, they are largely contextualized in the experience of the singer. While vocal performance is a multidirectional experience, the primary goal of this project is to thoroughly explore the ways in which singers experience voice in the negotiation of their identities. My interest in these experiences stems in part from my own singing life, and the ways in which voice and vocality have consistently formed the fulcrum of my self-knowledge. I do include descriptions of those processes at points throughout the book, though my own experience is not the primary focus; I represent only one in a sea of voices, in a multivocal body of narratives about singing. In the process of my ethnographic research, I reached out to friends and colleagues alongside whom I had studied in my voice-major years, as well as to singers whom I did not previously know, and I encountered consistently amid the myriad unique stories of voices this common association between voice and sense of self.

Brambilla locates the study of borderscapes in "the era of globalization and transnational flows" and cites its potential contribution "to the understanding of new forms of belonging and becoming" (Brambilla 2015: 14). *Multivocality* attempts a study of voices in such a context, located within and without bodies, at once confining and liberating.

Methodology: An Ethnography of Singing

My study of multivocality draws on discourses in the ethnography of communication, in that its goal is to understand how ways of singing might reflect and shape ways of living. My understanding of vocalities as ways of singing, or vocal ways of being, recalls the work of Dell Hymes, writing in 1974 in "Ways of Speaking." In that essay, Hymes explains his preference for studying *ways of speaking*. The phrase, for him, presents the act of speech as a "complex social act," and recalls both Whorf's "fashions of speaking" and the notion of "ways of life" (Hymes 1974: 445)—the latter understood to be the foundations of culture. Research in ways of speaking must address, he writes, not only "means of speech and their meaning" but also the "norms of interaction that go beyond choice of style, and the attitudes and beliefs that underlie both" (446). Hymes also references the roles that voice—its pitch range and contour, its timbre or loudness—can play in ways of speaking, using the example of Wolof communities in Senegal. He describes a contrast between two modes of speech—*restrained* and *unrestrained*—a contrast that, in part through distinct uses of voice, also divides the speech of men and women, adults and children, and members of low and high social castes (442). He urges ethnographers to study linguistic modes in addition to linguistic structure, noting that "It would be a mistake to assume that the essential principle of a form of speech is always structure, never mode" (443). Hymes turns to music here (as elsewhere in the essay), positioning practices as equally important to form: "one may sing something that is not a song, and present a song without singing it" (443).

Muriel Saville-Troike, elucidating the primary tenets and approaches to the ethnography of communication, writes that ethnographers of language tend to study how ways of speaking are patterned, and how those patterns interrelate and "derive meaning from other aspects of culture" (Saville-Troike 2003: 11). A handful of previous literature in ethnomusicology and folklore has employed the idea. It follows, then, that an ethnography of vocality should investigate ways of singing—not merely as modes of practice but also of meaning-making. Some studies, such as Edward Kerr Miller's dissertation *An Ethnography of Singing: The Use and Meaning of Song Within a Scottish Family* (1981), declare a focus on the singers. Others—for example, Mary Ellen Cohane and Kenneth S. Goldstein in "Folksongs and the Ethnography of Singing in Patrick Kennedy's *The Banks of the Boro*," emphasize "the description of song context" (Cohane and Goldsgein 1996: 426). In an unpublished paper presented as an "Embodied Approach to the Ethnography of Singing," ethnomusicologist Nadia Chana centers her research on a specific voice teacher's worldview, and on the relationship between vocal technique and personal emotion—embodied practice—that shapes it (Chana 2013).

Chana is part of the rising tide of scholarship in ethnomusicological voice studies, a field described by Eidsheim and Meizel as "work concerned with the material, sonorous and sensory voice as it made and imagined in human life" (Eidsheim and Meizel 2019). It is a transdisciplinary area of research stretching across the performing arts, humanities, and social sciences, and across medicine, physics, and the study of science and technology. Scholars in voice studies tend to rely upon multiple approaches from these areas in pursuit of a more holistic knowledge of voice in the world. That said, there is no unified way of doing voice studies, of asking or answering the flood of questions raised when we wonder what voice is. Contradictions abound—"The voice is both materially grounded and ideologically enacted. It is a sounded phenomenon... silently inscribed" (Eidsheim and Meizel 2019)—and to address them, voice scholarship must employ and celebrate a multiplicity of approaches. In *Multivocality*, I have applied methodologies rooted in ethnomusicology, literary studies, media studies, identity studies, disability studies, and, at times, voice science.

In the ethnographic study of singing, ethnomusicologists must aspire to the same kind of rigorous reflection as we undertake in other specializations. Though we avidly advocate the integration of emic terminologies in other areas of music culture, when it comes to vocal sounds we tend to fall back on the vocabulary of western classical singing. That reflex, without reflexivity or critical consideration of the discourse, can cause us to overlook the nuanced meanings of vocality in culture-specific contexts. Furthermore, much of the western classical vocal lexis lacks any standardized meaning or correlation to productive processes—for example, register terminology such as "head voice" and "chest voice" yields a stunning variety of definitions among practitioners, or may even be denied entirely by some western classical singers and researchers. Other commonly used descriptors, such as "nasal," do have standardized definitions in voice science—"nasal" refers there to a sound in which air flows through the nose—but we cannot confirm that quality without some form of acoustic or physiological measurement, and sometimes perceptual discourse and practice differ significantly. For example, when I have played for my students recordings in the *Mystère des Voix Bulgares* vocal *obrabotka* genre, they have consistently described it as "nasal"—a term that in western classical pedagogy describes the sound created when air is allowed to flow through the nose during vocalization. But I once talked with a Bulgarian singer of that style who teaches Americans, and who explained that the first thing she has her students do is hold their noses to prevent a nasal sound. Ingo Titze has written of a confusion among vocalists regarding types of nasality, particularly between what he calls "nasal murmur," in which acoustic energy is transmitted into the nose, and "twang," which he links instead to acoustic resonation in the epilarynx tube and which may be nasalized due to velar position (Titze 2001). So, it is clear that there can be a discrepancy between empirical and casual practical discourse, and between how we hear vocality and how we make it. Additionally, we should note that "nasality" is a culturally loaded concept, undesirable and maligned in western discourse and often understood as a marker of Otherness (my students often describe any non-western vocality as "nasal"). If we are aware of vocality's inextricable link with structures of power, we can neither imagine it independent of them nor allow familiar but unexamined frameworks to overshadow other culture-emerging ones. Though many participants in my study locate themselves within western discourses of singing, it is important to view those discourses as only part of the picture of voice. Because my work largely focuses on individual singers, in each chapter I strive to use the terminology they have used, within the framework of their own experiences.

Ethnomusicologists have long acknowledged a need to examine the processes of representation in scholarship. But, especially considering the rhetorical associations between voice and agency in political representation, I would suggest that a study of singers requires special attention to such issues. Representing the experiences of others through research is often positioned as "giving voice" (Ashby 2011). Bogdan and Biklen, for example, describe giving voice as "empowering people to be heard who might otherwise remain silent" (Bogdan and Biklen 1998: 204, cited in Ashby 2011). Though many of the singers I write about face a network of oppressive systems that work to suppress voice, by virtue of their resistance through vocalization, through multivocality, they are definitively *not silent*. Christine Ashby, whose research centers on non-speaking disabled people, critiques the concept of giving voice for its complex implications of agency and power. She cautions researchers against the belief that they must uncover or "excavate" an individual's authentic voice (Ashby 2011, after DeVault 1999), and urges them to hear or "read" silences, as well as speech. I have written *Multivocality* with these ideas in mind. Because the participating singers do their work through many voices, there is no singular authentic voice to locate. I have also tried to listen to the silences as they came—for example, as I discuss in chapter 5, one participant in my study withdrew entirely owing to a religious conversion, and another withdrew as a result of increased celebrity status—and I have tried to include my own singing experiences only where my voice seemed relevant. Overall, as in any ethnomusicological research, just as in any novel Bakhtin studied, it is only the multiplicity of other voices that allows the author's own to sound.

Overview of Chapters

Each chapter in this book highlights singers in motion, their voices delineating borderscapes that imply transitions and transgressions across genre and gender boundaries, cultural borders, the lines between body and technology, between religious and secular contexts, between foundness and lostness. The first chapter addresses Ms. Giddens's vital question, "What *is* my voice?," investigating how singers who practice multivocality answer it. The voice is often understood as a kind of sonic fingerprint, embodying a unique, unalterable, and authentic self. But what dynamic processes and ideologies are at stake when one body generates many voices? An African American opera singer changes her sound to record Appalachian repertoire; a Canadian-born diva learns a different way of singing through the traditional music of her parents' Korean homeland; a Syrian soprano and refugee uses a song that showcases multiple vocalities to negotiate her life in the United States. Such fluidity of genre and place necessitates the confrontation of racialized, ethnicized, and gendered stylistic boundaries, and indicates more than mere practical or aesthetic adaptability. More significantly, it points to the ways in which the voice figures in the infinitely complicated work of identity. Chapter 1 investigates how singers trained in western classical tradition create and experience this kind of multivocality, and explores the explicit and implicit sociocultural meanings they make in the process.

Chapter 2 examines a specific site of multivocality, a type of singing performance designated as "popera," or vocal "classical crossover." Identifying the various aesthetic characteristics and preferred repertories of popera, the chapter integrates the experiences of several participants in well-known crossover productions and groups. They have generously shared with me their methods and thought processes in choosing and performing certain types of repertoire, their ideas about vocal technique, and the roles multivocality has played in their careers. Their work reveals a complex process of code-switching, not only moving between vocal qualities and between genres but also highlighting and challenging existing social structures—cultural histories of class, race, and gender—just as both opera and popular music have always done. Popera, in the end, provides an acoustic space for the reunion of the two genres and their social registers, and for the negotiation of alterity.

Some performances of multivocality are quite literal: impersonator acts sometimes involve the adoption of multiple celebrity voices, all sounded from one body in an acousmatic sleight of hand (or larynx). Las Vegas has long been a national hub of impersonator culture, from its abundance of Elvises and its dozens of drag venues, to the perennial pop impressionists of the long-running show *American Superstars*. Theatrical transvestism in Vegas has performed and celebrated many permutations of difference (a Black Elvis, a male Barbra Streisand), at once underlining and undermining the fluidity of identity. Chapter 3 details the ways in which such disjunctures between bodies and voices are manipulated by Vegas impersonators, and how they paradoxically contribute to the construction of these performers' own identities.

Chapter 4 discusses the work of d/Deaf singers and their fraught relationships with voice, signing, and both hearing and Deaf cultures. For d/Deaf singers—who typically grew up culturally hearing before becoming physically deaf—singing can be a special locus for identity conflict, embodied in both the aesthetics that shape the vocal tract and the kinetics of sign language, and negotiated through a complex performance politics of inclusion and exclusion. This chapter highlights the problems of defining Deafness through a negative relationship with voice, and contends that d/Deaf singers' work in voice and sign constitutes a form not only of multilinguality but also of multivocality. Furthermore, it suggests the need for an extended definition of multivocality to include other embodied modes of communication; if multivocality functions as a strategy for identity building, I propose in chapter 4 that such a strategy need not be solely a sonic one. Other embodied forms of communication, such as signing, must also be considered as integral, and even sometimes integrated.

Chapter 5 deals with movement among styles of sacred and secular singing, focusing on the experiences of musicians who have performed across multiple religious contexts. One of my consultants, Anthony Russell, provides a glimpse into the importance of vocality in the embodiment of religious conversion and of intersectional identities. In his musical conversion, he has learned not only a new body of song but, through the act of singing, also the embodiment of a new culture—a new set of stylistic elements, timbres, and vocal gestures informed by both contemporary Jewish practices and historical cantorial recordings. But he has not abandoned—cannot abandon—aspects of his African American cultural identity, and in his creative endeavors he seeks points of musical, vocal, historical, and religious convergence that allow him to tell his own story and find his voice as a Black, Jewish, gay man. Other aspects of the chapter focus on the concept of *intent* in spiritual singing practices and the crossing of borders in the neoliberal religious marketplace.

Vocalities figure in the shaping of bodies and of performativities. Chapter 5 discusses the ways in which four transgender singers understand their relationships with voice in extremely individual ways, and how shifts in vocality impact their senses of identity. Two of them, as trans men, have experienced changes in their singing voices, a shift to more masculine sounds. One woman has maintained a career in opera as a baritone; another sang mezzo-soprano and soprano repertoire before coming out as female. Vocality has served different functions and generated different meanings for each of these singers, whose experiences collectively underline the idea of "transition" as an ongoing journey rather than a destination.

If one is to understand the notion of finding a voice, one must also address its loss. Chapters 7 and 8 discuss the political and personal implications of voice loss. I examine the loss of voice through and mediated by technology, tracing a history in American cinema and the shifting sociopolitical landscapes in which it has projected its visions and auditions, where the transformation of voices can be heard clearly. The singing voice in cinema has moved from symbolizing the vulnerability of identity and its susceptibility to manipulation, to embodying the affirmation of identity as a site of individual agency. Outside of cinema, voice loss in singers is subject to discourses no less suffused with ideas about identity and agency. Losing a voice can be, in some ways, losing one's self, or at the very least one's primary mode of enacting identity. Chapter 7 also explores the loss of voice one singer experienced through selling her voice to a digital sampling library. Chapter 8 focuses on the idea of voice loss, through trauma or illness, as a personal loss of control, and examines the ways in which singers negotiate such a loss.

Finally, chapter 9 highlights two case studies of multivocality in the political climate following the 2016 U.S. presidential election, specifically within the contexts of intersectional feminist activism and youth activism against gun violence.

Though discourse about singing tends to assign fixed, ostensibly biologically determined qualities and often value judgments regarding an individual's vocality, to a significant degree voices are made through choices. The borderscape of the human voice is, *within certain biophysical limits*, constructed, shaped in relation to individual, intersubjective, cultural experiences, and—like geographical borderlands—formed according to structures of power. As identities experience the flow and rupture of changing intersubjectivities, voices can, too. *Multivocality*, in its focus on the suppressions and soundings of voice in various borderlands of identity, works toward a deeper understanding of voice as a technology of the self[15] and of culture.

---

[15] I use this Foucauldian phrase with a nod to musicologist Nina Eidsheim and her dissertation (Eidsheim 2008).

1
Finding a Voice

> Find your own voice & use it
> Use your own voice & find it
> —Jayne Cortez, "Find Your Own Voice" (1994)

In opera, Wayne Koestenbaum wrote, "The singer's face is called a mask, as if a voice were never capable of telling the truth" (Koestenbaum 1993: 154). Western classical vocal pedagogy indeed often recognizes the upper half of the face as "the mask"—where a Venetian Carnival disguise might perch—and as the location where a larger portion of vibratory sensations should optimally be felt. Though this is a culturally specific view, Koestenbaum's play on words resonates in any discussion of voice and identity. If all vocalities, like all the identities they inform and implement, involve a fundamental element of performativity, their truths can perhaps most effectively be viewed in relative terms. Ironically, within the variable constraints of individual bodies, singers often explore the changeable nature of the voice in search of some deeply embedded, unchanging authentic self. But even if, as Deborah Cameron observes, "voices are made, rather than born" (Cameron 2001: 84, cited in Preston 2016: 48), singers often arrive at a *feeling* of genuine vocal identity. Only, as Katherine Preston has pointed out, "'genuine' does not mean the same as 'unwilled'" (Preston 2016: 48). This chapter examines some of the directions in which singers *will* their voices in the search for self, and the process of branding that self in the neoliberal music market.

Ultimately, finding a voice in that market means following a course prescribed for the neoliberal subject, whom Türken et al. explain as "increasingly construed as a free, autonomous, individualized, self-regulating actor understood as a source of capital; as human capital" and as an entrepreneur of the self (Türken et al. 2016: 34). And in order to maximize one's value, neoliberal subjectivity demands continuous self-development, self-monitoring, and self-improvement (34). "Largely responsible for her own successes and failures," Türken et al. continue, "the individual's wellbeing and development becomes the sole responsibility of the neoliberal entrepreneurial subject" (34). Most significantly, self-improvement helps the subject to fill the requirements of a "flexible and unstable market" (Türken et al. 2016: 34, after Olssen 2006). I suggest here that late 20th- and early 21st-century discourses of singing have highlighted voice as a technology of such self-development, and that both knowledge of classical singing and the ability to switch vocalities are seen as paths to authentic selfhood and vocal well-being, and therefore to marketability.

The concept of finding one's voice,[1] of recognizing one's individuality and self-worth, is at this point so deeply embedded in U.S. culture that it seems timeless, without history. But though individuality is a key element in the foundational mythologies of Americanness, and though the equation of voice with agency is in itself not new, the explicit articulation of the metaphor may be traced to certain trends in writing analysis and pedagogy, and to the pivotal identity movements that shaped the nation's social, economic, political, philosophical, and cultural climate in the late 20th and early 21st centuries. It is only a short distance between a narrative concept of voice (as in an author's voice) and an agentive one (voice as a way of authoring one's own life); both developments have dialectically contributed to the discourse of "finding a voice."

The 1970s social movements—including second-wave feminism—inspired by the struggle for African American civil rights in the 1960s were largely driven through the rhetoric of "gaining a [sociopolitical] voice" (Bauman 2008a: 3). Examining the writing of textbooks of this time, Darsie Bowden (1995) pinpoints Donald Stewart's 1972 *The Authentic Voice* as a seminal document. Stewart advised students: "Your authentic voice is that authorial voice which sets you apart from every living human being despite the common or shared experiences you have with many others" (Stewart 1972: 2, cited in Bowden 1995: 175). Other "voicist" (Bowden: 1995: 18) scholars turned to a more social, intersubjective view of language and of voice, where "all discourse is inhabited by meaning from other contexts and uses" (186). In their 1997 analysis *Femininity and Shame: Women, Men, and Giving Voice to the Feminine*, Barbara L. Eurich-Rascoe and Hendrika Vande Kemp offer a (third-wave) feminist perspective, defining literary voice as "*self-declaration in an interpersonal context that has the primary goal of maintaining interpersonal connection*" (Rascoe and Vande Kemp 1997: 7; emphasis in original). It is these formulations that shape my understanding of multivocality as the process of negotiating a personal identity through a network of vocal intersubjectivities.

By the late 1980s, when neoliberal individualism had secured a firm political and cultural foothold, journalists were asking writers and performing artists the question "When did you find your voice?," as in a 1989 *Time* interview with Ann Landers (Taylor 1989) and a 1990 interview in *Guitar Player* with the Kinks' Dave Davies (Resnicoff 1990). The concept rapidly made its way into advertising as well, and by 2000, the surgeon general's report on women and smoking

---

[1] A small amount of text in the following pages is drawn from Meizel 2019, used with permission.

called out the Virginia Slims company for exploiting the language of the women's movement in its global "Find Your Voice" marketing campaign, begun the previous year (Koplan 2000). That campaign also painstakingly targeted women of color, emphasizing themes of liberation and enfranchisement and infuriating many who saw the project as an effort to globalize addiction in women (Kim and Chung 2008). It is also telling that the ad campaign emerged during the infancy of the neoliberal twenty-first century internet culture—in which one's "voice" is synonymous with one's "brand."

The phrase "find your voice" has also flourished in vocal pedagogy, though extant evidence on the internet appears to date only from the early 2000s; and around the same time, the *Idols* franchise was encouraging young singers to make music "their own." It is worth noting that in 2007, Season 5 *American Idol* winner Taylor Hicks published *Heart Full of Soul: An Inspirational Memoir About Finding Your Voice and Finding Your Way* (Hicks and Wild 2007). I have written elsewhere about the *Idol* process of creating individualized performances, and I invoke the work of philosopher Charles Taylor as he connects the concepts of expressive individualism with the search for an authentic, "inner voice." Both are, he suggests, rooted in an entanglement of the Calvinist shift toward the establishment of a personal covenant with God with the impact of naturalist philosophy in the history of western thought. This convergence led to thinking in which "what is primary is the voice within, or according to other variants, the élan running through nature which emerges inter alia in the voice within," and God "is to be interpreted in terms of what we see striving in nature and finding voice within ourselves" (Taylor 1989: 371, cited in Meizel 2011b: 122–123).

Discourse in vocal pedagogy that locates such authenticity only in the classically trained voice has led many singers to restrict themselves to this single music culture. But I began my research talking with classically trained singers who have challenged the widespread notion that they can or should only sing in one way. In this study, I have encountered three overarching tropes. First, many entertain the notion that a singer's self can sound most authentic in a particular vocal mode, and that the search for such authenticity often occupies many years. Second, I heard repeatedly a related notion that the individuality of a voice, amid the babble of dialogic voices that shape the singing text, is usually socially suppressed and in need of liberation. While, as Nina Sun Eidsheim notes, pedagogical discourse typically identifies physiological "tensions" or psychological blockages that must be cleared (Eidsheim 2019: 44), both she and the team of Christian Utz and Frederick Lau point out that an imagination of voice as needing liberation is really a call for freedom from one or more types of hegemony, from musical and/or political subjugation (Utz and Lau 2013: 2). Third, the process of finding a voice is intertwined, often intersectionally, with other elements of identity—perceptions of the body, senses of place, and the oppressive systems of race, ethnicity, and gender that shape them—which in turn dialectically influences the process of finding a voice.

The interviews I conducted for this chapter and the next explore singers' discourses on authenticity and some of the borderscapes traversed by vocalists trained in the cultivated pedagogies of western classical singing. These pedagogies have occupied a privileged position in the history of voice discourse, and are often presumed to institute "correct" or "healthy" modes of singing, in opposition to other modes. As ballet has at times been understood as the foundation of any dance style, western classical vocal training has been positioned as the necessary groundwork for all singing, without which one cannot vocalize in a safe or acceptable way. Singing classically, our teachers told my student colleagues and me in the 1990s, was the only way to save our voices from damage; it was touted as "healthy" in the same moralizing manner as was disciplined awareness of one's body mass index.

In a compelling and elegant analysis, Afua Osseo-Asare draws a connection between the pedagogical turn to vocal health, the voice studio conceived as medical clinic, and western constructs of health as they developed in the 19th and 20th centuries. Osseo-Asare observes that the 19th-century medical gaze contributed to the construction of health and "*unhealth*" as purely biological, and therefore was "absolved of all relation to or consequence from social context," despite the disease- and violence-producing capacities of social contexts such as poverty and imperialism (Osseo-Asare 2018: 50). It is this same medical gaze that has helped to construct raced and gendered and dis/abled bodies; and with the emergence of Manuel Garcia II's laryngoscope in the 1850s, it turned to the newly visible internal workings of voice. Garcia's legacy has guided generations of voice scientists, voice teachers, and their students (though, I would amend, I have also encountered singers who reject it as a hyper-intellectual and anti-artistic approach). Osseo-Asare observes that, today in the United States, health is positioned both as a norm or neutral ideal and as a kind of ideological good. After Deborah Lupton (1995), Osseo-Asare notes that "health promotion discourses valorize and seek to produce white, middle-class, rational subjects with regulated, contained bodies." With the erasing of social and political context, health has thus become an individual responsibility: a manifestation of (I would add, quasi-religious) self-control and self-denial—it is "an achievement and a status symbol"; while unhealth is "the shameful result of indolence and irresponsibility" (Osseo-Asare 2018: 50). It is noteworthy that, as Osseo-Asare observes, a significant expansion of vocal pedagogy's clinical focus occurred during the 1980s and 1990s (for example, the work of Richard Miller at Oberlin, and of voice scientists such as otolaryngologist Robert Sataloff and acoustician Ingo Titze), a time when mainstream wellness was exploding in the ascendant neoliberal marketplace. The ideal millennial singer, like the ideal health subject, is expected to practice continuous self-improvement—in other words, to be an ideal neoliberal subject.

The historic timing of Garcia's laryngoscope is also significant, occurring as it did during the second half of the 19th century, at a peak imperialist and colonialist moment when concepts of race were crystallizing into the form that would shape social relations globally thereafter. Nearly 170 years later, Nina Sun Eidsheim suggests, the vocal-pedagogical concentration on health and individualism may be framed in terms of a still-racialized listening practice equating "honest" or "authentic" voice with a singer's race and ethnicity. She finds that some western classical voice teachers champion culturally constructed "ethnic" timbres as representative of a (particularly non-white) singer's "real" voice; the identification and cultivation of a student's "Korean" sound or "Black" sound is, she suggests, an effort by voice teachers to integrate multiculturalist ideology, and to avoid "'homogenizing' their students' sounds" (Eidsheim 2019: 45–46). It is a recognition of difference *within* the hegemonic classical vocality. And it might be seen as an offer of voice, literally, that reinforces a suppressive kind of listening and celebrates a superficial diversity that merely meets the needs of multicultural neoliberalism.

Liberating the Vocal Thumbprint

Many singers who move between vocalities sustain a kind of auto-essentialist discourse, positioning the voice as what opera and Broadway veteran Sean Cooper calls "a thumbprint" (interview, September 15, 2009), comprising a unique, unalterable, authentic self-ness that remains fixed, beneath any flexibility of vocality across genres or styles. Singers sometimes feel the integration of voice and self so keenly that they find homologous relationships between their vocal qualities and vulnerabilities and other aspects of their lives. Ellen Wolf, currently a cabaret and musical-theater singer in Paris, feels that she is "living in the wrong time" because, as she puts it, "I don't have a modern voice" (interview, June 7, 2011). (Kati Roberts also invokes this sort of temporal displacement—when singing jazz, she explained to me, "I'm often told that I sound like a voice right out of an old Victrola" (personal communication, July 7, 2011). In spite of her self-perceived anachronism, Ms. Wolf concedes that there are "people who love me the way I am." It's worth noting her wording: not "people who love my *voice* the way *it* is" but, rather, "*me* the way *I* am." Others have also considered and sometimes struggled with the interdependence of voice and self throughout their singing lives, or have at least assigned homologous properties to the voice. "I can't force my voice to do anything, and that's kind of *me* [as well]," muses Kristin Williams Baugher, seeing herself as a person who can't be forced (interview, June 20, 2011).

And Lara Bisserier speaks of a "warm" quality in both her voice and her personality (interview, June 7, 2011). Such connections, though, can be perilous. When I spoke to him, Gary Ruschman blamed recent changes in his voice on "an early midlife crisis":

> [T]he whole first third and a half of my singing career I've been really determined to negate the identity crisis or have the voice *be me,* because I think that's dangerous. And I think having to go through a lot of rejection professionally, because we have to, as a professional musician, it makes it much easier to say "this person might not like my voice, but that has nothing to do with me, it just means that what I'm selling isn't something that they want to buy." However, now, I'm in my late 30s, I think the change in my voice, or the changes that are just happening either biologically or you know, timbrally, that has created more of a problem, because the things that I used to do best, aren't—either (a) as easy as they used to be, or (b) are just inaccessible now. So I'm having to ... sort of shift my identity to what, over the next couple of years I'm going to have to figure out what it is I actually *do* best [now]. (interview, June 7, 2011)

Crossing out of classical singing, Mr. Ruschman adds, did *not* contribute to his crisis of identity—rather, he observes, non-classical musics can often be altered to fit the voice, "for wherever you are at a particular time, you can—the music is malleable enough to do that ... in pop you find your key," whereas in an opera aria, you are, as a rule, stuck with the key on the page" (interview, June 7, 2011). In other words, he feels able to make popular music fit *him,* rather than the other way around.

For some, like Mr. Cooper, vocal authenticity comes directly from formal (classical) instruction, which optimally yields "the openness of a classically trained, liberated voice ... someone's true voice ... people really find out what *their* sound is" (interview, September 15, 2009). Jimmy Kansau, instructor for the San Francisco Boys Choir, explains that society suppresses the voice and makes it "shy," designating when and where speaking and singing and other vocalizations are allowed or forbidden (interview, October 20, 2011). In order to find their voices, he asks pupils to try going back to "the primitive noises, like a calf or like a sheep," or to make a sound like a crying baby—sounds in which he identifies muscular coordination and acoustic characteristics desirable in classical singing. The use of infant sounds in vocal training is common—and Adriana Cavarero, after Julia Kristeva, writes about the infant voice that the eventual development of language "asks the sacrifice of their free vocalization, which is still rooted in the biological" (Cavarero 2005: 132). In classical singing pedagogy, the infant's bodily voice is often positioned as the freest, most authentic embodied sound.

If some assign redemptive qualities to classical training, others find their freedom in *non-classical* musics, locating their authentic voice in the popular repertories they learned before they were subjected to the rigors and rigidity of classical training. Mr Ruschman, a member of the cross-genre group Cantus for over a decade, reflects: "Well, I think there's a sense of freedom and individuality that is part and parcel [of] any popular idiom. And I think most classical programs will try to train those idiosyncrasies out of you" (interview, June 7, 2011). And Ellen Wolf actually believes she was a "freer" and more "natural" singer before she began operatic training. "You're born with the voice you have," she says, and hers was fine until she began studying, when she developed physical problems she believes stemmed from poor instruction.

Ideas about the body, impaired or unimpaired, can reflect and shape the work of vocal identity. For Kristin Williams Baugher, a singing instructor and musical-theater actress in California, the uniqueness of her voice comes from perceptual discourses about sonic structure and bodily dimensions. "[My voice] is big, and I'm small . . . 'that little girl with the big voice,'" she says she's heard all her life, "that's the one identifier since I was probably five" (interview, June 20, 2011). This kind of dissonance between the body seen and the body heard is a familiar trope, suffusing the reality-TV stories of singers like the 2009 *Britain's Got Talent* sensation Susan Boyle, who was received as a prodigious talent in an unlikely middle-aged package, and whose success was succeeded in 2011 by the development of the famous "blind auditions" in NBC's singing competition *The Voice*. The paradoxical interdependence and reification of the voice in the body and the body in the voice highlight the complexities of voice as a multisensory experience.

The choice of non-classical repertoire is not the only criterion for musical multivocality. It is more than what theatrical producer Marion Caffey terms "opera singers trying to sing other styles of music"; in addition, it requires attention to "*maintaining the integrity* of the other styles" (interview, November 11, 2009). Some singers remark on their conscious manipulation of different idiomatic timbres and vocal gestures in order to do just that—for example, adding R&B melisma, sliding between pitches, and sustaining a straight-toned timbre (or altering the incidence and rate of their vibrato) for popular repertoire.

But many singers I've spoken with have also suggested the importance of preserving certain practices consistent with operatic discourse, regardless of genre: primarily, what they call "low" or "non-clavicular breathing," a strong preference for higher pitch ranges, and the elimination of register breaks. Typically, these are identified as ways to foster vocal health, a theme raised often by my interviewees as important in finding one's voice. Limmie Pulliam believes that applying his classical training to what he labels the "growling or squalling" and "raspy singing" of gospel music allows him to execute potentially harmful vocal gestures safely. I also heard "safety" named as a benefit of applying classical training to pop, musical theater, jazz, and heavy metal. Because the instrument is the body, not just the larynx, formal vocal education usually includes extensive discussion of kinesthetic efficiency, or strain-avoiding techniques to maintain the health of laryngeal and pharyngeal tissues and muscles, the lungs that power the sound, the muscles of the ribcage and abdomen and shoulders and neck, and even the legs that support those structures. Mastery of all this physiology can play a role in the negotiation of the classical singer's "real voice," according to Jennifer Goode Cooper. When a singer simply mimics recordings of his favorite stars instead of finding his own voice, she says, undesirable muscle tension can result. But, she continues, with training, "when they're not doing anything to their musculature or not creating tension anywhere . . . it's honest . . . and it's not trying to be anything it's not" (interview, September 24, 2009). Her words recalls Eidsheim's association of vocal "honesty" with ethnic identity and insist upon a personal essentialism. On the other hand, many singers I spoke with about *American Idol* cited imitation as vital in the development of their individuality, and Rhiannon Giddens relates a similar experience, in which imitation served as "my template . . . and then," she says, "I just sort of put my own stamp on it" (interview, November 3, 2012).

High Lonesome Sound

Ms. Giddens relied on the imitation of recorded voices at the start of her classical studies, as well as after college, when she began to work in Celtic and Appalachian styles. In her work with Celtic singing, she was careful to keep in mind the issues of appropriation raised when imitating accents.

> I listened to Solas, an Irish band. Karen Casey was the singer for that, I can't really remember all the bands, Old Blind Dog . . . contemporary Celtic bands, and tried not to pick up their accents, but that was only sometimes successful.

As her research into the Black history of old-time music deepened, she moved away from imitating white Appalachian singers:

> I imitated Sheila Kay Adams; she's from Western North Carolina. I found my singers, and then as I started getting into the Black stuff, I started finding, like, Vera Ward Hall, and sort of trying to imitate her timbre and see where that fit in the whole thing. Just really listening to as many women as I could, and just—Bessie and Ma Rainey started creeping in there towards later years, and [I was] thinking about how I could open my throat like those guys. (interview, November 3, 2012)

She emphasized in our interview that imitating Black singers does not mean that their sound, or hers, necessarily represents a monolithic "Black" vocality. Genre, style, and regionalisms might influence a vocality more specifically than any generalized perception of "Blackness" might encompass, she explained. Any descriptors typically used to evoke Black voices might be attributed to place of origin, musical context, specific singers, and details of performance requirements, such as venue size or microphone use.

> It's not so much a race thing as it is—you know, Bessie Smith and Ma Rainey, they're from the city, and they're singing a different style. And Vera Ward Hall is from a different part of the country, and—at this point it's kind of the chicken and the egg, you know. What comes first in terms of some of these regional differences in singers? Did the race influence the style, or did the isolation, the regionalism influence [it more]? You know, it gets kind of difficult. It's really tempting to say Black singers do *this*—[but] even if there's any of them that do, how can you say it's because they're Black, physically, [or] culturally, or if it's just where they're from? But you know, you could also say "well, Black singers, they have a more robust sound," and that's kind of a larger sound—but Vera Ward Hall has a very delicate sound, you know. She sounds a lot like my grandmother, just kind of the way her vibrato came out, sort of natural, fast vibrato but not overbearing. And then you have Bessie and Ma, who are like, throats completely wide open, roaring, because the functionality of the music is different, as well. So they're up there on a theater stage, trying to project with no microphone, so that changes things. (interview, November 3, 2012)

Multivocality, for her, is not about code-switching between white and Black ways of singing but about acknowledging the Blackness in a vocal sound inaccurately coded as historically white. The context of this inaccuracy makes its way into Audre Lorde's poem "Coal," in which she considers "How a sound comes into a word, coloured/By who pays what for speaking (Lorde 1996[1976]).

Particularly because Ms. Giddens sometimes moves between genres and ways of singing within a single album or even a single concert, I asked her how she transitions between them. It isn't a focus on technique, she says, but a kind of aural imprint she keeps in her head that she can access when necessary.

> I'm a lot less of a technical singer than probably a lot of people who've had classical training. I'm very instinctual ... so when I slip into a different genre, I don't think, "OK, I need to slow down my vibrato" or "I need to do *this*," I just put myself where that genre would be. So whatever's coming out of my throat, that's how I'm in that space. But I'm not technically thinking, "Oh, I need to lower this down," or keep this up, or how to copy that, I'm just kind of like, "OK, I'm going

to sing 'Pretty Saro'" [an Appalachian ballad of English origin] . . . I pretty much find the "Pretty Saro" voice and then just put it out there. (interview, November 3, 2012)

The vocality associated with Appalachian singing was something that didn't take long to feel comfortable to her. She describes it as "that high nasal, straight tone, mountain ballad" timbre, "that high lonesome" quality (interview, November 3, 2012). Reviews of Ms. Giddens's work often specifically praise that "high lonesome sound" (Davidson 2017 and Simon 2012, for example) This descriptive terminology for Appalachian music has become standard in references to bluegrass, "Americana," and country music, particularly applied to the genre's preferred vocality(ies). When *The High Lonesome Sound of Bill Monroe* was released in 1966, the phrase gained public currency, though it had already been introduced in Alan Le May's eponymous 1950 film, *High Lonesome*. The Western, starring John Barrymore, Jr., is set in the Big Bend area of southern Texas, where, as a voiceover helpfully expounds, "it is high, and it is lonesome." But there are also mountain locations in the Southwest with the name High Lonesome, along the Continental Divide National Scenic Trail in Colorado and in New Mexico, settled in the 19th century. The phrase "high lonesome sound" made its way into bluegrass discourse itself through a 1963 documentary by John Cohen of the New Lost City Ramblers (*The High Lonesome Sound: Kentucky Mountain Music*), featuring white banjo player and singer Roscoe Holcomb. In Tom Davenport's 2003 documentary *Remembering the High Lonesome*, Cohen recalls his first musical encounter with Holcomb: "my hair stood up on end. It was the most moving, touching, dynamic, powerful song I—not the song itself, but the way he sang it, it was just astounding" (Davenport 2003). "High lonesome sound" has come to encapsulate the expressive, often mournful singing, especially with a high range and sorrowful lyrics, that characterizes Appalachian "old-time" or later bluegrass style, or a sound reminiscent of either. Because these genres have been popularly racialized as white and associated with working-class culture—historically due in part to the old minstrel-show traditions, white supremacy, the early recording industry, and white academic interest in American "folk music"—so has the vocality, and like the banjo Ms. Giddens champions, its roots in rural, southern, Black, and shared tradition have been nearly erased. Bill Monroe himself, though, recognized the connection. "Bluegrass music is a field holler, just like blues," he said (quoted in Tunnell 2008: 81), and attributed his high lonesome singing style to this powerful influence. Keith Tunnell theorizes that the vocality's origins are in the lined-out, long-meter hymns of rural southern Black churches—and this singing practice has also been part of tradition shared with rural white Southerners. (Cohen's film, incidentally, focuses some attention on white churchgoers singing in just that tradition.) Thus, just as Ms. Giddens's work reclaims the Black history of American banjo and string band tradition, it also reclaims the Black history of an American vocality that has been whitewashed and appropriated for more than a century. And this is her vocality, as multilayered as her identity—and embedded in racialized, classed social structures. She "embodies Affrilachia," Barbour-Payne writes, "her body transforms into a multifaceted catalyst through which individuals communicate their regional, racial, and national identity connections" (Barbour-Payne 2016: 46).

Ms. Giddens has been called "a one-woman definition" of the Americana music category (Farrer 2017), and she has been nominated for several awards by the Americana Music Association. Americana, which grew out of trends including "roots music" and "alt-country," is understood as an umbrella category including "country, roots-rock, folk, bluegrass, R&B and blues" (Americana Music Association, or AMA, cited in Farrer 2017). The Association, though it has honored some Black artists, has been sharply criticized for persistently excluding artists of color—90 percent of the acts scheduled at its 2017 festival, Jonathan Bernstein noted in *Rolling Stone*, comprised only white performers. Black singer-songwriter Adia Victoria, initially embraced by the AMA, has rejected its advances, uncomfortable with the prospect of being held up as a romanticized token, a "special exotic ornament that they can point to and say, 'See! See! That too is Americana!'" (Himes 2015). Giddens's audience is mostly white, and she told a *Guardian* reporter: "Trying to penetrate the black community has been really difficult. It's not enough to produce the work—you then have to connect it to the audience" (John 2018). But early in her work with the Carolina Chocolate Drops, featured in an album preview for *Genuine Negro Jig* on Nonesuch Records, she said:

> One of the things we love is when we do a show, and a Black person will come up, and they'll be almost furtive, you know, and they'll go, "you know, I've always loved this music." You know, it's almost like they're getting it off their chest—"I love country music!" It's just like, "I'm glad that we could help you with that," you know? (https://www.youtube.com/watch?v=XbcqGjeNz7w)

She and the Carolina Chocolate Drops are reclaiming not only a music's Black history but its present, as well.

Not Singing Like an Opera Singer

During my time as a graduate student in vocal performance, I had my own experience on the high lonesome road. I took a rare opportunity to enroll in an old-time/Appalachian ensemble course—to become acquainted with an aural/

oral tradition that required a new way of learning music and a new voice. What followed included a happy four-year stint in a band, some hard work learning to play the fiddle, and a lasting love of the vocality that characterizes the music. At the beginning of the semester-long course, I was warned: *remember, this isn't classical singing.*

"I know," I said.

No, really, you can't sing like an opera singer.

"I *know*," I said again, bristling a little at the implied insinuations about the inflexibilities of voice majors. There is something to that warning, of course. In the introduction to this book, I cited Edward Dent's class critique of opera singers attempting "folk" music (Bairstow et al. 1929). Nicholas Harkness has also written of a similar situation, in a very different national context; he describes the situation when a Korean opera singer was unable to successfully envoice a Korean folk song because her western classical training had become "a competing phonic habituation that was manifest corporeally in her throat" (Harkness 2013: 38).

A U.S. soprano might certainly experience such a disjuncture encountering U.S. vernacular singing. I was (arrogantly) sure that I could do it, but I didn't know *how* I would achieve a sound outside of the western operatic aesthetic, or outside its then slightly disparaged cousin, the ideologically laden "legit" sound of musical theater.[2] Because I knew that listening and imitation are essential practices in the acquisition of a vocality, I spent countless hours in the company of recorded voices—of the Carter Family, Iris DeMent, Gillian Welch—but the high lonesome sound still did not feel like part of my body in the way I was used to with my usual repertoire. I'd done some coursework and research in the acoustics of voice and language, and I'd read studies of the contributions made by vowel configuration to vocal timbre. Research by Ladefoged (2000) and Johan Sundberg (1987), for example, had affirmed that the first two acoustic formants[3] in a vocal sound correlate to vowel identity, while the third formant, usually determined by the portions of the vocal tract closer to the larynx, had been identified as key in the perception of speaker- or singer-specific vocal timbre (Sundberg 1987).[4] Classical voice teachers often instruct students to concentrate on Italian vowels to achieve the desired acoustic configuration for opera, so I thought that

---

[2] Robert Edwin has written in the *Journal of Singing* that "legit," or "legitimate," singing in musical theater is "most closely aligned with classical singing, and had its origin in early music theater" (Edwin 2007: 213). He also dismantles the "highbrow"/"lowbrow" dichotomy between "legit" and "belt" modes in musical theater, and argues that "belt is legit." For more on related dichotomies, see chapter 2, this volume.

[3] Intensified groups of overtones selected by the shape of the vocal tract, which contribute to the perception of vocal timbre.

[4] Ethnomusicologist Eve McPherson has also written about the contribution of vowel structure to vocal timbre in her studies of the Turkish *ezan* (call to prayer) (McPherson 2005).

if I started with vowels, I might arrive at an appropriate timbre. So, one day I sat down and tried speaking the texts of my songs in an accent with very broad vowels—a terrible exaggerated accent that I was fairly sure I'd performed once as Ado Annie in a community-theater production of *Oklahoma!*—and found that as I transitioned to pitched speaking and then to melodic singing, everything was different. An affected falseness, it seemed, had led me to something that felt true. After that, even though I never again affected an accent when I sang, it seemed that the exercise had helped me to shift register and tone color and style all at once. After one of my first performances, a musicology professor told me, "I think you've found your voice. Your *real* voice."

But even if it was a "real" voice, it was a stolen one. Unlike Ms. Giddens, I have no family heritage in the places where this music originated—though the multiple revivals of old-time music have certainly de-territorialized the repertoire in favor of a misplaced middle-class nostalgia for times of desperate inequality. How could this vocality be my "real" voice, and not just an appropriative imitation? But then, I had no Italian or French or German heritage, either, and did not live in the 18th or 19th century, so even with fifteen years of training, could I say that opera was my true vocal identity? I'd grown up listening to and performing musical theater, but to study voice at my conservatory in the 1990s, one had to set aside even "legit" non-classical repertoire as forbidden fruit. Could I sing Stanley Brothers classics without committing the sin of developing "nodes" (nodules on the vocal folds caused by excess friction)? As it turned out, I could, and the vocality remained a beloved if conflicted mode of singing for me over several years.

My studies in western classical singing had been infused with a pervasive discourse that assured me the training would lead me to find my voice, to identify some essence of my vocal being. If that didn't feel true, then I was a failure. And western ethnomusicologists who subscribe to the tenets of participant-observation, and to Mantle Hood's exhortations toward bi- (or multi-)musicality, often struggle to navigate the appropriative impulses and associations that accompany the acquisition of musical knowledge outside their usual cultural experiences. Given the central role voice plays in western understandings of identity, my adoption of another (Other) vocality raises special concerns regarding histories of colonization and representation. Even though I live in the same nation where the music developed, and speak the English language in which the texts are written, and even though I've studied the old-time canon and the social contexts of the music, have participated in festivals and camps, and have taken lessons from expert musicians, is this music my voice? Is mine a voice capable of embodying the "voice-of-the-people" significance assigned to a repertory often classified as "folk?"

On the heels of the late 1990s, and during the explosive growth of digital technologies that characterized the era, anthropologist Gordon Mathews described new trends in the constructive processes of cultural identity. *Culture* itself, he observed, was a term under fire in his discipline, because "in today's world of massive global flows of people, capital, and ideas, a 'culture' can't easily be thought of as something that people in a certain place on the globe have or are in common" (Mathews 2000: 3–4). He recognized that contemporary identity formation involves not only the conventional idea of culture as a shared way of life but also "the information and identities available from the global cultural supermarket" (Mathews 2000: 4, after Hall 1992). Mathews examined the fragmented and eclectic cultural practices set to mark the Zeitgeist of the new 21st century, and suggested that "people throughout the affluent, mass-mediated world today may be as molded by the material and cultural supermarkets as by the state" (Mathews 2000: 9). Those who can reach the wide array of consumer choices available in the cultural supermarket feel free to incorporate their selections into their sense of self.

Mathews surveyed anthropological frameworks of self. Clifford Geertz had famously asserted in 1975 that "the Western conception of the person as a bounded, unique, more or less integrated motivational and cognitive universe" becomes "a rather peculiar idea within the context of the world's cultures (Geertz 1973: 31, cited in Mathews 2000: 11). But scholars at the turn of the millennium saw an *un*bounded postmodern self heavily shaped by mass media—a "protean" self, as Robert Jay Lifton wrote, "fluid and many-sided" (Lifton 1999[1993]: 1, cited in Mathews 2000: 12). "Any one of us can," Lifton continued, "at any moment, have access to any image or idea originating anywhere in the contemporary world, or from any cultural moment of the entire human past" (Lifton 1999[1993]: 1, cited in Mathews 2000: 12). For Mathews, the eclecticism tied to such access—which Richard A. Peterson identified as a cultural shift to "omnivore" from "snob" (Peterson 1996)—is the "most shallow and most fully conscious" level in the shaping of the self (Mathews 2000: 15), the one experienced most clearly as free choice. The two levels before it he identified as the "deep shaping taking place beyond the self's control and beyond all but indirect comprehension," and the "middle-level shaping taking place beyond the self's full control but *within* its comprehension" (15; my emphasis).

Mathews's "shallow" end of self-making—essentially, consumer choice—can feel deep, though. Living in the rural Midwestern United States, I've encountered two types of supermarkets (the physical kind): tiny local stores whose aisles barely accommodate an entire person, and huge warehouse stores that seem to stretch the width of airports. In a small shop, I'll choose a tube of toothpaste from among two or three options; in a "big box" store, it will take me half an hour to find any toothpaste, and when I do, I'll be introduced to twenty new brands (not to mention several completely unrelated items on the way). My choice there seems somehow more significant, more personal, more considered, more effortful. I don't mean to position vocality here as an analog to toothpaste but, rather, to suggest that the profundity of the (problematic) investment some white, middle-class singers find in the global cultural marketplace might be attributed to the vast variety offered to them by neoliberal capitalism.

My privilege as a white, middle-class American woman at an institute of higher education allowed me to pick up the "high lonesome" vocality through academic study and feel as though I'd made it my own. There is precedent, of course, as in the folk-revival movements of the 1950s and 1960s, when some traditional musics were celebrated, even fetishized, among the white middle class (see Filene 2000: 75) Old-time music has a special place in the history of the popular recording industry as one of its earliest mass-marketing successes, and I was by no means the first singer to questionably shop the temporal (and racial) marketplace that recordings provide in the service of imagining authenticity.

Ethnomusicologists have long been occupied with self-reflexive questions of cultural appropriation, wrestling with our participation in oppressive power structures and wresting our focus away from the search for authenticity. In the groundbreaking collection *Performing Ethnomusicology: Teaching and Representation in World Music Ensembles* (2004), Michelle Kisliuk and Kelly Gross write about the postcolonial problems of representation in a BaAka ensemble at the University of Virginia. The embodiment of the music culture through music and dance is a primary pedagogical goal for Kisliuk, but she and Gross assert that such inherently appropriative work requires a redefinition of "authenticity" and an aspirational shift from imitative performance to interpretive (Kisliuk and Gross 2004: 253). And as I learned, the performative choices ethnomusicologists make should be carefully considered when both the fantasy of self-authenticity and the reality of power structures hang in the balance.

Those structures that underlie vocal borderscaping are key in any study of voices that shift among genres or styles or places. In the digital rush of the 21st century's globalizing culture, music forms a primary aisle in the cultural marketplace, and if any identity may be easily stolen there, singers must carefully consider the potential implications when finding a voice in that marketplace, as well. The multitudes with access not only to recent technological advances but also to older libraries of recorded song also have immediate access to multiple voices. Jacob Smith (2008), in the book *Vocal Tracks: Performance and Sound Media*, traces characteristics of 20th-century recorded vocal styles and their cultural meanings, and he discusses the impact of recordings on how singers learned (for example, see Smith 2008: 132, on the implications of microphone and amplification technology; and p. 136, on the transmission of vocal performances of Blackness). In other words, the voices singers listen to can inform their own, and a singer's access to voices of many cultures can provide ways to negotiate the crossing of cultural borders.

The following sections detail the ways in which two singers have made and carried their voices through geographical and cultural borderscapes. The first introduces the work of a Korean-Canadian-American mezzo-soprano, and the ways in which she has molded her singing for different contexts, for different audiences, as she manages the shifting shape of her ethnic identity. The second centers on the strategic uses of a song that requires dual vocalities, a multivocal song grounded in the globalizing influence of 20th-century film, and in the geopolitical interrelationships through which music moves.

Crossing Genre, Geographical, and Cultural Borders

Gloria Anzaldúa wrote, in *Borderlands/La Frontera: The New Mestiza*: "I will have my voice: Indian, Spanish, white. I will have my serpent's tongue—my woman's voice, my sexual voice, my poet's voice. I will overcome the tradition of silence" (Anzaldúa 1999[1987]: 81). The borderscape of Anzaldúa's voice is sounded in many ways, within and across boundaries of identity and of place. The silence she will overcome comprises an externally imposed and internalized silencing of self—of the space to sound all aspects of her identity, all of her voices.

If vocal genre-crossing can be instrumental in the shaping of a singer's self-identity, it is also essential to consider how other moving components of identity might impact the sense of personal voice as it moves between geographically grounded musics. Mezzo-soprano Charlene Chi Kim was born in Canada and has lived in the United States for more than twenty years. She grew up speaking Korean at home, and she learned French and English in school. She discussed with me how she became interested in singing Korean music, after discovering that ethnic difference could make a difference in casting decisions:

> A singer has to know the body very well—the physicality has a lot to do with technique. And then past that, a singer needs to know their own identity very well... [so] here I am coming out on stage, and no matter what wig I'm wearing, no matter what makeup I wear, I can not hide my ethnicity. And the fact is I don't want to hide my identity. So I started to question myself... and began to look into Korean music and Korean tradition. (interview, July 10, 2011)

For Ms. Kim, the experience of singing traditional Korean songs in westernized arrangements has figured strongly in her understanding of her own, gendered, ethnic identity. She estimates that in the past decade, around 40 percent of her performances have been for Korean or Korean American audiences whom, she says, ten years ago always requested Korean songs and *hanbok*, traditional Korean women's dress; but more recently, they have been asking for western formal gowns, famous opera arias, and classical-crossover repertoire. But no matter what the repertoire, she reiterates, it is imperative that she sing with a quintessential Korean quality, called *jeong*.[5] Ms. Kim,[6] observing that there isn't one English word that can define *jeong*, describes it as a cross-disciplinary term indicating "a very, very deep belief, or passion, or discernment, and identity awareness." Psychiatrists Christopher Chung and Samson Cho write that the idea of *jeong* also exists in Chinese and Japanese cultures, represented by the same Chinese character, but that it has broader meaning in Korean usage. There, in addition to "feeling, love, sentiment, passion, human nature, sympathy, heart," it also encompasses "attachment, bond, affection, even bondage," and is located both inside the heart and in the interaction between individuals, or between individuals and objects or individuals and places (Chung and Cho 2012). *Jeong*, then, is a powerful and multivocal concept that in many ways connects people with each other, and with Korea. It is honest, inimitable, Ms. Kim asserts, "something that is very authentic to oneself," and for singers it "is shared from the performer to the audience." When she sings with *jeong*, she relates,

> I feel that my entire body is involved and engaged. My entire body. It's something that the Alexander technique cannot define, or achieve. Because now your soul is integrated into the physicality of singing as well. (interview, July 10, 2011)

And when it comes to vocal performance, *jeong* trumps everything else. In Ms. Kim's experience, Korean listeners would never consider her mezzo voice ideal, as it does not conform to a Korean aesthetic that largely privileges high-pitched voices in women—young pop stars and other women in the media typically model high speaking voices as the epitome of femininity; in opera, the internationally celebrated Korean coloratura Sumi Jo (Jo Sumi)'s Queen of the Night aria ("Der Hölle Rache") is often lauded as the pinnacle of vocal perfection. But in spite of her own low range, Ms. Kim says that her performances are nevertheless received warmly because she sings with *jeong*. She explains, "All of those other things become very small, and they don't care. All they see is, 'Ah, she's Korean because she understands the *jeong*.'"

Ms. Kim articulates, as does Rhiannon Giddens, an understanding of discrete voices within her sense of self—voices separated not only by genre but also by context: for opera, for Korean songs, for Christian Contemporary, and for pop

---

[5] There are other romanized transliterations of this term, including, as Nicholas Harkness uses, *chŏng* (Harkness 2013). Harkness also discusses the perception among Koreans that the presence of *jeong* (*chŏng*) singing is in decline.

[6] Ms. Kim holds a doctorate of musical arts in vocal performance, but prefers the prefix "Ms." for this publication.

music, as well as one she uses "in the shower" or when singing to her husband, "my most intimate voice," as she names it. This is a useful example of register in its dual meanings, as detailed in the introduction: linguistic register, or the association of distinct speech practices with varying situational contexts; and singing register, according to western classical discourse, involving a change in vocal quality. Ms. Kim's vocalities are determined by genre, by language, and by her relationship with her audience. For her, multivocality is a conscious reality, marking, like Ms. Giddens's demo album, intertwined elements of identity: gendered ethnicity and place; religious and the domestic spheres; her self embodied and emplaced and sounded in the most complex of signals.

Ya Toyour

In 2016, I attended a Toledo, Ohio, event titled "Mideast X Midwest:[7] A Dialogue of Music, Food, and Fun at America's Crossroads." Detroit's National Arab Orchestra performed with the Toledo Symphony Orchestra, along with local school choirs and guest soloist Lubana Al-Quntar, billed as "Syria's first opera singer." A Syrian refugee living in the United States, Ms. Al-Quntar had taught both western operatic singing and *tarab*[8] at the Conservatoire in Damascus before the Islamic Revolution. She grew up singing Arab music, in a family related to the iconic Syrian-Egyptian star Asmahan[9]—her grandmother was cousin to the mother of siblings Asmahan and Farid al-Atrash. She says that her family, and eventually others, observed early on a likeness between Asmahan's voice and her own. Ms. Al-Quntar loved Asmahan's repertoire, and the ultra-iconic Umm Kulthum's, but she says she always wanted to do something "different" in singing. When the conservatory in Damascus opened an opera department, she jumped at the opportunity; though she didn't know much at the time about opera or western classical music, she did know that she wanted to learn about the process of singing: "I was fascinated about the idea of *learning* how to sing. It doesn't matter what style it is, but I wanted to know more about the voice and the breathing and all this" (interview, December 4, 2016). Ms. Al-Quntar studied in Damascus for four years, beginning in 1993, then for two years at the Royal College of Music in London, and attended the Maastricht Academy of Music in Holland. When she began to study opera, her teacher asked her to stop singing

---

[7] A play on the Austin, Texas, festival of technology and music, "South X Southwest."
[8] *Tarab* refers to both a repertory of classic songs based in Arab poetic traditions, and in the *maqam* or Arab modal system, and to the state of ecstasy a performance is meant to induce.
[9] Asmahan (born Amal al-Atrash) belonged to a branch of the politically significant Syrian Druze al-Atrash clan, relocated to Egypt. Her brother, Farid al-Atrash, became the renowned "King of the 'Ud."

Arab music or in any style other than western classical. She abandoned Arab music for seven years, but eventually felt that the technique she had learned, the awareness she had gained of her physical instrument's mechanics, had allowed her to improve her singing in *tarab* vocality as well.

Her history in two vocalities served her well when returned to Syria to head the opera department at the conservatory in Damascus. There, she taught western classical singing, but also established an "Arabic singing technique department" (interview, December 4, 2016). She applied western classical training techniques to Arab music, asking her opera and *tarab* students to practice the same kinds of exercises, including triadic arpeggios, though with distinct modes of resonance. The *bel canto* conceptualization of breathing, she says, and of vowels, functions well in *tarab*. The primary difference, she explains, lies in the corporeal location where the singer feels the strongest vibration:

> In opera I teach the same method in terms of breathing, of the vowels; there are specific rules you can follow at the same time with opera and with Arabic [music]. But in terms of the *place* of singing, like where the sound has to vibrate, it's different. In Arabic you are completely singing from your throat, exactly from the throat and from the chest. The vowels have to be with the mouth and the articulation the same as opera, but in opera you are using the head voice, and you use your body just to support your higher notes, and your resonance, and the vowels. In Arabic [music] you do much the same, but you open your throat. . . . Instead of making the head voice resonance, I tell my students to open the throat and the chest, so the chest is the place of the vowels to resonance. So it's the same method. (interview, December 4, 2016)

Her training in *tarab* had consisted primarily of studying the recordings of renowned singers, not only Asmahan, but also Umm Kulthum. (She also was told once that she sounded like Maria Callas, so she listened closely to her, as well as to Joan Sutherland and Leontyne Price.) In her youth in Egypt, Umm Kulthum famously studied Qur'an at village *kuttab*-s (primary religious schools), and absorbed the fundamentals of recitation there (Danielson 1997: 22); as with other singers of her time, her later reputation in secular music partly hinged on how strongly her expressive performance style was informed by her knowledge of *tajwid*, the rules of Quranic recitation. In her biography of Umm Kulthum, Virginia Danielson describes her singing as a combination of these qualities with "what the cognoscenti of Cairo taught as historically Arab aesthetics" (92). She demonstrated a range beyond two octaves, vocal strength, an admired ability to sing long phrases, and the meaningful changes in tone color that Egyptian listeners associate with religiously learned musicians—a hoarseness or break, *bahha*, a nasality called *ghunna* or *khanaafa*, and the judicious use of falsetto, vibrato, and trill.

Though not herself Muslim (her family, like Asmahan's, is Druze), Ms. Al-Quntar says that she analyzed and absorbed elements of Umm Kulthum's *tajwid* foundations. She considered these practices again when she began teaching *tarab* at the conservatory. In particular, she notes that *tajwid* study has historically had a useful impact on *tarab* singers' breathing, the long phrases of Qur'anic recitation allowing them to manage the similar demands of *tarab*. The breathing techniques required across *tajwid* and the music of *tarab* and *bel canto*, she believes, are one and the same. "You cannot divide one sentence, you cannot breathe in each word" (interview, December 4, 2016).

At the 2016 concert, Ms. Al-Quntar's showpiece was Muhammad al-Qasabji's composition "Taghrid al-Balabil" ("The Warbling of the Nightingales," with lyrics by Ahmad Fathi). More popularly known as "Ya Toyour" ("Oh, Birds") after its opening words, the song takes its singer through both *tarab* and *bel canto* paces, juxtaposing *maqam* virtuosity and light western coloratura in quick oscillation between one phrase and another. Al-Qasabji first offered his 1941 "Ya Toyour" to Umm Kulthum, in whose career he had become instrumental as composer and 'ud player—but, according to Samim Sharif, "her golden throat hadn't reckoned with the science of western music, solfegio [sic]" (Sharif 1981: 227, quoted in Zuhur 2000: 101). And al-Qasabji passed the song along instead to Umm Kulthum's rival, Asmahan.

Asmahan's film career coincided with that of her younger contemporaries in Hollywood, Deanna Durbin and her successor, Kathryn Grayson. Ms. Al-Quntar told me that al-Qasabji had been inspired to write "Ya Toyour" upon hearing Johann Strauss's 1882 piece "Frühlingsstimmen" ("Voices of Spring") waltz, a sweet and similarly nightingale-centered soprano showcase populated by trills, ornaments, and moments of staccato, an ornithological imitation on which al-Qasabji conceivably based his own. Though I have not found a reference, I wonder if it may be significant that Kathryn Grayson sang "Frühlingsstimmen" in her first film, *Andy Hardy's Private Secretary*, in 1941, the same year al-Qasabji wrote "Ya Toyour"; perhaps the film was an inspiration. Sherifa Zuhur suggests that the coloratura in "Ya Toyour," which she calls "The 'Queen of the Night' section of the song," demonstrated that Asmahan "could musically equal the Deanna Durbins or the Jenny Linds of any country" (Zuhur 2000: 101). In other words, she was film-worthy and could appeal to a broad audience—she was an icon of popular culture, to which she brought a classic quality.

Both al-Qasabji and Asmahan, especially owing to the success of "Ya Toyour," are considered to have masterfully integrated elements of European elite genres into Arab music. Ali Racy explains a dominant 20th-century Cairene musical aesthetic as a "neutral canvas" of Arab musical elements hosting patches of color, with musical forms on a continuum from wholly "neutral"—precomposed songs with *tarab* characteristics—to a linear structure with segments in contrasting styles. Western classical and film musics become significant sources of color, as in "Ya Toyour," which certainly exhibits stylistic contrast. Racy continues to explore the idea of sound color through the popular concept of *lawn* (in Arabic, literally "color") in the context of Arab music discourse. The neutral-canvas model, he writes, is often referred to as *lawn tarab*, and sounds from a western palette provide *lawn gharbi* (western color). Asmahan's use of *bel canto* might even be termed *lawn upira*, or operatic color (Racy 1982: 395–396).

Compositions in this model emphasize tradition, innovation, and an artist's individual special quality, or *lawn khāss* ("special color," *lawn* meaning "color," *khāss* meaning "particular"), which may concern vocal timbre or use of ornaments (Racy 1982: 400); Racy gives Asmahan as an example. She was "proficient in the area of *tarab*," and also "highly innovative" (393), able to "inlay the fundamentals of European singing into Arab singing," according to Ilyās Saḥḥāb (Saḥḥāb 1980: 64, quoted in Racy 1982: 393). Racy also defines *lawn* in his book *Making Music in the Arab World: The Culture and Artistry of Tarab* (2003), calling it a musical style or "flavor," but also noting that it may refer to "a stylistically distinct segment within an eclectic piece of music" (227). Zuhur, cautioning readers who focus on Asmahan's operatic abilities, asserts that Asmahan is too competent in *lawn tarab* to be associated simply with a westernized sound. It is also important to remember that al-Qasabji and Asmahan were not aiming to cross over into western markets but, rather, were experimenting with the kind of modern, eclectic Arab style that had inspired the musicians present at the Congrès de Musique Arabe du Caire in 1932.[10]

In Asmahan's recording of "Ya Toyour," she shifts between two *lawn*-s, two vocalities—within the *tarab* sections, a medium-to-heavy register typically heard in contemporary Arab film songs; and a consistently vibratoed, lighter register in the most Straussian moments of the song, such as the final cadenza, featuring a birdlike call and response between her operatic soprano and the violin (replacing the flute that plays a similar role in "Frühlingsstimme"). When she sings diatonic scales and triadic arpeggios with clearly western ornamental motives, she remains in that lighter register, even at lower pitches. In the *tarab* sections of the music, her passages (which take her up to D5) tend to involve her heavier register and a virtuosic modal exposition. Her performance goes as far as a staccato A5, though the highest segments mostly center on G5.

A significant difference between the vocalities may lie in the idea of vocality as vowel-ness (see introduction), with Italian vowels favored in western classical

---

[10] Al-Qasabji, himself, had a tense relationship with the Congrès. (Vigreux 1992, cited in Danielson 1994: 135).

diction, such as the singular open vowel for /a/, while Egyptian Arabic includes a range of /a/-related vowels between a front-positioned /æ/, to a back-positioned version (Cowan 1970: 96). There are places in "Ya Toyour," though, where East and West intersect—the final cadenza taking her operatic staccato into maqam modulation and the use throughout of descending and ascending portamenti—characteristic, if in distinct ways, of both Arab and western styles.

Lubana Al-Quntar has sung "Ya Toyour" many times, in many countries; and it has helped her to successfully cross borders throughout Syria, Europe, and the United States. Two very different performances are available as of 2017 on iTunes and YouTube: one, released on the official recording of the 2000 Queen Elisabeth competition in Brussels, where she placed fifth in singing; the other, recorded at the Festival de la Medina in Tunisia more than a decade later (https://www.youtube.com/watch?v=EPyMyrLgNiM). Typically, when she performs the song, she shifts between two *lawn*-s like Asmahan; however, in her Brussels performance, when she was participating in a western classical singing competition, she sang it truncated (but including the final cadenza), a cappella, and at a pitch higher than the other performance (and higher than Asmahan's recording), centered on B-flat instead of G. This change in pitch helped her to emphasize the high tessitura highlighted in western classical vocality, and she avoided any heavy-registered *tarab* vocalizations at all, finishing on a suitably operatic B-flat 5. Conversely, and more like Asmahan's rendition, the performance recorded in Tunisia showcases her ease with both *tarab* and *bel canto* singing—low and high pitch ranges, heavy and light registration, and ornamental practices specific to each style. Ms. Al-Quntar finds special meaning in this way of performing the song:

> Singing the *tarab* is very dear to me, because this is what we sing, and what we embrace, and this is our culture. And then to go to the opera part, I feel like the song was made for me. . . . I like the style, I like the idea so much, the East and the West in music. (interview, December 4, 2016)

I asked her whether she feels that one way of singing is more "her" than the other.

"Actually," she answered, "I ask myself this question a lot, and [other] people ask me this question, and always, I cannot choose. So apparently both are me. . . . I feel both actually. I really feel both equally" (interview, December 4, 2016). Two vocalities reside in one singer, wherever she resides, and "Ya Toyour" encapsulates them both. The dual *lawn*-s of "Ya Toyour" allowed Ms. Al-Quntar to cross borders, to negotiate a global career, and then exile.

Considering Judith Butler's question—"How do we read the agency of the subject when its demand for cultural and psychic and political survival makes itself known as style?" (Butler 2000: 36)—Ms. Al-Quntar's use of both *bel canto* and *tarab* singing becomes a means for her survival as a refugee. The original draft of this chapter also discussed a white American singer using "Ya Toyour" as an entrée into the Arab music industry, but the singer withdrew from the project for religious reasons. I nevertheless mention this here because it is important to note that the song's East–West in-betweenness makes it conducive for use in both directions—in order to find a place in a new cultural context.

To find a voice, a classically trained singer may navigate multiple vocalities. Despite pervasive essentialist discourse about voice, they may in some ways leave one vocality for another, though performative habits are often difficult to break—or they may feel that they embody two or more vocalities as they chart the borderscapes of their vocal identities. They may rely on shifts in vocality to negotiate the boundaries and intersections of different geographical, social, and cultural spaces, and to sound their intersubjective individualities in new places. Their choices may be guided by culture-specific discourses about self, about individualism, and/or about a relationship to broader cultural identity.

In many ways, the freedom to choose a vocal identity is a privilege in the increasingly accessible, increasingly messy global sonic marketplace. Sometimes, multivocality becomes a strategy for cultural interaction and sometimes a strategy for survival. It is important, in the context of multivocality and agency, to remember Judith Butler's question regarding political survival and style (Butler 2000: 36). The singers featured in this chapter have demonstrated that vocalities perceived as culturally homogenous—within the western classical context, for example, or in *tarab*—can hold extremely heterogeneous meanings for the complex individuals who employ them.

2
Vox Populi, Vox Divo
Voicing Genre Politics in Classical Crossover

> That's why I'm going to
> Sing in op'ra, sing in op'ra,
> Sing in op-pop-pop-pop-pop-popera.
> —Aldous Huxley, *Crome Yellow* (1921)

Four young singers with matinee-idol features stride onto the stage at the Fox Theater in Detroit, met by an explosion of flashbulbs and Beatle-maniacal screaming. But in spite of these pop trappings, and though they belt out a string of '90s hits from Mariah Carey and Toni Braxton, this is no boy band. Instead, the group, Il Divo, is known as a *popera* quartet—a portmanteau ensemble for the portmanteau culture of the 21st century—comprising two operatic tenors and a baritone, and a French pop star who is strikingly branded in the international press as "vox populi." The smoothing over of the internal division between opera and pop—what is being crossed in *Billboard*'s "classical crossover" charts where Il Divo is tracked—reflects more than just the transgression of genre boundaries. As I began this work, I envisioned finding intersecting ideologies of genre and class, and I have encountered some; however, it became clear that there is much more at stake. The genre-borderland of popera offers a tangle of interlaced ideological lines to cross: lines from old dialogues about class and culture, industry pickup lines to woo female consumers, and the gender and color lines woven through the tapestry of popular music history.

"Popera" is a neologism that over the past decade and a half has grown into an umbrella category applied by music critics to a number of different international, genre-bending contexts, old and new—for example, the Three Tenors, the Irish Tenors, the American Tenors, the Ten Tenors, the Twelve Irish Tenors (a record number of tenors!), Il Volo, and quartets like Spain's Compañía Lírica Pópera (one of two rare examples in which the term "popera" has willingly been appropriated by the singers; the other is the Bulgarian singer Krassimir Avramov)—as well as Il Divo. It is a voice-centric branch under the international music industry's umbrella category of *classical crossover*, which has encompassed myriad ways (instrumental and vocal) of combining western classical and popular musics.

Among many markers of the component genres and styles, popera singers and their audiences especially rely on the connotations of vocality, and they manipulate it to acknowledge and blur the imagined borders associated with related musical epistemologies.

This chapter examines how popera singers have negotiated intertwined social and aesthetic discourses through this multivocal work. Like much of mass-mediated culture in the 21st century, popera is a global phenomenon, sounding within local contexts. Among its roots are intertwined the geopolitics of European song competitions and the difficult politics of race and immigration that have shaped American popular musics since the 19th century. Because of the breadth and extensive timeline of vocal crossover, I have chosen to narrow my focus; though women's and children's voices have contributed vitally to popera, this chapter is concerned with the primacy of male singers—particularly those in the iconic tenor category. Tenors constitute an exceptionally poperatic area of study; in range, audience, practices, and cultural context, they provide a rich crossover nexus where the heroic idol of 19th-century opera meets the male pop idol of the 20th and early 21st centuries.

Classical crossover, as a product of the neoliberal global music industry, demonstrates Couldry's "crisis of voice" (Couldry 2014: 1–2), offering a panorama of often-marginalized vocalities yet simultaneously maintaining the classed, racialized, and gendered structures of power that have long kept marginalized voices from being heard. Importantly, though, some of those marginalized voices have chosen to capitalize on the borderland status of crossover to find a marketable artistic niche, and to resist the silencing force of market-centered art. In this chapter, I investigate popera as a space in which popular music is colonized at once by the voices and bodies that dominate conventional operatic spaces and by the voices typically barred from operatic spaces who create their own (see figure 2.1).

Defining Popera

The term "popera," of course, implies an elision or a hybrid form, and though it can be difficult to separate what is "pop" about it and what is "operatic," popera juxtaposes elements of distinct vocalities as genre signifiers. A significant history is at work here, of course: the codifying of opera as something other than popular is a relatively recent plot development, with the genre removed deliberately from its early duality as part of both public *and* elite life sometime between the 1860s and the 1930s, depending on which historians you follow. Opera, as John Storey writes, "did not become unpopular, rather it was *made* unpopular" (Storey 2002: 37).

Figure 2.1 Marquee announcing Il Divo at the Fox Theater in Detroit, May 17, 2009.

Though not all popera is American (for example, much of its canonic repertoire and several artists have emerged from the Sanremo Music Festival in Italy; the membership of Il Divo is international; their management is British; and many of their songs are written by Scandinavian composers), the mutual influences of American popular and operatic traditions are paramount. Nineteenth-century popular parlor songs, including some minstrel repertoire, became recital and later recording staples for opera singers (the Australian diva Nellie Melba, for example, recorded Stephen Foster's "Old Folks at Home" in 1905). And operatic singing had a place in the earliest American-grown forms of popular culture, particularly the minstrel show, as well as in the vaudeville formats that followed. In both contexts, the imagination of race through vocal expression played a significant role.

Allison McCracken traces a key shift in popular vocality that took place when the vaudeville circuit met the electric circuit: a popular vocal aesthetic known as "crooning," today understood as the singing of "popular, sentimental songs in a low, smooth voice, especially into a closely-held microphone" (McCracken 2015: 2). McCracken associates crooning with early 20th-century aesthetic constructions of whiteness and Blackness, gender, and middle-class identities, and identifies its sonic lineage in more recent popular microphone-based singing styles. Today, popera's multivocality combines *bel canto* singing with the crooning aesthetics that has informed popular music from the minstrel show to R&B, developed through decades of advances in the mediation of sound and to this day based in ideologies of identity. It is a borderland shaped and reshaped by the diasporic voices of the early to mid-20th century, by Black voices, by queer voices.

Vocality is one crucial site where the negotiation of this politics takes place in popera. I suggest that others include: (1) the marketing strategies that sell popera's multivocality as a neoliberal expansion of consumer choice by virtue of conflation—courting the tastes of pop fans and opera fans alike in one place—and simultaneously acknowledging, blurring, and manipulating the discursive divisions between opera and popular music; (2) the repertoire that showcases this multivocality; and (3) the technologies that mediate it. I also argue that popera has emerged as a (cross-)genre at once eclectic and narrow, balanced on a fulcrum of contrasting vocalities that are grounded in specific histories of race, class, and gender.

Marketing Strategies

Part of the "pop" in "popera" lies in the way it is marketed through methods typically used to sell commercial music and Broadway shows—in particular, television appearances as well as websites where singers can interact virtually with their fans (another line being crossed). Il Divo's U.S. publicist, Lois Najarian, described to me how the greatest challenge in promoting the group is "to get the music to people without the traditional venues"; you don't hear Il Divo on the radio, and you can't introduce them through videos on MTV. Instead, like the Three, Irish, and American Tenors, they've appeared at large stadium and musical-theater venues, and had a special aired in the United States on PBS, whose audience, Najarian says, is "slightly older, more sophisticated," and especially "open" to projects with classical-music qualities like Il Divo's. And, most frequently, the group does the daytime talk-show circuit, appearing on programs like *Good Morning America*, *Live with Regis and Kelly*, *The Oprah Winfrey Show*, *The View*, and *The Martha Stewart Show* (interview, March 23, 2009). They've also appeared three times on the daytime soap opera *The Young and the Restless*, in 2005, 2006, and 2007.

This strategy highlights the gendered construction of popera demographics. Daytime talk-show and soap audiences are understood in the entertainment industry as predominantly female (Shattuc 1997), and so is Il Divo's audience. According to Najarian, market research has shown that women 35 and older account for an overwhelming majority of the group's fans. It's two *generations* of women, as well, she says, the "moms and the grandmas" (interview, March 23, 2009). It is no coincidence that one of Il Divo's mainstays, from their first, self-titled album, is "Mama," written for the group as an emotional tribute to mothers. One woman I interviewed at the Detroit concert in 2009 said it was her favorite song; she was there with her son. Another fan had been given tickets as a Mother's Day gift by her husband (field notes, May 17, 2009). Homages to mothers thread through the world of popera and its progenitors—McCracken describes the mother songs of the vaudeville era as based in a prominent "Victorian cult of motherhood." Mothers are much lauded, especially by their sons, in early 20th-century popular song,[1] in part drawn from minstrelsy's adjacent fetishization of the mammy character, in whose nostalgic lullabies the "crooning" vocality was grounded (McCracken 2015: 17). Popera revives the celebration of mothers as nostalgic cultural icons and as target consumers.

As I noted earlier, Il Divo isn't a boy band—its members are not teenagers but, rather, men now in their 40s and early 50s, whose Armani image is more *GQ* than 'NSYNC. Many of their fans, of course, are mothers. Still, some of their most ardent female fans communicate their devotion in the same way as one might expect at a Backstreet Boys or, perhaps, a Tom Jones concert: they throw their underwear onstage. Branden James, a member of the Twelve Irish Tenors and a 2013 finalist in *America's Got Talent*, relates that one female fan was so taken with him that she attended show after show and made arrangements in Las Vegas, without his knowledge, to marry him. The attention from women, Mr. James suggests, makes the performer–audience relationship more "like a boy band" than opera, in his experience (interview, March 11, 2010). Knickers and vows aside, music associated with feminine taste has long been scoffed at as overly sentimental, artistically empty, and inappropriate listening material for cisgender, straight men. It is telling that Il Divo has collaborated with Céline Dion and Barbra Streisand, indicating the goal of a shared market with those artists, especially among women and gay men. (Mr. James confirms that in South Africa on a 2010 tour, the Twelve Irish Tenors amassed an impressive following among the gay community there.) The men seated near me at the 2009 Il Divo concert in Detroit were attending with their mothers or wives. As the lights dimmed before the show, I heard one of them ask, "Why am I here, again?" (field notes, May 17, 2009).

The primacy of the female demographic in the aesthetics of popera reaches far back into the formative years of American popular culture. McCracken writes about the ways in which vaudeville shows were marketed to women in the early

---

[1] As an example, I offer a song popularly performed by John McCormack, pioneer in the mixing of popular music and opera: vaudeville composer Frank Tours's setting of the Rudyard Kipling classic "Mother O' Mine" (published 1903).

20th century; in fact, she pinpoints the female audience as a key development in the formal shift from the minstrel show to vaudeville. "One way promoters wooed female audiences," she explains, "was by altering the structure of entertainment to feature the male solo singer and his [romantic] ballads" (McCracken 2015: 69), emotionally directed to women. And vaudeville touted its male singers as stars to be erotically desired. Women in vaudeville's heyday, McCracken continues, were symbols of a classed and racialized aesthetic—respectable but not elite—known today as *middlebrow*, and vaudeville strove to appeal to them. Today, journalists often couch their critiques of popera in this vocabulary.

Highbrow and *lowbrow* are concepts grounded in the racist and anti-immigrant pseudo-science known as phrenology, which in the 19th century, and later revived in the early 20th century, posited that the bodies of (non–Anglo-Saxon) populations phrenologically associated with low brow ridges demonstrated near-primate, less than human physiology, their brains of less than human intelligence—and therefore having poor cultural capabilities and taste (see Lipsitz 1991; Peterson and Kern 1996; Levine 1988). The term "middlebrow" emerged as a humorously conceived supplement to the previous "-brows," in the context of taste-making journalism, with editor Russell Lynes's 1949 piece in *Harper's* titled "Highbrow, Lowbrow, Middlebrow" (Lynes 1976[1949]). In a humorous but biting analysis, Lynes sorted Americans according to their habits of cultural consumption. A 1976 reprint of Lynes's essay in *The Wilson Quarterly* claims to reproduce the chart that was in the original in 1949, "with minor changes" (Lynes 1976[1949]: 154); it assigns customs of fashion, interior decorating, entertainment, and dining to highbrow, middlebrow, and lowbrow consumers. Within Lynes's subcategories for middlebrow, "theater" is assigned to the upper middlebrow consumer and "musical extravaganza films" to the lower middlebrow. Popera does count on attracting musical-theater audiences, fans of a middlebrow genre that today as in 1949 includes both stage and screen. Lynes's critique preceded the advent of rock and roll, the popular music that seemed to break most definitively away from the classical and deepen the discursive divide. The article was, not inconsequentially, published during the period that Keir Keightley identifies as the early years of "easy listening," when radio programming included a great number of both familiar classical works and "semi-classical" pieces influenced by Romantic composers (Keightley 2008: 316). By this time, Canadian soprano and film star Deanna Durbin was a household name, combining opera and popular culture; and tenor Mario Lanza was just about to burst onto U.S. movie screens and in records. Radios and phonographs had become fixtures in middle-class American homes, making such listening literally "easy" for middle-class consumers.

In a 2010 conference presentation, ethnomusicologist Jeremy Wallach, who has written extensively about hybridity in popular music (Wallach 2008), highlighted the inherently hybrid construction of "middlebrow culture. I talked with him about it many years later, and he reminded me that middlebrow is an ideological and practical mixture of high and low cultures and, he continued, self-reflexively seeks the affective expressivity that supposedly underlies all art regardless of genre or cultural status. Middlebrow forms "often provocatively juxtapose different genres" in order to "'reveal universal human themes'" thought to be lying below the surface of apparent disparity (personal communication, June 2, 2017). Popera fits this model well, too, its hybridities of genre and style searching for universals (love, sentimentality, motherhood) underneath the seeming disparity of opera and pop. Both the successes and the criticisms of popera today owe much to these notions of middlebrow culture. Additionally, in 1996, Richard A. Peterson and Roger M. Kern noted a distinct and recent shift in attitudes toward culture that took Americans from "snobs" to eclectic "omnivores" and a more accepting view of "low- or middlebrow" music (Peterson and Kern 1996: 900). The omnivory of multiculturalist consumption in the millennial years is strongly linked to the rise of neoliberalism (Melamed 2006). And it is perhaps significant that classical crossover singing blossomed in the early 1990s music market, generating the original popera ensemble: the Three Tenors.

Repertoire

Twenty-first-century popera includes a diverse set of repertoires, but certain trends stand out. First, there are new songs as well as pop ballads that have topped American or European charts, including Anglophone examples translated into romance languages (the Righteous Brothers' "Unchained Melody" sung in Italian as "Senza Catene"—a favorite in Il Divo's catalog). Second, popera repertoire involves the remnants of earlier crossover eras: (1) 19th-century songs popular at the beginning of the recording industry, associated with diasporic national, regional, or racialized/ethnic identities (for example, Irish and Neapolitan songs and, for Black singers, spirituals and sorrow songs); and (2) arias and songs associated with 20th-century musical films: (a) the repertoire of operatic singers popularized on the silver screen, such as Mario Lanza (his "La Donna è Mobile" in the 1951 film *The Great Caruso*), or standards from the American Songbook ("You'll Never Walk Alone" from Rodgers and Hammerstein's *Carousel*); (b) warhorse Puccini arias, especially those that might be familiar from films (*Turandot*'s "Nessun Dorma" as heard in the 1984 film *The Killing Fields*, or "O Mio Babbino Caro," the aria from *Gianni Schicchi* that appeared in the 1985 period piece *A Room with a View*); and (c) repurposed themes from cinematic soundtracks

("Nella Fantasia," based on a melody from Ennio Morricone's soundtrack for *The Mission*).

Anglophone Pop Ballads in Romance Languages

The music Il Divo sings is often on the nostalgic side, featuring songs with an already established presence in popular culture and expressive of heightened emotion and dramatic vocality—for example, Toni Braxton's "Unbreak My Heart" (by Diane Warren) or Sinatra's "My Way," or the iconically passionate "Unchained Melody." Popera artists have a predilection for singing in romance languages; Il Divo performs "Unbreak My Heart" and "Unchained Melody" in Spanish and Italian, respectively. The performance of originally Anglophone songs in Italian recalls the weight placed on the Italian language in opera. Sony/BMG executive Simon Cowell, who created Il Divo, explains his preference for translation this way: "the classical style loses its mystique in English, and can sound very old-fashioned" ("Simon Cowell" 2008). And turning a well-known pop song like "Unbreak My Heart" into "Regresa a Mi," Il Divo tenor David Miller suggests, makes it feel like a new song—at once familiar and something that must be listened to with "fresh ears." Two American fans told me that the Spanish and French and Italian enriched their experience, asserting that even if one can't understand the foreign language, "you can still feel the meaning" (interview with Linda Sears, May 17, 2009). Mr. Miller also sees *vocal* benefits in the language:

> The bonus to it is that Spanish is much easier to sing than English, operatically, anyways. Like when we get to the final ... choruses and stuff, with English there's a lot of /i/s and a lot of /ae/s and a lot of really unpleasant vowels to sing on a high C. So the bonus for me is, Spanish and Italian, I can let my [operatic] technique[s] show through in those moments, on a pure /a/ vowel, as opposed to an /ae/, you know, [it] makes my life a lot easier. (interview, March 10, 2009)

The idea that romance-language vowels are more comfortable in his operatic vocality supports the relevance of the vowel/vocality relationship I mentioned in the introduction, where the acoustic structure of a vowel contributes the first two formants (groups of overtones) of a vocal sound (Sundberg 1987).

Considering the issue of romance languages, I asked Lois Najarian about the ubiquity of the press describing pop singer Sébastien Izambard as "vox populi," as if it were a conventional way, like "tenor" or "baritone," of categorizing a vocal range or Fach. She dismissed the phrase vaguely as "something someone put in a bio sometime." But in fact, I wonder if it originated as a misinterpretation of Allegra Rossi's explanation in her 2005 Il Divo biography (early in their career), in which she describes Izambard in these terms: "A tenor in pitch, Sébastien's voice is the 'vox populi'—the pop singer, the popular voice—of the group" (Rossi 2006: 45). Sébastien's colleague David Miller calls the expression "snooty," and assured me that "it's the record company trying to [be] classy" (interview, March 10, 2009). It certainly holds *implications* of class, if conflicted. "Vox populi" is a phrase used in journalism to indicate "man on the street" interviews; it's Latin for "the voice of the people," but today that's a language linked with socioeconomically selective private education.

Vox populi also draws attention to two important concepts in popera: first, that *voice* is at the center of the genre; and second, that, like opera in its original form, popera is at once democratic and elite. Multiple examples of poperatic singing rely on the notion of voice as an identity per se—it is not mere chance that Malena Ernman sang a composition titled "La Voix" for Sweden in the 2009 Eurovision Song Contest, or that Ireland's song "The Voice" won the competition in 1996 (written by Brendan Graham, also composer of the popera standard "You Raise Me Up"). And Cezar "The Voice" Ouatu finished the 2013 competition in thirteenth place. In 2001, British crossover tenor Russell Watson released his first album, *The Voice*, and in 2010, a new one titled *La Voce* (also meaning "the voice"). In these ubiquitous appellations, voice becomes something both reified and conflated with an individual singer's identity. (Notably, there isn't a similar plethora of artists named "Vladimir 'The Piano' Horowitz" or "Sarah 'The Violin' Chang.")

Vox populi is not the only class-conscious (and class-challenging) moniker assigned to male popera stars. The international media has routinely bestowed the title "the people's tenor," in the early years of the 21st century, upon Andrea Bocelli (whose voice Céline Dion, perhaps contradictorily, also once imagined as God's [when she introduced him on *These Are Special Times*, CBS, November 25, 1998]), and on *Britain's Got Talent* sensation Paul Potts, as well as on Michael Amante, Alfie Boe, posthumously on Luciano Pavarotti, and retrospectively on John McCormack and Mario Lanza. Russell Watson is one of the primary recipients of the designation; the first application appears to have been a 2001 newspaper item in which his vocal coach, Bill Hayward, declared, "Certainly in England, the opera establishment... is very snooty and very cliquey. He's not part of that, and he does not want to be. He's the people's tenor" (Moody 2001). Watson himself has expanded on this narrative in multiple press interviews, including a 2016 appearance on *The One Show* (BBC, July 11, 2016) in which he took his hosts to Greater Manchester to visit his childhood home in a suburb of Salford. He discussed his father's job as a steelworker, his own as a boltcutter, and introduced himself this way:

> In my time I've sung for the great and the good, and in front of some very special crowds. But my background is far from grand. Maybe that's why they call me "the people's tenor..." (BBC, *The One Show*, July 11, 2016)

Watson, notably, titled his autobiography *Finding My Voice* (2008). He represents the crux of Lynes's middlebrow—a working-class man negotiating elite culture and, in the process, reshaping it into something new. And in Il Divo, the *vox populi* title separates Izambard from the other members of Il Divo, not only along sonic lines but also along social ones, the operatic singer's vocal paradigm relying on different institutionalized ideologies of training, talent, and authenticity from Izambard's. The group's official press materials do the same. Their website tells fans that David Miller and Urs Bühler, American and Swiss tenors respectively, attended conservatories to study classical singing, and Spanish baritone Carlos Marín had master classes with opera icons Alfredo Kraus and Montserrat Caballé. In contrast, Izambard is touted as "the only completely self-taught singer" in the ensemble. Autodidacticism, a property more discursively associated with rock than with opera, is given an ever increasing importance in the democratic configuration of the millennial music industry, as global reality TV formats like *Britain's Got Talent*, *America's Got Talent*, *The X Factor*, and the 2003 *Operatunity* scour the world for everymen (and women) with marketable—but as yet unmarketed—voices. Il Divo had its own kind of "Do It Yourself" experience. The singers were cast and thrown together with a list of repertoire, without any stylistic instructions from producer Simon Cowell, who, according to Mr. Miller, only told them "you guys are the singers, go make something we can all be proud of" (interview March 10, 2009). With a repertoire comprising both pop and opera standards, and their attendant ideologies of voice, they did just that.

Repertoire and Diasporic History: Irish Tenors

The regional, national, and ethnic repertoire noted here comprises a history of diasporic identities that is perhaps best exemplified by "You Raise Me Up," a song canonical today among Il Divo and other popera performers. "You Raise Me Up" came from the instrumental duo Secret Garden—Norwegian pianist Rolf Løvland and Irish violinist and singer Fionnuala Sherry—but spread internationally through Josh Groban's 2003 recording on his album *Closer*, and across Europe thanks to impresario Simon Cowell's Irish boy band Westlife, in 2005. The song is largely based melodically on the "Londonderry Air," an Irish tune collected after the famine in the 19th century and made popular in the Irish nationalist folk-culture movement.[2] That provenance, writes Helen O'Shea, established the original tune as part of a gendered view of Ireland, the idea of its Mother Ireland nationhood and its classic culture both associated with the feminine, with sentimentality, and with the parlor, the home (O'Shea 2009: 11–12)— not irrelevant in the feminized context of popera. Later the "Londonderry Air" became an international phenomenon after English songwriter and lawyer Fred Weatherly published it with his lyrics as "Danny Boy" in 1913 (O'Shea 2009)— and it is possible that Weatherly learned of the tune from his sister-in-law after she heard immigrant Irish miners sing it in Ouray, Colorado (Robinson 1997, cited in Russell 2006: 44–45).

The groundwork for "Danny Boy" as a crossover favorite through the 20th century was laid in a 1915 Victor recording by German American opera singer Ernestine Schumann-Heink (Audley 2000: 207), and other opera stars who followed in her footsteps. But the Irish tenor was a crossover role already firmly established in U.S. culture, a staple in the minstrel show (Giddins 1986: 206), in the vaudeville formats that succeeded it, and in the popularity of John McCormack, whose career began when he won the Tenor Competition in the 1904 Dublin Feis Ceoil, juxtaposing a Händel selection and Thomas Moore's "The Snowy Breasted Pearl," (McCormack 1918: 95). His international success encouraged the engagement of many more Irish tenor recitalists in the United States. For Irish Americans, McCormack supplanted the negative Irish stereotypes that had dominated vaudeville, and became a source of ethnic pride, at "the center of an evolving Irish-American middle-class sensibility" (Moloney 2006: 397). McCormack and his imitators favored solo performance over opera, and unfailingly included Irish popular and traditional songs in their programs. As do today's crossover stars, he sold out large stadiums (including the Hippodrome, multiple times) (McCormack 1918: 335). His legacy has become an important facet of the 21st-century popera ecology, especially since the group known as The Irish Tenors debuted in the late 1990s, in the wake of the decade dominated by the original Three Tenors, and only a short time after the emergence (through the Eurovision Song Contest) of the Irish dance and music spectacle *Riverdance*. The Irish Tenors performed a 2001 televised concert at Ellis Island, the point of entry for many 21st-century Americans' immigrant grandparents. Though the members of the original lineup of The Irish Tenors were all born in Ireland, their program at Ellis Island featured both "Danny Boy" and "God Bless America." This must have struck a chord, perhaps particularly

---

[2] Some researchers, such as Robinson (1997), Shields (1979), and Gilchrist (1934), suggest that the tune derives from one collected in the 18th century, titled "The Young Man's Dream" by Edward Bunting (Russell 2006).

following the events of September 11, 2001, and the Irish Tenors' music director Frank MacNamara assembled The American Tenors in 2002.

If popera included Irish Tenors and American Tenors, it was only a matter of time before *Irish American* tenors had their day. The Twelve Irish Tenors, created in 2006 by British producer David King (of Dublin Worldwide Productions, also known for projects such as the Irish spectacular *Spirit of the Dance*), were billed as "Ireland's Greatest Voices" in Branson, Missouri, (http://www.bransonquicktix.com/twelveirishtenors.html) and "Ireland's Finest Singers" in Chicago (Riverfront Theater). But when I attended a 2012 concert in Chicago, and each of The Irish Tenors introduced himself, only one was Irish and one was English; the rest were from the United States. (One did hail from Dublin, Indiana.) But all of them pointed to their Irish lineage, a "prerequisite," Branden James told me, for the cast (his lineage comes from his mother's side, the Kennedys from Shannon). The group first toured Europe and played Reno, Nevada, and their show became a fixture in Branson, Missouri, an entertainment destination infused with the long Scots-Irish history of the Ozarks. The tenors have toured all over the globe. In Chicago, they opened with the iconically Irish songs "Danny Boy" and "Molly Malone," but the show was a mix of songs from Ireland, British rock anthems from Queen and the Beatles, Neapolitan song, opera, American pop, and standards from the Rat Pack, and musical theater, as well as the 1913 Tin Pan Alley song "Too-Ra-Loo-Ra-Loo-Ral (That's an Irish Lullaby)," written by Michigan composer James Royce Shannon (the Irish "Shannon" was added for his *nom de plume*).

At the performance I attended, the tent-like Riverfront Theater was filled with white-haired men and women who had entered with walkers and canes, plus a few younger attendees perhaps in their thirties. I encountered a mother and daughter in line who had driven from McHenry, an hour away; they had never heard of The Irish Tenors, but had come across a Groupon deal for the show. They did claim Irish heritage, though, and the daughter had participated in Irish step dancing in her youth. But however pleased the Irish American contingent may have been, my concert companion's Limerick-born husband refused to accompany us. "The Irish American thing is overdone here" he said, "For Irish people in America, it's difficult. It's a cliché" (field notes, June 2, 2012).

Following his time with the Twelve Irish Tenors and a synchronous stint in the Chicago Lyric Opera chorus, Branden James came to broader national attention as one of the top twelve finalists in the 2013 season of *America's Got Talent*.[3] His greatest competition, as it was presented during the show, was a trio of tenors

---

[3] He had previously auditioned for other reality singing competitions, including *American Idol* and *The Voice*. In 2004, Rhiannon Giddens, Kati Roberts, and I encountered him at *American Idol* auditions in San Francisco.

called Forte. Mr. James's televised *AGT* audition presented "Nessun Dorma," and in his subsequent bid for the semifinals, he performed "You Raise Me Up."

Technique and Technology

Christopher Newell and George Newell have documented certain qualifiers that popera vocalities tend to negotiate, including the privileging of higher voice types, the ability to sing with both the lower larynx position of classical technique and the higher position of pop, the use of portamento as in pop, the use of vibrato, a breathy tone to indicate intimacy, virtuosity, and "microphone technique" (Newell and Newell 2014: 137–141). Mr. Miller's experience corroborates these observations. After Cowell sent Il Divo to the studio, and following much experimentation, Mr. Miller recalls, what Il Divo came up with was not simply an out-and-out performance of pop songs with an operatic sound but, instead, what he calls a "linear" progression *within each song* from pop to opera, from opening notes sung with an intimate, breathy tone carried by the microphone, to a robust operatic finish. In the beginning, he says,

> we sing maybe two or three shades quieter than a pianissimo that would be in an opera house. And, so then we kind of shift gears, and we kind of bring ourselves up to maybe a mezzo piano in about the middle of the song, and everyone's kind of, like, gearing up.... And then when we go to the final chorus, everyone just lets loose, and within the structure of the chord, everyone's using their fullest capacity possible. Carlos is a baritone; if he's on lead, he'll be singing something like A-natural, or A-flat, and I'll be on the high C or C-sharp, and we'll fill in the chord underneath with Sébastien and Urs, but everyone's really going for it, like a hundred percent, as if it were the finale of an opera. (interview, March 10, 2009)

Thus, every Il Divo performance begins as pop—signified by the raspy, airy tone, emotionally expressive use of vocal fry, and little R&B ornaments eschewed in classical singing—and ends as opera, complete with conventional and plentiful high C's. (Mr. Miller asserts that he sings more high C's on each night of their tour shows than he has in any opera.) It is the microphone that allows the presence of intimate vocal expressivity like vocal fry and breathiness, and this is part of the middlebrow, middle-class character of popera. McCracken observes that the "transformative effects of microphone technology ... put soft-voiced singers on equal footing with classically trained singers and Broadway belters" (McCracken 2015: 3). In a way, then, the microphone has served as an equalizing force in the accessibility of space; singers without access to training, or who wished to represent a non-elite identity, could vocally occupy a large theater as effectively as an operatic tenor.

Sometimes the mid-song transition from pop to opera takes place within a few phrases sung by one voice, leading to a full operatic ensemble sound. For example, at 2:03″ in "Regresa a Mí" (*Il Divo*, 2005, Sony/BMG Music Entertainment), Carlos Marín sings the lines, "No puedo más si tú no estás / Tienes que llegar / Mi vida se apaga sin ti a mi lado" ("I can't anymore if you aren't here / You need to get here / My life is extinguished without you at my side"). The second and third phrases in Marín's voice demonstrate a quick shift between a pop-influenced vocality and an operatic one. Pop vocality often features the application of "creaky voice" or "vocal fry," in which the vocal folds are adducted tightly, though part of their length remains open (Belotel-Grenié and Grenié 2004: n.p.). Creaky voice has been targeted in public media as an undesirable characteristic of a young woman's speaking voice in the early 21st century, a value judgment entangled with derisive attitudes toward contemporary pop and its female stars. This discourse emerged in 2011, with a study published in the *Journal of Voice* (Wolk et al. 2012, published online the previous year), and the *Daily Mail* in the U.K. even took up the conversation with an article titled " 'Vocal fry': The New Craze in Talking Inspired by Britney Spears, Ke$ha, and Kim Kardashian," noting that the study's authors call the practice dangerous and that many find it "annoying" (Vocal Fry 2011).

To visualize these distinctions in Carlos Marín's performance, I have included two spectrographic examples. In a spectrogram, the *x*-axis represents time and the *y*-axis frequency; this provides a kind of transcription of some of the vocal elements perceived as timbre. Figure 2.2 shows the waveform and spectrogram

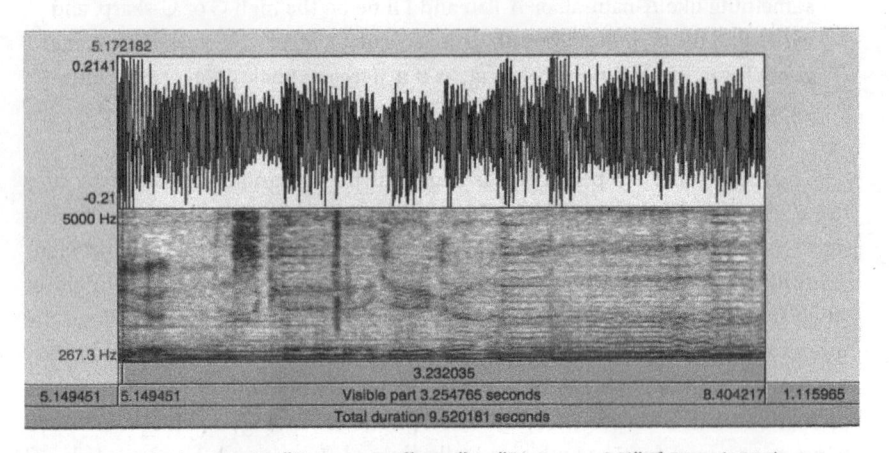

Figure 2.2. Carlos Marín, "Tienes que llegar," in "Regresa a Mí," *Il Divo* (2005). (Note that there is a sparse instrumental accompaniment in this example, though the trajectory of the voice is clearly visible.)

of the phrase "Tienes que llegar." Irregular pulses of sound are visible in the waveform and the spectrogram at the beginning of the phrase, where Marín starts the vowel in "tienes" using creaky voice.

This phrase is followed immediately by "Mi vida se apaga sin ti a mi lado," which begins in pop vocality but moves toward operatic singing in its final syllable. In the spectrographic transcription (see figure 2.3), the syllable "-do" in "lado" shows a melodic ornament, a lower neighbor indicated by a slight dip in the fundamental-frequency trajectory of the voice, and a subsequent blossoming of the vowel's acoustic structure into a tone with even, persistent vibrato cycles, and a strong amplitude in the "singer's formant" (the cluster of frequencies centered on 2800 Hz–3200 Hz that characterize male operatic voices, indicated visibly here by dark bands near those frequencies).

After Marín's lead-in, all four singers move into the louder, fully classical portion of the song. By the time the quartet reaches its vocal climax in any track, Mr. Miller says, the shift from pop to opera, from microphone-intimate to theater-extroverted, has been so gradual that the listener doesn't notice how or when things changed. Mr. Miller believes, based on comments from fans, that this stealth-operatic singing inspires listeners unfamiliar with opera to seek it out. The idea of popera as a kind of gateway drug to the opera house resonates with many. Il Divo biographer Allegra Rossi wrote in 2005 that "popera can introduce new listeners to more *hardcore* opera and classical singing" (Rossi 2005: 20; my emphasis). Curiously, four of the crossover singers I've interviewed to date did not care for the mixture of genres before they began performing it; they traversed the popera gateway in the other direction, with their minds newly opened to the

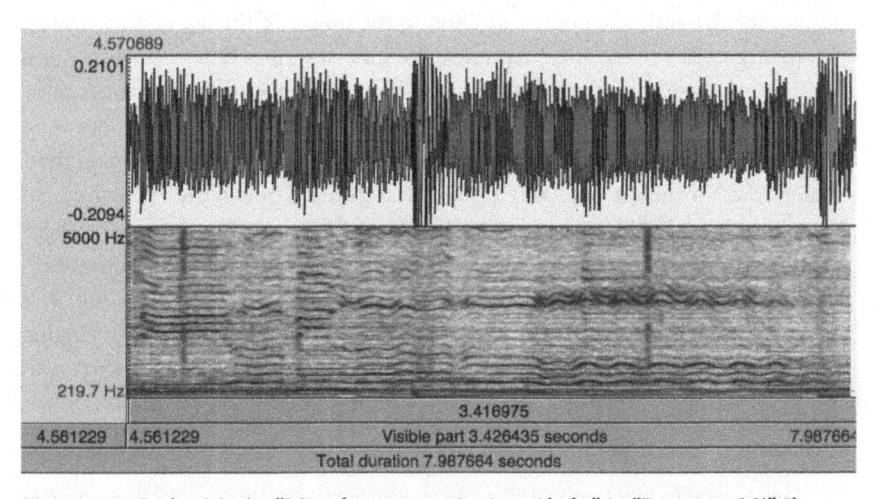

Figure 2.3 Carlos Marín, "Mi vida se apaga sin ti a mi lado," in "Regresa a Mí," *Il Divo* (2005)

possibilities of singing non-operatic repertoire. For baritone Sean Cooper, who sang in *Riverdance* on Broadway and in Baz Luhrman's Broadway production of *La Bohème*, crossover mitigates a public fear of opera—of live opera—through various forms of mediation, from the microphone to the television, and contradictorily offers a sense of direct communication (interview, September 15, 2008). In this way, crossover singing distances the operatic voice from the intimidating, institutionalized opera house etiquette established in the imagining of opera as "high culture."

Amplification and mediation are key signifiers of pop, or at least of negating operatic genre, for critics of popera. In a 2005 review in the *Washington Post*, Philip Kennicott critiqued Il Divo's sound this way:

> It's a weird non-style, distinguished by way too much electronic processing and consistently urgent vocal lines, hopped up to sound bigger than pop but far short of opera. Though they're being sold as "classically trained" singers, the men of Il Divo never really register as distinctive vocalists, perhaps because the end product is, electronically, so many generations removed from the simple, unadorned human voice.

For Kennicott, Il Divo, which he calls "cheesy," is neither pop nor opera, in part because he infers from the presence of technology that Il Divo's bigness of sound, the fullness that he associates with opera, is artificial. Microphones are necessary and common gear for popera singers, who often perform in enormous stadium venues[4] over heavy orchestration and in competition with each others' voices. Mr. Miller suggests, also, that amplification increases the voice's possibilities for dynamic nuance, in addition to the power of the big ending. Daniel Montenegro, one of the three American Tenors, describes how detractors point to his group's use of microphones as a sign that the singers' voices wouldn't carry in an opera house. It isn't true, he counters; all three American Tenors were "trained to sing in an opera house, and we all had appropriate voices to do that" (interview, November 11, 2008). (Even Pavarotti used one in the Three Tenors.) Amplification, then, becomes as much a part of popera's discourses of authenticity as it has been in popular music. And the crossover singers I interviewed—all indeed classically trained—expressed concern about the upholding of a personal, even essential vocal authenticity. I asked if they changed their singing techniques in order to sing into a microphone; the unanimous answer was no. Sean Cooper explained to me why keeping operatic vocal production is

---

[4] Large venues and broadcast audiences have featured prominently in the recent vocal crossover boom, since the Three Tenors (Luciano Pavarotti, Plácido Domingo, and José Carreras) turned to popular repertoire in their 1990 performance at the World Cup in Italy.

important. Otherwise, he believes, "you don't hear the true voice . . . the openness of a classically trained, liberated voice. . . . I think that's one of the most attractive things about opera . . . after all this training people really find out what *their* sound is" (interview, September 15, 2008).

Popera singers aren't only criticized for their perceived inability to render music *operatically* in an authentic way; pop authenticity is also in question. In 2009, Colombian online magazine *Semana.com* hyperlinked an article to Compañía Lírica Pópera's cover of the Juanes pop hit "A Dios le Pido," and asked its readers the rhetorical question: "*¿homenaje o agravio?* (homage or insult?)" ("Juanes a la Opera" 2009). In this case, a song associated with a specific pop voice was performed instead with operatic vocality, and they questioned that as a potential affront to Juanes fans.

At the core of all the discomfort with popera is an uneasiness with the contamination of opera and its high-culture status with the stylistic signifiers of popular music, and in the case of the Juanes cover, vice versa: it's a fear, really, of miscegenation. That fear isn't confined to connections between genre and class; at least in the United States, it touches on racialized discourses of opera and pop as well, with the former associated with Whiteness and the latter with Blackness (or appropriations of it). The vocalities that Newell and Newell identified as key in crossover singing are racialized, too—Il Divo's raspy pop tone with vocal fry is an R&B sound; yet their operatic timbres are European.

Popera as a Space for Black Opera Singers

If popera allows white opera singers (such as those in Il Divo) access to the vocalities of popular musics that are racialized as Black, it can also provide a much rarer entrée for Black opera singers to vocal spaces still largely segregated as white. In American popular musics, the embodied (or appropriated; see Meizel 2011a) vocalities of Black singers have historically been granted public space in ways similar to the bodies of Black athletes: as commodities. The ability to codeswitch between musics has always been required of Black classical singers to win over their predominantly white audiences. In the days when formerly enslaved soprano Elizabeth Taylor Greenfield became the "Black Swan," concerts by white opera singers included parlor songs, as well as Verdi arias. But Greenfield and the later star Sissieretta Jones, adept as they were with Italian repertoire, were also expected to satisfy white audience requests for minstrel songs (Eidsheim 2011b: 652). And Marti Newland has written about the strategic choices in vocality and diction that Fisk University's Jubilee Singers have made throughout their history. The touring ensemble, founded in 1871, initially eschewed spiritual songs as "customs which reminded them of slavery" and performed "white" songs during concerts (Wright 1911: 24, cited in Graham 2018: 43), but finally gained the interest and eventual support of white Congregationalists by including "Steal Away" in their program at a conference in Oberlin (Graham 2018: 52). Marti Newland suggests that singing spirituals either with or without the "dialect" that white audiences have historically associated with "authentic" Black voices,[5] and in an operatic style racialized as white, has served as a complex performance of nonviolence—as nonviolent resistance, as a way of protecting the singers from racial violence, and within the boundaries of operatic vocal pedagogy, as a way of protecting the singers' voices from the harm discursively associated with non-classical (non-white) sounds (Newland 2014: 42–43).

The management of white expectations regarding genre and vocality still impacts the decisions made by Black operatic singers. In 2001, playwright and theatrical producer Marion Caffey debuted the project he called "Three Mo' Tenors," a pointed response to the success of the Three Tenors (Pavarotti, Domingo, and Carreras) and the continuing scarcity of African American men cast on the opera stage. He followed it in 2006 with a new show, "Three Mo' Divas: A Celebration of Class, Sass, and Style." Caffey's singers were rotating casts of three, performing opera, soul, R&B, jazz, musical theater, spirituals, gospel, and blues. Another motive of Caffey's was to find singers who could "maintain the integrity" of several vocalities, a kind of genre authenticity he says the original Three Tenors hadn't managed in their forays away from opera (interview, November 4, 2009). All the Mo' Tenors were classically trained. Their shows not only traced the significance of Black music in the United States but also attacked old and persistent myths that position the physical capability of singing opera as the exclusive domain of white singers. Caffey says that the operatic capabilities were key for his intentions with the shows, when common American understandings of Black voices neglected the possibility: "without the classical, it's just Black people who can sing" (interview, November 4, 2009).

And his productions were intended to provide the opportunity for Black singers. "Most of them," he told me, "if they could sing classical music all the time, they would—but there's nowhere for them to work." He noted that the problem is particularly persistent for tenors, suggesting that there are more leading Black baritones on the opera stage than tenors because of racialized role expectations. "Tenors get the girl," he explained, and it's a "world that doesn't see Black males getting the girl" (interview, November 4, 2009). One Mo' Tenor, Ramone Diggs,

---

[5] The expectation that Black singers will provide the symbols of authenticity that white audiences imagine pervades the music industry even in the 21st century. My earlier study of *American Idol* began because of music critics' complaints that young contestants on the show did not perform "melisma" authentically, in the style of pioneering soul singers such as Aretha Franklin (Meizel 2011a). And during more recent field work, I witnessed a music executive comment to two Black singers that he was surprised they didn't "use Ebonics," like a group of blues artists he had worked with before.

stated on the *Today Show* that the group inspires African American singers, "opens their minds to other things, things that maybe you thought 'I could not do or I should not do, because I don't know of any Black people that do this'" (https://www.youtube.com/watch?v=PUp0aM0-ERk). But the Three Mo' Tenors audiences are not only Black. Caffey estimated that the racial makeup was sometimes up to 92 to 93 percent white females over the age of 40 (interview, November 4, 2009), and he viewed his work as an enlightening force in race relations. In 2008, Caffey told an interviewer that in Three Mo' Tenors shows, "Blacks in the audience give whites in the audience permission to have fun" (Infantry 2008). Caffey's declaration—which, he explained to me, referred to the limited relevance of audience participation in white Americans' everyday musical experience—also separates the idea of the tenor performance from the confines of its serious status in "high culture"; he names his show as popular music, on the other side of the binary from opera. The Three Mo' Tenors, though, didn't seem to care much what you called their music; in their introductory song called "Three Mo' Tenors, That's Us," they sang, "Highbrow, lowbrow, they all agree / We're the best in harmony" (*A Taste of Three Mo' Tenors* 2006).

The persistent dearth of opportunity for Black opera singers has a long history in the United States, as does the recourse of the popular music world. Naomi André, Karen M. Bryan, and Eric Saylor remark upon the intersection of "popular and highbrow theater" in the 19th-century minstrel show, and the ways in which minstrelsy and opera exchanged and mutually impacted ideas about staging race. They write, "Given the limited public performance venues deemed appropriate or suitable for African Americans prior to the latter half of the 20th century, it is not surprising that many Black performers who might have been involved with opera were funneled into minstrelsy" (André et al. 2012: 3). Today, as the number and overall vitality of American opera companies dwindle and many classically trained singers shift into crossover and popular genres, Black vocalists find themselves in a particularly vulnerable position; and some, like Marion Caffey, are driven to create new stages and new forms of music theater.

Another innovative artist is Chicago musician Adrian Dunn, who in the mid-2000s established HoperaWorld Entertainment, a company headquartered in Chicago. A neologism that Mr. Dunn created to integrate hip hop and opera, the designation "HOPERA" (capitalized in the organization's literature) serves not only as the name of his organization but also as a series title for his stage works and as a movement toward the establishment of a new genre.[6] Because of hip hop's location within popular music, hopera might be seen as another form of popera. Like Il Divo, Mr. Dunn's company markets multivocality—his own, first

---

[6] Mr. Dunn acknowledges that the phrase "Hip Hopera" preceded his work, coined for the 2001 MTV production *Carmen: A Hip Hopera*.

and foremost. The background information on his website lists his performances with The Roots and others as a background vocalist for pop, R&B, and gospel artists, as well as his work as an operatic, oratorio, and choral singer. The company's repertoire, written by Mr. Dunn, showcases this multivocality, particularly featuring his own voice in operatic and rap vocalities. Like other examples of popera, his shows rely on microphones, whether the singing is in hip hop style or not.

Mr. Dunn began by composing, co-writing, producing, directing, and conducting his shows, and now also counts singing and rapping among his onstage duties, in shows that aim to portray the lived experiences of young Black men in the 21st century. His characters confront difficult social issues such as suicide, alcoholism, teen pregnancy, grief, and violence, and the everyday anguish faced by many young Black men and their communities—themes which he feels have not been adequately addressed in the realm of classical music. Though Chicago's Department of Public Health partly sponsored the early HOPERA shows based on its commitment to these themes, Mr. Dunn worries that the focus on social justice might supersede the artistic value of his work, and the significance of the singers, instrumentalists, and dancers of color who bring it to life. Like Marion Caffey and the Three Mo' Tenors, Mr. Dunn also founded HoperaWorld with a view toward providing opportunities for musicians of color, to make classical music "a place where everybody feels welcome and valued." And, he told me, he is passionate about the "ability for Black men to be more than one thing."

Hopera asks this "more than one thing" of all its singers, who sometimes alternate among pop, gospel, and opera vocalities, in addition to rap. All of his performers use microphones, and while he is precise in setting the levels, he does not change them as they shift between styles and genres. He wants the audience to feel overwhelmed, and appreciates the effect of consistent high amplitudes. Unlike other crossover artists with whom I've spoken, Mr. Dunn advocates the use of microphones in the opera house, as well as in popular genres, noting the notoriously large size of U.S. houses.

Raised in a conservative Christian household and trained as an operatic tenor and gospel singer, Mr. Dunn came late to hip hop and rap, but upon studying it in college, he found the work of rap giants such as Tupac Shakur profoundly inspiring. He began rapping himself in his second series of shows, "HOPERA: Unleashed." He had been coaching both singers and rappers, trying to adapt their sounds to the needs of the production. Rappers in HOPERA do their work differently from rappers in "the industry"; he conceives their verses operatically, intertwined with the singing and grounded more in classical forms than in typical rap forms. As a composer, he has tended to treat his rappers like singers, demanding fewer pauses for breathing and requiring them to be heard above the amplified band and singers. To this end, he has coached the rappers (and himself) toward a "kind of operatic sound." In his own rapping, he remains extremely conscious of classical vocal technique, attributing to it his stamina and his ability to switch with ease between singing and rapping. He explains, "I think a lot about it like an extension of speech ... but I also think about it more from a vocal standpoint, in terms of placement and breath support" (interview, October 8, 2013). He also views classical technique as particularly important in his recent show "HOPERA: Unleashed," where he plays an emotionally demanding role that deals with his own grief at his mother's passing; concentrating on his classical technique helps to keep the emotion from disrupting his sound. But all of the vocalities represented in his work—opera, gospel, musical theater, pop, rap—are part of the multivocal Black experiences he wants brought to the fore. And they are all facets of his own experience:

> It's all a part of me. It's all a part of who I am and what I do, and then again, me being passionate about being a Black young gay man, as well. This is Black folks' story. This is our story in the 21st century, which looks a lot different than the 19th or the 20th century. . . . I think that younger contemporary Black voices deserve an opportunity to be heard. (interview, October 8, 2013)

This is one of the ultimate effects of popera, to challenge existing social structures as opera and popular music—and middle-class publics—always have. In this way, popera perhaps surprisingly stands as a subversive form of expression and of consumption, queering the popular and the operatic pitch simultaneously. Its voices do more than switch between two styles of music; they undertake a complex process of code-crossing between cultural histories, interrogating the racialization of genre in the global music industry. Like all recorded musics, popera serves as a sonic archive of these histories. Sébastien Izambard has called Il Divo "an arranged marriage" among the four singers; classical crossover in general might be seen similarly—a union of histories, of discourses, and a reunification of social registers that played the same stages before their separation. Il Divo, as of 2017, had sold more than 30 million albums, according to David Miller. If popera is, as Miller describes it, "the bastard child of music" (interview, March 10, 2009), then its voice has reached maturity in the 21st century.

3
Voice and Disjuncture in Celebrity Impersonation

> We're all impersonators in a way. We are all impersonating something, including ourselves.
> —Arthur Miller

Every year, millions flock to the Mojave to work, play, and lighten their wallets in the sands that span Nevada's desert of the real.[1] On the Las Vegas Strip, time and space collide and shatter, where "ancient empires" bracket a chaotic cartography of Venetian gondolas, lush Belle Époque Paris, and a century's worth of iconic New York architecture. Replicas of the Sphinx, the Eiffel Tower, and the Chrysler Building loom over the strip's 4.2 miles, from first to last resort. These monuments to monuments, still massive but largely in reduced scale, embody a central sensibility of Las Vegas as a site for re-mapping and re-sizing—the strip at once strips icons down to their most recognized features and paints them larger than life. Patricia Ventura recognizes Las Vegas as the epitome of a "neoliberal city," attributing this quality to the 1990s building boom that transformed Vegas from the Orientalist, colonial design (desert-themed hotels titled Sahara, Aladdin, Dunes, etc.) that had characterized it since the 1950s and '60s to its current reflection of neoliberal globalization—not only in its collection and display of global imagery but also in its shift from mob-dependent finances to late 20th-century corporate capitalism (Ventura 2012: 46). The topography of the world captured in a souvenir snow globe, Las Vegas offers visitors a set of intertwined performative layers, a collection of façades and masquerades that shape the city's distinctive character. Each casino compound is a palatial feat of placial transvestism, a city in the middle of nowhere always singing with someone else's voice, and along the way asserting its own voice. Las Vegas has claimed its place in the world by impersonating itself.

It is, of course, a premise that informs the city's entertainments as much as its architecture. On any given day, Vegas hosts hundreds of bejeweled and be-jumpsuited Elvii, while simultaneously, throughout its arenas, theaters, casinos,

---

[1] For "desert of the real," see Baudrillard 1988.

Multivocality. Katherine Meizel, Oxford University Press (2020). © Oxford University Press.
DOI: 10.1093/oso/9780190621469.003.0004

nightclubs, and even on its baseball fields, crowds might be applauding for a Dolly Parton, for a Barbra Streisand, for a Cher, Prince, Elton John, Madonna, Dean Martin, Frank Sinatra, or Marilyn Monroe—impersonators commemorating cultural history with performances of performances. And while many celebrity impersonators aim for impressions that are picture and pitch perfect, others (literally) capitalize on the features that most visibly—and physically—set them apart from their models, embodying both the star and *not*-the-star. As Freya Jarman-Ivens has suggested about Elvis impersonation, audience members may discover who they believe an artist is in recognizing what they believe he is *not* (Jarman-Ivens 2006: 223). So, instead of personifying some kind of intractable inauthenticity, the gendered transgression of a female Elvis, the racial complexities of a Chinese Elvis, the bodily implications of a Big Elvis, might help fans to more fully imagine an authentic original.

It isn't only the impersonator's audience who's struggling toward a sense of authenticity, toward an ordering of what Richard Schechner points to (after Goffman) as a "hierarchy of realities" (Schechner 1985: 96). Many scholars, including Schechner and Victor Turner (1982) have studied theater as ritual, and Kirsten Hastrup has built upon their ideas to propose it as a "site of passage" for those in attendance (Hastrup 1998: 29). But in the liminal space of the stage, impersonators themselves are also involved in an intersecting process. They are actors in more than one way: as they perform others, they are also performing the work of their own identity and vocalizing that identity—whether from their own throats or in (lip)-synch with someone else's. And those who ground their acts in their embodied distance from the stars, underlining instead of concealing unexpected incongruities between the visual and the aural, remind us that the work of identity is most plainly seen through the enactment of difference.

The impersonated voice is, at its core, acousmatic— separated from its source—and reunited with a different source, within what listeners know to be a kind of living simulacrum. Still, a sense of mystery persists, as the process is not entirely transparent: a voice is always hidden inside us; to borrow from Mladen Dolar's explanation of ventriloquism, a voice implies not only a body but, more precisely, "a bodily interior, an intimate partition of the body which cannot be disclosed—as if the voice were the very principle of division into interior and exterior" (Dolar 2006: 71). The mystery deepens when the body appears to be visibly distinct from the voice's original source, especially in the most broadly painted identity categories—skin color, size and shape, gender; and for bodies interpreted as disabled, the usually private, silent realm of imperfection is made noisily public. Recent studies of singing and disability (McKay 2013, Mills 2012) emphasize voice as an externalization of hidden internal states—damaged sounds emerging from a damaged body and/or psyche. But what if the voice sounding from the interior is heard as *un*damaged, non-disabled, even extraordinarily able? What if it is a voice previously associated with another body entirely—literally the voice of a superstar? If the voice, as Dolar suggests, can be "located at the juncture of the subject and the Other" (102), then it is also locatable in their *dis*juncture.

This chapter explores the experiences of celebrity impersonators who engage with such disjunctures, and who harness them as they negotiate their own voices through the performance of others' voices. They demonstrate singing impersonation as more than mimesis, as a sociovocal strategy in the construction of identity. Their work, in the end, illuminates the contradictory interdependence and reification of the enclosed aural body and the disclosed visual body as products of multiple subjectivities and multiple intersubjectivities. Returning to Anke Strüver's explanation of the borderscape as a site highlighting a confluence of processes that "takes place" through representations, through performative acts, through acts of narration, visualization, and imagination, including their interpretation," we can view both Las Vegas and the voices heard there as borderscapes, and as always borderscaping. If, as Lev Vygotsky claimed, "through others we become ourselves" (1998: 170; see also the introduction to this book), celebrity impersonators on the Vegas Strip have their work cut out for them, shaping a vocal way of being through the performance of others.

Singing Impersonation

Singing impersonators generally operate on a performative continuum that includes cover versions, tribute bands, and comedic parody. George Plasketes, in *Play It Again: Cover Songs in Popular Music*, writes about such forms as part of a broad turn-of-the-millennium "cover complex," which, he suggests, "may be viewed as a postmodern manifestation of rampant recontextualization in music" (Plasketes 2010: 2). But some artists, at least, differentiate each form very clearly. To voice actor and singing impersonator Jeff McNeal, "there are tribute bands and then there are cover bands. A tribute band usually picks one artist, and they do their best to look and sound like that one artist. . . . [C]over bands do lots of different songs, but they don't really sound like the original artist; they sound like a cover band doing all these different songs, and they put their own spin on it" (interview, August 22, 2013). I have written elsewhere about the "make-it-your-own" phenomenon in cover performance, noting that in a cover version, an artist attempts through various musical and vocal changes to "reach a precarious balance between . . . the need to live up to the work of a song's original artist, and an originality that is seen as an innovative expression of individuality" (Meizel 2011b: 63). Mr. McNeal describes his band as a tribute group, but instead of choosing one artist to emulate, he presents vocal impressions of nearly forty different artists. He develops his impressions using only certain singers and songs that he feels suited to, and, he says, "It's really about trying to reproduce the original recording. I don't try to embellish or put little flourishes in the vocals, or anything that wasn't part of the original song" (interview, August 22, 2013).

Because of its internal location, the voice is always fundamentally secret, and while an impersonator may rely on oculo-centric techniques to match the body language or superficial physical features of a chosen artist, they must also depend upon the imagination of another's interior space, the assumption of its familiarity and the perception of minute variance. The impersonator must be, as Mr. McNeal terms it, "a good listener," practicing a special kind of listening, attending not only to phrasing and diction and expression but also to hearing and imitating subtle internal adjustments in the shaping of the vocal tract—what Mr. McNeal calls "throat modeling" (interview, August 22, 2013). Music cognition scholar David Huron has identified a *kinesthetic* form of listening, "characterized by the auditor's compulsion to move." He explains that "feet may tap, hands may conduct, or the listener may feel the urge to dance. The experience is not so much one of 'listening' to the music, as the music 'permeating' the body . . . 'motivation' rather than 'contemplation'" (Huron 2002). Though impersonation may or may not involve dancing, it certainly constitutes a permeative experience of sound and a conscious, or perhaps semi-conscious, physiological response. Therefore, I suggest, we might look at singing impersonation as the result of a special kind of kinesthetic listening, one that translates—not in perfect mimesis but with an ear toward the meanings made during the listening process—the internal and external movements of one voice, one body, to another.

50 Voices

Tina Turner hasn't sung in Las Vegas for years.[2] But in October of 2013, I heard her voice there, anyway—issuing from a petite blonde French Canadian woman who strutted across the stage at Bally's Casino and filled Turner's legendarily high-heeled shoes, for an ephemeral moment. But this was only one of Véronic DiCaire's impressive fifty impressions. For ninety minutes, a packed audience gasped and sighed, and sometimes even cried, as they heard one throat produce the instantly recognizable sounds of Katy Perry, Adele, Shakira, Anita Baker, Whitney Houston, Taylor Swift, and Donna Summer. Véronic (her stage name) began her career as a solo performer in Montréal, and worked in musical theater, but because of a facility with altering her voice, she was soon paid to do

---

[2] A portion of the text in this chapter is from Meizel and Scherer (2019),, where we present a preliminary investigation into the acoustic analysis of singing impersonation.

imitations of French and French Canadian singers—including Céline Dion—for special events and television appearances. She became a protégé of Dion when she opened for the superstar on her world tour in 2008, impersonating her. Then she expanded her repertoire from a small number of francophone singers to dozens of transnationally known figures, including Tina Turner and other singers of color.

Véronic's 50 voices, in highlighting the visual disjunctures foundational to ideas about identity, raise some powerful questions about the fraught and ambiguous boundaries between imitation and cooptation, about the many (one might even say 50) shades of essentialism, and about what kinds of vestment exactly are involved in racial transvestism. When I asked Véronic about her Tina Turner performance, she explained that she is aware of the volatile sociopolitical implications of a white performer mimicking Black performers, and of the fine line she always walks between imitation and insult. It's part of the reason that she eschews the full wig-and-sequins effect typical of other impersonators (especially vital to drag performance), instead choosing to embody Turner in voice and posture and movement, without visual illusion.

The process of embodiment, though, is still thorny. In the development of each of her voices, Véronic told me, she locates it *in the body*, working carefully with her vocal coach:

> Let's say for this voice you need to place your voice there (points), or there, or there, or in your legs, or, you know, in your shoulders, you need to think about that. And other times it is only a thought . . . for Celine, my thought was to be very in the nose. Well, [my teacher] would say, for example, okay, the nose is good, but . . . she also sings with *this* [elongates neck, using hands] and the long neck, so *imagine* the long neck, and so that's how we are working . . . with the voices. (interview, October 11, 2013)

She went on to explain that when she was developing her Tina Turner, the body as a whole became a vital part of her vocal modification. She told me:

> I couldn't get her voice . . . I couldn't get her. I was listening and listening, and it was obsessive. . . . And then at one point I said, "OK, Tina Turner, I'm gonna get you tonight." . . . I went on YouTube, I went to watch her, and the thing that was missing was the high heels. So I went into my wardrobe and got my highest heels, I put them on, I double-checked on YouTube, and she had her knees a bit bent, and her shoulders, and her neck . . . and I went like this and I hold my mic

like her . . . and I was like, "OK, that's it, that's it. This is my Tina Turner." (interview, October 11, 2013)

In the show, when she sings the work of some African American artists, a photograph of the singer—of Aretha Franklin or Billie Holliday—often appears in the background of her set, as if to make each number a tribute rather than a parody, or to remind audience members to cognitively isolate the voice they hear from the body to which it should belong (see figure 3.1).

Véronic and I talked about the problematic notion of "Black voice," and her understanding—part of a shockingly persistent colonial discourse—that this idea is grounded in structural physiological variance between racial groups. When she imitates African American singers, she told me, she thinks about adjusting the soft palate and the position of the jaw, and imagining her sound "up front" to compensate for such differences. What is especially striking about our conversation is that despite her belief that a racialized voice lies in the structure of the bones, she arrives at her target sound simply by manipulating *soft* tissues and spaces in the vocal tract—a practice that *contradicts* her thinking and supports current scholarship *dismissing* the idea of racialized biological difference as a source for vocal diversity.

At a 21st-century moment when the soul-soaked voices of white British women like Adele and Amy Winehouse have provoked uneasy murmurs of a renewed appropriative cycle, Véronic's imitations of both further problematize old concerns about what kind of music belongs in what kind of body. Daphne

Figure 3.1 Véronic imitates Tina Turner's characteristic wide stance.

Brooks has written about the new wave of white British soul singers in the mid- to late 2000s, contextualizing their singing as part of a renewed "sonic blue(s) face culture." "Black women are everywhere and nowhere in Winehouse's work," Brooks observes, contending that Winehouse's vocality, in strategically evoking "1940s jazz divas and 1990s neo-soul queens," not only draws from their sound but also attenuates their crucial roles in the trajectory of western popular music (Brooks 2008: ??); rather than simply paying homage, paradoxically Winehouse was ultimately *suppressing* Black women's voices. Véronic, in covering Holliday and Turner, but also Winehouse and Adele, contributes another layer to the complex sociopolitical life of vocalities.

Especially because all of Véronic's voices are so heavily impacted by the body language, gesture, posture, and even dance moves of the artists she mimics, the space between tribute and disparaging caricature can be difficult to navigate. Her meta-disjunct version of Susan Boyle, for example, takes on a performing object already famous for a perceptual disconnect. As Boyle, Véronic stands stock-still and stares ahead, clenches her jaw, and squints a little between phrases, offering her audience what she describes as a "little wink" but, she insists, not "making fun." She'd want the singers she performs to come to her show, she explained to me; the stars who had attended previously had laughed at themselves and told her they felt honored to be imitated. Part of the challenge, she admits, is condensing all of the iconic characteristics of a singer into the one minute and thirty seconds her show allows each of her voices, without giving her mimicry an edge of mockery. Nevertheless, a certain level of essentialism seems to be essential to the act of impersonation. When it comes to voice, López et al., in a 2013 study of spoken impersonation, found that broader caricatures, meant to emphasize specific aspects of a target speaker, are better recognized by listeners as belonging to the target speaker than recreations intended to sound as close as possible to the target speaker (López et al. 2013: 3).

The Impersonator's "Own" Voice

Another challenge for Véronic is keeping sight of her "own voice" along with her impressions. She understands "her" voice as the foundation for all of her imitations, and she keeps it in mind even as she departs from it. She says:

> My voice is still there. It has to. Because it's the base of all of my other voices. When I started to work on my imitations, impressions, at one point I came back and I was like, where am I? I couldn't connect to the voices I had just worked on, and everything was lost, and my teacher said, "Véronic, I think you're lost. I think we should reconnect with Véronic['s] voice." ... So when I'm off, I sing as

myself. I, when I have doubts, I sing as myself, to reconnect, Because I find that I don't want to be Celine Dion, I don't want to be Pink in my real life, in my day to day life, I'm not them, I'm Véronic.... If I want to be strong for these voices I have to be strong for myself. I have to be Véronic. And that's why I don't dress up, because I don't want to transform *as*, I want the people to connect with the voice and let their imagination go where I want them to go. Come with me in this world, in this voice. (interview, October 1, 2013)

Conversely, Mr. McNeal thinks of his own voice as uninteresting. "To me, my voice is just ordinary, nothing special, you know, I hear it all the time and I'm just not that intrigued by it. But being able to manipulate it to sound like somebody else, to me, that's where the fun is" (interview, August 22, 2013). He has recorded hundreds of videos for YouTube that he has labeled "tribute covers" (voicing Johnny Cash, Eric Clapton, John Fogerty, Jim Morrison, Bob Dylan, Dennis Yost, and many others), but also a few non-tribute covers in his own voice ("The Girl From Ipanema," for example); he notes that these are mostly songs whose original artists are female, whose voices he cannot imitate. Most of his videos consist of close-ups, single-angle sequences that follow him recording a song in his studio to a pre-recorded backing track, with shades and headphones slightly obscuring his visage. He has occasionally received feedback from some of the artists he has covered, or their bandmates—guitarist Ray Fenwick praised his version of the Tee Set's "Ma Belle Ami," in tribute to the band's Dutch-born lead singer Peter Tetteroo—and from YouTube viewers. His video for Kyu Sakamoto's 1963 hit "Sukiyaki," which Mr. McNeal learned phonetically in Japanese, elicited dozens of kudos, one commenter exclaiming that they had been listening to Mr. McNeal "summon the spirits of many of my favorite singers" (https://www.youtube.com/watch?v=oYPqJPZgNMs 2012). Not only does he feel uninspired by his own voice, but he also finds it difficult. I asked him whether it is easier or harder for him to sing in his own voice, and he answered:

It's a little harder, because when I'm singing in somebody else's voice, it's almost like putting on a mask, and being able to lose your inhibitions and really get into that character without so much of yourself being out there. And when I'm singing in my own voice, then I'm much more self-conscious about it—"Gee, I wonder if people are going to like *this*," you know. I mean, I know they're going to like it when I sound like somebody they recognize. But I don't know if they're going to like how I sound just as me. (interview, August 22, 2013)

To Véronic, the voice she recognizes as her own, "*as* Véronic," sounds something like Sheryl Crow's. But she points to an individual idiosyncrasy in her instrument that allows her an unusual degree of vocal flexibility. She related to me a visit with renowned otolaryngologist Jean Abitbol, who told her, before he knew about her act, that she would make a good impressionist owing to an especially "uneven" (her word) set of cartilage in her larynx. It isn't the vocal folds themselves, he explained to her, but the cartilage that surround the muscles that are unusually flexible. In his book *The Odyssey of the Voice*, Abitbol attributes impersonators' talents to particularly powerful muscle and cartilage structures in the larynx, and to their uncommon flexibility. Observations he made with a video-fibroscope identify a "cross-eyed" larynx in which the arytenoid cartilage can allow one vocal cord to lengthen more than the other, and even permit the vocal folds to partially overlap (Abitbol 2006: 412). Impersonators also, as they remodel their vocal tracts for an imitation, may "contort" the epiglottis and its position in the pharynx, or reconfigure their soft palates (413). Acoustically, Abitbol writes, an impersonator's own "vocal imprint," or "fingerprint," will remain identifiable regardless of any mimesis (414–415). And the physiological qualities that support impersonation contribute to that imprint. Since learning about the larynx during her interaction with Dr. Abitbol, Véronic sees her own voice, her own body, as *meant for* the sounding of Otherness; its declaration of self might best resonate in the forms and formants of fifty other voices.

Of Note: Blind Auditioning

The premise of this chapter is grounded in the assumption that an impersonator's audience experiences connections with and divergences of the visual (the body) and the aural. But not everyone perceives sound and voice in the same ways. In the process of researching the sight/sonic disjunctures that characterize singing impersonation acts, I gave a joint presentation with my colleague Ronald Scherer (in the department of Communication Sciences and Disorders) to students and faculty in speech studies at my university. After I saw the rest of the audience respond with the expected surprise to watching video and hearing recordings of Véronic's impersonations, one attendee shared another, important perspective. For linguist, ESL specialist, and musician Sheri Wells-Jensen, who is blind, a voice does not necessarily imply any particular type of body. She acknowledges that upon hearing an opera singer, her thoughts might gravitate toward the cultural discourse of heavy female singers, but she does not generally hear voices as originating in large or small bodies.[3] If she perceives a singer as a large person,

---

[3] A 2016 study by Katarzyna et al. did find that blind listeners involved in the research accurately assessed differences in men's body size, and they suggest that "humans' ability to accurately assess body size from the voice may in fact be acquired without the need for visual input or is present at birth" (Pisanski et al. 2016: n.p.).

it may be either because in person she or he casts a sizable "sound shadow" (the change in acoustics when a voice comes from above and resonates broadly) or because she hears a labored breath *between* vocalized phrases that she understands as the result of health concerns associated with obesity (she offers Israel Kamakawiwoʻole as an example). She says that unless someone reminds her, she is never sure which singers she listens to are "supposed to be Black" (interview, April 16, 2015).

The most obvious differences she heard between Véronic's imitations and her target voices were not bodily but, rather, spatial. The examples I played, she could tell, were recorded in different rooms, and the divergent acoustic surroundings were "too distracting" for her to decide whether the voices themselves might sound similar. Though she notes that some blind people form "3-D" images in their minds upon perceiving sound, she does not, and she never pictures the body from which a voice emanates. In *Extraordinary Measures: Disability in Music*, Joseph Straus suggests that perhaps blind listeners and deaf listeners might "share an orientation toward the tactile and the kinesthetic" (Straus 2011: 169)—but Dr. Wells-Jensen's orientation is *synaesthetic*. In her early childhood, she could see light and color, and even though she does not anymore, color remains vital to her perception of the world. As a grapheme-color synaesthete, she associates any individual's voice with a color attached to the first letter of his or her name. Her daughter Claire, for example, seems and sounds yellow because, for Dr. Wells-Jensen, the letter "C" is associated with that color (interview, April 15, 2015). "I don't usually get good colors for voices unless I know the name," she says, "nameless voices don't always have color" (personal communication, April 17, 2015).

While we weren't able to pinpoint any correspondences between colors and imitated voices while listening to Véronic's examples, Dr. Wells-Jensen did remark that "Elvis impersonators have an Elvis-colored voice" (interview, April 15, 2015). But she sometimes experiences more than one color—a dual chromatic identity—when she hears mimicry. When her young children watched *Sesame Street*, she heard the Muppet character called Grover as red, but her children saw him as the blue he is onscreen. Her husband Jason's voice is always blue to her. But when he imitates Grover in a song for the kids, he can be either red for Grover or blue for Jason (she notes that she does not associate either of these synaesthetic experiences with the letters of their names, though she is not sure why that is the case). She further explains, "I think, in the end, [it] has to do with choices and perspective: I can listen to Jason doing a Grover voice as red or as blue depending on how I think about it. If I am thinking 'yeah, that's Jason,' then it's blue. If I think 'well, there's Grover' then it's red" (personal communication, April 17, 2015).

Voice, in this framework, is acousmatic in a uniquely individual way. A voice does not *seem to originate* in the colors Dr. Wells-Jensen perceives in the way it seems to come from an imagined body for sighted listeners to recordings. Voice is no less tied to identity for her, though. "I probably have friends I've never touched," she tells me, "I think I've got a couple of bandmates I've never touched . . . so it is *all* their voice; that's all there is, so that's absolutely who they are [to me]" (interview, April 16, 2015). Dr. Wells-Jensen's ontological understanding of voice is not uncommon (see chapter 4), but her listening practices are crucial reminders that voice, sound, and music are experienced in a wide variety of sensory and cognitive ways. They also highlight the significance of perceptual disjuncture in singing impersonation—even if it does not fit a visual/aural binary.

Size Matters: "Mini" Impersonators

In *Dumbstruck: A Cultural History of Ventriloquism*, Steven Connor notes that though a voice comes from the body, it can only exist in departing it, and is only recognizable as *belonging* to a person through "the ways in which it parts or passes from" them (Connor 2000: 7). The ventriloquial voice appears to come from a body that should not speak, a doll only animated when the breath of life seems to pour out of it in sonic humanity. When a listener is sure of the source, Connor writes, the voice serves to engage and unite the senses of hearing and seeing, but in its ability to "put its source in question" the voice may also keep them separate (43). If it is thus "a means both of integration and of disturbance" (43), then, I would suggest, a voice with an unexpected source, or a source with an unexpected voice, has a special capacity for transgressive work. The impersonating voice, unlike the ventriloquial, sounds from a body that is identifiable as human. But such a voice has already had a life, first embodied in an originating singer and then disembodied by the audiocentric recording processes of music consumption, or even, as in the case of Elvis, by death. It is then re-embodied, a kind of intangible organ transplant or trace reincarnation in the impersonator. In with this process, the shuffling of bodies and voices can produce more than an entertaining gimmick. When a human body, like that of the ventriloquist's dummy, is not expected to speak, let alone sing—a subaltern body, a disabled one—it is perhaps strategic to take on the voices of others in order to be heard.

Familiar tropes of 21st-century popular culture engage with ideas about bodies and the voices that "should" emit from them or, conversely, the bodies that should house certain voices. One of the most powerful consequences of the 20th-century rise of music television and video has been the increasingly intense scrutiny of mainstream pop artists' bodies, especially, though not only, female. The many singers who dance particularly call attention to the fitness and vigor of their bodies, and the bodies that do not match these expectations are often lambasted by press and fellow public figures; even the wildly celebrated Adele has been criticized for her weight.

But in the age of reality television and YouTube, when any ordinary individual might become an extraordinary star, another narrative has also emerged, centered on embodied difference. In the past two decades, myriad talent competitions have swept the globe, and the transformation of singing bodies has taken center stage. The 2009 season of *Britain's Got Talent* introduced the world to Susan Boyle, a contestant with a pleasing voice located in hardly a Hollywood body—middle-aged, dressed and coiffed accordingly; during her time on the show, she related a story of childhood brain damage, though she has since received a diagnosis of Asperger's syndrome in its place (Brocklehurst 2013). In the wake of Boyle's subsequently stunning success, other shows made an effort to recreate it. In 2010, *American Idol*'s runner-up Crystal Bowersox experienced severe difficulties during her time on the show, caused by her Type 1 diabetes. The following season James Durbin, a young Californian, shared his experiences of Tourette syndrome and Asperger's with millions of viewers. Australian *X Factor* contestant Emmanuel Kelly, born in Iraq with incomplete limbs, moved thousands to tears in 2011 with his cover of "Imagine," and progressed to the second phase of the competition.

In some ways, a new public focus on singers perceived as disabled was the most natural step for singing competitions at the time; as viewers settled into the familiar formats, producers needed a way to up the stakes. If they sought a transformation even more powerful than the ordinary becoming extraordinary, what could be more fitting than that of a *sub*-ordinary individual becoming a superstar? The disabled individual is never actually allowed to aspire to ordinariness, but it is acceptable, even expected, that they aim higher. Onscreen and offscreen responses to their performances have frequently hailed these singers as "brave," "inspirational," or comparative reminders of how "small" the problems of nondisabled people are (Seven Network broadcast, August 29, 2011). Such responses, though positive on the surface, have been largely repudiated in disability studies, as ultimately representative of ableist discourses that reify object and abject bodies, and that position them as a kind of foil, serving to reflect moral lessons for the nondisabled.[4]

Under the pressure of such agency-denying cultural attitudes, the assertion of an active personal voice—*voice* in its metaphorical implications of power—becomes especially complicated for many disabled performers. George McKay, in *Shakin' All Over: Popular Music and Disability*, explores the relationship

---

[4] For an argument supporting the "recuperation" of inspiration as valuable to disability studies, see Chrisman 2011.

between discourses of authenticity and sincerity in rock and pop, and how disabled voices, and disabled bodies singing, are heard. He reminds us (McKay 2013: 55), citing Simon Frith (1996), and Barthes (1977) that the singing voice in popular music is ultimately understood by fans as a sonic expression of the real singer, the "corporeal truth" (McKay 2013: 57) of the artist, a performance that is more than just performative. He discusses, too, voices that sound in audibly pathological ways, containing a singer's autopathography. What does it mean, then, when the voice coming from a disabled body sounds healthy, and when the artist chooses the purposeful, unconcealed inauthenticity of impersonation? I have elsewhere written about the varying degrees of liveness in 21st-century pop performances, the pervasive application of what Lawrence Grossberg has termed "authentic inauthenticity" (Grossberg 1993: 205), and the possibility of intention and personal agency even in the process of lip-synching—of a performer *choosing* the voice that others hear, and do not hear, from him (Meizel 2011b). Impersonators, whether singing live or lip-synching, make such choices.

On the Vegas stage, the uncommon bodies of disabled impersonators produce uncommonly beautiful sounds, brokering intertwining philosophies of advantage and disadvantage, fame and infamy, disability and the extraordinary ability associated with vocal talent. But even offstage, performativity, as Carrie Sandahl and Philip Auslander argue, is a daily part of the lives of disabled individuals, with a script authored by others. In the context of that sort of drama, purposeful theatrical work can be a way to take control of the performance (Sandahl and Auslander 2005: 4). By co-opting the staring that unexpected bodies tend to attract, a performer can exploit it for her own benefit. And in Rosemarie Garland-Thomson's view, "[t]he artistic genre of performance lends itself especially well to the project of renarrating disability, because the body is the artistic medium of performance" (Garland-Thomson 2005: 33).

"Mini" Impersonators

In 2007, the year that saw a record 39.2 million visitors to Las Vegas (King 2012), the Planet Hollywood Casino and Resort debuted a new impersonation extravaganza called "Little Legends," billed as "a show so big we have mini-performers," and advertising "Little People, Big Show." "Little Legends" and its average-height MC presented a cast of short-statured entertainers in roles such as Mini Elvis, Mini Madonna, and Mini Tina Turner, and even offered a striking sort of meta-impersonation of the nearly self-impersonating duo Milli Vanilli. Two years earlier, a group called Mini KISS was engaged for a time at Beacher's Madhouse, a Vegas burlesque experience that also featured short-statured wrestlers, exotic dancers, and flying drink-serving "Oompa Loompas" in what was advertised as a "midget bar."[5]

The "mini" version of a pop star is a concept rooted in a contentious and painful history in western popular culture, in which people with any of two hundred forms of dwarfism have been cast in roles from the imaginary, to the infantilized, to the hypersexualized, and as Rosemarie Garland-Thomson describes it, from the "cute to [the] grotesque" (Garland-Thomson 2009: 172)—from fairy-tale dwarves, mythological leprechauns, and Santa's elves, to the 19th-century sideshow, to Mike Myers's cloned doppelganger "Mini Me," played by Verne Troyer in two of the Austin Powers films. Even the designation "Little People" is a contested one; it originated when the organization Midgets of America revised its title in order to accommodate multiple labels for people with dwarfisms, but to some it evokes only crypto-folklore and diminishment. This network of stories is intricately tied to the complex place of diminutive bodies in entertainment, popular but persistently positioned as spectacle perhaps because, as Garland-Thomson has suggested, "they are unfamiliar as flesh and too familiar as narrative." (172). It is not so difficult, then, to draw a connection between the roles of leprechaun and pop star; both are creatures of fantasy, after all.

To further complicate these size matters, at the same time that acclaimed figures like actor Peter Dinklage (starring in the HBO series *Game of Thrones*) and the reality-star Roloff family (TLC's *Little People, Big World*)[6] have been reshaping public perceptions of Little People, many others still choose to base their entertainment careers in more traditionally available roles. Stances vary within the disparate Little People community, some viewing the perpetuation of fantasy roles as damaging and damning, while others understand it as a kind of strategic essentialism, a reappropriation and reworking of the old fictions (Adelson 2005a and 2005b). Though most short-statured individuals in the United States are employed outside of the entertainment field, those who do end up in the spotlight weigh the heavy cultural baggage carefully.

Little E, the Compact King

Larry Gawatz is an Elvis impersonator, a part-time actor promoted as "Little E: the Compact King." Mr. Gawatz has played Vegas eight times, travels to gigs, and is well known locally in his home base, Tulsa, Oklahoma. He is publicized

---

[5] Mini KISS and the Madhouse's successive tribute band Tiny KISS made headlines with a possibly fictional dispute in 2006 (Welkos 2006).

[6] As of 2019, there have also been several seasons and spinoffs of the Lifetime Network's reality show *Little Women* franchise.

by his manager as "a bona fide 31% of the real deal" with a caveat that "a full 26% of this entire 4'2" act is hair." Humor is implicit in this description, as is often the case in discourse about performers of short stature, but though Mr. Gawatz enjoys his work, he takes it seriously, too. He studies his moves and is careful to treat Elvis's image with respect. In fact, he says, fans demand this respect for the King. He and his manager, Jon Terry, had worried initially that Elvis fans might interpret his "compact" act as making fun of Elvis, but they soon discovered that concern to be unfounded. He describes an incident early in his career in which he was performing at a baseball game with another Elvis impersonator. While Mr. Gawatz offered his usual routine, the other impersonator had dressed as "fat Elvis" with a burger imprinted on his cloak and was made up like a corpse. A season ticketholder accosted the team owner as Mr. Gawatz stood nearby, furious at the other actor's irreverent treatment of the King. "Don't you *ever* bring this guy back again," he reproached the team owner, and then pointed to Mr. Gawatz as a more appropriate example. "You can bring *him* back any time you want. He is out there busting his you-know-what to give us a performance. And not one time did I think he was making fun of him. He can't help that he's short. But he is one heck of a performer" (interview, February 28, 2012). The jumpsuits and the hips, the intense hair and the historical-replica sunglasses were not a problem. Exaggerations of gestures and coiffures are par for the course in affectionate, slightly parodic tributes. But meanness is not tolerated in the world of impersonation.

Mr. Gawatz is in high demand as Little E. He says his act has taken him to the "four corners of the United States," including one memorable Vegas gig for which two cast members of Cirque du Soleil's 2009 *Viva Elvis* show flew him in from Oklahoma for their wedding. While it's not uncommon for a Little Elvis to perform *at* the proliferation of Vegas wedding chapels, Mr. Gawatz could offer the Cirque du Soleil couple something no one else could; he came to *perform this wedding* as a minister. He belongs to a church in Tulsa, but he had obtained his ordination through another in California for the purpose of officiating as Little E. (His first wedding was a mass vow renewal on a Tulsa baseball field in 2007.) After failing to convince a regular Vegas Little Elvis to apply for a quickie ordination, the bride and groom had located Mr. Gawatz on the internet—a compromise, they told him, because he wanted an Elvis impersonator, and she wanted a Little Person. Mr. Gawatz could give them both, and found his niche as a performer.[7]

The equation of shortness with whimsy and humor is not an easy discourse to shake, and some Little People are uncomfortable with the ramifications

---

[7] Another Vegas impersonator, Rev. Mighty Mike, obtained his minister's license in 2010.

when a performer relies on it. But Mr. Gawatz, who got his start in the leprechaun business, explains his decision this way: "I'm going to get made fun of, looked at, stared at, and all that, I'm going to get paid. That's why I do what I do. Because every day of my life there's someone out there that makes a wisecrack, or laughs... but you know what? I'm going to the bank" (interview, February 28, 2012). As for other responses to his work, he says that he's received only respect from fellow members of Little People of America (LPA)—he has entertained as Little E at LPA events—and emphasizes that no one there has ever called his act offensive.[8]

The reappropriation of such problematic essentialisms is a well-established performative tactic. At the time that I spoke with Mr. Gawatz, there had been recent headlines regarding a campaign in Florida to repeal the state's ban on "dwarf-tossing," a bar-room competition in which a Little Person volunteer (sometimes paid) is thrown into a padded wall. The activity has for decades incited a complicated controversy about human rights and civil liberties, evoking the carnival spectacle of small bodies still deeply ingrained in American culture and raising questions about social freedoms, strategic essentialisms, and ableist hegemony. Opponents of dwarf-tossing cite the painful history that gave rise to it and the continuing struggle of Little People against attitudes that treat them like objects—even as dehumanized objects to be picked up and moved about against their will.[9] Those who defend the practice protest the ban itself as prejudicial, against those who make a living being "tossed."

David Flood, a professional tossee, sued in 2001 to challenge the ban as discriminatory against those who voluntarily participate (Adelson 2005b: 364). When a torrent of letters and calls from short-statured professionals convinced Republican Representative Ritch Workman to drop his effort to repeal the ban in 2012, Workman stated publicly,

> I'm on a quest to seek and destroy unnecessary burdens on the freedom and liberties of people.... I find the practice of dwarf-tossing repulsive.... But what I found more repulsive is that in 1980, this state decided that a person of sane mind—a full human with a full human mind—could not make their own decision to act like a fool. (Moye 2012)

Workman's abandonment of the repeal campaign came "not because I'm wrong on the liberty issue, but sometimes human dignity needs to prevail" (Moye 2012).

---

[8] LPA was founded by an actor, Billy Barty—and the first meeting under that name took place in Reno, Nevada, known as "The Biggest Little City in the World" and located 450 miles from Las Vegas.
[9] Actor Peter Dinklage raised this issue in his 2012 Emmy Award acceptance speech, citing a case in which an individual was seriously injured after being thrown without his consent.

Mr. Gawatz does not agree with the practice of dwarf-tossing. At the time of our interview, he initially expressed mixed feelings about balancing its violence and bigotry with the agency of the tossee, but a few years later, he is crystal clear that it isn't acceptable to him (personal communication, January 13, 2019).

Short-statured performers, like impersonators in general, build on the demands and processes of ocular-centric culture. But they particularly play to, and wrestle with, what Garland-Thomson identifies as a culture of staring—"a kind of potent social choreography that marks bodies by enacting a dynamic visual exchange between a spectator and a spectacle" (Garland-Thomson 2005: 31). Disabled bodies are perhaps among the most taboo but inevitable objects of the "normative stare" that constructs the disabled object (32). In their navigation of ocular-centrism, the disabled body and the disjunct body of the impersonator both disrupt the process of listening. But vocal impersonation also encourages a kind of auditory staring, an oral/aural choreography that, although subtler, is no less complex than the visual. In 2013, Miley Cyrus promoted her *Bangerz* album and tour by appearing on stage with short-statured dancers costumed as mushrooms. The controversies that followed *Bangerz* around the world included accusations that Cyrus's show exploited the Little People who accompanied her twerking, dressed as plush teddy-bears. One dancer in Cyrus's notorious *Video Music Awards* performance, Hollis Jane, wrote in her personal blog: "I was being stared and laughed at for all of the wrong reasons. I was being looked at as a prop ... as something less than human" (Jane 2013).

Finding a Voice

Larry Gawatz has wrestled with the question of whose voice to use in his act. Many impersonators, including short-statured performers, prefer to lip-synch, though occasionally they sing live.[10] Though he sings in a church quartet at home, Mr. Gawatz chooses to lip-synch as Little E. In a feat of compound impersonation, he performs to tracks that have been prerecorded by a local Tulsa Elvis impersonator (singer) his manager hired. Mr. Gawatz says he isn't comfortable singing as the King, and from the beginning he preferred not to lip-synch to Elvis's own voice, "because" he says, "that to me is more fake than what I'm doing now" (interview, February 28, 2012).

He used to acknowledge to his fans that the voice they heard belonged to a friend and not to him, but he recalls how a disquieting experience one night

---

[10] One short-statured impersonator I spoke with consistently sings live. The person gained significant fame a few years after our interview, and withdrew from this project in its late stages owing to professional contractual obligations.

changed his mind. Between sets at a gig, he befriended an elderly couple attending his show for their fifty-fifth wedding anniversary. They had seen Elvis live seven times, they told him, and this show was bringing back happy memories. They complimented Mr. Gawatz's voice and later asked how long he'd been singing professionally. Not comfortable concealing the truth from his new friends, he explained the situation. They told him they wished he had lied to them, because now their anniversary night had been ruined. And since then, Mr. Gawatz's reply to praise for his voice has been "thank you" (interview, February 28, 2012).

On the other hand, Mr. Gawatz and his voice, Karl Suggs, ended up performing on stage together one night in Las Vegas, with Mr. Gawatz lip-synching and hip-swiveling to the live singer standing right next to him. But, he says, "People were coming up to us, and they were telling Karl, you have a beautiful voice, you sound just like him, but they would turn around and say [to me], but *you* got the moves" (interview, February 28, 2012). Each convincing in his own way, together they made an extremely compelling Elvis, their duo appearance encapsulating the performative complexities of impersonation.

Gawatz's and Suggs's fragmented Elvis presented the iconic voice in what might be the beginning of a dizzying infinite regression—the voice removed from Elvis's (absent) body, apparently relocated to Larry's body, then revealed to be external to Larry's body and visibly re-enclosed in Karl's body. This metaphysical mess illustrates what Slavoi Žižek proposes as the "spectral autonomy" of the voice, which, he writes, because of its fluidity, its mobility, really "never quite belongs to the body we see" (Žižek 2001: 58, cited in Dolar 2006: 70). The question, then, of what kind of voice should sound in what kind of body is unanswerable, nearly moot. And though both singers and listeners take it for granted, it is a complicated project to pinpoint an impersonator's—or any person's—"own" voice. A voice is full of possibilities; in certain ways, a voice is always *any* voice, and we are all endowed with a Schrödinger's voice box waiting to be embodied, encultured, inscribed. Jonathan Rée, writing on deafness, has offered this conclusion: "We are none of us linguistic islands, after all; more like lost swimmers out at sea, buffeted by waves and dragged by currents that have no regard for our carefully groomed individualities.... In the end, we have no such thing as a voice of our own" (Rée 1999: 375).

Yet our internal, intimate experiences of voice tell us that we'll know who we are when we hear it—and when we see it. It is important to note that a singing impersonator's body almost demands to be seen; it is the very act of re-embodiment that creates the magic of disjuncture; after all, if you just want to *listen* to someone who sounds like Céline Dion, you can listen to Céline Dion. The hyper-representational act of impersonation excises, almost violently, one of the primary organs of identity and exposes it as an exquisitely dynamic site for the negotiation of difference.

What I have presented in this chapter points to the impersonator's stage as a rich field for further inquiry into how voice figures in identity politics. The explicit division and juxtaposition of Self and Other, of the objectified and abjectified, of the real and the hyperreal, highlight the exquisitely complicated process of making identity. While the uniquely individual singing voice tends to be described as a phenomenon either natural and inimitable, or trained into a particularly desired framework of vocality, celebrity impersonators like Mr. Gawatz demonstrate the centrality of choice that ties the vocal process to the construction of identity. Certainly any voice encounters both physiological and psychological limitations of range, timbre, and power—Véronic DiCaire refuses to imitate male singers because, she says, "you can always tell" her sound isn't male (interview, October 11, 2013)—but impersonators show that even those limitations allow for more freedom than most suppose. They highlight how identity is a project not only "for more than one voice" (to paraphrase Adriana Cavarero [2005]) but also for more than one vocality; and for those who find their freedoms curtailed, multivocality can be a vital instrument of agency.

4

Two Voices

Singers in the Hearing/Deaf Borderlands

> She knew very well that the law of the land was that no bird who could not sing beautifully should be allowed to dwell within its limits.
>
> —Laura Redden Searing, *The Realm of Singing* (1871)[1]

On July 25, 2013, Mandy Harvey stood barefoot on the stage at the Kennedy Center in Washington, D.C. Ms. Harvey, who is profoundly deaf, stepped up to the microphone, lifted her hands, and began the Sinatra classic "The Song Is You."[2] This concert, simultaneously sung and signed, celebrated the anniversary of the 1990 Americans with Disabilities Act,[3] and Ms. Harvey had traveled to Washington as the protagonist in a success story, as one of the young musicians recognized by the Center's arts and disability organization, VSA.[4] But that story isn't a simple one, and the recognition juxtaposes difficult ideas about *singing* as an extraordinary, embodied ability and ideas about *signing* as a marker of extraordinary, bodily *dis*ability; this placed Ms. Harvey at the juncture of legal, medicalized, and cultural definitions of deafness. At the heart of this labyrinth lay notions of sonic voice as agency, the assumed universality of the sounded and heard voice, and the equation of its absence with silence in the world.

---

[1] The prose poem *The Realm of Singing* was written as an "autobiographical allegory" by deaf poet Laura Redden Searing (who used the pen name Howard Glyndon), commenting on the skepticism her work had met owing to societal preconceptions about her deafness. In the story, a bird's broken wing is substituted for Searing's deafness, and its singing for her self-expression in writing. I quote it here *not* to draw a comparison with the singers about whose experiences I write but, rather, as reminder of the difficult choices about voice that deaf (and women) artists faced in the Victorian era, and that they still face 146 years later.

[2] Written by Jerome Kern and Oscar Hammerstein in 1932.

[3] It should be noted that while Deaf culture rejects the sociopolitically diminishing implications of disability, deaf individuals are protected under the Americans with Disabilities Act.

[4] In the 1970s, VSA was originally named the National Committee-Arts for the Handicapped; it was renamed Very Special Arts in 1985, and then shortened to VSA in 2010. The following year it merged with the Kennedy Center's Office on Accessibility (http://www.kennedy-center.org/education/vsa/).

Voice, in all its material and metaphysical implications, is one of the most politically charged ideas in American Deaf culture.[5] In hearing discourse, sonic voice is conceptually entangled with the metaphor of agentive voice. But Deaf philosophies of voice must confront the oppressive systems that for centuries enforced oralism and disavowed both sign languages and Deaf identity; voice in this history is not an instrument of liberation; instead, it is one of erasure. As scholars in Deaf studies have observed, Deaf culture developed as a response to vocal hegemony and the institutionalized trauma of compulsory speech, advocating instead for the legitimacy of American Sign Language (ASL) in deaf lives. While other 20th-century social movements were driven by the rhetoric of "gaining a voice" and "speaking out," the deaf community's initial struggle toward the capital D, toward recognition as a culture, challenged the dominance of those expressions as primary metaphors of identity (Bauman 2008a: 3).[6]

The intricacies of voice and identity always make "discovering a voice of your own ... the task of a lifetime" (Rée 1999: 1). This kind of task is, as Jonathan Rée remarks, the particular work of actors and singers. No two Deaf musicians do this work in the same way. Jeannette DiBernardo Jones writes about Deaf rappers Sean Forbes, who signs and voices his lyrics, and Finnish rapper Signmark, who collaborates in American Sign Language with a Hearing vocalist performing in spoken English (2016: 64). Thus, d/Deaf singers like Ms. Harvey, who grew up in a hearing culture before becoming audiologically deaf, must navigate these clashing, but nevertheless intertwined, histories as immigrants to Deaf culture. For them, voice can become a special locus for identity conflict, embodied both in the aesthetics that shape the vocal tract and the kinetics of sign language, and in the performance of an intricate politics of inclusion and exclusion. It is this politics with which the present chapter is concerned, examined through the experiences of d/Deaf singers working on and across the borders of identity. I want to emphasize that I am not situating this chapter as a study of Deaf culture; rather, in what might best be termed an adjacent inquiry, I discuss several ethnographic case studies that explore individual, complicated relationships with

---

[5] In this chapter, though I later explain recent critiques of this model, I follow the common convention of referencing Deaf cultural identity with a capital "D," and the audiological condition of deafness with the lower-case letter—representing, respectively, social and medical models of deafness. Within Deaf culture, there are categories of identity including Deaf (individuals for whom ASL is the primary or exclusive language) and Hard of Hearing (may refer to individuals with some hearing loss who primarily speak English, but *may* also use ASL; or it may refer to a deaf individual who does not identify culturally as Deaf). (See National Association of the Deaf, http://nad.org/issues/american-sign-language/community-and-culture-faq.) I maintain the "d/Deaf" division because it is still important to many culturally Deaf people, but it is vital to acknowledge the emerging discourses in Deaf studies that critique the binary as outdated (see "Locating d/Deaf/DeaF Singers," later in chapter).

[6] Note: The sign translated as the adjective "hearing" in English is the same sign translated as "speak."

both Hearing and Deaf cultures, and the roles of singing and signing in their negotiation. I position these artists' practices in song and in sign as strategies of self, and I argue that their work supports an inclusive view of *musical voice* that encompasses multiple embodied modes of meaning-making. This chapter investigates the work of d/Deaf musicians for whom singing and signing are experienced as two voices, two vocalities—ideas at once a world and just one letter apart.

Phonocentrism

The equation of voice with agency is rooted in the long association, in western thinking, between speech and existence. Within such metaphorical frameworks, voice figures as a site of selfness and self-empowerment. Jonathan Rée, in his landmark work *I See a Voice: Deafness, Language, and the Senses*, considers this trope and the binary thinking that pervades voice discourse outside of Deaf experiences: "[voices] are both expression and communication, both feeling and intellect, both body and mind, both nature and culture. The whole of us, it would seem, is included in the compass of the human voice" (Rée 1999: 16). But much more than self-epistemology is assigned to voice: it has been positioned not just as a way of being but also *being itself*, as an index of, in Jacques Derrida's framework, "presence as substance/essence/existence" (Derrida 1997[1967]: 13).

Derrida, in *Of Grammatology*, employs the idea of *phonocentrism* to critique the privileging of speech over writing. Derrida attributes the history of phonocentric thought to a semiological and metaphysical association between voice and the concept of self-presence—an association that, as translator Gayatri Spivak notes, Derrida also observed in *Speech and Phenomena* (in French titled *La Voix et le Phènoméne—The Voice and the Phenomena*), his collection of essays on Husserl's theory of signs: "Why is the phoneme the most 'ideal' of signs? . . . When I speak, it belongs to the phenomenological essence of this operation that *I hear myself* [je m'entende] *at the same time that I speak*" (Derrida 1973: 77, cited by Spivak in her preface to *Of Grammatology*). For Derrida, phonocentrism results from a human desire to imagine some kind of "central presence at beginning and end" (Spivak, in Derrida 1997[1967]: lxviii).

Bauman quotes Derrida in his examination of voice: "it is the 'absolute proximity of voice and being, of voice and the meaning of being, of voice and the ideality of meaning' that has governed our onotological tradition" (Derrida 1997[1967]: 12; cited in Bauman 2008b: n.p.). This hegemonic tradition is foundational to the institutionalized trauma that has shaped Deaf history and which eventually led to the counter-movement of Deaf culture. Notably, the Derrida quote Bauman discusses, in its complete form, also positions "[t]he notion of the sign" within "the heritage of that logocentrism which is also a phonocentrism" (Derrida 1997[1967]: 12). It requires little effort to connect such a semiological model to the embodied signs of sign languages.

Writing on audism (discrimination against Deaf people), Bauman extends Derrida's critique to underscore the oppressive implications of privileging speech, not only over writing but also over *any kind* of non-sounding, non-phonemic language—sign languages, in particular. Bauman argues for a notion of the sign that is not bound to phonocentrism, a model that does not locate presence—being—only in the material voice; instead, he suggests a "theory of voice no longer beholden to sound, but to the gesturing body that may speak outside the reach of phonocentrism" (Bauman 2008b: n.p.). If the same can be done for a theory of vocality, and if, as I have argued in this volume, vocality functions as a strategy in the structuring of identity, I propose here that such a strategy need not be solely a sonic one. Other embodied forms of communication, such as signing, must also be considered as integral, and even, sometimes, integrated.

Locating d/Deaf/DeaF Singers

The significant but contested role of music in Deaf culture has been somewhat documented by music scholars (for example, by music therapy and music education researcher Alice-Ann Darrow [2006], with Gallaudet University's Diane Merchant Loomis [Darrow and Loomis 1999], and more; by Hash 2003; and Sheldon 1997), as well as Deaf scholars—particularly in the *Journal of American Sign Language* (http://journalofasl.com/articles/). Further, d/Deaf individuals are often capable of aurally perceiving some frequencies, though those may or may not fall outside the primary range of musical instruments and the human voice. Frequency vibrations may also be experienced through the sense of touch— and a brain-imaging study by neuroscientists in 2001 showed that for deaf people, vibrations felt through the skin are processed in the auditory centers of the brain, the same parts used in the auditory experience of sound (Klarreich 2001). Another study the same year revealed that deaf individuals may be able to identify more subtle changes in vibration frequency than hearing people (Levänen and Hamdorf 2001, cited in Klarreich 2001). Music is a part of life for many d/Deaf people, and in Deaf culture music is experienced in particular, intensely embodied Deaf modes of listening. However, for some, music retains too many ties to Hearing values to be of interest; in 1987, scholar and activist M. J. Bienvenu stated in a translated and published ASL presentation: "the hearing culture prizes things of no value to me, such as music and spoken

English"[7] (Bienvenu 1987: 5). Bienvenu, whose lecture originally addressed ASL interpreters, recognizes the intersection of Deaf and Hearing identities as a complex space that forms a *third culture*. A third culture, she explains,

> is not a full culture that people can identify as such. Third culture consists of people from two other cultures, for example, hearing and deaf people, coming together. Each of these cultures is different. Members of third culture bring their own cultural biases with them, but establish a temporary set of cultural rules and values (Bienvenu 1987: 1)

Bienvenu also distinguishes between "third culture" and bi-culturality, observing that a third culture "is neither permanent nor stable":

> People who are bi-cultural have a first culture which they temporarily give up in exchange for a second culture. In the move to the second culture, they take on the language, rules, and values of that second culture. Then they are able to return to their first culture. Being bi-cultural means knowing how to move comfortably between two distinct cultures. Third culture is special in that it represents the possibility of coming to a halfway point, making contact with members of the other culture, but maintaining all the while one's identity as a member of one's first culture. (Bienvenu 1987: 1)

For some, third culture represents the *necessity* of coming to a halfway point. That is, d/Deaf singers typically became deaf or hard of hearing postlingually, after the development of speech, in school-aged childhood, adolescence, or adulthood,[8] and they negotiate Bienvenu's halfway point in diverse ways, in speech and sign language. But their relationship to sign language is different from that of the interpreters to whom Bienvenu was speaking, in that, owing to non-normative hearing, they do not necessarily feel comfortable in their "first culture." Adapting a phrase from Bauman's discussion of sign literature (Bauman 2006: 360), I suggest that these singers live in "hearing/Deaf borderlands," and their movements across linguistic and cultural boundaries map the landscape of a unique frontier. It is especially noteworthy that both Bauman's borderlands and Bienvenu's third culture are grounded in ideas about movement across cultural borders, and about the mutability of identity.

---

[7] Bienvenu also wrote an essay titled "Stop the Music," but it is unavailable in English at the time of this writing.

[8] Donald Grushkin found in 2003 that in the United States, Hard of Hearing individuals she interviewed had a variety of responses to the idea of a third culture—some acknowledged the existence of a third HOH culture already, some saw it in the future and worried about further divisions among d/Deaf people, and some didn't see a need for such a space (Grushkin 2003: 134).

Guy McIlroy and Claudine Storbeck similarly emphasize this mutability, though they position the "deaf in my own way" stance as a specifically bicultural identity (McIlroy and Storbeck 2011: 495, after Ohna 2004). They critique as outdated the binary application of static medical or social models (and the d/Deaf duality) to deaf experiences, and they suggest instead a "dialogue model" that "embraces postmodern tensions between contradictory identities" (496). Their concept of *DeaF* identity—the capital "F" indicating fluidity—describes a cultural position that is neither grounded in Deaf nor hearing contexts but, rather, "represents the cultural space from which [Deaf, deaf, or hard of hearing individuals] transition within and between both the Deaf community and the hearing community" (McIlroy and Storbeck 2011: 497, also discussed in McIlroy 2010). It is a position that may complicate the neoliberal biosociality of which—like other U.S. identity-based communities—Deaf culture, according to anthropologist Michele Friedner (2010), is in part a manifestation. Friedner builds on Foucault's (1978) discussion of biopower and subject formation; on Rabinow's subsequent (1996) concept of biosociality, in which people form communities based on shared biological characteristics; and on the work of Nikolas Rose (1999), who argues that neoliberal government motivates and depends upon the formation of such communities as replacements for social welfare programs. Friedner, though she in no way denies or negates the significance of U.S Deaf culture as a community based in the use of ASL, understands power as both oppressive and productive, and she views Deaf culture as fundamentally a result of this neoliberal framework: "something produced by and through, and not in spite of, the existence of power" (Friedner 2010: 337). Resistance, as she summarizes Foucault, "exists and operates within power and should not be seen as the opposite of power" (341). I suggest that individuals who participate in both Deaf and hearing cultures, each community predicated on assumptions of discrete shared biological characteristics and linguistic practices, may confound and resist neoliberal biosociality. Furthermore, the singing, signing voice may serve as an especially notable vehicle for this resistance.

Though a relationship with music in general is not unusual in deaf experience, the work of singers who sign—who embody voice in more than one way—presents an important and unique opportunity for the study of deaf, multilingual, and polycultural identities.

Singing/Signing Bodies

"What do we miss if we reduce music to sound?" asks ethnomusicologist Matt Rahaim in his monograph on Hindustani singing, *Musicking Bodies*. His answer: "people, for one thing" (Rahaim 2012: 1). Rahaim links the separation of voice and body, in both Hindustani and western musical discourses, to late 19th-century developments in science and technology, including phonology, anatomical studies, psychoacoustics, and the phonograph (20-27). An invention of deaf educator and oralism advocate Alexander Graham Bell, the telephone has also had a significant impact on this way of thinking, and is known to have served as an isolating factor for deaf people in the 20th and 21st centuries (Lang 2000: 29).[9] The voice–body divorce ("still singers and silent dancers," as Rahaim writes [2012: 28]) in European musics has also been exacerbated by the classed, racialized split between high and low culture, the association of dancing with primitivized, hypersexualized ideas about Blackness, and further changes in performance technology. As operatic practices shifted in the late 19th century, the musicking bodies of audiences were also stilled as they listened. Alex Ross cites the first performances of *Parsifal* in 1882 as a pivotal moment, when an audience misunderstanding combined with the general sacralization of Wagner's music led to new silences in Bayreuth (Ross 2005). Wagner's operas are also often assigned the blame for the now-derided "park and bark" or "stand and deliver" method of opera staging, in which a singer remains stationary during an aria or number (for example, a Vancouver Opera communications manager blames Wagner for this; Steele 1997). Western *popular* musics, of course, place a higher premium on movement, particularly that of women's bodies, but it is typical for pop stars—though the practice is often reviled—to perform live with support tracks so that the voice is uninterrupted by the dancing body. In a music video, an artist is expected to lip-sync to his or her own voice, for the sake of both visual and auditory quality.

The bodies of singers, though, are always dancing, even when standing still, in an elaborate interior choreography of muscle and cartilage and space, in the tremor of bone and passing air. Though listeners cannot see these elastic contortions of the singer's inner self, singers know that hidden landscape intimately, having mapped it themselves over time in the process of finding a voice. Signing, when accompanying perhaps the only characteristically hands-free musical instrument, expands the cartographical terrain for both the listener and the singer, and it intensifies the dynamics of identity performance. Singing is engineered on the inside of the body; signing inhabits the outside. Singing involves not only the larynx but also hundreds of articulatory and respiratory muscles and the spaces in the body that serve as resonators. Signs are not only made with the hands; the hands touch the head, the torso, and sometimes the

---

[9] This isolation was the impetus for developments such as the teletypewriter (TTY); conditions have improved with computerized video conferencing and email, but as Ms. Spurlock pointed out to me, none of these technologies encourages in-person, face-to-face encounters (interview, July 20, 2014).

legs, and the face and body posture affect the meaning, grammar, and inflection. It would perhaps not be hyperbole to suggest that no body could be any more completely engaged in the performance of identity than the singing, signing body. Literally, for such a body, "The Song is You."

Mandy Harvey

In 2006, Ms. Harvey had begun college studying vocal music education; then, after a lifetime of recurrent hearing difficulties, she became profoundly deaf. She left school and her career plans behind in 2007, and she stopped singing for a year (Harris 2012), until the process of making a home recording with her father inspired her to return to music.

With that return, Ms. Harvey had to make adjustments to her musical practices. Eschewing shoes onstage, she can feel the vibrations of instruments through the floor. She gathers a great deal of information through this technique, including the pulse and the progress of the music[10]—"the differences between which instrument is playing, based off of how it feels and where the feeling is coming from" (personal communication, August 28, 2013). The importance of this practice in her singing journey is made clear in the title of her autobiography: *Sensing the Rhythm: Finding My Voice in a World Without Sound* (Harvey and Atteberry 2017).

She has also built upon the foundation of her preexisting talents. Her absolute pitch permits her to learn new repertoire directly from sheet music without the assistance of recordings, and once she has established middle C with the help of a tuner or an available human ear, she can be certain of any other pitches. Learning by sight has its benefits, she says. She can't rely on listening to others' interpretations now, so she is able to focus on cultivating her own. But the process of learning has changed in frustrating ways, too; though formerly she was able to memorize a song after one hearing, "Now if I am not paying attention I can forget the whole thing" (personal communication, August 28, 2013).

Vocalization is typically a heavily proprioceptive experience, in terms of both tactile and aural sensory feedback. As speech pathologist John A. Haskell wrote in 1987, "[a] speaker's perception of his or her own voice, as it has been experienced over time, becomes the basis for a vocal intention in communication and for self-monitoring of vocal production once it has begun" (Haskell 1987: 172). Yet, when confronted with a recording of one's own voice, in speech or song, there is always a degree of unfamiliarity; it sounds as if a stranger is imitating

---

[10] This tactic is also famously associated with deaf percussionist Dame Evelyn Glennie.

your patterns and inflections. Research posits that this common phenomenon is due to a key difference in hearing inside the body and outside—from inside, we hear our own voices sounding through bone conduction, as well as through the air, while the process of listening to a recording can only offer air conduction (Maurer and Landis 1990: 226). For hearing singers, this discrepancy can be problematic, splitting focus and creating an unreliable feedback loop. Western classical and classically based vocal pedagogies often address this issue explicitly. A 2011 episode of the BBC Two magazine *See Hear*—a television program designed for d/Deaf British citizens[11]—featured opera singer Janine Roebuck, who first publicly shared her deafness in 2007 (Roebuck 2007) together with her singing instructor Arwel Treharne Morgan. In the interview, they discussed similar concerns, as Morgan explained:

> Opera singers, the sound, you are inside, and you have no real idea of how the sound is projecting out into the auditorium or into the opera house, so therefore even as a hearing person it's all about the feel, because you don't have a concept of how that voice is travelling correctly into the auditorium. Because if you're changing acoustic all the time, and you're going from a dry acoustic like a studio, [to] a cathedral or a concert hall or an opera stage, all those acoustics are different, so if you go by sound, you've had it. (BBC Two, *See Hear* 2011, series 29, episode 32, accessed at https://www.youtube.com/watch?v=RG4-lXdFIJ4)

When Ms. Roebuck found her progressive nerve deafness worsening in her late 20s, she tried to adjust her technique so that she could hear herself better, but ended by paradoxically suppressing her sound. She told me:

> I have not been able to depend on what I hear for a very long time, and fell into the bad habit of trying to place the voice forward in certain resonators in order to better hear. This of course is counter-productive for any singer, as the more you hear of your own voice, the less it is likely to travel into the auditorium. (personal communication, July 20, 2014).

"Forward" is a concept related to what classical singers call the "placement" of the voice, the shaping of the vocal tract in such a way that sympathetic vibrations are felt most strongly by the singer in particular physiological locations—for example, in the area of the zygomatic arch and the nose, or "forward" in the face. By shifting the place she felt her vocal vibrations, Ms. Roebuck was able to hear her own voice more clearly, but the sound didn't reach her audiences in the same way.

---

[11] Broadcast in British Sign Language (BSL) with voiceover and English subtitles.

Ms. Roebuck participated in a 2011 study by Fulford et al. of "The Experiences of Musicians with Hearing Impairments," which documented the decision to stop listening as an important strategy. They identified Ms. Roebuck as a "listening" musician, in spite of her previous statement, owing to her reliance on hearing aids in performance, but for other cases the authors suggested the term "non-auditory attending" to replace the idea of a "non-listening" musician, identifying such musicians as those who have "developed the ability to attend, perhaps more closely than can people with lesser degrees of hearing impairment, to characteristics of sound *other* than those which can be heard, for example, the vibrotactile" (Fulford et al. 2011: 459)—as Mandy Harvey attends to the vibrations of the instruments in her band and Ms. Roebuck to those in her body.

It is perhaps not surprising, given singers' experiences of self-hearing and self-sensation, that it is a common practice among voice instructors to ask hearing students to place their fingers in their ears in order to interrupt the feedback loop, shift focus to the body's internal spaces, and facilitate vocal "freedom." T. L. Forsberg, whose work is detailed later, mentioned to me that just after college, in preparation for a Broadway callback, she studied with a coach who trained both d/Deaf and hearing singers with the assistance of earplugs.

Without full hearing, the phenomenology of voice is fundamentally different. Though she remembers what she sounded like to her own ears when she was 18, Ms. Harvey's experience of her singing has shifted from audiocentric to a focus on more internal sensations. She is "hyper-aware" of the relationship between sound and her body now, since her ears can no longer process her voice at all. While that perceptual absence can be troubling, she also indicates potentially positive effects. She believes that her voice has stayed the same, but that her confidence has grown; always a reluctant performer before her hearing loss, she says her relationship with her voice was "weak," but "now that it's more of a phantom feeling I have a deep respect for that muscle" (personal communication, August 28, 2013). She expands on this newfound confidence:

> It's funny how you do not worry as much about hitting high notes or what people think of you when you cannot hear yourself. [There's a] [g]reat deal of freedom to not go home and pick apart everything that I performed. (personal communication, August 28, 2013)

This view strikes a chord with fans, as well. A review in *Healing Path Magazine* seized upon that idea of freedom as a kind of metaphysical touchstone for its readers: "[Ms. Harvey] demonstrates the power available to us when we give up our attachment to outcome and focus only on what we do now.... We experience freedom to be all that we are" (Waterman 2009, cited in video at https://www.youtube.com/watch?v=EjtLkrh2ZEA).

As her sense of voice has turned inward, she has also carefully developed the more external, communicative aspects of her performing. Already a capable lip-reader owing to her years of hearing problems, Ms. Harvey had begun to study American Sign Language when things worsened in college. Since her return to jazz, signing has become an integral part of her performances. "Signing clarifies your tone," she says, "signing has more ways to say the same thing to really bring out the meaning of what you are trying to say" (personal communication, August 28, 2013). Interpreting, though, is not a simple process; it is complicated by the demands of live translation and by fundamental structural differences between ASL and English. As a result, interpreters may draw upon several different methods. For her Kennedy Center performance, Ms. Harvey relied, she said, on a combination what is known as "sim-com" (also SimCom, simcom), or "simultaneous communication," and ASL. In the controversial sim-com approach, English is spoken (or sung) and the words simultaneously are signed in literal, but un-artistic, translation, sometimes drawing from non-ASL systems such as Signing Exact English (SEE II.). Sim-com highlights disjunctures in the word order and grammar of the two languages, and frequently produces awkward or inaccurate results (Conley 2001: 154, cited in Brewer 2002: 30). Ms. Harvey supplement sim-com with ASL when she can, especially when the lyrics come too quickly for her hands to keep up (as in fast-paced songs like "In Walked Bud"), and she says that Deaf and Hard of Hearing (HOH) audience members are supportive of this combination (personal communication, January 21, 2014). When she later competed in the 2017 season of *America's Got Talent*, she signed infrequently with music, as she usually accompanied herself on ukulele, but when she interpreted her original song "Release Me," her ASL performance was as expressive and nuanced as her vocal one (for example, with each iteration of her repeated English phrase "release me," her signs were distinct). She also sometimes signs only a summary of a song, and she provides d/Deaf audience members with printouts of the lyrics. Some of her performances use a sound system that is connected to a hearing loop—an electromagnetic transmitter whose signal is received by hearing aids and cochlear implants. For d/Deaf audiences, she says, she additionally tends to use more drums and bass so that the sound can be felt more clearly through vibrations (personal communication, August 28, 2013).

Her singing makes her relationship with Deaf culture especially difficult. I asked her whether she considers herself part of it. "Yes and no," she answered. She does use ASL, but:

> There are some people within the Deaf community that do not agree that we should be promoting oralism (speaking/singing) and only allow ASL. My response to that is that singing is my dream and I would never suppress someone pursuing their dream. (personal communication, August 28, 2014)

When she appeared on *America's Got Talent*, she later told the BBC, she received "strongly-worded letters and death threats" for "promoting oralism" (Rose 2017). She understands this reaction from "a very small group of loud voices," she told philanthropist Jay Ruderman during a 2018 podcast, in light of the oppression faced by the Deaf community. But she asserts that there are "so many different forms of being deaf," and contextualizes her work within the cultural framework of "Deaf Can," an empowering discourse in 21st-century Deaf culture (Ruderman 2018). While signing is often positioned as an embodiment of cultural agency, Ms. Harvey also equates her singing voice with personal agency. For her, despite any controversy, the simultaneous act of singing and signing articulates both sonic and social voice, individual and cultural identity.

T. L. Forsberg

Actress and singer T. L. Forsberg finds her cultural position similarly complex, singing and signing at the halfway point of third culture. She has struggled throughout her career to balance her sense of self as dually envoiced—to reconcile across two social worlds what she calls her *singing voice* and her *Deaf voice*. Ms. Forsberg identifies as Deaf, having experienced hearing loss as a child, but she is not profoundly deaf and can manage her daily life using hearing aids in some situations. ("I am audiologically dependent for a Deaf person," she explains. "I hear it first, and then I say 'say it again,' and then my eyes will pick it up . . . because I was born hearing, I'm rigged that way.") In the 2010 documentary *See What I'm Saying?*, she expresses her discomfort with the need of others—directors, music producers, friends—for her to be "more deaf" or "more hearing," and, she has been a passionate advocate for the understanding of Deaf diversity. She points to the film as her "out-of-the-closet experience about my Deafness"—curiously, musicians who publicly reveal their deafness are often described as "coming out" (e.g., Fulford et al. 2011, discussing Janine Roebuck and others), a full embracing of her Deaf identity. At the same time, though, she feels that the hearing part of her identity was forced into that closet for the sake of acceptance in the Deaf community. "There was a lot of shame about being able to hear," she says, explaining that while hearing people who wear hearing aids often hide them from other hearing people; Deaf people who can talk on the phone might keep that ability from other Deaf people. To those who question her identity now, she offers this typical response: "I self-identify as Deaf, and I'm not a profoundly deaf individual. I'm not that kind of deaf. I'm *my* kind of Deaf" (interview, November 22, 2013).

Ms. Forsberg sang in a choir as a young teenager, but like many others, she remembers that her most formative vocal experiences came from singing along with the superstars of her youth—"singing along with what other people were already doing." She studied theater and dance in college, and for a long time felt that using her body allowed her to express more than using her voice. Now, though, she thinks of her voice and body as inseparable. She still turns to dance to facilitate her singing and her composing: "there's been times where I've been writing songs and I wasn't sure what the song was about, so I would dance to the music and then I would start to get a story out of it." And she eventually found a way to combine elements of voice and dance in a set of personally particular performance practices; her signing onstage integrates both her poetry and a choreography of her whole body.

She began signing during her time fronting the rock band Kriya. At first, she incorporated a style influenced by visual phonics (a didactic system of hand symbols representing English language sounds) and then, she notes, "as I grew in my cultural identity, I found it to be more respectful to learn the language ASL for myself and for my art" (personal communication, December 4, 2018). She was encouraged by the appreciation her d/Deaf audience members expressed; for some, she was offering deeper meaning to their typical experiences of music. Eventually, though, her motivation shifted. She noticed that, in the club scene, music was relegated to background noise, with the focus more on drink and dance and conversation than on the band. When she added signing to her performances, she found that bar patrons abandoned their chatter. They might still be drinking and sitting with friends, but now "[t]heir *body* was listening to what I was saying." Now, along with enhancing the music for deaf audiences, her new goal was to change the way hearing people experienced it:

> I thought, wow, hearing people don't know how to listen. They're more deaf than actual Deaf people! Because Deaf people are so tuned in to listening, like they're really hypersensitive, they pick up every little detail. But hearing people, they multitask, they don't make eye contact, but they're all over the place. I thought, I'm actually helping the *real* deaf people, which is the hearing people, learn how to *really* listen. (interview, November 22, 2013)

In other words, they *can* hear, but they *don't*. In a 21st-century culture where hearing people's entertainment is overwhelmingly oriented toward the visual—television, film, video games—perhaps signing can bring a necessary element of sight to the sound of music. Despite the rewards of Ms. Forsberg's performative path, it has been a rocky one, linguistically problematic, and physically and emotionally grueling. The structural differences between ASL and English are a primary concern.

For Jonathan Rée, such differences separate a spoken language that "forces us to consider ideas . . . one after another in time" and a gestural language that, in its complex vocabulary of hand movement, facial, and body affect, "make[s] us consider different ideas simultaneously, side by side in space" (Rée 1999: 86). Emphasizing that spatial element, Ms. Forsberg rejects sim-com, and draws on her training as a dancer to supplement ASL with her own movements—especially as it is imperative for her that the "choreography matches the rhythm of the word[s]," a requirement that sometimes makes finding appropriate ASL signs impossible. In line with her educational goals for non-Deaf listeners, she developed a way of interpreting that she describes as "visual phonics . . . and I still kind of do that. Like, I will do whatever I have to do with my body to communicate. I won't follow the literal rules of sign language." Hearing people often find her signing simply hypnotizing or aesthetically beautiful ("Deaf people hate that," she points out). But she has been told by directors in Deaf theater that her speech signing is "too musical" (*See What I'm Saying?* 2010), too lyrical and not precise enough—if signing enhances Ms. Harvey's singing, then conversely, singing is seen as having *attenuated* Ms. Forsberg's signing.

The issue of linguistic compatibility is further complicated by those elements of grammar and expression that fall outside the purview of the hands—called "nonmanual markers." Some of these signs are classified by linguists as "mouth morphemes," which J. Albert Bickford and Kathy Fraychineaud describe as "use of the mouth as an independent morpheme which combines with a variety of manual signs" (Bickford and Fraychineaud 2006[2008]: 33). In ASL, "[t]he grammar is in the face," Ms. Forsberg explains; to indicate an intensified degree—for example, as in "a lot" or "very," an unvoiced lip trill is required, a gesture that is not feasible while singing. My own ASL tutor, Michelle Spurlock, introduced me to other nonmanual markers that may interfere with singing, such as the nonvocalized plosive typically glossed as "pah!" in English that is used in the sign for "finally!" or "about time!" For "pah!" the lips purse and then open along with the jaw, sometimes allowing a puff of air to escape; this accompanies a manual sign.) (field notes, June 22, 2014).

"The interesting thing about my art form," Ms. Forsberg told me, "is that my two voices conflict with each other, because the ASL goes one way and the singing voice goes another" (interview, November 22, 2013). Finding a way to balance those "two voices" has been challenging, even at times devastating. In the early days, to sing and sign at once, she had to turn her head sideways to a stand-held microphone so that her hands were free and she could keep the space in front of her clear for signing—and unlike Mandy Harvey's controlled signing, Ms. Forsberg's interpretive style, forged during what she terms her "gothic phase," tended toward "epic" gestures (her word). The physical effort led to hoarseness, damage to a sternocleidomastoid muscle, and the temporary loss of her sounded voice. A doctor told her that what she'd been doing was "like singing and boxing at the same time." These linguistic and vocal-health concerns have, in the end, meant abandoning live singing for live signing, lip-syncing—and "sign-syncing," as she terms it—to the soundtrack of her studio recordings. Managers first encouraged this to ensure the best sound quality in videorecorded shows. But then, Ms. Forsberg recalls, "I realized it gave me more freedom to do my other voice, which was the sign language" (interview, November 22, 2013).

Like Mandy Harvey, Ms. Forsberg understands her voice as both material and metaphorical. Compounding her literal loss of voice, she worries that signing has compromised the sense of agency that singing affords her:

> I feel like, since I've been signing my music, that I kind of have lost my singing voice a little bit.... [T]here's a part of me, like, I'll come offstage and I get paid.... I'll do my autographs and get to look like a celebrity, and I come off stage and I go, "I'm a fucking puppet. Where is my singing voice?" Because when I was with a band, I could hold an audience. I was *commanding*.... And I feel a little bit like I've swallowed my singing voice to appease the Deaf voice. And that I'm being forced to make a choice between the two. (interview, November 22, 2013)

She has also, at times, hired "native signing" Deaf professionals to interpret her performances. Though she has enjoyed the experience, she has sometimes worried that "I was giving my artistic voice away to a more perceivably Deaf individual as an emotional shield to protect myself from the cultural bullying I often experience" (personal communication, December 4, 2018).

The dynamics of the music industry itself have provoked related anxieties for Ms. Forsberg. In *See What I'm Saying?*, she is in the process of recording an album with a strongly gothic character, in the style of the band Evanescence. When I made this comparison, she told me that this was a producer's choice, as Evanescence was a "flavor of the month." She is capable of changing her singing according to the tastes of producers she works with; she remembers as a teenager singing along with the rock tracks she heard through her headphones, and copying the singers closely.

> I can sing a Nelly Furtado track, I can do a No Doubt track, I can do Madonna or Cher, I can do Cyndi Lauper, I can do any of these, and vocally, the intonation, copy each one of them, because that's how I got my training. Like that's where it started for me, in my room, with headphones listening to this stuff. (interview, November 22, 2013)

But she found an important disadvantage to her flexibility as well, one that other participants in my project have also expressed: "The problem was, I got so good at imitating that I didn't know who I was. And it's taken me a long time to figure it out, to figure out what my voice is" (interview, November 22, 2013).

As she has worked toward finding her voice, she, like many singers, has received a great deal of input from external sources. We talked about this part of training, and I asked for her thoughts about why we rely on others—coaches, teachers, producers—to arrive at a vocal sense of self. "I know, right?" she exclaimed. "And it's usually a man!" Ceding the hearing and shaping of her voice to these others' ears, she feels, has been a disempowering series of transactions, tinged with the persistence of patriarchal relationships:

> They're always men. And one of my struggles has always been, certainly I know in the film my challenge was finding my own voice, showing up to it ... [but] the moment somebody wrote a check, paid for my rent, my clothes ... the dynamic became father-child. It's like, "Are you pleased, Daddy? Did you like what I did today?" "OK, OK, OK, OK." So my power just went out the window. (interview, November 22, 2013)

But voice, in Ms. Forsberg's work, is not only about her sense of self. In addition to singing and acting (recently she had a recurring role on ABC Family's TV show *Switched at Birth*), she is also a professional one-on-one interpreter (with the help of hearing devices and a headset) (personal communication, December 4, 2018). Some of her interpreting jobs center on music: in 2012, she signed for Cee Lo Green and contestants on NBC's *The Voice* (including crossover singer Chris Mann's performance of "You Raise Me Up"), and she interprets at an "LGBT church" (personal communication, December 28, 2018) in Silverlake, East Los Angeles, every Sunday. We discussed the unique demands of interpreting for other singers, which, in addition to the nuances of an artist's textual reading, also include the communication of extralinguistic information—in her hands, a kind of relocated embodiment of vocal qualities and specialized performance practices. It's "part of the responsibility" of an interpreter, she clarifies, to "capture the vocal intonation—we call it register— because deaf people don't have the vocal intonation, so you have to really capture the quality of what their voice is saying and doing" (interview, November 22, 2013). She can, for example, add a purposeful tremor to a sign in order to demonstrate a singer's use of vibrato.

Interpreters consider and embody other culturally embedded sounds, as well. Ms. Forsberg describes a recent church performance, sung in call-and-response by a white singer and an African American singer. To articulate the distinct signing styles of each performer, she incorporates racially coded body language into her interpretations. For the African American singer, she says, "I make it look a little more Black, like *oh yeah, girl*, you know, I'll snap my finger, I'll like, I gotta do anything to get in my body, "this is a Black girl" (interview, November 22, 2013). She accompanied the previous statement with a particular head-swivel, and another gesture, her right arm sweeping left to right in a narrow z, trailed by three snapping sounds.

A fair amount of literature has been devoted to this snapping gesture as part of American speech communication, both as a "nonverbal art form" and as a "contested signifier" associated with African American women's discourse and with camp performance in gay men's culture (Johnson 1995: 122). E. Patrick Johnson writes of the appropriations and reappropriations that have shaped the history of the snap (Johnson and others transcribe it as "SNAP!")—the gesture's pop-culture currency skyrocketed in the 1990s, when it featured prominently as a parodic stereotype in television shows such as the breakthrough Fox Network comedy *In Living Color*, in camp skits starring African American comedians Damon Wayans and David Alan Grier; or in equally camp segments on Martin Lawrence's *Martin*. Within the women's and gay communities he researched, Johnson found that the SNAP! was inscribed with gendered and racialized meanings, and sometimes classed. And in mediated popular culture today, it maintains appropriated versions of those meanings. *The Root* journalist Helena Andrews, for example, reviewing the 2012 TLC show *Here Comes Honey Boo Boo* (a spinoff from the previous hit *Toddlers and Tiaras*), remarked that its white, 6-year-old, snapping, head-swiveling star seemed to have lifted her entire persona from one of Martin Lawrence's camp, drag characters (Andrews 2012).

Figure 4.1 Still from *See What I'm Saying*, as Ms. Forsberg uses tuning software to check her pitch.

The SNAP! typically accompanies English words in speech, and it is also used in ASL, in the same emphatic role: to underline a statement or to comment nonverbally on a situation or person (Michelle Spurlock, interview, July 13, 2014). These interpretive methods underline (1) the important place sign-gestures have in the communication of hearing people, and (2) the essentializing role assigned to such sign-gestures in the imagining and performance of racialized and gendered bodies. Additionally, the translation of an individual's sonic identity *into* the embodied vocabulary of sign language at once supports and challenges Roland Barthes's famous complaint that language can only interpret music in adjectives, "the poorest of linguistic categories" (Barthes 1977: 179). Even if signed adjectives are no more or less successful than spoken ones in describing voice, they nevertheless add another, significant dimension.

Singing Interpretation and Sign-Singing

Michelle Spurlock interprets for musical theater and cabaret productions in the Sacramento area, in California. She identifies as Hard of Hearing, and we talked about how she communicates the extralinguistic sounds that are integral to the vocalization and hearing of identity. She identifies as Latina, and like Ms. Forsberg, is keenly aware of racialized body language in her interpretive work:

> if someone's singing something like, you know, a little kid very quietly singing "you are my sunshine, my only sunshine," we're gonna sign it like this, sort of sing-song [head tipping cheerily from side to side, her hands bouncing while signing], and happy, and [it will] match. But if I have a little girl with a lot of soul and a lot of rhythm, if some little Latina comes out, and she's like [sings phrase from "You Are My Sunshine" in a strong voice, ornamenting the melody with vocal "scooping"], I'm gonna sign [broader gestures, wider smile, head swivel], I'm gonna bring it, I'm gonna have to match her *intent*, what she's trying to emote [for] the audience, with her voice, with her intonation; I have to make my signs either bigger or smaller. (interview, June 22, 2014)

I also asked Ms. Spurlock how she indicates the vocal improvisations known as "runs," or "melisma," favored across many popular singing styles and carrying, as I have written elsewhere, all of America's racialized music history (Meizel 2011b). She explained: "You do something to show that the person is still singing and that feeling is continuing." And "my head might do it," she observed, demonstrating a version of the iconic head swivel (interview, June 22, 2014). As an example, we listened Whitney Houston's 1992 cover of the Dolly Parton classic "I Will Always Love You," a famously melismatic performance. At 2:55 in the track, Houston concludes the phrase "I wish you joy and happiness" with a short descending run. Ms. Spurlock, as she signed "happiness"—her hands vertically parallel, palms facing her chest, moving in small outward spirals—slowed the gesture down significantly, and her head swiveled, and her eyes closed and tightened at the corners as if she experienced deep emotion.

Like Ms. Forsberg, Ms. Spurlock finds that these embodied distinctions of vocal identity become especially useful when interpreting solo for a performance with multiple singers. She described to me interpreting for the show *Rent*, for the ensemble number "Seasons of Love," which features solos sung by separate characters, and a refrain typically voiced by the full cast. In addition to communicating distinct vocal sounds and expressivities, in such situations she also employs the technique of *role shifting*, used in everyday signing in a quotational context and in narrative context, allowing a signer to "embod[y] the event from the character's perspective" (Pfau and Quer 2010: 396). Facial expression, a change in gaze, body angle (e.g., a move to the side), and/or a change in head position may signal the narrative shift (Pfau and Quer 2010: 396). In "Seasons of Love," Ms. Spurlock had to convey the distinct identities, including implications of ethnicity, of each participating character and singer. Such interpretive performances throw a network of representational issues into stark relief, and they underscore just how centrally the body—the entire body, the sounding body, the moving body—figures in ideas about identity.

It is worth noting that in ASL, as public attitudes about race, ethnicity, and difference have shifted, and as global connections have formed between geographically and linguistically disparate Deaf communities, relevant signs have changed, too. Where signs earlier marked identities based on perceived physiological distinctions—a "K" made at the corner of the eye to indicate "Korean," or flattening the nose for "Black" ("Negro")—today they tend to focus on cultural attributes or geography, indicating a hat brim for "Mexican" or the shape of Japan for "Japanese." Many of the newer identity signs are adopted from the relevant culture's sign language, as well (interview with Michelle Spurlock, July 28, 2014; see also Senior 1994). Some recent signs, considered by many to be less offensive, still engender controversy and underline the problems inherent in embodied representations.

While professional sign interpreters are careful never to upstage a live voice artist, the phenomenon of "sign-singing" (sometimes referred to with other terms, such as "song-signing" or "signed song")—a tradition of performing an interpretation to a prerecorded track—does allow further opportunity for personal expression. Thus, like many singers, Ms. Spurlock has a "signature" song: the celebrated Kander and Ebbs composition "Maybe This Time" (the soundtrack recording by Liza Minnelli for the 1972 film *Cabaret*). She usually interprets for audiences with only a single or a few d/Deaf members, but in a special cabaret revue she has performed on her own for a mostly Deaf audience. She also finds that she functions as a peculiar kind of critic. Sign language interpreters are certainly no longer imagined to be "neutral conduits of language" (Metzger 1999: 1), particularly in the performing arts, but Ms. Spurlock is sometimes called upon to provide d/Deaf clients with judgments of taste. A d/Deaf audience member at a show might ask her whether a performer has a beautiful voice; Ms. Spurlock will answer with as many adjectives as she can: *beautiful, smooth, amazing, strong*—or, if a singer's sore throat has been announced to the audience, she might tell them "she doesn't sound as good as she did a few weeks ago" (interview, June 22, 2014). But either way, it is her opinion that matters, since she is both an interlocutor for the voice in sign and a kind of aural surrogate.

Sign-singing—a designation that directly compares the processes of signing to singing—has experienced a recent internet vogue, fueled by the DIY culture of YouTube, and perhaps most currently the work of Sean Forbes and D-PAN (Deaf Performing Arts Network, which creates music videos of both original works and popular songs, performed in ASL for a Deaf audience). But M. J. Bienvenu, nearly three decades before YouTube, identified the practice as a problematic one; in the third culture, she remarked, the participation of deaf people is "crucial," and singing songs highlighted a conflict in values (Bienvenu 1987: 3). At present, some sign-singing videos, featuring only hearing performers who have varying degrees of familiarity with a sign language, and often asking viewers for financial support, are triggering concern and even anger from the Deaf community. In September of 2014, Stephen Torrence, who terms his work "songsigning," posted a blog entry titled "On the Ethics of 'My' Art," addressing the many criticisms he had received for his videos based on his non-fluency in ASL, a lack of full understanding of Deaf culture, and his requests for monetary support. His early videos, beginning in 2008, mostly feature Torrence standing alone and signing in front of a wall; his latest examples are produced with dance movements (also from a standing position) and more cinematic detail. A video posted in August 2014, the Monkees' "Last Train to Clarksville," elicited both enthusiastic and angry comments. "I am a deafie and love your videos," wrote one commenter, before requesting that Torrence make a video of a favorite song; another comment from a self-identified Deaf viewer begged, "PLEASE stop oppressing and misappropriating our oppressed language!" (https://www.youtube.com/watch?v=T6EQEGk7cY4&google_comment_id=z133d1f45ybhx3r4b04chpa4knjpghxrenk0k).

Torrence's blog posting confronts and attempts to negotiate the complexities of cultural appropriation. He explains that his interest in signing songs stemmed from ASL classes in college and a fascination with synaesthesia and the visualization of sound, "the fuzzy boundaries between the senses and media that we often consider distinct" (Torrence 2014). The blog post concludes with an announcement that he will stop producing his videos, and that he will add links to Deaf and CODA (Child of Deaf Adult—another kind of native signer) videos to his existing productions online.

Anabel Maler has suggested that, despite the cultural conflicts that have arisen, the signed song "provides an invaluable opportunity to build stronger connections between hearing and Deaf artistic communities, and to showcase multiple ways of hearing" (Maler 2013: n.p.[12]). It also showcases, I suggest, multiple ways of singing. Sign-singing is a phenomenon that draws attention to the complicated relationship between material voice and agentive voice, to non-phonemic implications in the relationship between language and voice, and to the significance of cultural values in the construction and practice of vocality.

Janine Roebuck

Opera singer Janine Roebuck has taken part in some innovative projects conceived to integrate operatic tradition and sign performance, and to challenge conventional ideas about listening. In 2012, the Tête à Tête Festival in Hammersmith, London, England, premiered an opera, a work in progress, about Annie Jump Cannon (1863–1941), a celebrated American astronomer who became deaf in her late twenties. The composer, Stephen Bentley-Klein, has a daughter who is deaf; and one of the star singers has a deaf son. Janine Roebuck participated in the performance, and deaf choreographer Mark Smith worked with Bentley-Klein and leading experimental-theater producer, writer, and director Sarah Grange to create the work. Originally titled *A Quiet Life* (later *The Observatory*), the piece was advertised as "a multi-sensory opera . . . suitable for people who can hear and people who can't" (http://www.tete-a-tete.org.uk/the-quiet-life/). It was performed by singers with choreographed signing, and with captioning projected onto a screen at the back of the stage in varying fonts (see http://vimeo.com/47468818). The audience moved around the performance space, with no chairs to sit in, and could experience the music in a variety of ways at multiple locations. Some speakers positioned around the room held plates of talcum powder that formed shapes as the speakers vibrated, while further hanging speakers could be held for a tactile experience of the musical vibrations (Wilson 2012). Additional speakers were placed underwater in buckets so that, as Bentley-Klein explained in an interview on *Radio 3 In Tune*, hearing audience members could imagine a different experience of hearing, perhaps closer to that of deaf audience members (Rafferty 2012).

---

[12] Maler's piece on signed song details the process of Stephen Torrence's work, though it was written before he stopped creating new videos.

Musicologist Nina Eidsheim has previously written about an opera (Eidsheim 2011a) that sounded entirely underwater and was performed for hearing listeners, noting that sound waves travel faster through water and voice is generally heard differently in water because of water's increased density and reduced compressibility. She concluded from her experience of the work that "[t]he sound ultimately heard depends partly on what is sung, partly on the medium through which it passes, and how our bodies interact with that medium"— supporting the notion of sound as a multisensory phenomenon (147). Of course, the senses rarely work only one at a time, even in non-synaesthetic individuals. As Joseph Straus notes, hearing, by itself, is a multisensory experience, instead of a "one-to-one mapping of sense perceptions onto a single sensory organ" (Straus 2011: 167), it can also involve the tactile, the kinesthetic, and especially the visual. Straus refers to this in the context of what he calls "deaf hearing," as a mode of experiencing music in non-phonocentric ways. Sign interpretation, as Ms. Forsberg is aware, can broaden the act of listening for hearing audiences, and for singers as well.

In the radio interview about the project, Bentley-Klein also discussed how he composed with Ms. Roebuck's needs in mind, making sure to build her musical entries in such a way that she could find her starting pitch easily (Rafferty 2012). Still, she found that process difficult, especially as the inventive music did not follow familiar melodic or harmonic trajectories. "When we do it again," she says, "we will explore the use of in-the-ear monitors so I can hear my notes played by a suitable instrument— just as pop stars do!" (Janine Roebuck, personal communication, July 20, 2014). Her confidence in pitch depends a great deal upon capricious venue acoustics, the texture of the instrumental accompaniment, and the octave in which it is played. Recently, she has preferred recitals to the operatic stage, piano accompaniment to orchestral, and repertoire such as Mozart or French song "with tunes that I can anticipate," to the unpredictable melodic contours of many more contemporary works (personal communication, July 20, 2014).

Not all deaf singers habitually incorporate signing in their singing experiences. Ms. Roebuck has studied British Sign Language (BSL), and has sometimes performed with interpreters. Though she believes that sign interpretation is "a very beautiful thing . . . [and] it adds an emotional dimension" to singing (personal communication, July 20, 2014), she does not typically perform using both voice and sign. She is active in supporting U.K. institutions such as Action on Hearing Loss (formerly the Royal National Institute of the Deaf) and Music and the Deaf, which provides music education for deaf children. But she is also a patron of Auditory Verbal UK, a national charity that offers practical therapy in the interest of "[enabling] children who are deaf to learn to listen and speak without the need for lip reading or sign language" (www.avuk.org/about-us/avuk/).

Auditory-Verbal Therapy, which also promotes the use of hearing technologies including cochlear implants, is controversial in Deaf culture, both in the United States and in the United Kingdom. Ms. Roebuck acknowledges the delicate position of cochlear implants in Deaf culture, and professes her respect for individuals who decide against them. For her, though, the cultural framework does not fit her personal situation. She writes:

> I have total respect for those who choose to use British Sign Language instead— those for whom deafness is a culture with its own unique take on the world, a culture that in their view stands to be dissipated by implants. Deafness is not a disease, runs the argument. It does not need "curing." There are, however, millions who long to be cured. (Roebuck 2014)

With her hearing at 20 percent today despite her "state of the art" hearing aids (personal communication, July 20, 2014), she is currently considering the possibility of a cochlear implant herself.

Her advocacy of Auditory-Verbal Therapy is fueled not only by the thought of future deaf generations benefiting from the communicative practices of speech but also by the possibility of raising the voice in song; she believes that:

> all children should have access to the joy that singing brings. It is a quasi spiritual experience for me. Very uplifting, healing and beneficial, and a real privilege to touch and move others with my voice. (personal communication, July 20, 2014)

In this way, she supports voice as an extraordinary experience, one more than simply a given in the mundane dynamics of daily life. For Ms. Roebuck, the singing voice, though inextricably connected to the speaking voice, is also something separate from speech, with unique effects on both the singing body and the listening one.

These singers' experiences highlight the discrete political discourses of liberation and agency at work in both singing and signing, and complicate the practice of defining deafness through a negative relationship with voice. Instead, their work and their words, including Ms. Forsberg's "two voices," indicate that d/Deaf singers operate within a particularly comprehensive framework of voice, one that takes into account the physiological apparatus identified as voice, the metaphysical conflation of voice and being, the equation of voice with expression and with communication, and the understanding of voice as agency, as power. The multiple voices in their multivocality go beyond a distinction between singing and signing as modes of linguistic practice, and they underscore the significance of cultural discourse and thought in the construction of vocality. I might amend, then, my earlier definition of vocality (see the introduction) to encompass "the act of vocalization *and other embodied modes of communication in relationship with voice,* and the profoundly complex social world in which they resonate.... It is a set of vocal sounds, practices, techniques and meanings that factor in the negotiation of identity."

The work of the d/Deaf singers discussed here especially underline: (1) the complex relationship between speech and singing; and (2) the performance of singing and signing, of bodies in sound and bodies in motion, as an encounter not only between two languages but also between two voices, two *vocalities*—an intertwining within one body of two distinct ways of embodying and enacting identity. If vocality comprises a set of tactics in the construction of identity, perhaps it represents not just a way of being *for* voice but also a way of being *in relation to* voice. Then signing, specifically located within the context of a singing performance, should be considered in such a process. The d/Deaf singers whose work I have examined at once reinforce and trouble ideas about the relationship between phonos and logos and soma, between voice as a material technology and voice as a metaphor for power; and they refute the assigning of a singular, static vocality for every individual. Instead, their work effectively demonstrates multivocality as a significant strategy in the negotiation of cultural borderlands.

5
Spiritual Multivocality

Sing to the Lord a new song.
—Psalms 96, 98, and 149

Like many voice majors, I earned part of my income during my studies by singing in churches. Over the years I held steady section-leader positions in the choirs of a Jesuit church and later an Anglican one; I sang regularly for a Community of Christ congregation,[1] where I eventually became soloist and songleader; and at times I performed guest spots at Lutheran, Unitarian Universalist, Catholic, Presbyterian, and Seventh-day Adventist institutions. Because I grew up in a small-town Conservative/Reform Jewish congregation (there weren't enough of us at the time to divide into denominations), each of these jobs and visits became a kind of miniature ethnographic experience—participant-observation in a music culture half-foreign to me. Most of the time, a congregation's music director and even the congregation itself were aware of my Jewish identity, and though I often encountered some curiosity or mild tension, I was largely made to feel welcome. I was often told that I had a divinely given gift for choosing just the right song. And when I left for an academic job across the country, the Community of Christ congregation asked me after services to say a blessing over the challah they had purchased especially for me. I learned diverse musical worship practices, in multiple vocal styles, in repertoire from Bach to Bacharach and from plainchant to praise song. And, unexpectedly, at the Community of Christ Church, singing Sandy Patti or Twila Paris, I found myself experiencing the act of singing in a way that felt distinctly spiritual.

Singing at the Community of Christ Church, I was not interested in converting, and the sermons sometimes contained far-right political messages that unnerved me. I do not think I would feel comfortable singing there today, but still, in those years I looked forward to singing at the church every week. And when I thought about it, I recognized that it was not a new phenomenon for me. At my public junior high school, my mother complained to the choir director

---

[1] Formerly known as the Reorganized Church of Jesus Christ of Latter-day Saints, the Community of Christ Church is rooted in the heritage of Joseph Smith's theology and the Book of Mormon, but developed separately from the centralized Church of Latter-day Saints.

Multivocality. Katherine Meizel, Oxford University Press (2020). © Oxford University Press.
DOI: 10.1093/oso/ 9780190621469.003.0006

about the Christmas music our chorus performed annually, and two years later, when I was called back for the auditioned public high school choir, I alone was asked whether I would agree to sing Christmas music during the heavy holiday performance season. The choral judge didn't say so, but I felt that my acceptance hinged on my response. I stammered out something about the music addressing the "same God" and, pushing aside any church–state implications, happily (if perhaps naively) sang through all the required hymns and Hallelujahs until graduation.

Many western singers, professional and amateur, have performed the music of a religious tradition to which they do not personally subscribe, or even find anathema to their principles, or oppressive. Some are able to negotiate a way to do so, others are not; and some are forced out. Thousands of internet news reports detail protests and church closings following the firing of choir directors identified as gay (see St. John 2014, for an example). Others find ways to maintain their adherence and faith. Alisha Jones has written about the conflicts faced by some gay men in African American churches(Jones 2019), and details the speech and bodily strategies for heteronormative Baptist gender performance employed by countertenor Patrick Dailey in church.

For mezzo-soprano Kathryn Miller, "active disagree[ment] with a church's ideas is not a good place to be for making music" (interview, April 19, 2016). But even in the history of western classical music, rooted for many centuries in religion, there are examples of composers and performers working for institutions they did not attend for worship—particularly in pluralistic societies that comprised multiple religious practices. This was the case in Bavaria following the Protestant Reformation. Baroque music specialist Arne Spohr writes that during the counter-reformation, tensions led to the dismissal of Dutch Protestant singers from the Munich Hofkapelle—though, allowing for instances of compromise or conversion, the positions of Catholic musicians in Protestant churches remained somewhat safer (Spohr 2009: 44–45). In the United States today, Protestant and Catholic churches often hire music directors, keyboardists (pianists, organists, synthesizer), and singers from outside the congregation; Reform and Reconstructionist Jewish synagogues frequently do the same. Such decisions do sometimes generate controversy, but in many congregations the impact of 20th-century ecumenicism and interfaith movements, as well as the increase in interfaith marriages as that century progressed,[2] has demanded attention to the question of outsider participation in worship.

---

[2] In 2015, Pew Research reported that of married couples at the time of their survey, 19 percent of those married before 1960 identified as interfaith couples (including couples professing different denominations of Christianity), while for those married between 2010 and 2014, that percentage had risen to 39 (Murphy 2015). http://www.pewresearch.org/fact-tank/2015/06/02/interfaith-marriage/

Scholars often trace the history of interfaith efforts in the United States to the 1893 Columbian Exposition in Chicago, which included a World Parliament of Religions (Sussman 1982: 39). In considering that ultra-colonialist event, it is also worth remarking on the postcolonial trend of religious tourism in the East, which accelerated in the late 1960s. In his book *Spiritual Marketplace: Baby Boomers and the Remaking of American Religion*, Wade Clarke Roof writes that "American religion has long been known for its dynamism and fluidity, its responsiveness to grassroots opinions and sentiments, its creative capacity in relation to the cultural environment" (Roof 1999: 4). He notes the increased late 20th-century emphasis on self-knowledge in American religion, in part fueled by the psychological turn in the culture of baby boomers, and cites Martin E. Marty's observation that "the individual seeker and chooser has come increasingly to be in control" (Marty 1993, cited in Roof 1999: 7) of their religious experience. And this individualist, even consumerist approach reflects the widespread economic framing of religion in the late 20th century, associated with the neoliberal doctrine that also began to flourish then. In his work on the global New Age movement, Lars Ahlin traces its development from anti-materialist critique of capitalism in the 1960s to what he views as a spiritual legitimization of neoliberalism in the 1980s (Ahlin: 2013), much as capitalism was legitimized by Protestantism (Weber 2004[1930]). The kind of global choice spiritual seekers face recalls Gordon Mathews' global cultural supermarket, discussed in chapter 1 (Mathews 2000), and is intertwined with voice and vocality in related ways.

Spirituality is a concept with myriad definitions across cultures and throughout histories. In western discourses, it is today often balanced against that of religion, as evidenced in the 2012 report indicating that 7 percent of Americans surveyed by the Pew Religion and Public Life Project considered themselves "spiritual but not religious" (Oppenheimer 2014)—a framework with its own initialization (SBNR), in which religion is often critiqued as dogmatic, authoritarian, exclusive, and anti-individualist. Walter Principe also notes that writings on spirituality as early as the 9th century discuss it in the context of living according to "the Spirit of God" (Principe 1983: 130), but that around the same time there were also references to spirituality (*spiritualitas*) in Christian literature that define it in opposition to *corporalitas* or *materialitas*. This latter meaning gradually became a prevailing one in Christianity-dominated cultures, and contributed to the "disdain for the body and matter" that took root at the center of much Christian discourse (Principe 1983: 130–131). It is present in U.S. culture in the 21st century. The voice, though, has often been granted an exception—the most embodied of instruments, as material as any other (though perhaps less visible), but paradoxically inscribed with the highest spiritual value for the practice of worship. "O, How wonderful is the human voice! It is indeed the organ of the soul," wrote the poet Longfellow in *Hyperion*, "the soul reveals itself in the voice only" (quoted in Stras 2006). Mladen Dolar mourns the voice as "the flesh of the soul, its ineradicable materiality, by which the soul can never be rid of the body" (Dolar 2006: 71). And he explains that the voice both maintains a link with nature and "promises an ascent to divinity, an elevation above the empirical, the mediated, the limited, worldly human concerns. This illusion of transcendence accompanied the long history of the voice as the agent of the sacred, and the highly acclaimed role of music was based on its ambiguous link with both nature and divinity" (31).

The Decision Not to Sing

Even in the absence of voice, as in the silent worship at meetings of the Quaker Society of Friends, voice may be privileged, as human voices are hushed so that congregants may "hear more clearly God's 'still small voice'" (see http://www.fgcquaker.org/resources/silent-worship-and-quaker-values). And, as I approached the last stages of preparing this book, a singer I had interviewed the previous year about cross-genre performance asked me to remove all material drawn from our conversation. She had recently converted to Islam and decided to closely follow a rigorous interpretation of Sharia; because of the *sama'* polemic—the debate regarding the permissibility of music in Muslim lives—she had stopped singing, and felt that morally she could no longer take part in a project about music or allow a focus on her personal opinions. Nevertheless, though her voice does not appear in the book, it was foundational to my writing of it, and in a way still feels present to me in the multivocal lattice of my work.

As in other faiths, interpretation of religious law is debated wherever Islam is practiced, and it is practiced in multiple ways. In addition to the debate regarding music, women's voices in particular figure in the discussion of '*awrah*,[3] referring to the private parts of a woman that in the view of many are to be covered in the presence of men, the voice is often interpreted as an integral, intimate part of an

---

[3] From the root for *blemish*, and often translated in English as "nakedness"—though El Guindi notes that it is used in the context of "privacy," "weakness," and "vulnerability" in the Hadith, and interprets those terms as applicable specifically to men rather than to women (El Guindi 2005: 81–82). Ellen Koskoff has written of the corresponding concept of *ervah* (from the related Hebrew root) in Lubavitcher Jewish life and the associated dictum of *kol isha*, which prohibits men from listening to women's voices. That rule stems from rabbinic literature (the Talmud), where the Talmudist Samuel of Nehardea is recorded admonishing that "Kol b'isha ervah" (often interpreted as "a woman's voice is *ervah*"). Women typically may sing in each others' presence, but not in the presence of men. Ellen Koskoff transcribes an interview with a former conservatory voice major who had joined a Hasidic community in the Lubavitcher tradition. The singer details a set of gradations for contexts in which a man might encounter a woman's voice—a mediated voice, on a recording or even carried through a microphone, is not as problematic as a live performance, and much hinges on whether or not the man can see the body from which the voice emanates (Koskoff 2000: 136).

inherently sexualized female body that may distract men from their moral and religious pursuits (Hammer 2012: 144). Many Muslim feminist scholars caution against the view that following such strictures on behavior and dress is simply a capitulation to male oppression. I Fadwa El Guindi, writing about the *hijab* movement driven by young Muslim women in the late 20th and early 21st centuries, argues that "Reserve and restraint in behavior, voice and body movement are not restrictions. They symbolize a renewal of traditional cultural identity" (El Guindi 2005: 86). And Yvonne Yazbeck Haddad has positioned the wearing of *hijab* in the United States as an act of post-9/11 anti-colonial solidarity and resistance (Haddad 2007)not singing can make a similar statement. Though I cannot assign my own set of meanings to my former consultant's decision not to sing, and though it is complicated by the dynamics of religious law, her request reminded me that the conscious choice *not* to use one's material voice (and not to lend it to a researcher) can be an agentive act—and just as important a part of identity as making it sonically heard. Ethnomusicologist Jeff Klein has called this *negative voice*, in the context of celebrities who refuse the use of their voices in commercial advertisements for products they oppose (Klein 2014). As a "vocal way of being," silence can function as a strategic vocality.

Spiritual Mobility

Western spiritualities exist in overlap with religion, but they need not be attached to it, and a body, mobile and envoiced, may experience spirituality outside of any particular religious context. Furthermore, the interviews I have conducted imply that the perception of spiritual experience during the act of singing may occur not in spite of but, rather, *because of* the voice's embodied nature, in its vibratory sensory processes.

Many of those I interviewed for this chapter—self-identified as members of Catholic, Protestant, Reform and Conservative Jewish, and Buddhist faiths, as well as seekers (in Pagan, Buddhist, Greek Orthodox, Presbyterian, and other settings), agnostics, atheists, and the "spiritual but not religious"—asserted that even in unfamiliar religious settings, and sometimes in secular ones, they have experienced something they identify as spiritual during the act of singing. I suggest here that this is rooted in two important contexts: (1) a spiritual mobility that is mutually constitutive with vocality, and (2) the sensory experience of singing.

Sergei Shubin (2012) contextualizes the idea of spiritual mobility within the processes of transnational migration, in a study of the ways Eastern European immigrants to rural Scotland negotiate community reception and the maintenance of self-identity through religion. For Shubin, spiritual mobility is "linked to physical and corporeal dislocations of migrants and their possessions, but it is also related to faith-based sensations and performances of the spirit, movements beyond rationality and perception to the outside of knowing, and creation of new imaginations of our place in the world" (Shubin 2012: 616). In this chapter, I reconfigure the concept of spiritual mobility to indicate a kind of portable accessibility to spiritual experience, located and carried in the voice as borderscape. In the United States, the nation's history of colonization, immigration, and migration is one of the foundations of its religious fluidity. And the structure of American capitalism makes migration nearly a requirement: geographic mobility—the leaving of a home—to seek economic mobility. American singers, then, are particularly well positioned to negotiate their own communities and self-identities across cartographical and religious boundaries.

In Shubin's study, he categorizes the sensory aspect of religious experience as "faith-based sensations." Barbara Mundy writes about the primacy of sensory experience in religion: "ritual practice is *felt* more than it is ever *thought*. It is felt in the register of experiences received by the body, like the smell of burning copal incense or the sight of elaborately garbed ritual specialists. Or it is felt in enacted ones, as in moving through the steps of a dance learned through kinesthetic apprenticeship or singing a song so long remembered that it is deeply intertwined with one's sense of self" (Mundy 2014: 516). Singing is an exquisitely sensory, vibratory experience, as Nina Eidsheim has discussed in *Sensing Sound: Singing and Listening as Vibrational Practice* (2015), and a singer's sense of self is entwined with those sensations. Singing is, like the performance of ritual, also a kinesthetic experience. Thus, the sensory phenomenologies of singing, of spirituality, and of self-identity may intersect easily and be conflated or experienced together.

Several singers I interviewed discussed changes in religious context catalyzed by the movement of their own lives, as they left their families of birth to attend college or moved for work to a new city, state, or country, or joined a partner in a new religion. Many moved from institution to institution, as I did, to find steady musical employment. A few moved from institution to institution, searching for a religious practice with which they felt a connection—experiencing Roof's (2000) "spiritual marketplace," or what one seeker called a "smorgasbord" (anonymous interview, July 13, 2016)—ideas that both imply a form of consumption.

Another interviewee, who asked to remain anonymous, told me that he has taken hallucinogenics since he was 15, and after a hiatus while he served in the Marine Corps, he said, he moved in a spiritual direction with the practice. He began to understand psychoactive mushrooms and other psychedelics as *entheogens*—not experienced as recreational or party drugs but, rather, as substances that generate an experience interpreted as divine. After he moved from the United States to Finland, it was difficult to acquire entheogens, until he discovered an emerging, imported practice there: the Church of Santo Daime.

Daime refers to the plant-based substance (not legal in Finland) also called *ayahuasca*, a sacred mixture traditionally part of indigenous religious practices in the geographic borderlands between Brazil, Bolivia, and Peru[4]—the church is a syncretic religion with Catholic and indigenous shamanic elements, and in my interviewee's church, many practitioners are immigrants to Finland. Santo Daime ceremonies (for healing, concentration, or meditation) comprise a recitation of Catholic prayers, ingestion of daime, and then hours of singing in Portuguese (7–10 hours, my interviewee told me). The songs, from three books each filled with hundreds of hymns, are nearly the entire content of the practice. There are no sermons, there is no preaching; all information about beliefs and practices are transmitted through participatory singing. The grueling length of time occupied by singing is "absolutely essential for the spiritual connection," and listening is also vital—practitioners are encouraged not to look at each other but, rather, to listen as they sing. Describing himself as "spiritual but not religious," my interviewee says that he never felt a spiritual experience in the Catholic churches he had previously attended, or in singing the Renaissance sacred music he loved, or in meditative singing while under the influence of other drugs. But in Santo Daime, he has had "a feeling of intense spiritual experience" in which the sensation of singing a single, particular word can be so powerful he feels physically weak. "It's not the sound of the word, but what the word generates in your solar plexus" (interview, April 13, 2016). He says that he can trigger the same feeling singing the songs without the use of daime, because it is a learned sensory experience.

The singing ritual can be a practice of deep self-reflection, but also it relies on the communal connections forged in homophonic or (perhaps accidental, he adds) heterophonic singing. Among those I interviewed, many mentioned communal singing as a particular catalyst for spiritual encounter. For Adam O'Dell, a Lutheran who worked for several years as a cantor and choral section leader in a Catholic church, the social and musical aspects of singing in a choir offered him more of "an authentic connection to the music in a spiritual way," while as a soloist "It felt more like I was doing my job." He continued, "We hope to see God clearly in the next life, but here and now, we have human interaction. For me, the feeling of transcendence, of being connected with God, comes from being spiritually connected with other people" (interview, May 26, 2017).

Ethnomusicologist and singer Nadia Chana underlines the importance of communal singing in her own spiritual practice. Raised by one Muslim parent and one Sikh parent, whose marriage had been contested, she identifies as

---

[4] The church's founder, Irineu Serra, was an Afro-Brazilian Catholic who took ayahuasca in the early 1910s, among indigenous and mestiço populations in the borderlands between Brazil, Bolivia, and Peru (Dawson 2016[2007]: 71).

spiritual but not religious. She has sung at Anglican churches in Edmonton, Canada, as well as in Lutheran, Catholic, and Presbyterian congregations, and at St. Kateri, a Native American Catholic church in Chicago; she feels most at home at St. Kateri, she says, because members of the congregation, like her, "are used to being some sort of racialized Other." In church or in secular settings, she finds spirituality in singing "to people, for people, towards . . . something broader" (interview, May 1, 2016).

This gesture, toward "something broader," is common among those I interviewed. Polina Proutskova, who refers to herself as "quite atheist now," says that she can achieve a transcendental state in either religious or secular music: "you experience something which goes beyond you and is very powerful, and you wouldn't otherwise reach that state" (interview, April 19, 2016). Melissa Canaday, trained as an opera singer but happiest now in a choir, also feels that the act of singing with others engenders a connection that feels like "creating something bigger than you could ever do alone." The acoustic structures created by voices in harmony also facilitate her sense of spirituality:

> Certain chords, the hair on your neck stands up. It's almost like you didn't realize that you were uncomfortable until you hit that perfect chord and . . . everything settles in the right place, and you just kind of sink into it, and you think, "that's where I was supposed to be all the time." (interview, April 10, 2016)

Ms. Canaday harmonizes constantly, she says ("I will harmonize with a vacuum cleaner"), whether out loud or even in her head, which she denotes "singing without my voice." To her, the production of acoustic beating that sometimes occurs in choral harmony affects her similarly to the recordings of "isochronic tones" marketed as a wellness and sleep aid. Susanne Vanderhoef, no longer religious, has sung sacred music in choirs and also participated in meditational chanting at a Buddhist temple. The social aspect plays an important role in any transcendent vocal experience she has had:

> Singing solo is certainly an act of devotion, but in a sense it's also an act of . . . it's "I'm good enough to do this on my own and make you pay attention." Performing alone you are thinking more about details and making things perfect. You're spending a lot of time in your body. . . . I can never get out of my own head. Singing in a chorus I don't have to do that. (interview, April 10, 2016)

Ms. Vanderhoef's description reminds me of worship during my early teenage years, when I took my first voice lessons. My town's congregation, until shortly after that time, had no rabbi or trained *hazzan* (cantor) or choir, and most of our davening was done in unison. When I sang as I was taught, there were looks thrown my way, in subtle chastisement for standing out in a manner perceived as arrogant—it was, a little, but I felt a desire to use my "whole" voice in prayer. I did not feel a spiritual experience singing until we had a (7-member) choir that programmed Louis Lewandowski's setting of Psalm 13. Western choral singing, of course, is focused on a unified sound, and this implies a particular kind of social meaning in a religious space. Nicholas Harkness, writing on voice and sociality in Korean Protestant Christianity, argues that "in orienting to and cultivating particular shared qualities of voice, these Christians orient to and cultivate their individual and collective relationships with their deity and with one another" (Harkness 2013: 81) in church and in school. The same might be said for other religious choral traditions, many of which have been influenced by Protestant musical values. Louis Lewandowski (1821–1894), a Prussian Jewish choirmaster of the Neue Synagoge in Berlin, who studied composition at the Berlin Academy, even advocated for the use of the church-associated organ with the synagogue's congregational singing.

Ms. Vanderhoef's recollection of practicing Buddhist chant strikingly matches that of Mahayana Buddhist opera singer and teacher Heather Sung. Ms. Vanderhoef told me that at first she kept thinking "as a singer," and then felt bored, and then "moved past the boredom" to feeling that she was part of a larger whole (it's not her "preferred method of transcendence," however). Ms. Sung related her favorite ritual at the Hsi Lai Humanistic Buddhist Temple (in Hacienda Heights, California), the Great Compassion Repentance ceremony, which she feels is like "an oratorio" or "an operatic experience." Compared to other Buddhist sects, she says, Humanistic temples focus on longer sung phrases, more melodic and with some ornamentation—other sects tease them that "they go to temple to sing rather than chant." She finds her western classical technique useful for the demands of chanting—"the same diaphragmatic support"—and used it to help a nun in her voice class at the temple who had developed vocal fold nodules from chanting for hours at a time.

The Great Compassion Repentance ceremony contains a passage called the Heart Sutra, which involves faster and more repetitive chanting; "the ear will get almost bored," but then Ms. Sung finds a feeling of great clarity. "Boredom is the mind preparing to open," she explains. And for her, listening is as important as singing in finding her spiritual connection to the ritual. Nina Eidsheim cites Charles Hirschkind's work on performative and "ethical" listening in the context of Muslim sermons on cassette, highlighting the multisensorial and embodied qualities of such listening (Hirschkind 2006, cited in Eidsheim 2015: 151); with caution regarding the drawing of universalizing conclusions, it seems that something not unrelated can occur in other religious practices, as well.

Several singers described to me in detail their phenomenology of spirituality in singing, in both sacred and secular contexts. In chapter 8, I discuss the voice-loss experience of Jewish writer and composer Joel Derfner. But before Mr. Derfner developed a medical condition that prohibited it, he told me, singing had previously felt like an ecstatic experience. In his memoir *Swish*, writing about a performance of Händel's aria "Gentle Airs, Melodious Strains" (from a sacred—Christian—oratorio), he describes how his voice "caress[ed] every molecule of air in the room . . . and the melisma on the word 'woe' floated higher and higher and then higher still, and I felt I could sustain it forever, and my body disappeared and I understood what it is to be eternal" (Derfner 2009: 139). That ecstasy, he says, came to him not because of the sound of his voice but, rather, through the physical, and perhaps metaphysical, sensations of singing, and a feeling that his voice, like a consciousness, had left his body.

We spoke about the different ways in which voice has figured in his work, first in his singing and then in composing and writing. In his book, he returns twice to an idea his college-director friend had introduced him to: a biblical discourse regarding the English translation of two Hebrew words found in the description of Creation in Genesis. The meanings and nuanced implications of *bara* and *asah* have been much debated by Jewish and Christian theologians concerned with whether or not they indicate two distinct types of creative act by God. Following one significant line of thinking, Mr. Derfner's friend explained *bara*, in the first line of Genesis, as an act of bringing to life, of "bringing something in to being out of nothingness." *Asah*, though, is an act of shaping "something out of something else that already exists" (Derfner 2009: 144). Mr. Derfner himself associates *asah* with his singing, with his material voice, and an immediate kind of creation that involves the interpretation and the reshaping not only of preexisting music but also of the singer's body: "*you* are what is being molded. You are creator and created at the same time" (151). But his writing is *bara*, where he is the source of that which is created. Curiously, it is only *asah* that brings him ecstasy, as he understands transcendence to be impossible when your creative material does not come from outside of you:

> You're either the source or the vessel, and those are two different feelings. Being the vessel is literally ecstatic, and being the source is a much more—it's not just cerebral, it's also—what you're creating comes from inside you, and you cannot transcend yourself. (interview, June 7, 2014)

Another common theme among my interviewees was space, architecture, and the shaping of acoustics on the experience of spirituality. Ms. Canaday recalls an occasion in high school when the members of her choir, momentarily on their own during a tour, stopped to sing Norman Dinnerstein's "When David

Heard" in Philadelphia's acoustically generous Independence Hall: "There was definitely more at work there than just eighteen kids, who on the whole didn't all even like each other very much" (interview, April 10, 2016). Kathryn Miller, though not religious, loves church architecture, loves spaces that create "a hushed feeling that 'this is something else, this is something different.'" She distinguishes between sacred and secular performances in churches, noting that when she has sung a recital in a church, "it's a building, an object, as opposed to the thing that is *church*" (interview, April 19, 2016). Lilah Greendale Shapiro, a religion scholar and conservatory-trained singer who identifies as a Jewish "traditionalist," if not religious or even particularly spiritual, is nonetheless more comfortable attending synagogue for the sense of community than singing in church to earn money. She also appreciates that her singing helps a synagogue congregation "feel whatever it is that they need to feel"; she is less comfortable with that process in a church. However, she remarks: "I always love the way my voice sounds in a church," especially in stone buildings." The synagogues she has attended, she says, have always been carpeted, with seats instead of wooden pews, and the sound of her voice is absorbed. (Some synagogues, particularly in large cities, do feature aesthetically impressive architecture comparable to that of classic church design; the buildings that house suburban or rural congregations more often do not. Churches have also been built in diverse styles.) Because of the difference in sound, she likes the act of singing better in church, though she does not feel an emotional connection to Christian music (interview, April 19, 2016).

It is noteworthy that the history of church architecture is suffused with attention to sensory stimulation—especially visual and aural, enhancing the perception of light and sound. A 1993 report by the National Conference of Catholic Bishops, for example, insists that the liturgical climate requires "the beautiful in its environment and all its artifacts, movements, and appeals to the *senses*" (cited in Kieckhafer 2004: 98, my emphasis). Thus, the sensory realm of spirituality for a singer in a church may be underlined by the visual and acoustic results of a building's design.

In Jewish contexts, Dr. Greendale Shapiro says that it is harder for her to connect with sacred music than with Jewish secular music (for example, Yiddish songs).It wasn't always that way for her, but her life experience now makes her feel more attuned to symbols of Jewish history than of Jewish religious practice (interview, April 19, 2016). I asked other singers about how they have comparatively experienced the performance of sacred music and of secular music. For many, what makes the experience different, or for others makes it the same spiritually, is a concept I heard identified in the same way over and over: *intent*.

Kavanah

In our interviews, Anthony Russell, cantorial soloist, and Sharon Azrieli-Perez, cantor—both trained as opera singers—framed intent within the Jewish concept of *kavanah* in prayer. In *The Lord's Song in a Strange Land: Music and Identity in Contemporary Jewish Worship*, ethnomusicologist and rabbi Jeffrey A. Summit, in brief, defines *kavanah* as "Sincere devotion, concentration and intention in prayer" (Summit 2000: 178). Throughout his study, though, he discusses the more nuanced meanings he encountered in his ethnographic work. For one student, it entailed "personal confrontation and interaction with the text of the liturgy," the consideration of the text's meanings his own life and his historical connection to it (114). A rabbi told Summit that in the application of *nusach*—a Hebrew term, in this context, understood as the melodic modes specifically assigned to liturgical chant (105)—" 'the music gets the words across and your kavanah in tefillah [your intentions in prayer [are] much stronger'" (125).

Mr. Russell, comparing sung prayer in his Christian experiences with his Jewish ones, feels that *kavanah* has been present for him in both settings:

> I'd say it isn't different. I'd say it's the same. I'd say the same feeling kind of falls over me. When I recall how I used to feel about singing in church, it's that combination of text with melody and both those things coming together to create intention, you know, *kavanah*, as you would say. (interview, January 29, 2014).

When I asked Dr. Azrieli-Perez, whether she felt any differences between sacred and secular singing, she brought up the concept of *kavanah*, explaining that the job of a cantor in a Reform synagogue is not only to lead a congregation—especially one who may not understand Hebrew or Aramaic—but also to help those praying do so with the proper *kavanah*. A cantor's role is not intercessionary between congregant and God, but "he is supposed to be helping us like an operator with the telephone," she says. She acknowledges that in opera, one might have a spiritual moment—for example "in a particularly gorgeous phrase where you somehow access God"—but that prayer sung with *kavanah* is more "directly" spiritual. Evoking a similar historicity to Summit's student, she observes the impact of one particular aspect liturgical singing on prayerful intention: the knowledge of a mode or melody's age, passed down from generation to generation. "It's not possible to accomplish what that does viscerally to your gut just with words" (interview, January 26, 2014). In spite of her earlier participation in the tradition of classically informed cantorial singing, in the congregation she has brought together herself in Montreal, she prefers to sing "as a folk singer... with different production," and in a lower range, in order to make sure everyone can sing comfortably together.

This shift in vocality demonstrates an important element of North American Jewish practices, in which cantors and soloists may apply a variety of vocalities to the same melodic material across congregations. As many congregations use a mix of traditional *nusach* (here indicating both chant modes and metric melody) and the "American *nusach*" developed by Debbie Friedman in the late 20th century, a service may even contain multiple vocalities in one space. Friedman's liturgical music, first encapsulated in her 1972 folk- and pop-influenced service titled *Sing Unto God*, originated when she worked in her early 20s as a counselor at a Wisconsin Reform Jewish summer camp. Judah M. Cohen writes that the guitar-supported style known as "song leading" had become the preferred musical expression of Reform Jewish youth by the time Friedman was one of them in the 1960s, and she built on it to develop her own original Jewish service. Friedman's music quickly gained a place in Reform, Reconstructionist, Conservative, and even Orthodox synagogues, and largely because of it, by the turn of the 21st century, "song leading had developed a parallel system of pedagogy and apprenticeship to the cantorate, with an articulated theoretical approach to worship, and prayer, an expanding repertoire, and an idiomatic sound" (Cohen 2009: 219). That sound infused synagogues with vocal and guitar styles recalling those of Joan Baez and Judy Collins, and though its use often caused antagonism among traditionalists, it is now embedded in American Jewish participatory worship.

Some synagogues combine older and newer melodies in their worship, older and newer musical styles, and even disparate vocalities. If there is a classically trained cantor, the cantor may pray in a conventional, operatically informed mode of singing, but lead the congregation with a different sound. Sometimes, as in the Central Synagogue in New York City, a large congregation may hire multiple cantors, who pray in different styles. And some institutions, as the congregation in my hometown currently does, hold separate services for those members who prefer more traditional prayer. Synagogues are accommodating not only a taste for tradition but also an aesthetic that may include vocality.

As of 2017, the website for the Central Conference of (Reform) American Rabbis (CCAR) provides an adult-education curriculum on the topic of "Entering *Mishkan T'filah*" (*Mishkan T'filah* means "The Dwelling Place of Prayer," and is the title of the *siddur*, or prayer book, the CCAR released in 2007). "Session 3" presents a Reform approach to the kind of "multivocal" and "polyvocal" worship the book promotes:

> **Integrated Theology**—In any worship setting, people have diverse beliefs. The challenge of a single liturgy is to be not only multivocal, but polyvocal—to invite full participation at once, without conflicting with the *keva*[5] text.... This

---

[5] Fixed liturgical text

is the distinction of an integrated theology: Not that one looks to each page to find one's particular voice, but that over the course of praying, many voices are heard, and ultimately come together as one. (https://ccarnet.org/ccar-press/mishkan-tfilah-resources/adult-ed/three-part-study-module/session-3/)

This kind of dialogic multivocality, in the denomination's directives for worship, matches the material multivocality performed during prayer.

Conversion and Convergence: New Voices in Jewish Song

Anthony Mordechai Zvi Russell is, in his words, "African American by birth, Jewish by choice." Raised in Baptist and Pentecostal (Assemblies of God) traditions, Mr. Russell converted in 2011, and in the years since he formally became a Jew, critics have already appointed him "the new voice of Yiddish song" (Chesnoff 2012). Though he is quick to dismiss any such titles, his relationship with Yiddish repertoire *is* intense, and it has become central to his identity. For Mr. Russell, Yiddish song is as much *his* new voice as he is *its* new voice.

His self-description, "African American by birth, Jewish by choice," emphasizes the ways in which his identity complicates reductive understandings of Ashkenazi (Eastern European) Jewishness as white, and as an ethnic heritage only genetically transmitted. It provokes questions about identity and choice, history, and lived experience. "As far as African *American* culture is concerned," he told me,

> I'm not *deciding* to be part of it, I opted in just by being born . . . [but] it's really important for me to establish the fact that Judaism is a choice for me, is a choice to accept the texts and the experiences that connect me with a continuity of the Jewish people. . . . I chose it. Just like I chose these songs to represent a part of me. My voice. I chose these songs to be my voice. (interview, January 29, 2014)

The idea of choice has always been important to Jews, the "chosen" people, but the 21st century, in its ideal form, has so far been about *choosing* people—people making choices. And it's noteworthy that with the songs, Mr. Russell has chosen as a Black man and as an out gay man to take on yet another history, to shoulder the additional weight of Jewish suffering. His singing thus illuminates a particular position of intersectionality, his voice a multivocal instrument and one of many that must daily confront multiple oppressive systems that span the globe, as well as the past and present.

Voice and Embodiment in Conversion

Ethnomusicologist Eve McPherson has written about the role of the muezzin's voice as a catalyst for conversion to Islam (McPherson et al. 2014). In Turkey, she explains, it is believed that when a "beautiful voice"—one which meets certain aesthetic and spiritual expectations—is heard reciting the call to prayer, it has the power to draw listeners into the faith. But if voices can *sound a religion* in this way, I suggest that they have not only an aural impact in initiating conversion but a performative one in its process, as well. Religion scholar Rebecca Sachs Norris has noted that for converts, the "performance" of Jewishness can be especially imperative, "since they are forever denied the possibility of being Jewish by birthright" (Norris 2003: 174). For Mr. Russell, as a former opera singer, the idea of "performance" has especially keen connotations. To him, the act of singing is fundamental to the religious practice of Judaism. Though he can relate his memories of praying in church to his experience of *kavanah* (the intention, or mindset, for prayer in synagogue), he sees the function of singing as different across religions; it is so critical in *davening* (praying), he says, that he does not think a Jewish service could exist without it, whereas he believes that a Protestant service might. The significance of voice in Mr. Russell's journey to Judaism and Jewishness supports the important notion that conversion entails a reorientation not only of ideals and language and texts but also of embodied experience (Norris 2003). The convert's *body* must learn the new tradition through ritual, where, David Levin writes, "[t]he sacred language is woven, is insinuated, into the very fibers and bones of the body" (Levin 1985: 215; Norris 2003: 178). The kinesthetic adoption of new ritual gestures—the sign of the cross, the act of prostration, or in Judaism, the physicality of *davening*—is key to the process of conversion, and I would suggest that the negotiation of new sonic gestures, of new vocalities, constitutes an equally essential (if sometimes essentializing) enactment of embodied change. Furthermore, the purposeful alteration of vocality undermines discourses of identity—"the Black voice" for example—that are fallaciously predicated on assumptions of fixed bodily traits.

(En)voicing Intersectionality

The story of Mr. Russell's encounter with Yiddish song illustrates how shifts in vocality serve as indicators of multivocal identity work, and for the performance of intersectionality—of how voices have been sounded, and silenced, and reshaped through interlocking systems of oppression and hegemony. Classically trained since his teens, Mr. Russell felt constrained by the gendered performative prescriptions for his *Fach* (voice and character type). He wanted to vocalize the true complexity of human emotion through a broad range of dynamics and articulations, but found himself constantly reprimanded by directors whenever he ventured away from the amplitudes and aggressions assigned to bass singers. "You are not a soprano," he heard, over and over. "Don't sing like one." And once, when he was in college, he came into possession of a cache of sheet music for bass voice, including an edition of Brahms's *Zigeunerlieder*. As he learned them, though, he was told the songs were only to be sung by women. At first he worried that his failure to execute a codified operatic masculinity was some sort of subconscious performance of his identity as a gay man. But ultimately, he says, he just wanted something opera couldn't offer him: a way to tell his own story. While he sought an outlet for expressive honesty, he met his husband, now rabbi of an unaffiliated[6] Massachusetts congregation, and came to a new religion. At first, he did not gravitate toward Jewish musical repertoire because, he told me, "I didn't hear anything that sounded like me." The singing of cantorial repertoire seemed to be "a tenor's game," and, often compared by listeners to Paul Robeson, his singing elicited othering tropes about "Black voices." So, Mr. Russell recalls, "initially I thought there really was not a place for me in Jewish music" (interview, January 29, 2014).

And then he heard Sidor Belarsky. The Ukraininan American's rendition of the *Yiddishe Lied* "Dem Milners Trern" issued from a phonograph in the 2009 Cohen Brothers film *A Serious Man*, and Mr. Russell was captivated. At first, he was sure the voice belonged to a Black man. "It was a very low voice . . . it was a very covered voice, it was a dark rich voice. And those are things which are prized as being aspects of the African American trained voice." Mr. Russell imagined that he was listening to Paul Robeson; his discovery of the real source led him to a fascination with Belarsky's legacy, and the voice that gave him permission to sound as he did—Black and Jewish.[7]

Belarsky's songbook[8] and Mr. Russell's both include Yiddish-language traditional songs, on themes of everyday Jewish life, and *khazonus*, the Hebrew-language liturgical and paraliturgical repertoire of cantors. The "symbiotic relationship" (Levine 2010: 4, discussing Wohlberg 2010) between those genres reflects a blurring of the sacred and secular for many Jews (Wohlberg 2010); the most beloved recorded Yiddish voices in the 20th century applied the same vocality to "Dem Milners Trern" and the holiest of recitations, "Kol Nidrei." When he sings secular Yiddish song, Mr. Russell says,

---

[6] Outside of the traditional categories of Reform, Conservative, Reconstructionist, Orthodox.
[7] Note the history of Black Jews in the United States and elsewhere, as well as the conflicted relationship between African American and Jewish communities.
[8] "Songbook" in a figurative sense, not published as such.

in my mind, it's not really secular. There's a great continuum of Jewish life, specifically the late 19th-, early 20th-century Jewish, Ashkenazi Jewish life that I'm describing in these Yiddish songs. And as far as I'm concerned, [when] I sing, I'm describing moments in Jewish lives and in my mind, I don't really separate those moments from some of the more religious songs that I do. (interview, January 29, 2014)

He acknowledges a greater "intensity" in the liturgical context because, as a cantor, "you have an entire synagogue's spiritual hopes and intentions projected on you"; but, he says, "enacting a secular Jewish moment in the context of secular Jewish songs, is very much for me like enacting a religious Jewish moment. The only difference is the context" (interview, January 29, 2014). This is a subject also broached by other singers I've interviewed; some conceptualize Jewishness as an identity in which worship and philosophy and history and daily life are so intertwined that it is impossible to draw a line between "sacred" and "secular" expressive forms.

As he has learned the songs, Mr. Russell has also had to learn the singing. Because many performers of Yiddish and cantorial[9] music have relied on western classical technique, he has been able to draw from his own training. His cantorial style, he says:

involves using very specific kinds of ornamentation, some of which I've developed from my opera background. Like, passagework is not really a problem, [not] so much of a problem for me because of my training in [singing] Händel. So you can imagine where one can obviously be used for the other. (interview, January 29, 2014)

Despite the development of a classical cantorial sound in the 19th and 20th centuries, cantors have diverged from operatic style, too. Early 20th-century artists like Yossele Rosenblatt[10] popularized certain vocal practices that came to be understood as iconically Jewish; for example, a kind of brief downward slide between pitches—something, as Mr. Russell observes, that "you would just never ever, ever do as an opera singer." There is also the ubiquitous *krekhts*[11]—literally "moaning," the momentary, sobbing, melodic disruption that Rosenblatt made

---

[9] Mr. Russell is careful to say that he is not an ordained cantor (*hazzan*), and does not call himself a cantor, though others have applied the title to him casually.

[10] Rosenblatt was also Ukrainian, and his voice was featured in the Al Jolson film *The Jazz Singer*. I like to think of the *krekhts* as a Jewish yodel, old-country music—like the cry-break in country music. It's emotional.

[11] Note: the gerund *krekhtsing* is an expression in "Yinglish"—a combination of Yiddish and English—that Mr. Russell used in our conversation.

de rigueur (a sort of yodeling moment, like in country music—only, as Mr. Russell puts it, it's "old-country music!") The reworking of his voice to produce these gestures became a vital concern as he moved into Jewish repertoire or, rather, as he became a Jewish singer.

> I had to learn how to assimilate those sounds and abilities in order to create an authentic sound for what I was doing. I had a couple reasons for wanting to do this. I didn't want to just get up and be like a Black guy singing Kol Nidre, I wanted to give the people—who were listening and projecting their intention upon me as someone who was singing that—a good simulacrum of cantorial style. The way things should be done. The way it should sound. You know, I've been very concerned about authenticity. It's unusual because it predates my Judaism. I've always been a very big fan of early music, because I very much wanted to know what the music sounded like in its original context. And I've applied some of that obsession to my work in Jewish music because I want to assimilate the style of what I'm doing—as opposed to just singing things in a very general "classical singer" style. (interview, January 29, 2014)

Still, his work isn't only about reconfiguring his voice to be a Jewish one. It is also important to him to reconcile the multiple facets of his identity in performance, and to address the interlocking, unique histories of oppression that accompany them: the systematic denial of human and civil rights against which African Americans have fought for centuries, and Mr. Russell's newly adopted history, as he lives his life, as he puts it, "in continuity" with the repeated cycles of suppression, violence, and flight that ordered the Ashkenazi past. Anthropologist Diane Austin-Broos has written that "rather than simple cultural breach, the voiding of a past social self, the language of converts expresses new forms of relatedness" (Austin-Broos 2003: 2) In 2015, Mr. Russell premiered a concert called "Convergence," subtitled "Spirituals from the Shtetl. Davening from the Delta." The project, now an album as of 2019, juxtaposes Belarsky's material with African American sorrow songs forged in the crucible of slavery. Each of Mr. Russell's arrangements is structured as a kind of mashup—not an attempt to blend two traditions (I noted something similar in Bakhtin's use of *multivocality*, and in chapter 6 I discuss Joshua Klipp's similar genre combinations) but, rather, in a very 21st-century sensibility, to *layer* them and to acknowledge what they share: first, through parallel narratives of upheaval; second, through manipulation of musical (modal) sites of convergence; and third, through vocal sites of convergence.

In one track, he matches "Mikdash Melech,"[12] "whose Hebrew text is extracted from the Sabbath *piyyut* (liturgical hymn) "L'cha dodi," with the spiritual "Poor

---

[12] From Belarsky's *Hasidic Melodies*.

Figure 5.1 The pitches used in "Mikdash Melech."

Figure 5.2 The pitches used in "Poor Mourner."

Figure 5.3 Ahava Rabbah mode, on E.

Figure 5.4 Ukrainian Dorian, beginning on D, the 7th degree of Ahava Rabbah.

Mourner." The spiritual follows a minor pentatonic mode, and the other a *shteyger* (mode), often referred to as Ukrainian Dorian—a variation of a primary cantorial mode called *Ahava Rabbah*,[13] which is the foremost foundation for Hasidic melody (see figures 5.1 to 5.4). The two melodies, like their difficult histories, interlock neatly, the space between the first and third scale degrees in "Poor Mourner" leaving potential space for either a natural or lowered second degree.

[13] Meaning "Great love," associated with a melody for the "Ahavah rabbah" blessing sung before "Sh'ma Yisrael" in morning services.

Listeners get both, in part because the *nigun*—the wordless Hasidic tune—at the start of the recording uses a natural second while the Hebrew, texted portion of "Mikdash Melech" relies on the *lowered* second characteristic of Ahava Rabbah, sometimes also called "Freygish," or Phrygian. The spiritual plays with the seventh scale degree, as well, which is omitted in "Mikdash Melech."

Mr. Russell also draws attention to the use of nonverbal utterances, a practice shared by African American and Yiddish vocalities. ("Black people like melismatic singing; and traditionally, Jewish people definitely like melismatic singing. They both like melismatic singing. It's an ethnic indicator to me" (interview, January 29, 2014)). He puts the two songs together line by line—he describes this progression as "Black-Jewish-Black-Jewish-Black-Jewish"—and interposes improvisatory passages of the *nigun* and the moaning or humming characteristic of African American Baptist "lining out" traditions (Dargan 2006).

He finds additional commonalities in cultural responses to change in the 19th and 20th centuries—two songs that he combines relate to train travel, as he explains:

> There's an early blues song called "When the Train Comes Along," and then there's this 19th-century Yiddish song called "An Ayznban" where there's just this description of a train, and every car is a year and every seat is a minute, and the conductor of the train is God—and some people get on the train, and some people get off, and you can't choose what class of seat you get. So, when I was reading the description of this, I said "God, this is so didactic, I feel like I'm in church." Like, there's this big train, and everyone gets on, and the descriptions, and it's very, there's all of these wonderful parallels in this period between these modes of ethnic expression, so I've put them together. (interview, January 29, 2014)

Likewise, he presses together the anthem "Lift Every Voice and Sing" and the Yiddish labor song "Hof un Gloyb" ("Hope and Believe"), set to the lyrics of Yitzhak Leybush Peretz. In an interview, he told the *New York Jewish Week* in 2015 that the two songs "are all about these rhapsodic visions of what the future can be and the triumph of that over generations of death. . . . Our history has been horrible, so we are saying 'Let us lift our voices and find a space where we can move on without forgetting the kinds of things we came from'" (Winston 2015). In the same article, and in others, he has professed the urgency he has felt since the development of the Black Lives Matter movement, whose views on Israel have conflicted with those of some American Jews. And his musical identity negotiation has not proceeded without antagonism; he wrote an essay for *Forward* in 2015 to address it: "I'm Here to Perform Yiddish Music—Not Cater to Your Idea of Blackness" (Russell 2015).

As it turns out, the previously mentioned, curious aural connection his audiences have made to the voice of Paul Robeson has enhanced his work in the area of Yiddish song. It is not incidental. Robeson was the son of a minister father who had been born enslaved. He was a polymath who, among other significant cultural contributions, recorded sorrow songs and spirituals, and then folk songs from around the world, including the Yiddish lullaby "Shlof mayn Kind," as well as the 1943 partisan anthem from the Vilna ghetto, "Zog Nit Keyn Mol," and famously a setting of an 18th-century rabbi's sermon sometimes known as his "Lawsuit with God." Robeson began performing this "Kaddish," also called "Hassidic Chant," in 1938, and he described it as a "tremendous sermon-song-declaration-protest," a "protest against age-old persecution" (Karp 2003: 54). In 1958, after a long period of McCarthyist persecutions, Robeson performed this "Hassidic Chant" at Carnegie Hall. The previous year he had told an audience at Howard University that it was "close to my heart" and "means much more than just another song" (remarks recorded at Howard University, cited in Karp 2003: 54). This allusion to Jewish thought and history, along with an intimate relationship between his own and Jewish involvement in Leftist and antiracist activism, made him a darling of many American Jews. He was one of my grandmother's favorite singers. At the back of our family Passover *haggadah*, the song "Go Down Moses (Let My People Go)" was included along with other holiday-relevant songs. As Vivian Eden writes,

> The link between black history and Jewish history, as condensed into the song, made a great impression on many American Jewish young people and some community leaders or Socialist-Zionist persuasions of the late 1950s and early 1960s, who were involved in the Civil Rights movement and subsequently the campaign for Soviet Jewry—which chose as its slogan "Let my people go." (Eden 2015)

Though other singers, such as Louis Armstrong and Marian Anderson, also performed the song, in my family we associated it with Paul Robeson. And we were not the only ones; Mr. Russell recalls being invited to Passover seders where his hosts enthusiastically assumed that as a Black bass he could sing "Go Down Moses"—but he did not know the song. Considering the connection especially older Jews seem to make between himself and Robeson, he says now:

> What's interesting is to [have heard] about Paul Robeson a lot before I was a Jew, and then to hear about Paul Robeson a lot after I was a Jew. The interesting thing about hearing about Paul Robeson after I became a Jew is that the experiences and things that people have to say about Paul Robeson are much more personal. People are like "I saw Paul Robeson when I was a little girl" or "My family

were cultural movers and shakers in New York in the thirties and we had Paul Robeson over for dinner." So it's not like the very generalized effusions of admiration for Paul Robeson that I got before I was in the Jewish world where people were like "Oh, you sound like Paul Robeson because you're Black and you're a bass." Like people, and in a way it's heartwarming because people want to connect me with very personal experiences that they had in their life with the African American trained voice in the form of Paul Robeson. (interview, January 29, 2014)

If Robeson used Yiddish and Hebrew song as a way to negotiate the intersections between his cultural heritage and his own experience of oppression with other forms of oppression tearing the world of his friends and comrades apart, Mr. Russell has done something similar. Echoing the significance of Mr. Russell's "Black-Jewish-Black-Jewish-Black-Jewish" mashups, Robeson's Yiddish and Hebrew recordings have been understood as "performing Black-Jewish symbiosis" (Karp 2003: 53). With these songs, Mr. Russell says he aims to bring together Jewish and African American musical texts to tell one, seamless story—*his* story. In the end, he says, "I've tried to . . . create a repertoire of music in which it cannot be said my voice is not relevant."

This chapter has explored some of the modes in which voice and vocality figure in the construction of spiritual experiences within and outside of religious identity in the United States. Like vocality, those modes are relational, involving dialogue among internal and external sensory input, space, feelings of community, discourses which oppose the material (the body, the idea of earning money in a religious space) and the spiritual, and which locate voice at the center. Like the voice, these modes are mobile but embedded in the body—and partly dependent on the sensations of singing. An individual may carry the spiritual experience of singing across religious and cultural boundaries, renegotiating vocality as a strategy of borderscaping, of reworking the borders of belief, of corporeality, and of materiality in the voice. These processes are evident in Anthony Russell's religious conversion and in the adoption of his new culture, as music and language and discourse reshaped his sonic, agentive voice to accommodate multiple perspectives. The compound songs he creates, and his performance practices, illuminate the significance of this plurality as a kind of identity layering informed by the fluidity of the self.

6

The Journey

Voice and Identity in Gender Transition

> "It's not worth the sacrifice,"
> you've heard that line a thousand times.
>
> —Joshua Klipp, "Little Girl"

In Hans Christian Andersen's enduring 1837 tale "The Little Mermaid," a voice is famously sacrificed for the acquisition of an immortal soul. The protagonist is told that as a mermaid, she cannot live for eternity in heaven; but if a human man were to love her enough, he would marry her, impart his soul to her, and thus grant her immortality. To accomplish this, the little mermaid, who has "the loveliest voice of all, in the sea or on the land" (Andersen 1983[1837]: n.p.), becomes human through a set of painful and permanent bodily changes purchased from a sea-witch, paid for with her voice. The sea-witch warns her that if the prince marries another, the mermaid will become nothing but foam on the ocean. "I shall take that risk," the mermaid answers. The story nearly ends in hopeless tragedy, but at the last moment the mermaid is swept away by "daughters of the air" for a second chance to earn a soul—this time, instead of through marriage, through three hundred years of good deeds. She has a newly transparent body, and a new voice—one "so spiritual [in Danish *aandigt*, the adjectival form of *spirit*] that no music on earth could match it" (Andersen 1983[1837]: n.p.). A final moralizing statement entreats listening children to be good, lest their misbehavior add to the mermaid's three hundred years.

Andersen writes the little mermaid's happy ending as a kind of liberatory ghostdom, her voice a revenant to haunt children's moral consciousness, her new teleology not an arrival but a long journey of becoming. As a *transparent* being, she is *gjennemsigtige* in Danish, see-through—the world around her is visible through her body—and she must see the journey through. In the English language, the Latin prefix *trans-* is also, of course, used to mean "across," and -*parent*, from *parere* means "appearing," so that in translation the mermaid might also be *crossing appearances*. She is still her own self, and her voice will now sound in freer ways along her new transformative journey.

Multivocality. Katherine Meizel, Oxford University Press (2020). © Oxford University Press.
DOI: 10.1093/oso/9780190621469.003.0007

This journey *across* has not gone unremarked as allegory for transformation in human lives. Leland G. Spencer offers a close "transgender reading" (Spencer 2014: 113) of the tale. For Spencer, though the story was not purposefully written about transgender identity, it contains significant parallels between the mermaid's experience and transgender experiences. Most broadly, he points out, the little mermaid performs a gender identity "other than that which is socially assumed or assigned for her character" (113). Grounding his argument in the Butlerian tenet that all identities are "fabrications manufactured and sustained through corporeal signs and other discursive means" (Butler 1990: 173), Spencer writes that:

> The mermaid's performative permeability on the nature/human-culture divide suggests that identity performance drives the narrative.... From the mermaid's fascination with humans, to the painful changes she decides to make to her body, to the challenge of coming out to her family and friends, to her relationship with the prince—in one case [Andersen's version], the ultimate rejection of her identity and, in the other [Disney's film], a consummate acceptance—both stories reflect the excitement, anticipation, struggle, pain, silence, and beauty of coming out, of performing transgender identities, and of the search for love and the identity that seems to fit best. (Spencer 2014: 124)

Spencer focuses on the voice as a metaphor for identity and agency, and compares the mermaid's silencing to the social and self-censorship experienced by transgender individuals. He also positions the material voice on the same level of significance as the metaphorical—the physical/physiological intertwined with the cultural. For some transgender singers who choose to transition, the journey of engendered voice is similarly, if less fantastically, entangled and complex. The mermaid may give up her voice to get a man, but there are many nonfictional people who are willing to take grave risks in order to be or *not* to be one. And in late 2018 the risk has become excruciatingly more literal, the White House planning an erasure of transgender identities no less devastating than relegation to ocean foam.

Transvocality

Though it is with caution that I began this chapter with reference to such a work of fiction, trans musician Simon de Voil has called himself "an accidental real-life fairytale" ("Peter Pan," in *Funny Kinda Guy* documentary [2005]). When he wrote those words, in a song titled "Peter Pan," he was living a narrative that he had not exactly heard told before—he has been called the father of the trans movement in his native Scotland. Until recently, most of the literature to date about transgender voices grew from research in speech therapies aiming to elicit the desired perception of the speaker's gender identity. But in the study of singers, several key authors have been developing new concepts of *transvocality*.

For Holly Patch and Tomke König, transvocality ("trans* vocality") is the "embodied trans* being *in* and *of* the world. . . . There is no ontological trans* voice," they assert, "but in trans* people enacting singing—and thereby determining the phenomenon of trans* vocality—the trans*ness of the singing comes to matter and trans* singers become subjects" (Patch and König 2018: 33). Shana Goldin-Perschbacher's seminal writing on Jeff Buckley considers Buckley's "transgressive" vocality as multiply-gendered or transgendered, a voice that "resists" identification with his presumably cisgender, heterosexual male identity (Golden-Perschbacher 2008: 35). In her more recent work addressing the experiences of trans and non-gender-conforming singer-songwriters in country music, she reminds readers that while decisions about transitioning are individual, "staging a professional music career draws attention to these choices" (778). Musicologist and performer Alexandros Constansis has used the term *transvocality*, along with *hybrid vocality* and *hybrid vocal personae*[1] in his groundbreaking work—groundbreaking especially because transmasculine singers had virtually no literature to turn to before it; it now turns up in online discussions among transitioning singers, and one of my consultants cited it. Constansis understands transvocality as "non-binarian vocality," and notes that during transition it "behaves in a less conventional manner than standard adult or other types of changing cisgender vocality, such as those encountered during male adolescence or female menopause" (Constansis 2013: n.p.). And in their pivotal 2014 dissertation "Singing Strange: Transvocality in North American Music Performance," Elías Krell investigates transvocality in the context of affective experience, and as a theoretical framework that "asks how and why we hear sound as sexed, gendered, sexualized, raced, and so on—and allows sound to speak back to enculturated practices of hearing/seeing identity" (Krell 2014: 13). For Krell, the sensory experiences engendered by the embodied voice "(re)constitute[s]" the body, rendering transvocal performances "trans/formative" (35).

---

[1] Constansis explains his understanding of "hybrid voice" and "hybrid vocal personae" this way:

the terms "hybrid vocality" and "hybrid vocal personae" tend to focus on the effects of non-binarian, i.e., non-strictly "male" or "female," endocrinological and gender formation in singing vocality. Subsequently, these particulars are integrated and reassessed under a wide range of Humanities perspectives, apart from Musicological ones, with the incorporation of recent developments in Gender/Queer Theory and Social Sciences. This allows the drawing together of vocal personae from a variety of contexts without resulting in the pathologisation of human variation. Hybrid vocal personae, despite the presence of terminological changes, have been discovered in all civilisations. As such, their phenomenon has not been attributable to parameters, such as chronological and local convergence or divergence. (Constansis 2013: note 41)

Transvocalities also figure as what Krell calls "sonic borderlands" (Krell 2015: 95) after Gloria Anzaldúa, and what I have termed vocal "borderlands." For Anzaldúa, a Borderland is "a vague and undetermined place created by the emotional residue of an unnatural boundary. It is in a constant state of transition. The prohibited and the forbidden are its inhabitants . . . those who cross over, pass over, or go through the confines of the "normal" (Anzaldúa 1987: 3). And, as Krell summarizes, Anzaldúa positions the border as an open wound, a place where "established zones of power grate upon each other and bleed" (Krell 2015: 107, on Anzaldúa 1987: 3). This chapter presents the multivocal nature of transvocality not as merely double-voicedness and not inevitably about leaving one voice and one identity entirely behind for a newer, "truer" one. Instead, it is a space in which a fluid continuum of selfness, embodied and performed, vibrates uniquely in every throat. I suggest that transvocality may be viewed as a specific kind of multivocality that illuminates, rather than the flexibility of the embodied instrument in moving between voices, the capability of the individual to deeply identify with more than one vocal way of being, to sense a compound Self that has been, is now, and will be voiced in multiple ways. Even if one vocality is in a singer's past, it does not necessarily disappear from their sense of Self. As other chapters have discussed, the question "What *is* my voice?" is often answered in the plural.

Defining "Trans"

Current gender discourse—both academic and public—encompasses a wide range of identities that can both undermine and underline binary male/female categorizations. The descriptors "trans" and "trans*" have come to encompass multiple ways of identifying, including transgender, transsexual, trans man and trans woman, agender, genderqueer, non-binary, genderfluid, and more (You Know You're Trans* When, also cited in Krell 2014: 25). Typically, these terms are used by individuals whose gender identities conflict with the identities they were assigned at birth, and whose survival, eventually, may depend upon some degree of transition to another way of embodying and performing gender. Not everyone transitions. Transitions may or may not lead to a permanent change in public identity, may or may not fit binary performativities, may or may not include medical transition through hormone treatments and/or surgeries, and may or may not involve a shift in preferred pronouns—"he/him/his" and "she/her/hers" but also "they/them/theirs," "ze/hir/hirs," and other configurations.[2]

---

[2] See the website from the University of Wisconsin, Madison, for a broader, more recent list of pronouns in use: https://uwm.edu/lgbtrc/support/gender-pronouns/

(In this chapter I use the gender identity terms and pronouns my consultants and other sources have each individually applied to themselves.)

Notably, the word *transition* itself is a contested one; it implies a liminal phase within a direct teleological shift, but stories of a "journey" away and return to an authentic bodily home also occupy a prominent place in transgender narratives. Aren Z. Aizura cautions that the notion of the journey tends to be too-neatly packaged for the context of free-market democracy (Aizura 2011: 267)—a narrative of movement, self-improvement, and self-authenticity with a distinct endpoint that reaffirms the binary model of gender. Cael M. Keegan writes that this version of the journey, frequently offered in recent films and television programming, typically positions transgender difference as "liberal-sentimental" (Keegan 2013: 29), as "something that can be unproblematically folded into heteronormative familial and social structure" for a cisgender audience" (Keegan 2013: 28). For Keegan,

> These texts thus resignify a significant source of transgender unfreedom into the matrix from which Western culture may continue to fashion triumphal narratives about the constantly expanding nature of its democratic liberty. The "moving" experience of such texts is not a centrifugal journey outward to the margins of what is humanly imaginable, but instead a centripetal return—to the phantasmic vision of "liberation" that fuels the neoliberal future. (Keegan 2013: 29)

For many, whether within a binary framework or not, transition can be an ongoing process with no more absolute finality than any other aspect of identity. Because the corporeal/performative voice is always already somewhat unfixed, because it can only to a certain extent be anchored in flesh and in ideology, it can play an especially significant part in that ongoing process. Lee Tyson notes that the past several years have seen an increase in media made by and for transgender consumers and a call for agency couched in terms that encourage transgender individuals to "find their voices." Tyson writes that the search for one's voice is often framed as "a search for congruency between internal gender identity and external gendered vocal expression, to produce a voice able to articulate the so-called authentic self vis-à-vis gender-coded sound" (Tyson 2016: 2).

Each singer who chooses transition—medically assisted or not—lives the process uniquely. If a transmasculine singer receives testosterone, the voice's pitch range will drop, but how much depends upon the hormone levels prescribed and tolerated, and how long one has been undergoing treatment. The two singers I interviewed who identify as trans men both noted that their comfortable range had eventually dropped exactly an octave, though this is not a universal experience. For transfeminine singers, however, hormone replacement therapy (HRT) has not been shown to significantly impact the range or quality of the voice. Some desiring vocal change choose voice feminization surgery that, for example, thins and shortens the vocal folds, and increases their tension (known as Wendler glottoplasty); that stitches the cricothyroid cartilages together (cricothyroid approximation); or that diminishes and sometimes lifts the larynx, shortening the pharynx (feminization laryngeoplasty).[3] Though I do not know of any research published regarding voice feminization surgery and singing, at least one surgeon recommends against cricothyroid approximation for patients whose "singing voice is very important" to them (Haben http://professionalvoice.org/feminization.aspx). Professional voice therapy may also be available for those who aspire to feminine-identified speech—inflection, timbre, slightly higher pitch—without surgical intervention. Significantly, not all transfeminine singers begin their singing lives by using a vocality typically gendered masculine by listeners. Breanna Sinclairé, for example, an opera singer based in California's Bay Area, already sang as a mezzo-soprano before she began hormone therapy, and eventually extended her *Fach* into a higher lyric soprano (Bravo 2013). Singer, composer, and scholar Xavia Publius, in hir master's thesis on transgender inclusion in western classical music, explains that though ze sang as a tenor for several years due to "transphobic training," (Publius 2015: 130), ze has preferred a higher range since hir voice broke in adolescence. In hir own music for the thesis project, Publius wrote across binary ranges, in high and low tessituras that together erase gendered pitch, allowing hir to "finally sing in the tenor range without being a tenor" (131).

The case studies discussed in this chapter underscore the individuality of transition experiences—in particular, the ways in which trans singers understand the potential risks regarding voice in their personal negotiation of gender identity. Along their journeys, some seek a singing voice that matches their sense of self, and some cannot or do not need to find one. And even a medically supported transition undertaken to cross binary gender borders does not necessarily mean a complete practical or psychological cession of one vocality for another; rather, voices can form layers in a singer's identity—as sonic bodies that remain audible even when the visible body has changed, or as enduringly embedded deep in a life's archaeological strata, foundational if no longer in use.

---

[3] Constansis (2013) also mentions a surgery called Thyroplasty Type III, discussed in N. Isshiki et al., "Surgical Alteration of Vocal Pitch," *Journal of Otolaryngology* 12, no. 5 (1983): 335–340.

Singing Along with a Ghost

In 2007, Showtime's drama *The L Word* (Season 4, Episode 8), featured an R&B song called "Little Girl," as the soundtrack to an intoxicated hookup between characters Kit and Papi. This exposure brought a great deal of attention to the song's creator, Bay Area musician and dancer Joshua Klipp. "Little Girl" was subsequently touted, on the *Tyra Banks Show* and MTV LOGO, as a history-making phenomenon: the first commercial recording to feature an artist in a duet between his pre-transition voice and his voice after the process of medical transition had altered it.

The vocal changes experienced by trans men can be difficult, and singers usually require a long period of adjustments to their practice—the testosterone injections and/or pills often involved in medical transition do instigate a major shift, as the body moves into a kind of "second puberty" (Constansis 2008), in which the vocal tissue—muscle and membrane—is re-formed, reformatted, as the vocal folds, and to degree the larynx, actually grow.

Voice specialists to whom Mr. Klipp went for help were unfamiliar with gender transition, and told him that his hormone-induced voice change would likely parallel that of a boy's puberty. But he found the shift between singing as a woman and singing as a man to be embedded in social and psychological processes little resembling a child's move to the baritone section. In some ways transition for trans men constitutes a reversal of female puberty, or a replacing of its effects with male identified ones. It changes the performance and perception of sex and gender through all senses, not the least of which is hearing, and social interactions also change in gendered ways. A young boy tends to be treated like an as-yet incomplete person, like a potential man, like a seed of the male identity he will "become" in the future; a person externally perceived as a woman is approached as a woman, and their social preparation for the transition to manhood is very different. Discourse about boys' and cisgender women's voices, though there is some overlap, does understand them in distinct ways. The voices of children and adults are known to be anatomically, functionally, and acoustically distinct (Welch and Howard 2002: 106). And boys' voices (as well as, sometimes, those of young girls) are often de-gendered, or temporarily gender-suspended, even gender-transcendent in song, positioned as suited for classical and religious choral work and imagined in consort as the divine voices of angels. Martin Ashley calls attention to the widespread western idea "that the treble voice represents a brief and final flowering of purity and innocence before a necessary, although transitory, dark age of tempestuous, immature adolescent sexuality," and emphasizes that this belief operates within an adult gaze (Ashley 2006: 197).

Alexandros Constansis was also told that his vocal transition would be comparable to a boy's, and he began reading pedagogical and otolaryngological studies of young male voices, but he posits that the physiological distinctions between "bio-female"[4] bodies and boys' bodies are great enough to make the vocal impact of puberty quite different. Constansis has found that trans men's larynges tend to be only slightly larger in size than those of non-trans female sopranos, and theorizes that many trans men encounter vocal challenges because the vocal folds develop further than the cartilages of an already mature, and therefore less flexible, larynx can accommodate.

Additionally, if they have access to it, trans men may respond physiologically to HRT in different ways, and prescribed dosages may need adjustment to prevent severe side effects. Lower dosages may prolong or indefinitely postpone the kind of total vocal transition expected. And many do not have access to HRT at all, and may attempt to compensate by lowering their voices through damaging practices. Lee Tyson has written about such difficulties in transmasculine voice:

> the very *failures* or *insufficiencies* of FTM [female-to-male] vocality produced by the realities of gender dysphoria, as well as socioeconomic and material realities, are lodged in the voice; the power dynamics underpinning the material and social constructions of gender are indexed in the very sound, or lack thereof, of certain FTM voices. (Tyson 2016: 7)

Some voices take time to settle, and singers may experience them as out of control. (In chapter 8, I discuss the perception of vocal control as important to singers' sense of self.) Simon de Voil, during the first years of his slow vocal shift, found that he had "very little control over my vocal cords" and very low vocal stamina. He kept singing, though, he says, "[i]t took a long time to build my voice up again" (interview, September 13, 2013).

Mr. De Voil didn't intend to be a singer. But as a songwriter and guitarist, he found performing what he wrote gratifying, and found that it was "difficult to give my songs away, actually, to other people," afraid that "they wouldn't sing them right." His voice, then, became a vehicle so intertwined with his songs and sense of self that he sometimes feels physically uncomfortable singing in other contexts. Now an ordained interfaith minister, during his spiritual journeying he noticed that if he felt no connection to the meaning of the words he sang, he could experience pain. Living for a time in Iona Abbey in his native Scotland, there was singing every day, but, he says,

---

[4] Constansis' preferred terminology, equivalent to cisgender or non-trans female identities

if I didn't identify with the song and I didn't feel it to be true, my voice was much more likely to hurt. And it's like I just don't want to sing something if it's not true to how I experience the world. I find that absolutely fascinating. How come I can reach that high note because I really, really want to, whereas if it's just in the music and it's just pretty, it will make my voice hurt? ... [I]f I love something and believe it, I want to sing with my whole being, and if I'm just singing with my throat then my voice is sore. I don't think other people have that in quite the same way that I do; I think there's something about being authentic that I was just born to do, that my body just does not let me [be inauthentic]. (interview, September 12, 2013)

Mr. de Voil—the subject of the 2005 documentary *Funny Kinda Guy*—discussed his own transition with me, and said that a number of cisgender/non-trans men have asked him why he saw his voice change as such a sea change, when they had uniformly undergone it in youth, as an expected, accepted part of the journey to manhood. He tells them, "it was because it represented me; your voice represents how we understand ourselves. And the choice to change that was very scary for me" (interview September 13, 2013).

I think I identify very strongly with my voice. You get used to it ... it's psychologically quite difficult to separate me from my voice. Like, we get very attached to our body, we see our self in our body—we match—we're more, the voice especially. I was very attached to my alto voice that I had before. It was one of the things I felt was true about me, I think that that is to do with the fact that I was singing songs that were attempting to be an honest expression of who I was. And my voice enabled me to connect with others, and to sing the songs of who I was. Therefore, the idea of losing that was very distressing. (interview, September 13, 2013)

He explained the difficulty of his own decision further to me; he was reluctant to risk his sound and all it entailed—his musical partnerships, the vocal qualities his fans admired. But, he says, "I'd weighed it up and I was like, 'no, I need to do this. My soul needs me to do this, even if I'm worried about losing my voice. ... [T]here's something deep in my body that I need to honor'" (interview, September 13, 2013).

For some transmasculine singers, along with this common and intense association of voice with self and with identity, comes a keen awareness of what is at stake when they begin taking testosterone. Some, even as they celebrate the prospect of living as the person they feel they are, agonize over the loss of the voice that they have learned to know as their own, and over the possibility that the new voice may not retain the capability or talent they have come to depend upon. For Mr. Klipp, it was:

> hands-down the hardest decision I've ever made in my life. It wasn't [even the] decision about transitioning itself, it was sort of the subdecision of that, which was to have to be OK with that, knowing that I may not be able to sing. . . . [T]here is almost nothing more important to singers. And to me it felt like a choice between singing or living. You know? And I had to choose living, and I didn't know if singing was going to be a part of that in the future. (interview, August 26, 2013)

Part of that uncertainty came from a dearth of available information. The only literature he could find at the time he began the transition was scholarship about hormone use in athletes, or online discussions of individual's personal transition experiences. Today, years later, Constansis's publications have taken an important step toward filling in the gaps for *transvocal* singers (a term favored in Krell 2013), but published singing guides have been slow in coming,[5] and there is no standard training system in place among singing pedagogues.[6] Transition is an extremely individual process, anyway, both in terms of experience and of hormone dosages and effects, and some singers share their questions and advice with each other in online forums in the hope that someone else has had similar challenges.

Mr. Klipp and Mr. De Voil have each described to me his personal struggle with vocal realignment, with relocating both the kinetics of singing and the sensations of singing, as well as the shift in imagined and bodily space that came with the precise octave drop both experienced. "I love having the rumble in my chest," Mr. De Voil says, but it took several years to rebuild his vocal stamina so that he could make it through a gig. For Mr. Klipp, even as he grew to feel that his new voice for the first time fit his true identity, he had to reacquaint himself with an instrument that had become a stranger, its muscles and ligaments suddenly moving in new ways, and it took years for him to be in control of it again. Much of the problem in the first years of his transition, he believes, pertained to a lung

---

[5] In May 2018, Liz Jackson Hearns and Brian Kremer's book *The Singing Teacher's Guide to Transgender Voices* was published (San Diego, CA: Plural Publishing). It was listed at $129.95, perhaps not an easily accessible price.

[6] This is not to say that no work has been done, especially recently; for example, the website of the National Association of Teachers of Singing offers an article on the topic (Davies 2016), "Training the Transgender Singer: Finding the Voice Inside," and in 2017 its journal published several pieces on teaching transgender singers (such as Sims 2017). Earlham College also held a Transgender Singing Voice conference in 2016.

capacity that hadn't grown to accommodate the needs of his now thicker vocal folds, and he also found his pitch range and stamina suddenly and significantly reduced. His efforts to circumvent these powerful, if temporary, limits indirectly led to the production of "Little Girl," as Mr. Klipp left his first love, jazz, for pop during the years he spent rebuilding his voice. He replaced the sustained melodic lines, wide range, and demanding gigs he was used to performing in jazz with the shorter phrases and smaller melodic arcs of pop, where he could also write his own material to accommodate his vocal needs.

"Little Girl" was a track he and his producer and co-writer, Khristopher Cloud, had written prior to his transition, and then, as his voice began to settle, they were searching for repertoire his newly limited range could manage, and came across that track. Originally the song told a story of domestic abuse, later he and Mr. Cloud reworked the lyrics to allude instead to Mr. Klipp's transition. Where the first version offered a voice of counsel and warning to a woman in an abusive relationship, the new one allowed Mr. Klipp to address his younger self in retrospect, providing a kind of temporal rupture that let his present visit and redress his past. The break in his voice during transition became for him a literal embodiment of a break with that past, and the production of "Little Girl" allowed him to directly bid his former self farewell and move on.

> Hearing my old voice in my headphones and singing along with it was—that is a day that I will never forget... Oh, it was like—hearing a ghost, it was like—but it was me. It was like hearing this person that I had been and had let go of, this voice that I had said goodbye to, um, and singing along with it; it was like telling my old self who didn't know what to do, and who was terrified and scared and didn't know what was going to happen that it was going to be OK. (interview, August 26, 2013)

Notably, several trans vocal artists have written about ghost selves in the context of their gender identities. A 2012 track by Canadian singer-songwriter Rae Spoon, who eschews binary gender categories (they explain that they have "retired from gender" [Spoon 2014: 17]), opens with melismatic, ethereally processed, and difficult-to-gender vocalizations. The song promises, "Ghost of a Boy. / Hard to catch like light. / I'll hide you in my body. / I'll keep you alive" (Spoon, "Ghost of a Boy," on *I Can't Keep All of Your Secrets* (2012); lyrics printed in Spoon 2014: 31). In their chapter for *The Oxford Handbook of Voice Studies*, Elías Krell studies a composition by transmasculine singer Joe Stevens of the band Coyote Grace—a song called "Ghost Boy," which narrates his class reunion at a boarding school where he had been gendered female, long before his medical transition. "She is everywhere.... I wish she hadn't left so soon," Stevens sings (Coyote Grace, "Ghost Boy," on *Boxes and Bags* (2006); discussed in Krell, 2019). Krell points out that these lyrics challenge common public narratives that assume all trans persons hate their bodies and identities before a medical transition, and feel that they have come home at last after such a transition (Krell, 2019) Instead, the spectralities that haunt these songs are as nuanced as transition itself; they, if not *embody*, then perhaps *enspecter* the totality of western ghost discourses: of the threatening spirits of European superstition, the welcomed comfort of ghosts returning to their loved ones at 19th-century séances, the obscuring/clarifying presences in Marx's work on egoist-anarchist philosopher Max Stirner,[7] and, in the scholarly "spectral turn" inspired by Jacques Derrida, the ghost becomes not merely an echo of an individual life, but a manifestation of thoughts and ideas that stays with us.

In his 1845 book *Der Einzige und sein Eigentum* (*The Unique One and Its Own*, often translated as *The Ego and His Own*), Stirner presented the self as a unique, but undefinable reality recognizable only by its creative actions—"I am nothing in the sense of emptiness but I am the creative nothing, the nothing out of which I myself as creator create everything" (Stirner 1907[1845]: 6). He also used singing to exemplify the individual's inherent exploitation of others—"I sing because—I am a singer. But I *use* you for it because—I need ears" (395). The State, and society were "ghosts" to him, only illusions, and individuals the only reality. This is where Marx came in, and later, Derrida, confronting the construction of selves and bodies of ideology.

Ideas are not made flesh, Derrida explains, interrogating Marx, but spirit, producing ghostly bodies we call "the Emperor, the State, the Fatherland" (Derrida 1994: 163). For Marx, when a ghostly body—an emperor, a State—is destroyed, the generative body, the "real" body, remains, "more real than ever," its true power revealed (163). Marx's ghost is a mask, a screen that shields the truth about power and society. Diverging from Marx, who championed the exorcism of such spirits, Derrida proposes that we should live with the ghost, as it "ceases to be seen as obscurantist and becomes, instead, a figure of clarification with a specifically ethical and political potential" [Blanco and Peeren 2013:7]).

> For there is no ghost, there is never any becoming-specter of the spirit without at least an appearance of flesh, in a space of invisible visibility, like the disappearing of an apparition. For there to be a ghost, there must be a return to the body, but to a body that is more abstract than ever. The spectrogenic process corresponds therefore to a paradoxical *incorporation*. Once ideas or thoughts (*Gedanke*) are detached from their substratum, one engenders some ghost by *giving them a body*. Not by returning the living body from which ideas and

---

[7] All discussed in the editors' introduction to Blanco and Peeren 2013.

thoughts have been torn loose, but by incarnating the latter in *another artifactual body, a prosthetic body*. (Derrida 1994: 158)

Perhaps for Mr. Klipp and other singers, a previously gendered voice, as significant as (and not entirely separate from) a State, might be seen as a ghost—ideas and thoughts and performances, a construction of individual and social will—detached from the living body and returned to the abstract body of the recorded voice. This ghost is not some essence left behind, but something that remains, in an altered form, with the body that generated it.

Mr. Klipp's relationship with his voice was always, as he terms it, "complicated." It gave him an essential and precious avenue for self expression, but before his transition, he recalls,

> It didn't sound like how I felt—I mean it was very pretty, very feminine, you know ... [it was] a nice voice, but it just didn't fit how I felt ... it felt almost like it was betraying me every time I sang, yet at the same time it was the only way that I know I sometimes lived, through times of my life, because I was able to say things musically I could not—was not allowed to say out loud. (interview, August 26, 2013)

Though he is happier now with his new voice, he acknowledges that both his pre- and post-transition voices share some stylistic characteristics, which he says listeners describe as "smoothness" or "a romantic sound."

Mr. De Voil's sense of his two voices is different; listening to the work he recorded with his pre-transition band Icarus, he hears his former vocality as "small Simon," the way one might look at one's childhood photographs. There is continuity in this hearing, not a dramatic break, and when I asked him whether both of his voices were his, he responded: "Absolutely. They both feel true." And, perhaps paradoxically, the very fact that his voice had changed allowed him to disentangle his sense of self from the sound of his voice:

> I think that having my voice change so dramatically was helpful in stopping me identifying too much with the sound of it. You know, who we are changes. We think we are the same but we're meant to change.... I think the reality is we adapt, we adapt to whatever our voice is, even if that's sad. (interview, September 13, 2013)

It is key to recognize that not everyone who hears Mr. Klipp or Mr. De Voil is aware of their transitions, so they are not always heard as transvoiced. Strangers often interact with them as cisgendered men, and perceive their romantic partnerships as heterosexual relationships.

Duality is a crucial concept for both of these singers. Mr. De Voil, the interfaith minister, understands himself as "two-spirited" (invoking the premise of the important Native American transgender movement), not simply someone who has become male, but someone whose lived experience encompasses both masculine and feminine ways of being in the world. And Mr. Klipp, his voice now stabilized, has returned to jazz—currently a San Francisco fixture with his band the Klipptones—but he is working on something new, too. He has begun structuring many of his arrangements in performance as mashups, combining pop or R&B with the American Songbook—especially titular homonyms like Hoagie Carmichael's "Time After Time" with Cyndi Lauper's similarly titled 1983 hit, or Cole Porter's "Night and Day" with Al B. Sure's song of the same name (1988). (He also does "Let's Fall in Love" with Katy Perry's "Teenage Dream.") "It's just the coolest shit," he says. With these combinations, Mr. Klipp is able to reconcile the multiple genres that have shaped his voice, and the distinct but interwoven periods of his life associated with those genres, that have shaped his sense of self. His remixes, significantly, do not represent an attempt to blend two musical categories, or two experiences, but, in a very 21st-century sensibility, to layer them, and to both acknowledge their uniqueness and celebrate what they share. Likewise, in the chorus of "Little Girl," Mr. Klipp's two voices sing together, but each is clearly distinguishable—both his, and, however conflicted his first voice might have been, both him. This is the work of transvocality—not the replacement of one voice by another, but learning to balance the discrete but interconnected parts that make a whole life, to negotiate the self-knowledge of two voices, to embody both in the sounding of one.

An Unchanged Singing Voice: Lucia Lucas

The use and perception of trans women's singing voices can be complicated by a lack of the sort of dramatic change associated with trans men's voices. Certainly there can be effects from hormone treatments, but the size of the larynx and thus the vocal range are not impacted. Some must contend with a different kind of duality, in which listeners hear a typically masculine voice emanating from a feminine body. In some cases that stability benefits a singer—fans of Laura Jane Grace, of the Athens punk band Against Me!, have remained supportive following her recently publicized transition, and reviews of her work frequently note that she "sounds the same as ever" (Edwards 2014). Ethnomusicologist Revell Carr has written about the late singer Louisa Jo Killen, renowned as a male sea chanty performer, and who only in 2010 at the age of 76 began living and performing publicly as a woman. In the sea-music subculture, where authenticity has habitually been located in masculinity, the reception of Killen's female identity was mixed.

Some, Carr reports, saw the change as a loss to the sea-music community, and spoke as if Killen had died (Carr 2013: 8). But supporters pointed out her vocal continuity—"she's still got that voice; it's still the voice we love" (9).

Singing in the same voice can stretch and challenge traditional genre structures. Lucia Lucas, an American opera singer working in Germany (a border crossing), began publicly living as a woman in 2014, when she had already established a successful early career as a leading baritone. Despite dire warnings from American colleagues that transition meant an end to that career, she continues to perform the signature repertoire of her baritone *Fach* (voice and role type) in major opera houses throughout Europe. She seriously considered the potential impact on her work, but ultimately felt that her career would suffer anyway, if she couldn't live as herself. She didn't expect that the jobs would keep coming, but they did. In fact, sometimes the gap between her offstage and onstage gender presentations provides artistic inspiration—for a production of *Samson et Dalila* in Darmstadt, her role as the High Priest was reworked as a High Priestess, and by playing with inflection, she and her directors were able to turn the character's words from misogyny to critique. Ms. Lucas has also created her own spaces for performance; in 2016 and 2017, Ms. Lucas collaborated with writer and director Finn Beames (known as FXXX BXXXXX), and his "alter ego" Oedipa, for a show titled "Binary Optional" in London. The project was billed as "an evening of song in transition: from masc to femme, classical to queer and oppression to freedom" (www.cptheatre.co.uk/production/binary-optional/), and featured classical music in three languages, plus performances "flirting with Sarah Vaughan and Rocky Horror." Among the repertoire were the Cold Genius's aria from Henry Purcell's *King Arthur* (from a role often sung by a baritone, though countertenors, famously including Klaus Nomi, have also frequently been associated with the aria), and "When I Am Laid in Earth" from Purcell's *Dido and Aeneas* (from a female role typically sung by a soprano).

Though transgender singers have been excluded from classical singing in many ways (Publius 2015), in some senses opera has set the perfect stage for the undoing of vocal gender binaries. The history of high male singing and of roles "en travesti" for women already encourage 21st-century performers and audiences to trouble hegemonic models of gendered voice. However, the ubiquitous Cherubino and Octavian and Oscar characters are written as young boys and performed in treble registers, while Ms. Lucas sings mature male characters such as Monterone (in Verdi's *Rigoletto*) and Ford (in *Falstaff*), with an appropriately deep voice. For some time, she felt the identity conflict keenly—her made-up image in the mirror as an old man became a catalyst in her decision to transition; with penciled lines on her face, she was looking at a future self who was not her at all. But she has negotiated the division between her onstage and offstage presentations in a practical way that emphasizes performativity. Though young opera singers, she observes, sometimes feel a need to act out the personality of their assigned *Fach* in their offstage lives, character categories are not intended to guide one's everyday persona. "Yes, your voice is a *Fach*, but your personality is not a *Fach*" (interview, January 11, 2016). In other words, singers should not aim to live in the mode of their archetypical operatic role but, rather, should maintain a separation between personal and theatrical ways of being. Her transition allows her to make this distinction. And when others comment that she plays a man well on stage, she responds that it is because "I learned, my whole life, how to play a man" (interview, January 11, 2016).

Ms. Lucas has said that as a child she prayed at night to wake up a girl, and we talked about the role of voice in her experience of male puberty. For her, the change of voice did not feel as striking as other changes in her body—while her body betrayed her in other ways, she says, the voice seemed wrapped up in the masculine speech and movement she was coached into performing as a child assigned male gender identity. It was part of the role she was always studying. Adolescent voice change can be experienced as traumatic by cisgender male and trans female singers, though. Xavia Publius discusses the change in hir[8] own adolescent voice as traumatic, writing that the break made it "a voice not my own. I felt disembodied from my voice, which was in the service of music not meant for me" (Publius 2015: 7).

Unlike the masculine speech patterns and deportment, Ms. Lucas has no desire to abandon her baritone as part of an identity isolated in the past. For her, transition does not comprise a simple beginning and endpoint, but, as with any other aspect of identity, is an ongoing process. To accommodate this framework, Ms. Lucas has offered an important neologism (see Clarke 2015)—for more nuance than the frequently used *Geschlechtsumwandlung* (sex conversion or sex change), she suggests the neologism *Geschlechtsreise*, to indicate that her experience has been a *journey* rather than a direct, sudden shift from one identity to another. This is an important distinction, she notes, because some people (she cites a U.S. politician) still believe that the change is made on a whim for deceptive and nefarious purposes.

She aspires to more a more feminine speaking voice, but she is gratified by her operatic accomplishments and the voice she has crafted through years of training and practice and performance:

> My speaking voice, I'm not necessarily happy with where it is right now. My singing voice, my baritone singing voice, I'm extremely happy where it is right now. Is it me? It may be a side of me. I think that if you live in a framework of

---

[8] In hir thesis, ze informs the reader that ze uses she/her/hers pronouns in speech but ze/hir/hirs in writing (Publius 2015: 65). As this is a written document, I follow that practice.

male for, let's say twenty-five years, or over ten years of your adult life in this box, it's hard to do away with it completely. And that's something in my transition, specific more to me than most trans women. I don't need to give up the past, I don't need it to be gone. I don't get rid of old pictures; it's still there. There are people who try to delete their old identity, and I don't consider my old—how I used to present myself as genuine me, but there are a lot of things that I did accomplish before that I don't necessarily want to get rid of. And one of the things that I'm very proud of is this baritone voice that I built. (interview, January 11, 2016)

Though there can be no broad hormonal pitch change in her voice, there has nevertheless been change. The work she has done to alter her speaking voice, progressing gradually in order to avoid potentially adverse effects on her singing, has nevertheless impacted her onstage voice. First, she has found that the effort she has made to raise the pitch of her speaking voice benefits her singing. Adult male larynges are larger and the vocal folds longer and thicker than those of females, and they typically vibrate more slowly. Researchers in vocal acoustics have identified an average range of between 100 and 120 Hz for male speakers, and 200 to 220 Hz for female speakers (Weirich and Simpson 2013: 2965). Now, Ms. Lucas says, her average fundamental frequency in speech has gone from a low male range to an average of 180 to 200 Hz. She aspires to 220 Hz. She has not lost any of her low baritone range, but believes that her speech work has raised her tessitura, the range where she is most comfortable, at least a whole step. "It's much easier to sing the high notes now," she says, "because I'm sitting up there" (interview, January 11, 2016). She is approaching her longtime goal to sing the high Verdi baritone roles, and feels that she has "freed up my voice and freed up my acting, and I feel much more comfortable in myself. So I think my performances are actually better just because I'm more relaxed. I'm not fighting anything internally" (interview, January 11, 2016). Ms. Lucas describes including "more air" in her speaking voice, as well, but she does not include that difference in her sung performances. She thinks that in the future, though, she would like to perform some of Sarah Vaughan's repertoire, and that the intimacy of a microphone might allow her to make musical use of the new qualities in her speaking voice.

In addition to the practices she has adopted in her speaking voice, the facial feminization surgery she underwent demanded some adjustments to her singing. A lip lift resulted in a resting position with lips slightly more parted than she had been used to, which meant that she needed to accommodate a different shape at the front of her vocal tract. She told me:

I would say that it probably took me at least six months to get used to my new lip position and how it really affected the overtones. And I had to record myself all the time, and listen to it back multiple times to figure out how to deal with that, and how to sing. And some people say, well you want the top lip to cover the teeth, and I can't do that. If I do that it, makes my sound forced. So I could do the—if I did the exact same movements that another baritone did, it wouldn't necessarily result in my sounding good. (interview, January 11, 2016)

I asked Ms. Lucas if she had advice for other singers who might be in similar situations. Her answer underlines the way she positions her singing voice as both part of a performative masculinity and of her sense of genuine identity:

You have to find out who you are, and that will influence your voice. My voice is my voice. My baritone voice is my voice. It really does belong to me, and now more than ever it has me in it. But it's not because I fit this masculine person and I bring that on stage ... your private self is not going to make your stage self better. You don't have to live privately how your character is on stage for anything to match. It's acting. It is acting... The more authentic you are with your self, the more authentic your voice will be. (interview, January 11, 2016)

Unchanged Voice: Breanna Sinclairé

The story of Breanna Sinclairé's voice follows a different narrative; its range also stayed fundamentally the same as she began her transition—but she was already singing in a high tessitura, first in the operatic countertenor *Fach* and later as a mezzo, then as a soprano.

As a child, Ms. Sinclairé had identity thrust upon her in multiple ways. She was assigned male at birth (amab). Attending a Southern Baptist church, she was assigned a religious identity that would not recognize her true self. Singing there, she had been assigned a career path in singing by the age of five. With a four-and-a-half–octave range, Ms. Sinclairé never experienced a dramatic adolescent break and her speaking voice was always pitched high. She could "technically sing all vocal parts," she says, "accurately, and efficiently, and with power" (interview, March 9, 2017). She recalls listening to her grandmother's recordings of African American opera singers, including Marian Anderson, and Grace Bumbry, imitating and playing with the sounds they made—"the vocality, the vowels"—because she felt she could relate to them. Nevertheless, when she began formal vocal training at the age of 12 with the renowned instructor Dr. Nathan Carter of Morgan State University, she was assigned the tenor voice type. She dutifully suppressed her desire to practice the timbres of Shirley Verrett or

Leontyne Price, though she still felt a "deep burning inside... to just bust out and sing those sounds in that female register" (interview, March 9, 2017). As Xavia Publius writes,

> the assignment of voice parts is not a neutral process; it is intricately involved in ciscentric, heteronormative modes of bodily regulation, such that all people whose voices are stable below a certain point are automatically assumed heterosexual cisgender men, and all people whose voices are stable above that point are automatically assumed heterosexual cisgender women. (Publius 2015: 6)

And tenor opera roles are typically voices with narrow heteronormative, cisgender narratives. Trans identities—in either characters or in singers—have been largely, at least until recently, erased.

Ms. Sinclairé associated her higher, feminine voice with an authentic self she had to suppress, a self which she says in spite her adolescent work as a tenor, "never left me as a boy in high school; that was Breanna in there" (Bravo 2013). Because she maintained her extensive range when she attended high school at the Baltimore School for the Arts, she endured difficult lessons and doubt from her teacher, as well as teasing from her peers—was she really a tenor? Would she be better off singing in the countertenor operatic *Fach*?. In addition, she herself did not feel like a tenor. "The timbre was not of a tenor quality," she explains, "I couldn't fit in that mold that they wanted me to . . . I would be assigned these tenor roles, you know, and I just never fit in with those, because I always wanted to be the damsel in distress or the Carmen or the Dalilah, or the Tosca, or the Dorabella. I wanted to be those women" (interview, March 9, 2017). Though she did experiment with countertenor repertoire in her senior year, the roles associated with that voice type—for the most part, male characters originally written for castrati in the first two centuries of opera—did not feel any more appropriate to her than tenor roles. She considered quitting music.

But when she was 19 and a student at Bethany Bible College in Sussex, New Brunswick (Canada), a moment onstage unexpectedly changed her life. For a school talent show, she and a group of friends decided to lip-sync to a Tina Turner recording of "Rollin' on the River (Proud Mary)." Ms. Sinclairé, given the leading role, donned a Turner-esque dress and a brown wig and channeled the female singer so convincingly that audience members asked each other who the new girl on stage was. Though she was performing a caricature, the experience convinced her of something, too—she felt incredibly comfortable. The school's sanctuary, where the talent show was held, became a different kind of sanctuary, where for five minutes and forty seconds she was able to perform femaleness, and be seen as a woman. "God," she recalls thinking, "I wish I could just leave the sanctuary and have this on for the whole year.... I felt like I could actually walk out of the building and be a female."

It wouldn't be that simple. After leaving Canada and spending some difficult months in New York, she attended the California Institute of the Arts, and then earned her master's degree at the San Francisco Conservatory of Music. At 21, she began hormone therapy and had gender confirmation surgery while still in school. In 2013, the owners of the vintage furniture store where she worked hosted a private benefit concert for her. Advertised irreverently as "Opera's Greatest Tits," the event featured Ms. Sinclairé in a two-hour recital to raise funds for her breast implants. As the conservatory's only openly trans vocal major, she encountered some discomfort among students and faculty. "My transition was exposed," she explains, and not everyone approved of it, or knew what repertoire to give her. But she did have support from her studio teacher and others, and eventually she was given opportunities to sing mezzo roles—including Carmen, a role she had long coveted. And singing became easier, her voice more powerful. She is not certain whether the hormones made a difference, or whether her technique simply improved at the time, or whether it was an effect of being more able to live as her true self, but her voice "kind of aligned" (interview, March 9, 2017) and settled into mezzo and even some lyric soprano repertoire. She does not sing in the male countertenor *Fach*, but is sometimes still assigned music for countertenors and feels that she still constantly needs to prove her authenticity in female roles. When we talked, she considered the "triple whammy" of her African American, female, and trans identity in the world of opera, noting that one has to work "twice as hard" as an opera singer who identifies in any single one of those ways.

Her feminine-pitched speaking voice and her mezzo-soprano/soprano singing are integral to Ms. Sinclairé's experience of "passing," of being perceived as a woman. At 6'2", a height often associated with masculinity, she says that she is particularly grateful for her already feminine speech register. Stephan Pennington writes about transgender vocal passing—an idea that reworks the notion of racial passing—observing that it sets up a kind of epistemological catch-22. It "puts the lie to the convenient fiction that while gender might be a social construct, sex, especially as represented by the voice, is biological and unalterable" (Pennington, forthcoming), but the malleability of the voice can also lead to delegitimizing misconceptions of transgender identities as always only performative. He points to the danger that non-transgender people may process trans identities as deceptive, received not like the celebrated sort of deception at the center of staged impersonation performances—the disjunctures discussed in chapter 3—but instead as one that is purposefully fraudulent. And because such misperceptions can and often do lead to transphobic violence (Pennington, forthcoming), vocal passing becomes as integral to survival as visible physiological features. With this in mind, Ms. Sinclairé has imminent plans for facial feminization surgery: "It is hard, girl, when you're transitioning. The world makes it hard. I try to—and especially with these killings that are happening... for my safety, that's why I'm getting these surgeries" (interview, March 9, 2017).

Not long after she finished her degree, Ms. Sinclairé made international headlines as the first transgender person to sing the U.S. National Anthem at a major league baseball game. The Oakland A's invited her to open their home game against the Padres, scheduled in coordination with one of the team's "LGBT Pride Night" events. Singing to a crowd of 30,000, she could see over a phalanx of photographers and journalists to the stadium's balcony, to where a row of gender nonconforming and trans women of color were seated. She nearly burst into tears.

> While I was singing I was thinking in my head, I have this voice for a reason, and it kind of brought us together. And it might sound cheesy and corny but you know with all these deaths that are happening within our community and everything, I felt like singing the national anthem was my way of saying I am not going anywhere. I'm an American just like everybody else. And I—it was kind of like a way of stating that I'm a part of this country. I'm an American citizen, and just because I'm a woman of color and trans doesn't mean I'm an alien. And I felt like singing that gave me the power to solidify that meaning and that feeling, that understanding, knowing that, you know, I am an American citizen. And that's it. (interview, March 9, 2017)

Cisgender preconceptions often assume that singing voices displaced through transition were necessarily "lost" voices. But the experiences included in this chapter demonstrate the multiplicity of ways in which voice figures in the processes of gender transition, in its myriad presences and absences. The voice, as both biology and culture, reflects and contributes to the diversity of gender variance in human life. And on the journey, transvocality, instead of providing a map between one place and another, inscribes a network of paths to navigate the borderscape of voice. It does not necessarily represent a vocal liminality between two states but, rather, an instrument through which an individual may embody and identify with more than one sonic expression of self. Like the little mermaid's, it can represent a voice regained, and reclaimed, through trans*formation. Vocality can be a strategy for self-identity, and a strategy for survival—and so can risking its material and sonic integrity.

7

Voice Control

> she of the echoing voice, who cannot be silent when others have spoken, nor learn how to speak first herself.
> —Ovid, *Metamorphoses* Book III: 339–358

"I sold my voice," my friend casually told me in 2013, slipping the news into the middle of a Facebook chat (personal communication, June 10, 2013). Caught in the time lag common to instant-messaging conversations, I was still writing something about my dog when her comment posted, but I quickly backtracked.

"What?" I typed, baffled.

"I sold my voice and now people all over the world are composing random things with it," she supplied.

I wrote, less than articulately, "Wait, what??? omg, what???"

A successful singer and teacher in California, Nichole Dechaine had signed a contract that allowed the use of her voice as the basis of a sampling library called *Voices of Rapture*. The software, by Soundiron, provides building blocks of vocal music to composers, so Dr. Dechaine spent three long days in a Bay Area recording studio improvising, working through all twelve keys and her entire range, producing sets of single pitches sung on vowels, melodic phrases without text, and phrases sung or spoken in English, Latin, and French. She sang for hours at a time, *pianissimo* and *forte*, with and without vibrato, legato intervals from half step to octave, chromatic and whole-tone scales. Now, anyone with $119 to spare can borrow her acousmatic voice from the library—a sounded body detached from her performing body—and shape its 17,310 samples at will to produce music that has never actually issued from her throat.

Her experience is that of a quintessential 21st-century neoliberal subject—a subject Türken et al. explain as an "entrepreneur of herself" (Türken et al. 2016: 34; my emphasis). As noted in chapter 1, the neoliberal subject is "increasingly construed as a free, autonomous, individualized, self-regulating actor understood as a source of capital; as human capital" (34) and as such is expected to practice continual self-development, "to act to increase her value" (34). I argued in chapter 1 that knowledge of classical singing and the ability to switch vocalities are both understood as paths to continual development, and thus to marketability. Though her singing for Soundiron did not venture outside of classically associated timbres and techniques, it did vary among more operatically and more chorally conventional practices, and her digitized voice continues developing its expressive range in new ways outside of her body. It is a situation that highlights the ways in which vocal disembodiment can complicate notions of voice and agency. The idea of "self-entrepreneurship" implies that the subject is exercising intensified agency, but when the voice is in some way controlled by another party, that agency is in question. In Dr. Dechaine's story resonate myths deeply embedded in western cultures—colonial anxieties about the nature and nurture of humanity, the encroachment of technology, about Otherness, about the dangers of and the dangers to (especially women's) bodies. This chapter addresses the transfer of voice control from one body to another in two particular contexts, drawing parallels between the sale of a voice to 21st-century digital thrall and the fictional ceding or appropriation of in film.

The Soprano

Voices of Rapture features the voices of solo singers classified according to choral voice categories; Dr. Dechaine is *The Soprano*. The producers at Soundiron distinguish their library from others, like the global juggernaut Vocaloid systems, saying that their package focuses on "true legato"—the provision of all those intervals means a consistently smoother, more human-sounding transition between pitches. Vocaloid voices capitalize on and tend not to disguise their technological manipulation; the transitions between phonemes, their onsets and offsets, can sound mechanical to listeners. It's important to note that *Voices of Rapture* users *cannot* shape Dr. Dechaine's voice into lyrics not already recorded—a function that Vocaloid does offer— and this leads composers to write a lot of vocalizations on vowels and to use only words within the limitations of the pre-packaged poetry.

Legato is only one of many ways in which Soundiron emphasizes the *humanness* of their virtual voices. Nina Eidsheim (2009) writes about the humanizing marketing of Zero-G's early Vocaloids (2003–2004), whose voice providers were profiled (in multiple senses of the word) in the product's packaging—for example, recording artist Miriam Stockley was pictured on her system's box. Soundiron's website offers biographical information and photographs of Dr. Dechaine in the studio.

In our first Facebook chat about *Voices of Rapture*, Dr. Dechaine expressed anxiety about the images of her on the site and about sounds that had been sampled without her explicit knowledge. There are currently (as of 2017) fourteen demo tracks on Soundiron's web page for *Voices of Rapture: Soprano*, created by thirteen composers, accessible through Soundcloud (as are other compositions outside of Soundiron's purview). In these compositions, Dr. Dechaine's voice soars over digital piano or orchestral accompaniment, or in a multivoiced choir of one. But one example, a quasi-operatic scene ("L'Opera de l'Amour de Dieu," whose composers are listed as "Firoze, Kaizad, Maliki") includes the sound of her clearing her throat, reciting French poetry, singing in manipulated layers with an artificially wobbly vibrato, whistling, and at the end, laughing.

When she first listened to the sample compositions, she was startled to hear not only her voice but also these other incidental sounds she had made during recording: " that's not something that I thought would be included in the library," she told me.

> I thought it would just be the exercises that they asked for, and the improvisations, minus, you know, where it was an obvious sort of outtake. In another composition there's a—a composer used an excerpt where I'm improvising, and I had to clear my throat, I had phlegm, and so—my voice didn't really crack, but you can hear that there's something, there's a flaw, right? So I had stopped in the recording and I thought, "Oh, they'll edit that out," made an assumption, and no, and I guess the composer liked that sound or that quality and he used it in the composition. So that was surprising. (interview, July 7, 2013)

I asked whether she felt that those sounds were *part* of the voice contracted to record for the library.

"No," she said. "I felt that was just me being a human." And she considers the appropriation of her laugh more personal than the sampling of her singing:

> Because I think it reveals more of my personality—it's attached to my personality, and to my own expression as a human and not as a singer, where my voice, you know—I am attached to it, it is my identity, but I'm kind of used to sharing it with others, and being paid to share it with others [laughs], where I haven't—I've never been paid to laugh [laughs] or to give that up for someone to use in a way that I wasn't expecting. (interview, July 7, 2013)

Later, she added that although she has two graduate level degrees in classical vocal performance, "I haven't had any *training* in throat clearing."

The developers of Soundiron—Mike Peaslee, Gregg Stephens (editors and recordists), and Chris Marshall (programmer)—position the non-singing sounds not only as signs of general humanity but also of an especially living sound, and of Dr. Dechaine's unique individual identity. According to Mr. Peaslee:

> All those pieces are so integral to a vocal performance. They're used a lot in pop recordings and modern recordings. They're the things you kind of would exclude from a symphonic recording, usually, because they're—you'd consider them impurities, but those are things that . . . to make it sound like it was convincingly sung by a live performer, those breaths need to be there. A user might put them really low in a mix, but just before a line, you know, that can add tension, it can add weight to the line that's about to be sung. So that's—in that way, we actually include a section of playable breaths with each subset of phrases and sustains that we offer in the different presets within the library, so that they're always right there ready for you. . . . And it just—it makes it that much more alive. Throat-clearing and all that stuff—some of it's kind of for fun, but a lot of it really is also—you know, people use it. It gives that much more life. It adds that much more personality to it. (interview, July 11, 2013)

Mladen Dolar, in *A Voice and Nothing More*, examines a famous case of hiccups that interrupts Aristophanes in Plato's *Symposium*, during a celebrated speech. About the hiccup, Dolar suggests that:

> the involuntary voice rising from the body's entrails can be read as Plato's version of mana: the condensation of a senseless sound and the elusive highest meaning, something which can ultimately decide the sense of the whole. This precultural, non-cultural voice can be seen as the zero-point of signification . . . the point around which other—meaningful—voices can be ordered, as if the hiccups stood at the very focus of the structure. The voice presents a short circuit between nature and culture, between physiology and structure; its vulgar nature is mysteriously transubstantiated into meaning *tout court*. (Dolar 2006: 25–26)

The incorporation of Dr. Dechaine's non-singing sounds in the *Voice of Rapture* library might be understood to provide this kind of central meaning, across genres, offering tiny, ephemeral short-circuited sites where the human and posthuman intersect.

Our initial Facebook chat about the vocal venture took place a few months after her marathon recording session. She hadn't thought much about the process since, until just before our conversation, when she heard the sample compositions on the software's website. Now, she was unnerved, listening to the manipulation of her voice. Thinking of Nina Eidsheim's work on the marketing of Vocaloid's voice providers, I wondered aloud (or in the chat version of aloud) whether there mustn't be a support group for singers who'd sold their voices to sampling libraries? If there is, Dr. Dechaine mused, "It's probably open to prostitutes, too." Her statement was not meant as a condemnation of sex work or a light treatment of trafficking, of course, but it pointed to parallels in the complications of selfness that may arise in the neoliberal commodification of an embodied voice or a body. Anxiety about such technology is certainly not unheard of in the second decade of the 21st century, when a number of technologies are capable of manipulating the acoustic materials of voices. In April 2017, an online service project called Lyrebird (after the master imitator of the animal kingdom) was announced, whose purpose is to learn the acoustic structures of a speaker's voice, and then when any text is entered, produce a "recording" of that voice speaking the words. News sites like *The Register* panicked immediately, declaring: "Lyrebird Steals Your Voice to Make You Say Things You Didn't— And We Hate This World" (Claburn 2017). Though partly tongue-in-cheek, the *Register* essay responds to Lyrebird as if it will lead to the kind of identity theft internet users often fear—a mutilation of self that is, in a way, a metaphorical mutilation of the body.

It isn't only the body that's at stake for Dr. Dechaine, either; she says, "I do feel like I sold a piece of my soul or something" (June 10, 2013). Some of the most persistently sounded stories in western cultures engage with frequently gendered discourses of voice and agency in relation to body and soul—with the metaphorical location of identity in the voice and the idea that, although a voice is *in* a body, it is not quite *of* a body and that it is something ensouled enough, spectral enough to be detached, stolen, corrupted, or even transplanted. Ovid's *Metamorphoses*, for example, tells the tale of the nymph Echo, who when the epic introduces her has been punished by Juno for prattling on in order to stall her while other nymphs, who have illicitly lain with Juno's husband (and brother) Jupiter, escaped the scene. Echo's chattiness is at the center of Juno's chastisement, and as punishment, her vocal freedom is severely limited so that subsequently she can only repeat what others say. Unable to control her own voice, she can't effectively pursue her crush (Narcissus), who is afraid when he hears her, and the shame of it causes her body to waste away. After that, her remaining bones turned to stone, Echo exists only as a disembodied voice bouncing among those stones, inert and only pitched into motion by, and always subject to, the force applied by others. Her condition is also explicitly described by Ovid, in the words of A. S. Kline's translation, as "no longer to be seen on the hills, but to be heard by everyone. It is sound that lives in her" (http://ovid.lib.virginia.edu/trans/Metamorph3.htm). She is condemned not to *speak* in another voice but, instead, to *be* the voice of anyone at all and to be heard in her humiliation by absolutely everybody. Dolar writes that her voice "continues to echo our own voice, the voice without a body, the remainder, the trace of the object." The echo is the constant opposition of the voice of self-presence and self-mastery, he continues, "the intractable voice of the other, the voice *one could not control*" (Dolar 2006: 40; my emphasis). As Leslie Dunn and Nancy Jones point out, in western discourses about voice, "like the body from which it emanates, the female voice is construed as both a signifier of sexual otherness and a source of sexual power, an object at once of desire and fear" (Dunn and Jones 1994: 3).

Nearly two millennia later, Echo's genetic material, carried by generations of vocally intact Melusines and Undines, spawned Hans Christian Andersen's sacrificing sea-maid, who has become a kind of patron saint of lost voices (see chapter 6). The voice of Andersen's little mermaid is taken from her when the sea-witch cuts out her tongue—it's not a complete voice-ectomy but, rather, a removal of part of her body, prohibiting her voice from serving as an instrument of speech. Disney's sea-witch Ursula summons mermaid Ariel's voice whole out of her body and captures it in a small vessel, separating it from the mermaid's body and later re-embodying it herself in order to sabotage Ariel's love affair. It is her voice that Ariel's princess has fallen in love with, and it encapsulates her identity so completely that the physical presence of her body and personality mean nothing to him without it.

Another of the sea-maid's daughters stars in the play *Ondine*, by Jean Giradoux (1939). She does not give up a singing voice, but the play does present a different loss of bodily control; when the nymph Ondine's husband betrays her, he is cursed with a failure of autonomic function—he must consciously control his automatic processes—so that when he falls asleep and cannot concentrate on breathing, he dies. There is a disorder of the autonomic nervous system called central hypoventilation syndrome,[1] a rare cause of apnea until recently referred to as "Ondine's curse," in which patients stop breathing when asleep, and typically require mechanical ventilation at night.

Thomas Mann's *Doctor Faustus* centers on a fictional composer, Adrian Leverkühn, who purposefully contracts syphilis and its attendant madness in an attempt to become a great artist, and then sells out in the usual ultimate way, to a demon. His friend Serenus Zeitblom, whose voice narrates the novel, recalls his deep identification with Andersen's sea-maid—juxtaposing the mermaid's

---

[1] CHS is distinct from the more common disorder of obstructive sleep apnea, and may be triggered by brain injury. "In 1962, Severinghaus and Mitchell coined the term Ondine's curse to describe a syndrome that manifested in 3 adult patients after high cervical and brainstem surgery. When awake and needing to breathe, these patients did so; however, they required mechanical ventilation for severe central apnea when asleep" (Chin and Bye 2014: n.p., http://emedicine.medscape.com/article/1002927-overview).

sacrifice of her envoiced body to *obtain* an immortal soul with Leverkühn's *cession* of his soul for the price of temporary genius and artistic immortality.

All these tales demonstrate abiding anxieties about the entwinement of voice, identity, body, and soul—about agency and, more specifically, about who is in *control*. A sampling library's singing voice is procured through much less dramatic and more painstaking means than the little mermaid's—it is copied, pitch by pitch, utterance by utterance, until it has been deconstructed sufficiently to be rebuilt and manipulated in new ways. But still, control is yielded to others, and as Dr. Dechaine's response indicates, that surrender can feel total.

Sometimes, I hear from Dr. Dechaine when she thinks she has identified herself in a television soundtrack or video game, but she is never quite sure. She still sings, of course, but she is always looking over her shoulder, haunted by the life her own voice is living outside her, a vehicle driven by anyone who pays for a license. It is not a ghost but an echo in the machine, gone out of her control. Her feelings are complex, though, and she acknowledges the potential for a kind of immortality. Michal Grover-Friedlander suggests that "sound recordings, at times, are voices surviving the body that once produced them; invisible and devoid of body, the singer is somehow there in the presence of voice" (Grover-Friedlander 2005: 36). But sampling libraries like *Voices of Rapture* offer something beyond the possibilities of simple recording. "I like certain aspects of this project," Dr. Dechaine says; "I like that long after I am too old to sing, I can still use my voice and so can my kids." If *Voices of Rapture* were to persist long enough, it is conceivable that the vibrations of her raptured voice might be actively singing for years after her death, an echo of the voice *within* her reverberating among the stones *without* her. And like the nymph's voice, like the little mermaid's, it may be sounded and resounded however and wherever it is made to in the future. Her multivocality is, in fact, temporally distorted. She is in control of her vocality within the customary temporal framework of singing, where she can make choices as time progresses, but she cannot control it as it is manipulated in compositions borrowing from the library, beyond the choices she made and was coached to make during a Bay Area studio one weekend. Hers is a multivocality that stretches time and space.

Stolen Voices

The Walt Disney Company, in August 2013, held an online singing contest titled "Find Your Voice."[2] The competition invited fans who were registered as

---

[2] I wrote similarly on this topic in Meizel 2019, as well.

members of the website Disney.com to submit a video covering one of three songs from the 1989 Disney animated film *The Little Mermaid* (see figure 7.1). It was the site's "Disney Princess" page that hosted the contest and displayed the winning entries, and eight out of the ten videos awarded came from girls and young women between the ages of 4 and 21. The animated film is, of course, girl-centric, presenting the struggle of a teenaged (mer-)girl toward her goals of love and adventure outside of her familiar world, as well as sexual and social maturity—concerns certainly intimately familiar for youngsters in the film's audience. Six of the winning submissions offered covers of "Part of Your World," the ballad that introduces mermaid Ariel's personality and goals—the goals in pursuit of which she gives up and then regains her voice.

The Little Mermaid's continued success today, after more than twenty-five years, is not only owed to the universals of adolescence but also to longstanding discourses about singing voices and identity in western literature and cinema. As this book has discussed, the search for a voice indicates, even demands, a precedent loss. As the response to Lyrebird shows, western culture has often explored the hypothetical implications of voice control by external forces. In one of this notion's most common literary iterations, an individual's material voice is controlled by another person and, with it, their agency. This imagined

Figure 7.1 Still from *The Little Mermaid* (Disney, 1989) as Ariel signs away her voice. (An audience member at my panel noted that the scroll looks strikingly similar to the contract a young musician might sign before a label takes control.)

situation highlights another kind of multivocality—not entirely dissimilar to the impersonations discussed in chapter 3, but in the extreme. And in the context of cinema, it is women's voices that have been most coveted, most often stolen, most often lost. They are understood to hold, as Jennifer Fleeger has argued, dangerously seductive power over men (Fleeger 2014: 12), and thus a site where cultural anxieties about morality and the erotic can be inscribed. If an audience feels that a voice and body are "mismatched," Fleeger writes, as in the case of Susan Boyle on *Britain's Got Talent* or the prodigious young soprano Deanna Durbin in the 1930s—the kind of disjuncture also discussed in chapter 3 of this book—singers have often been pressed for proof that their voices belong to their bodies. This is not unrelated to the disability-studies concept of *biocertification* (Samuels 2014): the demand that disabled people must provide scientific evidence of their disability to earn belief (a tenet applied especially to women with invisible illnesses). Here, I examine some lost voices in the medium of film.

Acquired Voicelessness in Film History

The early years of the film industry thrived on silenced voices, and directors and producers were captivated by the simultaneous substance and insubstantiality of vocality. Oddly, though silent film inherently unvoiced singers, the blatantly performed drama of opera—which Paul Fryer calls "the semaphore art form" (Fryer 2005: 3)—became one of the most beloved sources for cinema. When film emerged in the early 20th century, it entered the vogue for interplay between popular literature and theater. For example, *The Girl of the Golden West* was first known as a play in 1905, then as an opera in 1910, then as a novel in 1911, and finally as a 1915 film. In 1915, Cecil B. DeMille created cinematizations of several operatic sources, including *Carmen*. Operatically trained performers like Geraldine Farrar were well versed in the broadly visible and emotionally specialized gestures of the Delsarte method of dramatic expression, very suitable to the needs of the silent screen. And, as surprising as it might seem from a 21st-century perspective, Michel Chion suggests that audiences who watched singers silently perform onscreen enjoyed the experience for its encouragement of "dreaming" (Chion 1999: 9). Still, given a medium in which all voices were equally heard in their equal silence, stories of voice loss were perhaps inevitable.

The theme grew popular beginning in 1915, with two films that capitalized on the fin-de-siècle mania for George du Maurier's 1894 novel *Trilby*. The eponymous Maurice Tourneur film[3] and Frank Crane's *The Stolen Voice* built on the

---

[3] Published in 1894 as a serial in *Harper's Monthly*, then as a novel in 1899.

novel and the Paul Potter dramatization that followed it. In *Trilby*, the nefarious Jewish hypnotist character is (metaphorically) enthralled by the voice of a French-Irish grisette (Trilby) who is a captivating singer, aside from her inability to carry a tune. Through a process like mesmerism on Svengali's part, she is (actually) enthralled and becomes the most beloved touring singer of her time. Trilby is portrayed as an ultimate naïve, who works as an artist's model without realizing the moral implications of such nudity until someone tells her. Svengali hooks Trilby by curing her dreadful recurring headache through hypnosis, so that she ends up trading the loss of control effected by her illness for the cession of her agency to Svengali. While she is controlled by Svengali, she is unaware of her actions, including the act of singing. As Jennifer Fleeger remarks, in the book testimony is included by "real composers and skillful fictional characters" seeking to identify a physiological source for Trilby's virtuosity (Fleeger 2014: 15). They little imagine that the source is less physiological than metaphysical, and lies in another body entirely. But when Svengali suddenly dies, weakened by his literal abuse of power, Trilby's voice loss is just as sudden and as complete. She only finds it again when, soon after, she herself dies.

From a distance, it seems that the story is about voice that is *given*, rather than stolen, but at its heart it is a story in which a woman's wild and out-of-control voice is subdued by a man, who controls it so that it meets a particular social standard of beauty and market value. Fleeger also suggests that the gendered cultural anxieties reflected in Trilby's story are intertwined with the drastic novelty of the phonograph, and the heretofore unknown implications of recorded sound's disembodied voices on the way embodied voices developed (Fleeger 2014: 1 and 18).

The other 1915 film on this topic, *The Stolen Voice*, functions as a kind of reverse-*Trilby* (it was also co-written by an actor in that film). This time, Svengali's victim is a man, deprived of his voice and his lover by the evil hypnotist, and only able to sing again at Svengali's sudden death. The singers in *Trilby* and *The Stolen Voice* are only instruments of Svengali, who is himself an unsuccessful singer (Coll 2010). In the novel, in his Victorian context, as a Jewish man he is only allowed to dominate a particularly weak non-Jewish woman (it is noted in the book that he had tried and failed to hypnotize a Jewish woman, as even a Jewish woman is stronger than this emasculated depiction of Jewish manhood). French director Tourneur's American film, which opened after a major influx of Jewish refugees from World War I, replaces du Maurier's anxieties about the invasion of British culture with worries about the threat to white American culture by foreign influences. Significantly, in 1915, D.W. Griffith's *The Birth of a Nation* was also released—wherein a girl symbolizes "both the culture being contested and the promise of a new world"—as well as *A Girl of Yesterday*, whose star Mary Pickford preserved older modes of femininity against encroaching modern trends (Driscoll 2008: 16–17). The voices of girls, as imagined and manipulated by the male minds of the early film industry, became embodiments of conservative American culture.

As synchronous sound entered the picture and young women's voices were no longer literally silenced, they provided less suitable victims. Instead, cinema moved on to silencing them in the context of moral warning. In sounded stories, voice loss became a fateful punishment dealt to women for errors of principle, for wandering from certain socially paved paths. Louise Dresser plays opera singer Marie de Nardi in *The Goose Woman* (1925), made voiceless after the birth of her illegitimate son. The film opens twenty years later, as she is nostalgically looking through reviews and photos of her days in the spotlight; one headline, dated 1902, is shown to the audience: "Great Artist Will Never Sing Again: Marie De Nardi Sacrifices Voice for Motherhood." Viewers learn that after her sin and her loss of voice, she had changed her name in shame, moved to the country to raise geese, became an alcoholic (during Prohibition), and began listening obsessively to a particular cylinder recording of her own vanished voice. Her son breaks the cylinder by accident, and she throws him out of her house. "Wasn't it enough to break my voice—" she cries, "without smashing my last record of it?" She tries to reenter the spotlight by lying about witnessing a murder,[4] and gets her son arrested. She does not sing again. She is a woman who has sinned and has lost her self-control, and her voice loss is penance.

During the Depression and just before the United States entered the Second World War—a time that demanded a drastic reconfiguration of women's social roles—*A Little Bit of Heaven* offered a fresh vision of the dangers of fame. Gloria Jean is Midge in the movie, a tweenaged girl from New York whose shocking rise to fame as a soprano causes tension among her Irish working-class family. The sins in this story are actually her relatives' as they begin to spend the money she earns without thought, and they excise old friends from their lives. Midge, infuriated, pretends she has lost her voice to teach them a lesson and to convince them to return to their former values. Voice loss here serves as a strategy—and it is truly her family that loses her voice—to rebalance the moral scales.

Films about women's voice loss seem to have faded for some time after the Second World War. One striking exception is the noir feature *A Woman's Secret* (directed by Nicholas Ray, 1949), in which a singer's loss of voice unhinges her and leads her (she claims) to attempt murder. Marian, played by Maureen O'Hara, gives up her singing career after an illness robs her of her talent; thereafter, she makes the decision to manage an ambitious ingénue, Susan (played by Gloria Grahame). Susan, from the religious crucible Azusa, California, is at

---

[4] *The Goose Woman* was inspired by an actual contemporary murder.

first naïve, but by the time she is shot, she has become a kind of femme fatale in her own right, fighting to escape Marian's clutches. In a way, the film gives a new angle to du Maurier's old story; Svengali is replaced by Marian, who selects Susan as her surrogate voice. But when Susan slips out of her control, Marian supposedly feels that she must silence that voice. (It is revealed at the film's end that Marian's confession was false, and that the gunshot that killed Susan was accidental.) Curiously, in the source novel, *Mortgage on Life*,[5] it is Marian's looks rather than her voice that desert her; the film, where an actress's looks sell the picture, perhaps required the other narrative.

The theme of women's voice loss did not entirely disappear from film. A renaissance of sorts occurred in the 1990s (perhaps coincidentally, or not, after Disney's 1989 *The Little Mermaid*) and early 2000s, in the same years that saw the emergence of "postfeminist" cultural studies, riot grrl culture, Mary Pipher's *Reviving Ophelia* (1994), and the Spice Girls' "girl power." *The Little Mermaid* also initiated what Cassandra Stover has termed a "'New Wave' of princess films," in which the teenaged girl and her voice embody feminist ideals, striving to leave pre-feminist culture behind (Stover 2013: 3–4). Late-90s psychologists discussed adolescence as a crisis of voice (Gilligan 1997), an age when girls in face specific social pressures and choices about agency, speaking, and silence. The 1999 novel *Speak*, by Laurie Halse Anderson, became standard high school reading, and it addressed the silencing effects of sexual assault. A deluge of movies about teen girl singers followed on the heels of these revelations, at the same time that a great enthusiasm for singing swept the world. The *Idol* shows launched in the U.K. in 2001 and a flood of vocal-centric television programming that followed has still not faded (and *American Idol* returned in 2018). *American Idol* produced three young female winners and an assortment of teen-girl finalists, and galvanized new generation of aspiring pop stars. Simon Cowell, the foreign (British) force behind the *Idol* and *X Factor* formats, is frequently casually referred to as a "Svengali" in the press (for example, Hogan 2013); even marketing theorists have adopted the habit (Hackley et al. 2012).

American pop idols have contributed their voices to this conversation, as well. Before pop sensation Beyoncé asserted that girls "Run the World," she recorded a freshly written dramatic ballad added to the score of the film *Dreamgirls* (2006). In character as Deena Jones (modeled on Diana Ross), she escapes her manager's strict control. She sings to him: "I followed the voice you think you gave to me / But now I gotta find my own."[6] Though she has not lost her sonic voice, Deena

---

[5] Published serially in *Collier's* in 1946 as "The Long Denial."
[6] "Listen" was composed by Henry Krieger, Scott Cutler, and Anne Preven, with contributions by Beyoncé Knowles.

feels that her Svengali-like manager has suppressed it, along with her sense of individual expression.

A string of films throughout the 20th and 21st centuries reiterate and reconfigure the mythological narratives of voice loss mentioned in the previous section. In a common trope, a young woman—a singer—departs her home and family with the hope of advancing her economic station; she loses her voice because of supernatural intervention and/or a life-altering trauma, and must attempt to find it again in the experience of love, faith, and/or a return to her moral values. In part, this trope recalls Sigmund Freud's first case study of "Dora" (Ida Bauer), whose attacks of coughing and aphonia (loss of voice) Freud declared psychogenic, grounded in her feelings about her father's relationship with "Frau K" and the sexual advances of the husband "Herr K" toward Ida herself (Freud 2001[1901–1905]). In film, the aphonia is often similarly associated with family relationships and/or sexual trauma, or trauma otherwise attached to sexuality.

In *Raise Your Voice* (2004), a young singer named Terri is unable to sing following the death of her brother, until her mother and aunt send her to a Los Angeles summer camp to find her lost voice. In *Hounddog* (2007), set in the 1950s, a young white girl escapes from her abusive home life by listening to and singing along with Elvis Presley's songs. After she is raped, her friend, an African American religious snake-handler, helps her to find her voice and sing again. In the television movie *Pure Country 2: The Gift* (2010), a baby is given a beautiful singing voice by angels, with a moral caveat, which she breaks as a young woman. She must make moral amends to regain her voice.

Many voice-loss stories in film, like *Raise Your Voice*, position stardom and capitalism as threats to morality, reworking the American Dream myths familiar from Hollywood's golden age. Others, such as the 2010 film *Pure Country 2*—in which angels literally gift singer Bobbie Thomas a beautiful voice that she may only keep if she fulfills a set of moral obligations—plainly evoke the Christian morality of Andersen's original "Little Mermaid." Readers are not privileged to witness that mermaid's final achievement of her immortal soul, after she has lost her voice, experienced the pain of walking on her own two feet, and given her life for the man she loves. This is what, to Andersen, it means to become a woman. In *Hounddog* (2007), protagonist Lewellen finds an emotional escape from her abusive home life through Elvis Presley's songs. After she is raped by a local teenager, it takes the guidance of her friend Charles, a religious snake-handler, to help her find her voice and sing again (*Hounddog*, 2007) Lewellen's journey to find her voice again involves harassment by serpents—those biblical pushers of feminine knowledge—as does that of Andersen's protagonist. But Lewellen is also special, like Terri and Bobbie; the sea-witch asks for the mermaid's voice in payment for the commodity of humanity because she sings the most beautifully. In the Disney film, the villainess actually sings using the appropriated voice, transforming herself into a paragon of human beauty and effectively controlling her rival's identity. At the end of Andersen's story, the little mermaid not only regains a sounding voice but also has earned a better one than she had before, one that matches those of the daughters of the air: "so lovely and so melodious that no human music could reproduce it" (Andersen 1983[1837]).

The little mermaid, though, is only one thread in the tapestry; today's tales of girls' voices weave together several crucial cultural themes, particularly: (1) the metaphorical/metaphysical location of individuality and agency in the voice; (2) the related idea that the voicing of difference can serve as an affirmative utterance of individuality; (3) the idea that a voice is the central locus of identity, but though *in* the body, is not quite *of* the body—spiritual enough, separate enough to be stolen, replaced, or even transplanted into another body.

In *Pure Country 2: The Gift*, as in *A Little Bit of Heaven* (2012), the loss of voice is brought about through the dangerous abuse of fame, when Bobbie (Katrina Elam) gives in to the allure of money, neglecting, faith, family, and the Shakespearean directive to be true to herself. Losing control of her voice, really of her identity, is presented as a critical sign of weakness. In this mostly unrelated sequel to the 1992 George Strait film *Pure Country*, the singer is gifted her voice as a baby by two angels who are in charge of cartoonishly squealing balls of light, which they identify as character attributes—including one they note as a beautiful voice. They send this particular ball of light careening down to Bobbie as she comes into the world. After her mother's death, Bobbie, who is white, is raised by a single Black woman and grows up singing in a Black Kentucky church. Aunt Ella, her adoptive mother, repeats to her frequently the mandate the angels included as conditions of the vocal gift: she must not lie, she must be fair, and she must never break a promise. Bobbie becomes a country singer, and she inevitably fails all the conditions: she lies to obtain a job, she leaves her band and her friends for the temptation of a solo contract, and she breaks a promise to her estranged father. The gift, her voice, is revoked by the angels. In a dramatic twist, doctors discover a congenital deformity in her larynx, and they tell her that she should never have been able to sing in the first place. Later, as Aunt Ella dies, she convinces Bobbie to make amends. Bobbie moves on to work with disabled children and horses, and learns once again to sing "from her heart." All of her good deeds move the angels, and in the middle of a hoarse performance for her clients, her voice is suddenly restored. Like Andersen's little mermaid, she has earned an even more beautiful voice through sacrifice and morality.

Global Voice Loss

The abovementioned movies are American, but the theme of women's voice loss has circumnavigated the globe. The Bollywood flop *Gazal* (1964) follows singer Naaz, whose suitor falls in love with her voice. She loses that voice in her fright when they are surprised mid-rendezvous by her father, and she only sings again when she is allowed to marry the man she loves. Another Indian film, *Dance of the Wind* (1998), tells the story of Pallavi, who, like her mother, sings Hindustani music; she loses her voice following her mother's death and is aided in her search to reclaim it by her mother's guru and by a little girl he teaches. An opera singer in *Sonata* (2013, by Peque Gallaga and Lore Reyes, renowned directors in the Philippines) loses her voice, returns to her home province of Negros Occidental, and in the filmmakers' words, "rediscovers her life" by connecting with a young boy there (Ventura 2013). The less fortunate opera singer in *The Voice Thief* (a 2013 short film by surrealist director Adan Jodorowsky) is strangled by her husband and her voice is destroyed, so she must comb Miami for a supernatural replacement.

The Iraqi/Belgian short film *The Lost Voice* (2013, directed by Bavi Yassin) traces the fictional journey of Salma Jasm (played by Darina al-Joundi), a renowned Iraqi singer who loses her voice as a refugee in Belgium. While living a refugee facility, she rarely speaks and never sings (the first nearly three minutes of the film contain no speech or song at all). She is befriended by a young man, Hassan (Muhamad Muktar), who seems to care for her. He buys her a cassette player, and as she listens to her acousmatic voice from an old recording, he suddenly attacks her. It is revealed that Salma had, during her long and successful career, sung for and been friendly with dictator Saddam Hussein. "We were dying for thirty years, and you just sang your songs," he spits at her. In a voiceover as the film ends, Salma explains, "Yes, I went along, but only to sing. I wanted to sing with my soul. Not with words, nor with music. Nothing mattered, except this singing. Only this singing." Director Bavi Yassin includes a note to viewers:

> From 1979 to 2003 Saddam Hoesein [sic] ruled over Iraq as a dictator. During his reign many artists were active in support of his dictatorial Ba'th Regime. Some of these artists participated willingly, some were forced to do so. Others were prepared to do anything to make their dreams come true. All those artists today are lost voices. (Bavi Yassin, *The Lost Voice*, Flanders Image 2013)

In *The Lost Voice*, it is implied that Salma is left without a home, without agency in her life, in cosmic punishment for her transgressions in sacrificing ethics for the sake of her art. This is not so far from the situation in *Trilby*, though du Maurier perhaps shows a great deal more sympathy for her than Yassin does for Salma.

Why Are Singing Voices Lost?

By the time these films emerged in the late 20th and early 21st centuries, singing had come to be heard as a predominantly feminine attribute. In 1989 (the same year Disney's *The Little Mermaid* premiered), J. Terry Gates outlined the gendered practices of American public singing beginning in the 18th century, arguing that as women gradually took on traditionally male social roles, they also began to dominate public singing as well (Gates 1989). In schools, Gates wrote, girls and boys joined choir in equal numbers in the 1930s, but after the upheaval of the following years that sent young men to war and women to work, singing came to be understood as a woman's pastime. Gates also worried that women's adoption of male values—such as an enthusiasm for public singing—would paradoxically lead to an eventual decline in women's singing: because men had become disinterested in singing, women would follow suit.

In her 1998 book *Frock Rock*, Mavis Bayton observes the prominence of women vocalists (rather than instrumentalists) in popular music—technologies such as electric guitar conventionally belong to men, while the feminine voice is seen, theoretically, as the only instrument that *only* a woman has. Since women's bodies are viewed as desirable in popular music, and the voice resides *in* those bodies, women are allowed to sing, even expected to do so (Bayton 1999). Women's bodies are also often expected to dance, even while singing—a test that has frequently led to lip-syncing and attendant scandals about liveness and authenticity. In lip-syncing and the much-maligned guiding tracks commonly used by dancing singers, a technological Svengali replaces a woman's voice with a more perfect simulacrum of her own. The bottom line is that if women's bodies must be policed, then their singing voices must be, as well. And if women want to recover and affirm their *own* control of their bodies, finding a singing voice onscreen meets is an effective mode of resistance.

Conclusions

Importantly, though the little mermaid surrenders all vocal communication, none of her cinematic daughters seems to lose the ability to speak. Marie de Nardi shouts at her son; Marian argues with her protégé; Bobbie talks with her dying Aunt Ella; Terri's cessation of singing is self-imposed; Lewellen is subdued but still speaks when she is spoken to. This pattern suggests the question of why women's singing voices are so often silenced onscreen, rather than their speech. The loss of a singing voice, onscreen, produces a kind of vocality in negative.

If there is anything to learn from the history of lost voices in film, it is that a woman's voice sounds in, and is silenced within, discourses about gender and agency. Onscreen, the singing voice has symbolized the vulnerability of identity and its susceptibility to manipulation. It has embodied the *declaration* of identity and has functioned as the seat of individual will. Entangled with 20th-century power structures, the lost voice, which once, like the little mermaid's, could only be regained through death and transfiguration, has become a found voice that resists tampering by external forces. Today, women singers onscreen are responsible for their own voices—are charged with withstanding corruption by fame and wealth, by shady music producers, by peer pressure, by men. The story of Nichole Dechaine's voice, and of films dealing with the loss and rediscovery of voices, serves as a reminder that control—*power*—and sound are intimately intertwined and dialectically constitutive in vocality.

It's noteworthy that recent protest culture, on and off the screen, has been suffused with the little mermaid's legacy, invoking the misogynistic, colonialist, and racist control of material and agentive voices. Social-media photographs of signs carried at the Women's March rallies in early 2017 included several with variations on the words "I'm not the little mermaid—you can't take away my voice" (see figure 7.2), and a T-shirt sold by internet celebrity Chris Crocker

Figure 7.2 Signs at the Women's March in Olympia, Washington. Photo by Madison Irizarry. Used with permission.

the week before the march proclaimed the same, with his customary signature "bitch" added for emphasis. In May, education scholar Jamila Lyiscott noted in an essay on decolonizing pedagogy that students of color, in order to benefit from the educational opportunities offered by and for white Americans, are expected to suppress any culturally specific modes of speech in favor of the language—and, really, the voice—of white institutions. In "The Little Mermaid," she wrote, "the protagonist is offered access to a desirable world by the sea witch only if she is willing to give up her voice in exchange" (Lyiscott 2017: n.p.). Global discourse about agency has grown into the 21st century entwined with the same brand of morality to which Hans Christian Andersen subscribed, offering millions the same Hobson's choice the mermaid must accept.

8
Lost Voices

> "But if you take my voice," said the little mermaid, "what will be left to me?"
>
> —Hans Christian Andersen, *The Little Mermaid*

When I was 16, I left my family for the first time to go to a summer arts camp. At night in my narrow dorm room, I began to have a recurring nightmare in which I was murdered. That wasn't the scary part, though. It was that dream-me understood I was dead, but my family wouldn't believe me, so I tried to stay with them and live my life as I nevertheless slipped away, little by little. *I think I've died*, I told my family, but they wouldn't believe me. After a while, I would realize that my parents and sister couldn't see me anymore. For a while things went on in a sort of facsimile of normality, but one day in the dream I realized that while my mother, my father, my sister could still see me, they'd stopped hearing me—first, my singing voice, then my speaking voice. I felt unmoored, somehow existing and not-existing in air that felt like water, horrified as my voice made no sound, and then I eventually faded into nothing. When I was 20 and at college, the dream came true.

At least it was the truth I lived, for nearly a decade, as a then-undiagnosed connective-tissue disorder pulled me apart from the self I thought was mine, and I fought to adapt and to be believed. And I lost my voice. Or maybe more accurately, I held onto it desperately as it fell away from me in slow motion. It took years for me to let it go, and then years after that to *let it go*. I wasn't exactly silenced. My vocal cords are fundamentally fine, have never been anything other than fine, while my body grew less and less able to compel them to produce a consistent sound. I had no trouble speaking, though others, including my family, constantly asked me to repeat myself at a higher volume. I could make singing sounds, but I could no longer trust the voice that emerged from my body, alien and outside of me, each time I opened my mouth. I had far less power than necessary over the multiple sets of muscles involved in singing, and their weakness compounded the problem. Even after I had a diagnosis and medical treatment, I still didn't have much stamina, and I couldn't shake the feeling that no one could hear me. I was living with an unwanted multivocality: the voice *before* and the voice *after*, one I nostalgically idealized in my head and struggled to return to, and one hated voice in which resided all the fear and shame of *unhealth* (Osseo-Asare 2018: 50; also see chapter 1 of this book). Singing, in the end, came to feel like a form of self-torture. When I told my teacher that I thought I needed to stop, her response was almost horrified. "You won't feel like you anymore," she warned. And I didn't.

I found the psychological trauma of my voice loss baffling and embarrassing, when I knew others who had dealt with severe dysphonias, even resulting from thyroid cancer, stoically. Those individuals had incurred real losses of voice, I told myself, unable to *speak* the way they wanted to, let alone sing, and mine was nothing in comparison. But in my research over the past few years, I have encountered a number of singers with experience in losing a *singing* voice without a loss of speech. I've heard their borderlands-voices, consistently, tell of crossings—between geographical spaces, between ways of singing, between ways of being. Chapter 4 of this book discussed T. L. Forsberg's voice loss as she tried to negotiate the Deaf and Hearing aspects of her identity and song and sign. Joshua Klipp and Simon De Voil, in chapter 6, experienced a kind of double voice loss in the process of affirming masculine identities—a temporary loss of range and flexibility, and a permanent loss of their pre-transition sonorities. This present chapter includes a voice lost in a silencing marriage, the voice of a Syrian refugee who could not sing for a year after she immigrated to the United States, and a voice lost in the crossing of both the Atlantic and the musical borders between genres. Finally, it discusses the work of a singer-songwriter/ activist who is attempting to give chronically ill singers like herself back their sense of voice, in the face of epistemic injustice. Nearly all of these individuals are singing again now, having experienced voice as a part of the self that can be both lost and found—sometimes at the same time. Like me, they did not lose all phonation or the capability of speech but, rather, they lost another kind of *voice control*, required to produce both the broad and the delicate sonic strokes that make up a singing style. The experience of loss when a professional singing voice is disrupted is entangled not only in the expressive and embodied nature of vocality but also in neoliberalism, in which labor and its value are understood as core components of identity. In a neoliberally grounded music industry, losing a voice can feel like losing one's value, and like a devastating loss of identity. Additionally, voice loss is often understood as a health-related deficit, and health in a neoliberal society can become a kind of moral imperative. As David T. Mitchell and Sharon Snyder assert, in neoliberalism "nearly all bodies" are sites continuously in need of improvement, and "are referenced as debilitated and in need of market commodities to shore up their . . . shortcomings" (Mitchell and Snyder 2015: 12). "[I]ncapacity," they write, "has become an increasingly fluid, shorthand term for individual citizens' responsibilities within biopolitics for their own body management" (12). If singers don't protect their voices, they have failed as commodities, but as neoliberal subjects, they must continue striving to improve.

In this chapter, I suggest that *control* is where the material voice (physiological and acoustic) and the metaphorical voice (embodying agency) intersect in the experiences of singers, and that the crossing of borders creates sites of instability where this control is particularly challenged. I've learned that in many lives, voice and agency are so tightly intertwined that a break in one may be felt as a break in the other. Those who experience trauma or another intensive impact on their sense of identity may find themselves unable to sing; and in a vicious cycle, those who suddenly cannot sing may feel a loss of self. The singing voice, for those who depend upon it, serves as an ontological and epistemological crucible. As such, singing is often thought to communicate a more fully authentic self than speech, and to forge more intimate relationships with others. So, when a voice escapes control, the failure can seem catastrophically total.

The chapter also juxtaposes the ideas of ability and disability that pervade western understandings of music, and that intersect in the borderscape of voice. Western classical and capitalist frameworks—and the popular-music discourses they have impacted—position musical ability as rare and valuable, as extraordinary, as *extra*. It is something not required, not expected, and that is cultivated in places and in ways that exclude many. Vocal ability, as supremely embodied, is given its own distinct character, though, it is simultaneously understood as universal ("everyone can sing") and as exceptional (only a few are marketable). Disability is also perceived as simultaneously universal and exceptional—something that happens to everyone, especially if the individual is fortunate enough to survive to old age, but at the same time pushed aside, along with the people who experience it, into the margins. Thus ability and disability are both, in overlapping and discrete ways, stories about people seen as exceptional, who may or may not be allowed a place in the space of musical labor. Laurie Stras (2006) has argued compellingly for the integration of the social and medical models of disability in the study of "damaged" voices, whose perceived flaws are rejected in some musical contexts but assigned certain aesthetic value in others—and therefore may disrupt the lives and careers of some singers, while adding to the celebrated individuality of others. A voice with a pathology identified in the medical model may or may not cause functional impairment or socially constructed disability for the singer. "In the case of the voice," she writes, "the significance of vocal disruption or damage to an individual will be in proportion to his or her reliance on vocal function for daily activity, and the more significant it is, the more disabled that person may be seen to be if afflicted by vocal pathology" (174). The experiences recounted in this chapter serve as examples of disabling voice loss, or as intertwined with particularly gendered ideas about ability.

Crossing 1: Life Stages

California jazz singer Sandy Cummings grew up in a house where children were to be seen and not heard. She says that outside her house, as a New York kid, her speaking voice developed a stridence, but she felt that no one heard her at all—until she started singing. She knew that singing could project a different part of a person's character from speaking; her mother, too, "spoke harshly" but "sang softly." And Ms. Cummings was able to express her gender identity differently, too: "People listened to me when I was singing," she says, and she was able to "become all those things I imagine[d] I want[ed] to be—the delicate, feminine female." Listeners have been constantly amazed throughout her life that the sound they hear in her singing voice is so different from her speech. "I would never have guessed it was you [if I hadn't seen you]," they would tell her (interview, May 18, 2015).

But when she married in her 20s, her husband didn't want her singing professionally. This was one kind of loss, she says. "I felt a loss of a part of myself, but I didn't understand it to be that at the time" (she was 65 years old). She developed a vocal condition that a doctor diagnosed as "globus hystericus," telling her that all her tension was gathering in her throat and the muscles were constricting, "and the result was that I sounded kind of like—if I started to sing I started to squeak. It was the strangest thing. A note would take off on its own. It scared me." Her voice suddenly beyond her control, she didn't sing for six months, terrified of what she would hear. Eventually the tension lifted, but she didn't sing professionally again until after her husband's death many years later, when the children were grown and out of the house. In the meantime, though, she had what she calls a "nervous breakdown," and with therapy, realized that "so much of my identity is wrapped up in being a singer. It's not just *that* I sing, it's that I *am* a singer. And if I stop singing, who am I?" For Ms. Cummings, singing has a Cartesian significance—less a way of making a living than an act that *engenders living*. Her boundary crossings came with the transition from career to marriage and family, and then the grief of widowhood and an empty nest. Now, facing the advent of her 70s and the accompanying changes in her vocal ability, she tells me that she is more afraid of losing her voice than of losing her life (interview, May 18, 2015).

Ms. Cummings is not the only female singer to tell me of a silencing effect experienced through the decision to marry and raise a family. Sometimes, the silencing comes from a partner's controlling behavior, and sometimes from the need to create a steady, better-paying career to support that family. Nearly all the mothers I spoke with—especially the operatically trained—laughed about their young kids not wanting to hear them sing around the house, covering their sensitive ears at the intrusive sound. None of this is to say that the singers necessarily regretted their choices, or their relationships, or their families; it's only to underline how shifts in social role can impact both material and metaphorical voices in very real ways.

Crossing 2: Across the Pond and Back

Áine Uí Cheallaigh became a sought-after singer in the Irish *sean-nós* tradition in the 1980s and '90s, winning the celebrated Corn Uí Riada competition in 1990 and 1992. In 1995, she ventured across genre lines and soloed in *Riverdance*'s initial Dublin run before it moved to Broadway. Then she traveled the world concertizing, and returned to Broadway in 2007 to originate the role of Evleen in *The Pirate Queen*. But when I talked with her in 2014, she had not sung publicly in over a year.

Ms. Uí Cheallaigh told me that she'd always felt "most validated as a singer." It was the one thing she could count on, and it was "effortless, absolutely effortless. I could open my mouth at nine in the morning and this voice came out." She found that traditional singing suited her best, but her career did not truly begin until the end of her marriage. "I found my voice when my marriage was in tatters and breaking up, and that's when I really said, 'this is something I can have for me, and nobody can take it from me'" (interview, April 29, 2014). She remembers that she "ate, breathed, and slept" traditional singing, and that she'd proclaimed more than once, "I'd rather lose my right hand than lose my voice. And then I lost my voice."

Ms. Uí Cheallaigh recounted to me an incident seared in her memory when, during a concert, as she was "relaxing into the very last notes of the second to last bar of a song with a very big range," her voice disappeared. She whispered instead, and hoped that the audience would interpret it as an expressive choice. Then, she was fine. She got through other performances, sang in *The Pirate Queen* for a year, but on her return to Ireland she knew that something was different. On Broadway, her songs (such as *Riverdance*'s "Lift the Wings") had sat low, and she had felt pressured to sing the way Broadway singers were expected to, with a big sound and a consistent vibrato—a "warble" in her words. The brutal hours of singing didn't bother her; she'd sung for "twelve hours out of twenty-four" in her competition days. But she had traded the intimacy of *sean-nós* style for the demands of theatrical performance, and the shift in genre aesthetics was hard to unmake. Now back in Ireland, she tried to sing the way she had before, in "that pure trad [traditional] voice," but she never quite managed it. She felt that her ability to sing on pitch was weakening, and the vibrato, now involuntary, distressed her.

When we spoke, she said her decision had come after a concert for which she had been forced to choose only songs with a small range. The performance was a struggle, and she was unable to control the delicate ornamentation that characterizes *sean-nós* singing. She thought her face must have been a "picture of misery," and resolved not to sing in public again. Doctors could not identify the source of the problem, so she thought she would try not singing for a year, hoping that she'd "open her mouth and it would all be better," but she was still waiting. "It's as if I've forgotten how to sing," she told me.

Ms. Uí Cheallaigh grew up in Belfast, Northern Ireland. It was her father's home; her mother was from County Waterford in southeastern Ireland, where Ms. Uí Cheallaigh herself now lives. Though her youth intersected with the onset of the troubles in Northern Ireland, she recounts a generally apolitical upbringing. In the summers when her family traveled to her mother's home county, they spoke Irish; when they were in Belfast, they did not. In a culture of intense geographical anxieties—she explains that people whose lives, like hers, cross borders often wonder, "Where will I be buried? Where will I go in to the ground?"—she has not experienced them. She attributes this stability to her singing, and to the traditional music in both Irish and English she has learned and loved. "In my songs, I belonged everywhere," she says. Moreover, it is her voice, she believes, that kept her from having a crisis of identity; rather, it was "my unity, my unifying force." Her speaking voice never pleased her, but singing gave her a way to communicate that seemed to consistently make others happy. "When you take away my singing voice," she admits, "I have a crisis of identity left, right, and center."

Her worries are sometimes existential. She observes that "dying is a very living thing in Ireland," and the idea of it has colored her understanding of her life. "I used to say to the lads [her sons], 'when I die,' [it's] like 'I was no good as a mother, I wasn't great as a teacher, but you just write on my gravestone, Our Aine: singer'. That's it. That's it" (interview, April 29, 2014).

Crossing 3: Border Control

The first time I heard Lubana al-Quntar, she was singing with the Toledo Symphony and the National Arab Orchestra in Toledo, Ohio. The resident conductor of the Toledo orchestra, Sara Jobin, introduced her as she made her entrance, telling the audience—a theater full of local residents, including several invited refugee families—of Ms. Al-Quntar's journey from Syria to the United States, and of her official refugee status. After her arrival in the United States, Jobin continued, Ms. Al-Quntar had "lost her voice" for a time, but had found it again and would share it with us.

A few weeks later, I spoke with Ms. Al-Quntar and asked about her experience. She explained that when the war in Syria began, she had come to the United

States on vacation to attend a film festival. She and her family in Syria felt that it wasn't safe for her to return, but that the conflict would be short-lived. It wasn't. She waited a few months, she says, and the wait became a year, and then two, and she was eventually able to attain approval for refugee status. When the fighting started, her Druze family left Damascus for As-Suwayda, in southwestern Syria, near the Jordan border. They are safe there, she says, and relieved that she is far away from the bloodshed; she is sure that if she had stayed, her outspokenness would have meant detainment or death.

But the trauma of her exile left her feeling voiceless:

> I was really in complete shock. Now, when I look to the news and see my country destroyed completely, I feel like—you know, it's very, very, very difficult. I'm sitting here in a country—I'm still adapting . . . everything is strange to me, and looking to the TV and seeing [it], it's so difficult. So for the first two years I could not sing. I could not. I did not. I was—even, I forget that I am a singer. (interview, December 4, 2016)

She explained further, "I did not want to sing; I did not lose my actual voice, but I had no passion of singing. I felt like there's no meaning, anything. Why I'm singing; why is there music in life? Everything had no meaning" (interview, December 4, 2016). Gradually, though, her friends and acquaintances in the United States encouraged her to find a new focus because, she says, "I live here, but all my thoughts are there." Despite her previous success in Europe, she did not have much luck in American auditions; though she received positive feedback, the world of opera in the United States simply does not offer the level of opportunity she had encountered across the Atlantic. "Everyone is always saying America is a place for dreams to come true," she observes, "but for me it was a place where my dreams were shattered."

> So I decided to sing to help the Syrian refugees. So my voice came back, I was feeling that again, my voice now has a purpose. My singing has more value. This idea itself—"OK, I can help, I can do something with my voice"—this is my only tool, the only thing that I have to help. So that gives me energy. . . . If I can help just one family with my voice—one family living in a shelter in Lebanon or in Jordan. Just a little money to help this people, I will sing again. And this idea just gave me the energy back. (interview, December 4, 2016)

As discussed in chapter 1, Ms. Al-Quntar has experienced performance as a cultural bridge, both for herself and for those listening. Her singing voice provides a way to connect with people, a connection felt on a deeper level than typical spoken interaction. Like others with whom I've spoken, she has met audience members who feel that they *know* her from her singing, and that allows her to know them as well.

> You know, this is a very fascinating, a beautiful thing that I'm experiencing, that I always experienced when I sing—[even] before the war, since my career started. When I sing, in any concert, or in any performance, any role in opera, people cry. First I did not think about that a lot, like OK, people felt that the music was good. But now I'm more like in contact with [something] more spiritual—I see people when I sing—for example, I did a concert at Aga Khan museum in Canada.[1] I was singing Arabic actually, the Syrian traditional music and when I finished, people came to congratulate me, and some of them were crying, Canadian [people]. And they said to me, "Well, I did not understand what you were saying, but there's something in your voice, something that makes us very emotional and we felt you." And that keeps happening, every time, even in a small group. So I feel like singing, when you are very—I have this connection with people; it's so amazing, I feel like really music and singing have united people. We can be from so many different countries but we can feel, share a moment together, a moment of truth that is like true art or true feeling. And really this idea makes me—I want to sing more. I just want to have this feeling over and over again, like we are one, in our way. (interview, December 4, 2016)

Ms. Al-Quntar's sense of unity is striking. It does not emerge merely from popular platitudes that position music above politics and conflict but also speaks of a real, practical experience felt by two parties who have, each in his own way, reached across cultural lines. For Ms. Al-Quntar, singing for diasporic Arabs and North American non-Arabs becomes a strategy in negotiating her identity as a Syrian dislocated from and yet tied to the Arab world—an identity she had been negotiating for decades already as she sang across international borders.

During the time she did not sing, her voice, if not lost in terms of material functionality, was essentially lost cartographically. But, as discussed in chapter 1, she had already mapped both Arab and western aesthetics onto her voice, as a site of cultural construction. As Áine Uí Cheallaigh's experience also indicates, singers employ changing performance strategies in the navigation of geographical borders and shape the voice itself as a borderscape.

---

[1] A museum of Islamic art and heritage located in Toronto.

Crossing 4: Different Voices

Author and composer Joel Derfner, in his debut book *Swish: My Quest to Become the Gayest Person Ever and What Ended Up Happening Instead* (2009), writes of his devastation upon losing feeling in his throat during his junior year in college. An aspiring singer of Baroque music whose career prospects had seemed positive, he struggled to sing until he was told that acid reflux had caused too much damage to be reversed. He could still make sound, could speak, even produce a "pretty tone," but he lacked the sensory feedback he had relied upon while manipulating the fine muscles in his resonatory tract. Speech, he explained to me years later, only requires the kind of blunt instrument he has, but the way he wants to sing needs fine motor control. In *Swish*, he recounts with bitter humor his heartbreak, which left him waking each morning in tears, and writing "overwrought letters to my friends during the summer about how my own body was cutting me off from my destiny" (Derfner 2009: 139). Reading this, I felt a pang of experiential (and vocal) resonance. "It made me feel shackled," he told me, when I asked him about it.

> Before, I could do anything—I mean I couldn't do *anything*, I had a lot of limitations as a singer—but . . . the vessel was free, it was clear . . . and then it started to get gunk in it . . . and trapped is not the right word, but shackled I think maybe is the right word. (interview, June 7, 2014)

He apologized for his poetic words, before adding, poetically, "it's like, you know, you got your wings clipped. And I'm now very happy with the life I created with my clipped wings." However, he reflected, though his life now is better than it would have been with unclipped wings, "having wings was nice. Nice is a gross understatement. Glorious" (interview, June 7, 2014). In chapter 6, I quote Mr. Derfner describing the ecstatic sensations he experienced while singing, before his voice loss, and the feeling that his body had disappeared. The nerve damage paradoxically made him less and more aware of his body as he sang—less because of the numbness, but aware of the failure of his body to provide him with feedback in the process of shaping his voice.

I asked Mr. Derfner the same question I asked the others: *Since you've lost your voice, do you still think of yourself as "a singer"?* Unlike others, he answered no. "You sort of spend your life becoming more and more who you are. . . .I [I]t would have been impossible for me to become more and more a singer, because I don't have the resources anymore. So I'm looking at myself, looking at my identity from a different angle." However, he amended, his past identity "suffuses" more than informs his work as an author and composer. "Everything that I write is based in the fact that I'm a singer" (interview, June 7, 2014).

Crossing 5: Ability/Disability

> Chronic fatigue is the accumulation of time in the voice, an accumulation that bids fair to remove it eventually from time altogether. The arc of the voice will always drag it back down to earth, a declension that is implicit in the steepest slope of its parabola. This is why fatigue is not simply the contrary of the voice, against which the voice must strive as an alien principle and which it might hope to expunge. We may think of the fatigue that is always gathering in the voice in Sartrean terms as the way in which I transitively "exist" my body: the for-itself "loses itself in fatigue . . . in order that this in-itself may exist to the fullest" (Sartre 1984: 456).
> —Steven Connor, "The Chronopher" (2009)

Kaeley Pruitt-Hamm recalls the moment that sparked her love of singing. She was 3 years old and on the way to a birthday party in the family car, when her teenaged sister suggested a song from *The Little Mermaid*, and taught her to harmonize with the melody (so the music from the film about a lost voice helped her to find hers). Ever since, she has used her voice in the service of harmony both aural and social, singing in folk-rock bands and even co-founding a women's a cappella group at Willamette University, where she majored in conflict-resolution studies. Applying what she learned, she has worked as an advocate and lobbyist in Seattle and Washington, D.C., for multiple nonprofit organizations, including the Friends Committee on National Legislation and the Fellowship of Reconciliation.

After graduation, she worked tirelessly for progressive causes; she sang, she gave testimonials to Congress, and her voice became sought after for radio interviews. People always complimented her voice, she says, "I kind of built my identity around people saying 'Oh, you have a nice voice,' even speaking." Then, after a lifetime of unexplained recurrent health issues, she became extremely ill at the age of 25. Within two years, Ms. Pruitt Hamm was diagnosed with Ehlers-Danlos syndrome-hypermobility type (a synthesis disorder of the connective tissue type known as collagen), postural orthostatic tachycardia syndrome (a type of dysautonomia, or autonomic nervous system dysfunction), mast cell activation disorder (which impacts the behavior of a kind of cell important to the immune system), and Lyme disease (caused by the *Borrelia burgdorferi* bacterium). Now, she told me, even though there are times she cannot sing due to pain or weakness, listeners seem to locate her identity in her singing voice alone and do not hear her speech the same way they used to. When her health began to decline, she explains, "People told me, who kind of didn't know me very well, 'you know, it's so funny, when you talk I can tell you have something to say, but it's not really connecting with me. But when you sing, I really feel like your soul comes through.'" As for her own relationship with her voice, "it's complicated.... I like my voice sometimes, but sometimes I wish that I had a little more control over it" (interview, April 28, 2017).

I share the first three of Ms. Pruitt-Hamm's diagnoses, as well as a lifetime of unexplained symptoms. In the long years before anyone could tell me what was happening to me, I experienced a similar loss of voice control—not only literally but more broadly as well. When I finally had a full explanation, and felt able to speak about it, I entered a resistance movement already in progress, led by women like Ms. Pruitt-Hamm with chronic illnesses who also suffer from the chronic disbelief afforded those with hidden disabilities. The movement has been largely virtual, taking place on blogs and sites for public writing and support, such as *A Mighty Girl* and *The Mighty*, and disseminated through social media.

In 2016, in an invited piece for Stanford University's medical blog, I wrote:

> The worst experience I've ever had—worse than the most debilitating symptom—was not being believed, over and over again, for decades. It's not only fellow females who know what I mean, but it's especially endemic in our culture for women (and anyone marginalized) to be denied this way, to have our experiences invalidated in all kinds of contexts, including the medical (Meizel 2016).

Though it certainly isn't only the female-identified who experience medical marginalization, many illnesses do disproportionately affect women. As discussed by Fairweather and Rose in 2004, autoimmune diseases, for example, impact between 5 and 8 percent of the American population, and over 78 percent of those affected are women (Fairweather and Rose 2004: 2005). And illnesses that primarily impact women have tended to initially be judged as psychogenic; women whose psyches are suspected of deviance or corruption are judged at fault within the same kind of moral framework that supports restricting the bodily agency of women in other contexts. The *Journal of the American Medical Association*, in 1900, contained a description of multiple sclerosis (MS)—which impacts more women than men—as "like hysteria, common in women at puberty; a history of some moral shock often precedes both" (Eskridge 1900: 583). It was decades before the disease was disassociated from hysteria, and even in recent years some patients have reported that their early MS symptoms had been misdiagnosed as conversion disorder (Dolce 2013)—a diagnosis in which a lack of "organic" evidence is interpreted to indicate that symptoms are psychogenic. The idea of conversion disorder descended from 19th-century theories of repression, at least one of which suggested that a patient was unable to organize their psyche due to "a special moral weakness" (Janet 1907, cited in Nicholson et al. 2011: 1267).

Twentieth-century women live amid echoes of Sigmund Freud and Pierre Janet that assign blame to patients who fail to either die or recover from their illnesses. Numerous studies show that medical professionals respond differently to men's and women's experiences of pain (see Hoffman and Tarzian 2001). In 1991, Dr. Bernadine Healy coined the phrase "Yentl syndrome" to describe the different treatment women receive for heart attacks. In the 1983 musical film *Yentl*, the title character, an Orthodox Jewish woman played by Barbra Streisand, must pretend to be a young man in order to attain the education she seeks in the study of Talmud. In the context of cardiac emergency, Healy writes, women must prove that their symptoms are as serious as those a man might experience (Healy 1991). Additionally, a recent study highlighted the pervasive presence of racial bias in pain treatment (Hoffman et al. 2016).

The U.S. presidential election of 2016 has galvanized new feminist activisms. The year-long campaign was perceived by many Americans as a battle of gender, pitting an unapologetically misogynist candidate and his cohort against an unapologetic woman and her self-identifying feminist cohort. Early 2017 saw a surge in public feminist discourse and activism, notably leading millions to participate in the post-inauguration Women's March on Washington, D.C., and its "sister" marches across the United States and in cities around the world. Despite the numbers, many responses critiqued the January 21 March—for lack of inclusivity or intersectional focus, for privileging cisgender femaleness, for marginalizing women of color and people with disabilities. Marches, by definition, imply the requirement of able-bodiedness, or at least access to other appropriate modes of mobility, and march-based activism can feel exclusionary to many. Just before the event, a group calling itself "Disability March" took a cyber step to encourage activism among those who found the women's marches inaccessible. Over 3,000 participants uploaded their photos to the Disability March website, along with their reasons for virtual marching. The week following Donald Trump's inauguration, the site asserted:

> In the days since the election there have been reports of hate speech directed at the disabled. Trump has vowed to repeal the Affordable Care Act, which many disabled people and those with chronic healthcare conditions rely upon. (https://disabilitymarch.com/2016/11/15/first-blog-post/)

Kaeley Pruitt-Hamm contributed another significant effort toward accessible activism, recording an EP titled *Hi From Pillows*, from her bed. When her illness compelled her to return to her parents' home in Washington state, members of her band had sent her a microphone, and she combined it with GarageBand software to record and edit. "I vomited out the songs," she told *I'm Music* magazine (Tillman 2017), applying an illness metaphor to her creative work. The album features a track titled "Believe Her," a sharp commentary that recalls the musical and lyrical intimacy of Fiona Apple's late 1990s work. Frustrated that her illness prevented her from marching in January, Ms. Pruitt-Hamm began work on a music video for the song and released it in March 2017. She had created it "for survivors who were doubted by people in power—by doctors, insurance companies and by presidents" (Video Premiere, 2017).

She says that she had originally written "Believe Her" as the long presidential campaign came to a close. She had been thinking about the physician who had just facilitated the denial of her application for disability benefits, thinking about a man who had exploited her trust in her teens,[2] and about the practices of disbelief and silencing that had suffused public discourse for the preceding year—the silencing of women representing the Black Lives Matter movement when they interrupted a Seattle rally for Democratic-primary candidate Bernie Sanders; the light sentencing in June of Stanford University student Brock Turner, convicted on three counts of sexual assault for raping an unconscious woman; the repeated airings in October of a "leaked" 2005 conversation between presidential candidate Donald Trump and *Access Hollywood* host Billy Bush, featuring the infamous lines, "And when you're a star, they let you do it, you can do anything . . . grab them by the pussy." Though these situations took place in separate contexts, they all highlight the importance of intersectional perspective, and the inextricably intertwined co-construction of oppressive systems such as misogyny, racism, and ableism. And so does Ms. Pruitt-Hamm's song, which she says underscores how marginalized communities are denigrated in medical and political contexts as hysterical, or as overreacting, "when people in privilege can't see why they're in pain" (interview, April 28, 2017).

In May 2017, Ms. Pruitt-Hamm also co-organized a virtual music festival titled "BedFest," featuring videos submitted by musicians with chronic illnesses—all recorded from the musicians' beds. Kicked off by a live video conference call for participants, the festival drew dozens of entries by musicians, visual artists, and activists. Those who did not submit performances or artwork had the option of sending a photo in which they held a sign with the words "Believe Her," to be incorporated into a reworked video of Ms. Pruitt-Hamm's song. BedFest built on the precedent of a 2016 concert called Bedstock, where celebrity musicians played from beds to support children dealing with serious illness, who could not attend a concert venue. However, BedFest created something new in offering

---

[2] Ms. Pruitt-Hamm is careful about discussing this incident publicly, typically describing it as "a breach of my and my family's trust."

a virtual venue to *musicians* who themselves were too ill to play at a physical concert site.

Looking for a relevant activist organization to collaborate with for the event, Ms. Pruitt-Hamm settled on ME Action, a group dedicated to the support of people with myalgica encephalomyelitis (ME), also known as chronic fatigue syndrome (CFS). She was drawn to the group upon viewing a January 2017 talk online by ME Action founder, filmmaker, and TED Fellow Jennifer Brea (who is also a woman of color), titled "What Happens When You Have a Disease Doctors Can't Diagnose" (Brea 2016). Discussing the concert, Ms. Pruitt-Hamm invokes the effective artistic advocacy of activists during the early years of the HIV/AIDS epidemic, and ME Action has made the connection as well; Jennifer Brea has conducted an interview with ACT UP's Peter Staley for her site (Brea n.d.).

The diagnosis of CFS or ME is a complicated one. Patients given this diagnosis generally also have diagnoses of one or more (other) physiological illnesses, but the multiple streams of rheumatological, psychological, immunological, neurological, and endocrinological research that led to and away from them have unintentionally resulted in a muddy (mis-)informational swamp. Though some medical discourse positions it as a *discrete* disease or disorder with an organic cause—possibly viral or bacterial—it is also often seen as simply a name for a set of symptoms underlain by any of a number of potential etiologies. Additionally, it has frequently been described as a diagnosis of exclusion, and in many patients' experiences it is sometimes conflated with, overlapped by, understood as caused by, or eventually replaced with other diagnoses. When "chronic fatigue syndrome" first entered public discourse in the early 1990s, often attributed to the Epstein-Barr virus, it was quickly mocked as "yuppie flu"—classed and racialized as a disease made up by young socioeconomically mobile white people (the "millennials" of the previous generation), though evidence indicates that neither racial identity nor socioeconomic status has any bearing on susceptibility to CFS/ME (Blease et al. 2016). Surveys of British general practitioners even in the mid-2000s showed that half of the respondents (80% male) did not believe CFS was a real illness. Blease et al. note that

> This degree of scepticism towards the existence of the condition could lead to testimonial injustice because patient reports would not be seen to have a genuine medical cause. It could also lead to hermeneutical injustice because patient complaints may not be interpreted as cohering into a set of recognised symptoms, nor given meaning as clustering around CFS/ME. (Blease et al. 2016: 5)

Today, many people who have received a CFS/ME diagnosis are later re-diagnosed or given underlying diagnoses of Lyme disease, one of the

Ehlers-Danlos syndromes, mast cell disorders, autoimmune thyroid disease, and/or one of several types of dysautonomia (disorder of the autonomic nervous system). In the interest of full disclosure, I was diagnosed with CFS in the 1990s—my doctor told me it was a "garbage can diagnosis," but all he could offer me at the time. But in the 2000s I was emphatically told that I absolutely did not have CFS; instead, I was re-diagnosed at Vanderbilt University's Dysautonmia Clinic with postural orthostatic tachycardia syndrome (a kind of dysautonomia), later with the Ehlers-Danlos syndrome Type III that caused the autonomic disorder, and even later with mast cell activation disorder, which the diagnosing physician feels is the root cause of the other two.

These three disorders are now found so commonly occurring together that some researchers believe that collectively they indicate a "new, unique phenotype" (Cheung and Vadas 2015). I was told there is likely a genetic cause, though it has not yet been pinpointed. My sister's teenaged daughter also now has two of these diagnoses, and my sister has most of my symptoms, as well. We've apparently had the disorders all our lives, and thinking retrospectively, a lot of things make sense now. In our teens, we were all told by doctors that we must be faking or exaggerating when we fainted or complained of intractable pain. My family now has a hermeneutical framework with which to understand our experiences, and this has been a powerful change in our lives.

After years of disbelief and continually disabling symptoms, I was relieved to discard the name of a disorder that wasn't taken seriously. I am not at all sure, though, that all these diagnoses might not belong together, might not refer to related problems. In any case, they certainly have engendered similar experiences for millions of people worldwide, and similar struggles with belief among medical professionals. These are diseases and disorders that impact the body in comprehensive ways and cause symptoms across multiple systems—including chronic pain. Patients often must see multiple physicians in multiple specializations before the pieces are all put together to reach any kind of treatable diagnosis.

Susan Sontag wrote of the ways in which tuberculosis, cancer, and HIV/AIDS became metaphors for social ills in their historical contexts, creating severe stigma, both medical and social, for patients. Similarly, "syndrome," which in medicine refers to a set of symptoms, has in American public discourse come to encompass implications of feigning, of fad, of exaggerated self-centeredness—this is one reason why some patients with a diagnosis of chronic fatigue syndrome prefer the term "myalgic encephalomyelitis," a name that implies specific physiological impact. Anna Mollow notes the common association of "syndromes" with controversy, and with the absence of measurable physiological signs (Mollow 2006: 296n28). Peter Conrad observes about cancer that if patients move into remission, their subsequent (re)construction of self—achieved in an "active voice"—is a postcolonial process, undoing the ways in which "modernist medicine [had] claimed the body of its patient as its territory, at least for the duration of the treatment" (Conrad 2009: 187).

And it isn't only the institutions of medicine that colonize, but also the public stigmas produced by the power structures within that colonial framework and that, in turn, reinforce it. Many do not find remission. Many are dismissed by doctors, family, and friends as attention-seeking or drug-seeking, and are told their symptoms are "in your head." I was told by a physician that in order to get better, I had to *want* to get better, as if I didn't—a common form of advice based in Talcott Parsons's "sick role" theory, in which patients must negotiate a set of social benefits and obligations presented by chronic illness (Parsons 1951). And though some of these illnesses, like ME, may not directly lead to death, a 2016 study found that ME patients are six times as likely to end their own lives as those without that condition (Roberts et al. 2016). Not only the illness itself but also the loss of agency, the loss of metaphorical voice effected by medical and cultural responses to syndromes, can be deadly.

Given the silencing of women with chronic illness in the medical office, it isn't surprising that the "active voice" that leads the self in resistance might take the form of an agentive material voice—a singing voice. Ms. Pruitt-Hamm's song "Believe Her," completed just before Election Day in 2016, warns listeners to "just keep an eye on kings / so they don't play you." "This is a pattern that happens," Ms. Pruitt-Hamm explains, "And we need to think twice" when our experiences are denied by representatives of white, heteronormative male institutions. "This is the power dynamic. . . . It's not anyone's fault and it's not meant to blame anybody," she says; the problems are systemic (interview, April 28, 2017).

The systemic problems at stake include an overwhelming social demand for proof of disability. Disability studies scholar Ellen Samuels calls this requirement *biocertification*, after the body of legal documentation pertaining to identity that citizens of many countries must obtain. "The overmastering fantasy of modern disability identification," she writes, "is that disability is a knowable, obvious, and unchanging category," a fantasy that leaves disabled individuals with a "kind of bodily/textual dissonance, in which their experiences are displaced and superseded by a written authentication that palimpsestically overwrites their own bodily knowledge" (Samuels 2014: 131). Charlotte Blease, Havi Carel, and Keith Garaghty write in the *Journal of Medical Ethics* about the results of such overwriting, which they identify as deeply rooted practices of *epistemic injustice* (Blease et al. 2016). A concept put forward by Miranda Fricker, epistemic injustice indicates "a wrong done to someone specifically in their capacity as a knower" (Fricker 2007: 44). The two subtypes she describes constitute *testimonial injustice* and *hermeneutical injustice*: the former occurs when prejudice reduces the credibility of a speaker's words, and the latter when a person is disadvantaged by the lack or inaccessibility of interpretive resources, so that the individual cannot make sense of his or her own experiences. Testimonial injustice might occur when a person speaking of her or his experience as a survivor of sexual assault is met with disbelief because the speaker is a woman and assumed to be at fault for leading her assailant on, or is a man and assumed to have been a willing participant, or is transgender and assumed to have intended deception. Hermeneutical injustice, Fricker explains, might have occurred if a woman was sexually harassed before the concept of sexual harassment existed and had no way to contextualize her experience in her social framework. In the context of CFS/ME, Blease, Carel, and Garaghty argue that (1) patients' testimonies are disbelieved, and (2) the uncertain etiology of the diagnosis "translates into uncertainty about its sufferers" (Blease et al. 2016: 2).

In health care, studies have shown that gendered prejudices, among others, do impact the ways in which medical professionals respond to female chronic-pain patients (see Newton et al. 2013 for a review). Female and other marginalized populations disproportionately experience disbelief and the assignment of blame for their conditions, as well as explanations that attribute their symptoms to emotional, psychological, or psychiatric causes. It is important to note that although mental illnesses are not any less real or organic than infections, prevalent medical and public discourses nevertheless can misdirect both diagnosis and patients' feelings of stigmatization. Ms. Pruitt-Hamm recounts one of many encounters she has had with testimonial injustice, involving treatment for an illness she contracted during documentary work in Rwanda, at the age of 19.

Already sick upon her return to the United States, she began displaying neurological symptoms which, despite a high fever and blood-test results that indicated she was fighting an infection, emergency physicians interpreted as signs of mental illness. Over her protests, they sent her to a psychiatric hospital. Ms. Pruitt-Hamm's cognitive functions, speech, and writing were affected by her symptoms, as well as her short-term memory. She had no personal or family history of mental illness, and no experience with excessive drink or any drug use, and she believed that the symptoms were related to the fever. When physicians dismissed this idea, they disregarded her own knowledge of her body and of her bodily experience, resulting in testimonial epistemic injustice, which she faced again years later when her application for disability was denied.

After her release from psychiatric care, singing played a central role regaining her sense of self. She reports that, immediately following her departure, someone brought her a keyboard, and after a fumbling start, she found that though her speech and writing had been severely affected by her illness, she could surprisingly play and sing as she had before. "I kind of turned off the thinking part of my brain that was trying so hard," she recalls, "and a completely different old part of me came forward, and I was able to sing and play the piano as clearly as I used to when I was lucid." She added, reiterating her earlier statement, "So my relationship with my voice is very complicated."

I asked Ms. Pruitt-Hamm how her relationship with her voice has changed over the years, thinking of the "before" and "after" of her most severe symptoms. She replied that receiving her diagnoses "gave me more context for my own voice in a way," because she had lacked a way to hermeneutically frame her construction of self. "I was blaming myself," she says.

> And doctors were blaming me, schoolteachers were blaming me, well meaning family members were blaming me, P.E. teachers were blaming me for just being kind of a wimp and not trying hard enough, having a weak immune system, feeling—you know, complaining of pain that clearly everybody was feeling too but they were powering through it. And so finally after getting these diagnoses of hypermobility Ehlers-Danlos, and POTS and Lyme disease, I drastically changed the way that I feel about everything. I'm kind of going over my whole entire life reassessing, "Oh, wow, that's what happened." But depending on how severe my symptoms have been, I have had times when I'm completely unable to sing, unable to hold my head upright or sit upright at a piano, unable to accompany myself on instruments because of Lyme arthritis—so it has been a very interesting changing relationship with my voice the last couple years in particular. (interview, April 28, 2017)

"Believe Her" and BedFest provide virtual space for her to make her voice heard, which she indicates is "a life or death thing" (interview, April 28, 2017). Others clearly feel the same, as submissions to the event came from all over the world. Some entries consisted of photos featuring the entrant lying in bed holding a sign with the words "#BelieveHer" or "#BelieveME"—the latter a play on the abbreviation for myalgic encephalomyelitis. Some showed visual art created by a person with ME, as did many videos, and dozens of videos showcased music—particularly cover songs and original songs. The seventy-nine videos posted on YouTube originated in the United States/Puerto Rico, the U.K., Canada, Australia, Spain, Germany, Norway, Sweden, and the Netherlands, telling the stories of teenage girls and grandmothers alike. A few came from men. Nearly one hundred participants and organizers in BedFest met on a conference video call using BlueJeans Video Communications, and the artists introduced their entries and their experiences to each other. As the event took place just after the U.S. Congress passed a controversial health-care bill, some participants related their difficulties finding and paying for care. A woman who identified herself as a veteran using the Veterans Administration health-care system, recounted the multiple appointments during which doctors told her she was a hypochondriac. One submission showed a choreographed routine performed underneath bedclothes. Another came from a virtual ensemble in the U.K. called Chronic Creatives Choir, whose artist's page at the festival counted seven singers, flute, and harmonica. "The group is described there this way:

> We're a choir made up of people with chronic illnesses (most of us have ME). Although we're not well enough to join ordinary choirs, we've been able to make music together long-distance. We each record our parts at home separately, in some cases from bed. Some of us have to record in short sessions due to the illness, rather than doing the whole song at once. I then combine all the parts on the computer.[3] (https://www.bedfest.meaction.net/chronic-creatives-choir)

Kandice Dickinson, a formerly professional classical singer with ME—and, she explained, a cousin on Emily Dickinson's family tree—sang, unaccompanied, Ricky Ian Gordon's setting of the poet's "Will There Really Be a Morning?" Her BedFest artist's page paraphrased Itzhak Perlman; a perhaps apocryphal, much-repeated story has Perlman in 1995 playing a violin concerto at Lincoln Center with a broken string, and telling the audience, "Sometimes it is the artist's task to find out how much music you can still make with what remains" (http://www.itzhakperlman.com/home/news/page/5/). Dickinson was performing, she wrote, "'with what remains' of my voice" (https://www.bedfest.meaction.net/kandice-dickinson).

As Conrad et al. point out, the 21st-century development of internet communities centered around shared health conditions has shifted the experience of illness for many from private to public (Conrad et al. 2016). And just the provision of listening ears, however digitally mediated, encourages members to use their voices publicly. BedFest realizes this potential in a newly literal way, allowing people who may feel silenced by those meant to help them, and even by their loved ones, to not only speak but also sing.

The crossings discussed here underline how for singers, the processes of finding and losing a voice can be inextricably intertwined with each other and with gendered and ability-centered negotiations of agency. Ms. Cummings feels that she lost her voice when she surrendered her career plans at the request of her husband; Ms. Uí Cheallaigh recounts that she first found her voice at the end of her marriage; Ms. Al-Quntar found her voice again when she found a new sense of purpose. Mr. Derfner entered a new career, and Ms. Pruitt-Hamm had given up her ability to work full time. All these singers' losses occurred

---

[3] The artist's page does not indicate which choir member wrote the description, and the "I" is unattributed.

at or brought them to borders in their lives where decisions were made—for or by them—that led to movement across musical and social boundaries. In these situations they lost or surrendered control of their most intimate sonic selves, of their vocal lives, but were eventually set to searching again. Together, they demonstrate that singers can navigate the borderscapes of ability and disability, suppression and agency, by acknowledging and allowing their changed voices to keep sounding.

9
Final Reflections
Hear Our Voice

> My voice has a quiver.
> That's where you store the arrows
> Before you shoot
> —Jim Carroll, "The Child Within," in *Void of Course: Poems 1994–1997* (1998)

The idea of voice as agentive value has had a powerful influence in western and global politics, as well as a deeply intertwined relationship with discourse about democracy. Voice and democratic agency are imagined so closely together that in multiple languages the nouns *vote* and *voice* are indicated with the same word. (In Germanic languages: in German, *Stimme*; in Norwegian and Danish, *stemme*; in Dutch, *stemmen*; in Afrikans, *stem*; and in Yiddish *shtimen* [עמיטש]. In Slavic languages such as Russian, Polish, Belarusian, Czech, Bulgarian, Serbian, Macedonian, Slovak, Slovenian, and Bosnian, the noun *voice* forms the root of the noun *vote*—for example, in Bulgarian гласуване [vote], is grounded in глас [voice].[1] Likewise, in Bosnian, the same word, written *glas* [voice] is the basis of *glasanje* [vote].[2]) In the late 18th century, the rhetoric of nascent democracy assigned legal authority to "the people" as the true authors of a nation (Looby 1997, Zink 2009). Thus, to James Wilson, on the U.S. Supreme Court's first significant case (*Chisholm v. Georgia*, in 1793), it was the people of the United States who "spoke it [the republic] into existence" (Zink 2009: 452)—as in the Old Testament, God is said to have spoken the world into existence—offering a new Enlightenment implication for the Latin proverb *vox populi, vox Dei*. And through Johann Gottfried Herder in the late 1770s, the "voice of the people"[3] and its song, its *Volkslied*, emerged as tenets of nascent Romantic nationalism (Gibson 2015).

---

[1] *Glasnost*, a term referring to a policy of public openness, became familiar to English speakers during Mikhail Gorbachev's use in the 1980s; it ultimately derives from this root, and its predecessor, *gal* (to call), as well.
[2] In English, the word *vote* is derived from the Latin *votum*, meaning a "vow."
[3] From *Stimmen der Völker in Liedern* (*The Voice of the People in Song*), 1778–1779.

Multivocality. Katherine Meizel, Oxford University Press (2020). © Oxford University Press.
DOI: 10.1093/oso/9780190621469.001.0001

But this rhetorical voice has not been fully, meaningfully recognized in western, colonizing, capitalist cultures. To Nick Couldry, writing on what he identifies as the pressing 21st-century "crisis of voice" (see this book's introduction), voice is "the normative domain that neoliberal doctrine casts into shadow"—voices of a diversity of people pushed aside in favor of that which supports a market-centered political, social, and economic system (effectively, colonization of civil rights by the market) (Couldry 2010: 103). Nevertheless, rhetorical offers of voice constitute a common neoliberal—and also authoritarian-populist—practice. Donald Trump, advocate of a neoliberal world order, proclaimed to his followers upon his Republican nomination for the U.S. presidency, "I am your voice." On January 25, 2017, five days after his inauguration, he demonstrated exactly whose voice he wasn't when he signed an executive order that led to the establishment of the Victims of Immigration Crime Engagement, or VOICE (https://www.ice.gov/voice), as part of his administration's intensified pursuit of undocumented immigrants.

Facing renewed assaults on the agency, and even the existence, of non-white immigrants, of women, LGBTQ + people, people of color, non-Christians, and disabled people, many Americans have responded by literally raising their voices. Those voices have sounded individually and en masse, on the street, on the air, and online. Nick Couldry's model of voice is inclusive of these multiple modes: "Voice," he suggests, "requires a material form which may be *individual, collective,* or *distributed*" (Couldry 2010: 9; my emphasis). The individual form of voice retains its intersubjectivity. It must also be recognizable in a collective voice (a person must recognize his or her individual voice in a collective voice). Couldry's voice applies his concept of the "distributed" voice to internet-based political activity, considering anthropologist Jeffrey Juris's description of a network that demonstrates social reorganization "based on horizontal collaboration, participatory democracy, and coordination through autonomy and diversity" (Juris 2008: 17, cited in Couldry 2010: 102).

In the late 2000s, Americans have met a surge in political, legislative, and physical violence with a surge in the disruption of silence. There are voices at work, tirelessly calling out the interlocking racist, misogynist, homophobic, ableist structures that have fueled and enabled the continuation of oppression. When lives are in danger and legislators send quiet, safe thoughts and prayers, U.S. communities are responding with voices raised in speech, poetry, and song. They *take* to the streets and they *take* the mic and they *give* voice to those erased from the world—gagged, stifled, strangled, torn apart by bullets. They entreat each other, as survivors of the 2018 school shooting in Parkland, Florida, did, to "be the voice for those who don't have one," for those from whom all future singing was taken. Voices might waver in mourning. But then they rise.

As in previous times of American civil unrest, singing has played a prominent role in the recent multifarious resistance movements, resonating in all three of Couldry's forms of voice. Individuals have expressed their personal perspectives—the individual form. They have sung in groups toward a common goal—in a collective voice, singing *with*. And they have together created, documented, and posted networks of songs on the internet. They have sung in their own voices, and metaphorically in silenced ones—singing *for*. They have tweeted and retweeted the voices of others. This chapter presents examples of singing in two recent movements, to highlight the multivocality of 21st-century musical resistance.

Taking the Mic

The expression "taking the mic" has long served as a metaphor for agency and for declaring a shifting balance of power. It's a way of making one's voice heard. But when there's no actual mic to take, a different kind of electric current can signal, even effect, that shift in power. Political demonstrations in the 21st century have highlighted a method of address known as the "people's microphone" (also called the "human microphone" or "human megaphone"), in which an individual speaker's words are repeated by nearby listeners in the crowd to ensure that the message reaches those at the back. Though versions of the system have been in use since at least the 1970s, it has gained special currency in the United States since the Seattle World Trade Organization protests in 1999, and in the age of social media, the Occupy Wall Street movement, for which it was famously implemented in Zuccotti Park owing to the policing of electronic amplification in public spaces.

The people's microphone is not an *echo* of voices, gradually fading away in the distance. Rather, each repetitive wave of speech is meant to strengthen the message, with perhaps even more clarity than a megaphone would offer. Homay King calls the practice "less a tool than a mode of speech." She continues, "It involves a special kind of speech-act, an actualization of principles *in viva voce*"—in living voice, or in *live* voice (King 2012: 239). Furthermore, King writes, after J. L. Austin (1975), the people's microphone is a performative utterance: it enacts that which it invokes. As an example, she invokes the popular chant, "*This* is what democracy looks like" (King 2012: 239). I suggest that it is likewise the enactment of agentive political voice, one voice amplified by dozens or even hundreds more—Couldry's "distributed voice"—to form an literal "voice of the people," sounding in *viva voce*.

The increasing use of social media as a revolutionary platform has greatly extended the reach of such voices, allowing them to resound (re-sound) and resonate beyond physical sites of resistance, in cyber spaces. As Alexander Halavais and Maria Garrido argue, though some frame the analog people's microphone in *opposition* to the digital world of social media, tweets and retweets might equally be seen as *extensions* of it (Halavais and Garrido 2014: 119). And because social media is now a significant driver of music culture, it is not so surprising that in addition to speech and Twitter posts, a *song* of resistance might work in this way, as well. When a song is articulated by a singer at a demonstration, then repeated by others in progressive waves of performance around the world, encouraged and perpetuated and posted on social media, the message is transmitted for the people in the back through a kind of global people's microphone. This section discusses the envoicing power of one such song, in its dialogic iterations of voice and virtual vocality.

January 21, 2017

The event known as the Women's March on Washington, D.C., held on January 21, 2017—the day after the inauguration of the 45th U.S. president—became a global network of protests involving an estimated 4 million people in the United States and an estimated 300,000 in other countries (Chenoweth and Pressman 2017). Despite its popularity, it generated controversy from its early days. Its initial organizers were white, and the protest's original name, "Million Women March," was criticized for appropriating the previous work of Black women in a 1997 protest project; its subsequent title criticized for copying the 1963 March on Washington. The 2017 march's official platform had to be amended several times to address issues of inclusivity and especially the demand for a shift to focus on intersectional feminism, but even then many participants experienced marginalization. And many in activist communities for Black, queer, trans, disability, and sex workers' rights still felt that millions of white women who had never before protested were usurping and receiving credit for others' work (Mosthof 2017). (As of 2019, many of the "women's marches" organized around the U.S. have disassociated from the original Women's March organization.) Eventually, the 2017 project's website offered a mission statement that concluded:

> We support the advocacy and resistance movements that reflect our multiple and intersecting identities. We call on all defenders of human rights to join us.... We will not rest until women have parity and equity at all levels of leadership in society. We work peacefully while recognizing there is no true peace without justice and equity for all. (https://www.womensmarch.com/mission/)

The statement ends with this enjoinder:

HEAR OUR VOICE. (https://www.womensmarch.com/mission/)

When a plural pronoun is applied this way to the singular noun *voice*—as also in the notion of "the voice of the people"—it implies a monolithic, collective vocality. But when groups of singers come together to represent communities in protest, what is really at stake is a network of distinct multivocalities in the model developed by Bakhtin—a "communion of unmerged souls" (Bakhin 1984: 26).

#ICan'tKeepQuiet

Despite the controversy, members of marginalized communities were present and vocal at the march. Well-known speakers and singers—Angela Davis, Linda Sarsour, Janelle Monáe—took the stage throughout, but the unfamous made their own spaces to be heard, as well. On the evening of January 21, film director Alma Har'el posted a recording on social media of a flash-mob a cappella performance. She had happened upon the performance in the street, and she wrote, "These women are from different states and never met till today. They practiced this song online. I was crying the whole time I filmed this" (Har'el, on Facebook, January 21, 2017). The video became viral, with over 6 million views by the morning of January 22. Then, it was hailed as the unofficial "anthem" of the Women's March (Flores 2017), and became identified with that countermovement. It has been performed by choirs and at public gatherings around the world.

The video featured a combination of two D.C. a cappella ensembles: Capital Blend and the GW Sirens (from George Washington University); and singers from Los Angeles, led by California singer-songwriter Connie Lim under her stage name MILCK (her last name backwards, plus her first and last initials). The ensembles backed Ms. Lim, all in the handmade pink "pussy hats" that had galvanized craftivists in the month or so before the march. The women performed an arrangement of a single MILCK had written the previous year and released the week before the march, titled "Quiet." She had written the song, "Quiet," with assistance from Adrianne Gonzalez, in the process of coming to terms with an abusive situation in her past, with depression, and anorexia, and with the goal of "developing her unique voice" ("MILCK—'Quiet'" 2017). But in the context of the women's march, its meaning expanded, and it became a multivocal symbol encouraging women to make their voices heard.

In the flash mob, Ms. Lim stood with a choir of twenty-six women from Washington, D.C., and Los Angeles, with "a beautiful range of backgrounds, shapes and sizes, from the out of state 18 year old to local, working, mother of three," a student a cappella group and a professional one (https://www.icantkeepquiet.org/the-choir/). The song features the following chorus:

> I can't keep quiet, no oh oh oh oh oh oh
> I can't keep quiet, no oh oh oh oh oh oh
> A one woman riot, oh oh oh oh oh oh oh
> I can't keep quiet
> For anyone
> No, not anymore. (MILCK and AG, https://icantkeepquiet.org/song)

Though the idea of not keeping quiet, of not letting anyone keep you quiet, implicitly references the act of speaking, communicating the message through sung vocality enhances it—singing is one of the least quiet ways possible to make a point heard. The guerilla flash mob rehearsed in separate cities and by Skype. On the day of the march, they performed under the name "#icantkeepquiet choir," and partnered with the Pussy Hat Project[4] to pass out hats in the crowd when they weren't singing ("How This Song Became" 2017). After the song caught global attention, the group was invited to sing on TBS's *Full Frontal with Samantha Bee*. The song had a website to encourage its use in protest, and as requests poured in for sheet music, MILCK and company provided it. Performances taking place all over the world quickly made their way onto YouTube— notably the video featuring MILCK with 1,300 participants in a Choir!Choir!Choir! performance. Choir!Choir!Choir! is a unique organization made up of thousands of singers who attend various meetings, pay a small fee for scores, and learn and perform music together; the "Quiet" video was made on February 6, "to protest the current US administration's threatening action on global liberty, women's rights, healthcare etc." Proceeds went to support the American Civil Liberties Union ("MILCK + Choir! Of 1300 Can't Keep Quiet," posted by Choir!Choir!Choir!, https://www.youtube.com/watch?v=1cc_neVdjb4, Feburary 17, 2017). International Women's Day on March 8 sparked a new round, and MILCK designated April 8 as "icantkeepquiet Day" for further performances. Videos of "I Can't Keep Quiet" flash mobs in Sweden, the Netherlands, Switzerland, Ghana, England, New Zealand, Canada, and the United States (in English and Spanish) were passed around social media. They took place, and space, in train stations, public squares, and streetcorners. In another month, May concerts and

---

[4] One of the Pussyhat Project's co-founders, Krista Suh, is also Asian American

Figure 9.1 The #ICAN'TKEEPQUIET T-shirt.

graduations at high schools and universities, private and public, began to include the song. A new flash mob, with orchestra, took place on June 11 as part of a resistance march associated with L.A. Pride. The Icantkeepquiet.org website includes a space for women to tell their stories. Fans may buy a T-shirt (see figure 9.1) with the phrase, in which the capital letters include a "Q" replaced by the "Venus" female gender symbol ♀. Those who purchase the shirt can dress their bodies in the message, but that isn't all. On MILCK's Facebook page, a number of women have posted that they chose to be tattooed with the words "I can't keep quiet," literally inscribing vocality on their bodies. In the January 21 performance, and in the call-and-response resounding through social media and live singing, "Quiet" has grown from a performative utterance by a single voice to become aggregately more and more multivocal each time it sounds.

An Intersectional Voice

Ms. Lim has recounted how she began to use singing to navigate a youth in which she felt pressured to suppress any external evidence of her internal struggle, and not to express what her "inner voices" needed to:

> People could not notice my struggles from the outside, as I was student body president and homecoming queen. I dealt with my misfit-ness internally,

and my inner voices were literally and figuratively starving to be heard. Once I found that I could play piano and sing at the same time, I immediately started to write lyrics to the piano parts I was composing. I no longer felt trapped. I felt free, and I owed it to music. (Lim 2015)

"My voice is my freedom," she told me, in a June 2017 conversation. Before "Quiet," she had "compartmentalized" her voice; her singing voice was where she could express what she needed to when she could not access her "real-life" voice—the voice that "speaks up when something's uncomfortable, or states my truth," she explained—to do so. Singing and writing songs allowed her to "say the truths that I was afraid to say in real life." When a period of personal development occurred simultaneously with the intensifying political environment in the United States (an intersection of two "growing forces," as she put it), with "Quiet," she was able to unify her divided voices (personal communication, June 20, 2017).

One of her early successes had come in 2011 when she made the top 60 contestants in the first season of NBC's singing competition *The Voice*—a show initially titled *The Voice of America*,[5] implying that a winner's single voice would represent the nation. Reality TV singing competitions have been enjoining citizens to elect a national pop star for nearly two decades, as a new kind of "voice of the people"—a singer carrying the voices of millions. But the kind of voice offered to the voting public matters. Ms. Lim has spoken of her television experience as a frustrating one in which she was made uncomfortable when *Voice* staff overheard her doing an impression of her mother and tried to push her into doing the Chinese accent on camera (Barlow 2017).

Shortly after her stint on *The Voice*, Ms. Lim was told by a manager that as a Chinese American musician, she might be more successful with the Chinese market. She was recruited for China's version of the show, which has a practice of holding auditions not only in China but also among the Chinese diaspora. (At the time, *The Voice of China was* part of the global *Voice* franchise, though it is now separate and is called *The New Voice of China* or, in English, *Sing!China*.[6]) Ms. Lim had to suddenly shift her focus from her songwriting to learning Chinese songs. She was born in California, and her habitual vocality was based in the aesthetics of the American (especially African American) genres she heard during her musical development. She expressed her misgivings in an interview for the website Ravishly.com:

---

[5] As part of the global franchise that began with *The Voice of Holland*.
[6] My thanks to my advisee Xinxin Jiang, who has written a splendid dissertation on the show (Jiang 2018), for sharing this information with me.

> I like the opportunity to learn about my culture, but I'm not a Chinese musician in that sense. I'm a Chinese American musician. I grew up listening to blues and jazz and folk music. So that would be almost completely going a different way just because of how I look. (Gloudeman 2014)

In other words, she was uncomfortable with the idea that racialized perceptions of her body positioned her voice as most appropriate for consumption by other, similarly racialized bodies. In this way, her voice is politicized by virtue of its association with her body, and she has recognized this: "As a minority female, everything I do is inherently political" (Barlow 2017). The Women's March performance, though, positioned her body and voice at the vanguard of contemporary intersectional feminism.

When PopMatters.com previewed "Quiet" on January 13, 2017, she articulated this position:

> I finally made a song that is 100 percent undeniably, my truth. In this time of polarized politics, propaganda, and discrimination, I am saying: no. I am not a delicate, Asian flower girl that can fulfill commodified fantasies. I am not the model minority who is going to stand by and watch my brothers and sisters of color be scapegoats. I am not the girl who is going to stay a victim, even after sexual and physical abuse. I am not the woman who is going to stay quiet in this era, where there are figures of power in today's world who promote scarcity, fear, and oppression. No. I can't keep quiet. ("MILCK—'Quiet'" 2017)

She sees her status, like many musicians, as at once marginalized and, particularly because she has made a place for herself in the music industry, privileged. She gets to hold the microphone sometimes and amplify her voice. Ms. Lim further explained her individual intersectional perspective to me: "I'm an Asian American, I'm an artist, I have depression, anxiety, an eating disorder that I survived, and lived through abuse.... I was shouting out *I can't keep quiet,*" she said, "as all of these different forms of myself that have been silenced." And her voice itself—material and metaphorical—is intersectional, she said:

> almost like those Venn diagrams, where you draw one circle, it's abuse; another one eating disorders; the others, Chinese American and another an artist; and the last circle would be a woman—and I think all of those experiences come to a head at an intersection and they surge into my songwriting. (personal communication, June 20, 2017)

Deborah Wong, in her essay "The Asian American Body in Performance," remarks that "[t]he social drama of the body" is, in the 21st century, the focus of "new ideas of performativity linking corporeality and social transformation" (Wong 2000: 60). Ms. Lim's embodied voice is the site of such a social drama, suggesting that the material/corporeal and the social/metaphorical might themselves constitute dual vocalities—and once again, if vocality is a "vocal way of being," then using one's voice to both sound and transform oppressive social structures might be seen as a form of multivocality.

Singers and Political Vocality

Musicians are often positioned, or position themselves, as sociopolitical leaders. Singers, in part owing to their use of language in performance, have particular potential to act as what Seth Hague and colleagues call "truth-bearers" for causes, "authoritative and representative voices" for their fans (Hague et al. 2008: 20–21). But as Bakhtin argued, "Truth is not born nor is it to be found inside the head of an individual person, it is born *between people* collectively searching for truth, in the process of their dialogic interaction" (1984: 110). So as truth-bearers, perhaps most importantly, a singer-leader may act as a community organizer for those audiences, encouraging *their* voices in public participation—as in flash-mob experiences—or in the offer of assistance on MILCK's website for the organization of choirs and performances of "Quiet."

Ms. Lim herself feels a connection between her own intersectional voice and the voices of those who sing with her. When she sang "Quiet" with Choir!Choir!Choir! in Toronto, *her voice was both reflected and carried forward*:

> The idea of thousands of other voices singing my song is a tremendous concept, way beyond my own expectation and understanding. And I thank the universe every day for the opportunity to feel that type of energy . . . having 1300 Canadians sing the lyrics I worked so hard to create, back to me. . . . And coming up with the phrase *I can't keep quiet* really took me years to get to. I think I had been trying to express that feeling for a very long time. So I just feel really grateful and really in awe of the power of song, and I also feel like there is this confirmation that we are all more similar than we think, and that at the core of it we are all very emotionally intelligent beings who can understand each other's experiences no matter how different we are. (personal communication, June 20, 2017)

In the time since the Women's March, MILCK has gone on to release a Spanish-language version of "Quiet"; she's joined Michael Moore on Broadway and Jason Mraz on tour; and she has included "Quiet" on an EP with Atlantic Records, titled *This is Not the End*. The song continues to resonate through her own voice and others,' with women taking the mic at political rallies and online. A performative utterance ever enacting that which it invokes, this people's microphone can't keep quiet.

Raise Your Voice

On March 24, 2018, the reach of "Quiet" extended to a whole new resistance movement, when a Massachusetts high school choir sang it at the March For Our Lives in Washington, D.C. A nationwide protest led by students and supported in part by those responsible for the Women's March, the March For Our Lives was one of a series of national events after a gunman killed seventeen students at Marjory Stoneman Douglas High School in Parkland, Florida. Among the issues the young leaders of this movement raised, the capitulation of U.S. policymakers to the National Rifle Association featured prominently. Parkland survivor Emma González, in a public speech three days after the shooting, criticized President Trump for accepting $30 million in campaign contributions from the NRA. When that amount was divided by the number of gun-violence victims in the first weeks of 2018, González noted, each victim's life was worth $5,800. "To every politician who is taking donations from the NRA, shame on you," she said (González 2018: n.p.).

Studying gun-control discourse after the 2012 shooting that killed twenty-six at Sandy Hook Elementary School in Newtown, Connecticut, sociologists Luigi Esposito and Laura L. Finley pointed to the ways in which opposition to firearm policy reform is supported by, and intertwined with, neoliberal ideology. The "anti-statist individualism" that fuels much gun rights advocacy, they observed, is tied to neoliberalism's focus on competitive individualism, its rejection of "big government" interference (for example, interference in the Second Amendment right to bear arms), and thus to its prioritization of private responsibility over social justice (Esposito and Finley 2014: 75–76). In this political environment, the intersubjectivity of voice is illuminated in its use as a counter-rational tactic against such neoliberal hyperindividualism. This section of the chapter highlights the multivocality particular to a recent resistance movement, a multivocality that carries the burden of lost voices and works to move others to sound their own.

The youth movement that arose in 2018 has included memorial events, rallies, and marches to demand new policies from lawmakers, and new voices have suddenly had the world's ear. The gatherings within the United States were joined by others in solidarity around the world. Hundreds of thousands attended the National School Walkouts on March 14 and April 20, 2018, and it is estimated that more than 2 million participated in the March For Our Lives on March 24 (Sit 2018). "Never Again," proclaimed protest signs and hashtags, "Enough Is Enough."

The largest events were organized and supported by different individuals and groups—the March 14 school walkout by students along with the Women's March and the ACLU, the March For Our Lives on March 24 by Parkland students, Everytown for Gun Safety, and the Women's March, and the April 20 walkout on the anniversary of the 1999 Columbine High School shooting organized by Connecticut high school student Lane Murdock and the progressive group Indivisible. On March 14, thinking of my own university students and revisions to the week's lesson plans, I surveyed social-media posts for examples of the musical soundtrack to the gatherings. Asked to contribute a related piece to NPR's website that night (Meizel 2018b), I corralled the mass of links I'd found into five categories: (1) songs that, fifty years ago, drove the Civil Rights movement; (2) in a meta, millennial twist, recent songs that reference that fight; (3) songs about peace; (4) anthems; and (5) what I felt were among the most moving examples, original songs. The relationship between the movement against gun violence and the Civil Rights movement is multilayered, intersubjective, multivocal. The student voice—especially the Black student voice—was one of the most powerful in the Civil Rights movement, and new efforts like this one owe a great deal to the young people of color who came before. Songs associated with the earlier peak years of the Civil Rights movement, such as "We Shall Overcome," "Will the Circle Be Unbroken," "Peace Like a River," and "Amazing Grace," made multiple appearances on March 14. Hearing "We Shall Overcome" reminded me of the story activist Jamila Jones has told (Jones 2014) about that song. When she was 14 years old, she attended a Highlander Folk School meeting in Monteagle, Tennessee, that was raided by police. As law enforcement entered the venue, the Highlander group began singing "We Shall Overcome." Jones felt moved to add a new verse that declared "We are not afraid," and as she lifted her voice, an unnerved officer, shakily holding a gun, asked her, "Do you have to sing so *loud*?" At that moment, she has said, she realized the power of the movement's music (Jones 2014). That power resonates in the throats of young people fifty years later, raising their voices in the embodied political space painstakingly opened by Jones and her colleagues—in a temporal, aggregate, collective multivocality.

Initially, media coverage of the 2018 movement against gun violence neglected to include the work of many students of color, not only survivors of the Parkland shooting but also young people who had already been fighting gun violence for years in different contexts. Calls for the movement to be more inclusive led to a new focus on non-white participants in the March For Our Lives events (Johnson

2018), on the relevance of police killings of young Black men (often teenagers or younger, and students themselves), of the Black Lives Matter movement that has grown in response, and activists fighting violence in Chicago's Black community (Minutaglio 2018). The second category of songs I noted—compositions that reference the Civil Rights movement—more specifically tended to highlight the continuing struggle. For example, "Glory," a track contributed by John Legend and Common to director Ava DuVernay's 2014 film *Selma*, was performed by students at the Chattanooga School for the Arts. Though *Selma* addressed the well-known 1965 marches for voting rights, the lyrics of the song (as John Legend noted publicly at the 2015 Academy Awards) reference the 2014 protests that took place in response to the shooting of 18-year-old Michael Brown in Ferguson, Missouri, by a white police officer. Legend and Common plainly draw the connection, and remind listeners that the struggle isn't over: "That's why Rosa sat on the bus / That's why we walk through Ferguson with our hands up." Another song frequently performed at the walkouts and March For Our Lives events was Andra Day's 2015 "Rise Up," which had become an anthem in the Black Lives Matter movement. Day sang it herself at the primary Washington, D.C., March For Our Lives event, with the Cardinal Shehan children's choir. The protestors who chose to perform these songs made the important statement that Black children continue to be at risk from gun violence.

Songs about peace, love, and healing drew from multiple sources, including John Lennon's "Imagine," Michael Jackson's "Heal the World," and Jackie DeShannon's 1969 anti-war song "Put a Little Love in Your Heart." At the March 14 walkouts, primary-school children performed some songs in this category, such as "Let Peace Begin With Me," written in 1955 for the International Children's Choir, and "Prayer of the Children" by Emmy-winning composer Kurt Bestor. Bestor originally wrote the "Prayer" about the Yugoslavian civil war, though it has also been used to commemorate the deaths on September 11, 2001, the Oklahoma City Bombing, and the Columbine shootings.

The U.S. national anthem ("The Star Spangled Banner") also featured in several videos posted on March 14, including one rendition by a seventh grader in Michigan and one by a police officer supporting children who walked out of school in York, Pennsylvania. Another anthem of a kind was posted by students in Alabama, who had learned the alma mater of Marjory Stoneman Douglas High School.

The following summer, that 2018 essay gave me the opportunity to curate an album of original songs and poetry performed by students at these events. The album, produced by the nonprofit label Little Village Foundation (Jim Pugh, CEO), allows the students to retain the rights to their work. All proceeds are donated to Everytown for Gun Safety, an organization that supports victims of gun violence, advocates for firearm safety, and works toward policy reform. *Raise*

Your Voice: The Sound of Student Protest comprises eleven tracks. Most are the contributions of then–high school students, with one track written by a college freshman. From survivors of the Parkland shooting to the nephew of the principal killed at Sandy Hook Elementary School in 2012, to at-risk students attending a St. Paul school for recording arts, many of these students have been personally affected by gun violence. Some of them had already, before we contacted them, been targeted and harassed on social media for their activist work. All of the singers' protest performances were accessible online before we began work with them, but we re-recorded most (though the School for Recording Arts and one individual singer allowed us to use previously recorded tracks, and the Parkland students sent us a new version of theirs). All of the songs, the performances at protest events, and the recordings are vocal acts of courage.

We named the album *Raise Your Voice* after a track composed and performed by 16-year-old Madison Yearsley. Throughout the project, one thread stood out: almost all of the students, either in their interviews with me or in their lyrics, alluded to some sociopolitically agentive connotation of "voice." Student lyrics include the following references:

"Gonna raise up our voices so we'll never, ever fall."

"Be the voice for those who don't have one" (this line from the CNN Town Hall performance, February 21, 2018).
-"Shine" by Sawyer Garrity, 16, and Andrea Peña, 15, Parkland, Florida

"So raise your voice for the ones who can't."
-"Raise Your Voice" by Madison Yearsley, 16, Seneca Falls, New York

"We spit our words to ignite the rage/And raise our voices to fan the flames."
-"Renegades" by Amalia Fleming, 15, Morro Bay, California

"We have a voice/We have a choice. Do our differences even matter when the world is shattered?"
-"The Separation" by Ashlyn Flamer, 16, and Christopher Doleman, 17, Phenix City, Alabama

In these lyrics, voice holds people up. It fuels social fury and encourages unity in the face of violence. The students invoke both individual and collective voice, but also, significantly, point to an impulse to take the mic in order to *give* voice—to offer one's own, when voice has been permanently denied to those killed. In a way, this also implies a multivocal taking up of others' voices, carrying them and carrying on. In the album's liner notes, I quote Sawyer Garrity and Andrea Peña as wanting their listeners to know that "Shine" is "for the 17 [who were killed at Parkland], to make sure that their voices are never forgotten" (Meizel 2018a).

Some students I spoke with called attention to the importance of individual voices in resistance. Madison Yearsley suggested, "I think that people underestimate the power that their voice has, because, 'Oh, it's just one voice.' But that's how things start, that's how movements begin—it's with one voice" (interview, June 21, 2018). And 18-year-old Ben Soto feels that this is especially consequential for individuals with minority identities, like him. Living in a politically conservative area, graduating from a school struggling with racism and bigotry, he particularly wants other young people in his position to know: "your voice does matter. And you *can* get it heard—you just have to fight for it. And anything you contribute matters" (interview, July 10, 2018).

Tyler Suarez still has a pile of napkins and scraps of paper at home, fragments of the words that he and his grandfather spent five years trying to put together, trying to put *themselves back* together, to compose themselves, and a song, after a terrible loss. They started the process in 2012 while visiting New York for the funeral of Tyler's aunt Dawn Hochsprung, who was killed along with 20 children and 5 other staff members during a mass shooting at Connecticut's Sandy Hook Elementary School, where she was principal. Tyler was 13. The students killed were 6 and 7 years old. For Mr. Suarez, the movement in the aftermath of the Parkland shooting is offering voice to young people. That realization motivated him to organize Hartford's March For Our Lives event on March 24, and to subsequently establish a Connecticut chapter of Students Demand Action. He says:

> [A]s an eighth-grader, you really—you think you don't have a voice, or you don't use it as often as older people, because you think that the older people should get the spotlight. And obviously that's changed since the Parkland tragedy—that was the biggest thing that I think came from that, is that students—kids—now realize that they do have a power in their voice. So I decided to use mine, and my experience, to organize the march. (interview, June 21, 2018)

Several students emphasized that their songs were intended to defy the social and political denial of voice to young people. Their generation, born at the turn of the millennium, has often been dismissed as lazy and self-absorbed, they said, and addicted to social-media activism without real-world impact. But they, and the rest of the movement, are changing these misconceptions. Sixteen-year-old Ashlyn Flamer (Phenix City, Alabama) explained that the school walkouts inspired her because: "It was the first time people started listening to teenagers," she noted. "And we're going to be able to vote in the next election. So I don't understand why we're being written off now, when we're really of age to understand politics enough to form an opinion" (interview, July 12, 2018). The seniors in Kyle Fackrell's AP music theory class (New York) expanded on this concern. They found motivation listening to the speeches of Parkland survivors such as Emma González and David Hogg—teenaged leaders of the movement powerfully speaking out—and wanted to "make [their own] voices heard" in the March 14 walkout. Lyricist Jerramiah Jean-Baptiste even included a reference to González's iconic February 17 speech: "Fifty-eight hundred dollars ain't enough for a life." Though their instructor helped minimally with the song's arrangement, the students stress that the song was their idea, and their work alone.

Discussing responses to the video they posted in March of "The Truth: We Need Change," 18-year-old Aeva Soler told me that "People are saying that we're being used as propaganda against the NRA." She and another student added that this implies "that we can't form thoughts of our own," and that "our morality doesn't come from us." Aeva asked, "If we don't have our own morality [at 18], when does that start to form?" (interview, June 21, 2018). In other words, high school students are cognizant that, even at voting age, they are denied voice—and recognition of their voice—and perceived as incomplete agents in the world. Instructor Kyle Fackrell supported the students' songwriting project, he says, because "it teaches them how to have a voice in the world" (interview, June 21, 2018).

When I asked students what they thought the role of music and poetry might be in the movement against gun violence, several of them contrasted singing with speaking, suggesting that a message sung had a better chance of reaching listeners than one spoken. They attributed this power to music's association with heightened experiences of emotion (Tyler Jenkins and Tyler Suarez, interviews, June 21, 2018), and to its potential to get "stuck in [people's] heads" in ways that speech typically does not (Ashlyn Flamer, interview, July 12, 2018). Additionally, two students suggested that discourse on social media, audible speech, and singing—in that order—carry an increasing level of connection between words and emotion. The meaning of social-media messages might be "twisted" more easily than speech (interview with Lavelle Preparatory Charter School students, June 21, 2018); social media can leave people "disconnected from genuine feelings that you feel when you listen to music" (Tyler Suarez, interview, June 21, 2018). Musical voice, in their understanding, is the most effective way to transmit their messages about gun violence.

Saida Dahir, whose "Poem for the Fallen" is the album's only non-singing track, describes the work she does as *artivism*—art as activism. Art, she says, is what stays with people long after the events of a protest. Her intersectional voice as a young, Black hijabi Muslim woman who came to the United States as a child refugee (she was born in a Somali refugee camp in Kenya) has been received as one of the most powerful on *Raise Your Voice*. It critiques the racialized responses to violence in the United States that position non-white perpetrators as part of the monolithic national experience of "terrorism," but white shooters as individual young men whose difficult lives and personal struggles with mental illness are to blame.[7]

Her performance of the poem at the March For Our Lives event in Salt Lake City went viral, and this video inspired my invitation to participate in the album. When eight of the students on *Raise Your Voice* performed at the Hardly Strictly Bluegrass Festival in San Francisco (on October 7, 2018), her poem moved the crowd to a standing ovation. But it has also garnered negative attention online. Following her March For Our Lives performance, a clip from her appearance on the Salt Lake City show *Radio From Hell* was reposted on AJ+, a news site from Al Jazeera. It was viewed over a million and a half times, and while most comments were positive, there were several on AJ+'s Facebook post suggesting that if she did not like the gun violence in the United States, she could return to "Africa." "Can we start sending these refugees back before it's too late?" read one post (https://www.facebook.com/ajplusenglish/videos/1915436632088180/). Sometimes, in the social-media iterations of the people's microphone, voices in the call-and-response attempt to disrupt the message.[8] But Ms. Dahir's persistent performances in social-justice contexts continue to raise her voice above theirs.

Four of the album's songs are literally multivocal—two sung by high school classes, and two duets. "Shine," by Sawyer Garrity and Andrea Peña, was first performed by several soloists and a chorus from Marjory Stoneman Douglas High School's drama club, replaced by just the composer's and lyricist's two voices on the album. Ashlyn Flamer's and Christopher Doleman's "The Separation" was also debuted by a performing-arts class, though only the two of them sing on *Raise Your Voice*. Lavelle Preparatory Charter School's song, structured with Macklemore and Ryan Lewis's "Same Love" in mind, includes two distinctive voices in a melodic hook sung by Aeva Soler and rap verses by Jerramiah Jean-Baptiste. And one track ("We Can"), contributed by the High School for Recording Arts in St. Paul, Minnesota, is written for the voices of three separate characters: one in favor of tighter gun control, one against it, and one observer.

Ultimately, the album was produced with two primary goals: (1) to document and amplify the voices of students fighting for their lives; and (2) to help them encourage other young people to use their own voices to reshape the spaces

---

[7] Though Esposito and Finley acknowledge that persistent rhetoric blaming incidents of gun violence on the increasing lack of access to mental health services does critique the neoliberal defunding of government programs, they also caution that attributing mass shootings to ill persons tends to shift the focus quickly from social to individual responsibility (Esposito and Finley 2014: 92).

[8] After Little Village Foundation posted clips of the students' performances to Instagram, a user whose account was titled "Antijüdische Aktion" trolled one with a white-supremacist comment, using triple parentheses. The post and account were reported and later removed.

in which they sound. The donation of all sales proceeds to Everytown for Gun Safety became another aim, though the tracks are also offered for free streaming on Spotify. *Raise Your Voice* was released in October 2018, one month before the ever more crucial midterm elections.

As I began writing this section a few weeks after the release, the midterm elections were nine days away. In the week immediately before, a memo had leaked from the White House detailing a plan to narrowly define gender, to erase transgender and gender nonconforming identities from policy and protection. Fourteen pipe bombs were sent to politicians and public figures outspoken against President Trump and/or targeted by far-right media. A shooting in Louisville, Kentucky, in which a white man took the lives of a Black man and woman at a grocery store after trying unsuccessfully to gain access to a Black church, is being investigated by the FBI as a hate crime. And eleven people were killed at a Pittsburgh synagogue by a man who railed against Jews and immigrants on white nationalist social media, and who told the police who apprehended him that he wanted to kill Jews.

But the midterm elections in November 2018 saw increased numbers of voters between 18 and 29—31% of eligible voters in that age range, as opposed to 21% in 2014 (Sanders 2018)—and more than two dozen NRA-backed members of Congress lost their seats. Bump stocks were banned as of March 26, 2019. But at the end of that month, in the space of a few days, two teenaged survivors of the Marjory Stoneman Douglas shooting died by suicide, as did the father of a child lost at Sandy Hook. So in April students walked out of school again, this time to demand mental health support for survivors. The 2018 movement was only a beginning, but now Americans know who to listen to.

Fiona Magowan and Louise Josepha Wrazen propose that singing can "offer an emotional catharsis that also transforms the singer into an active agent through the possibility of reimagining current realities" (Magowan and Wrazen 2013: 9). Aiming to experience and promote healing, and to reshape a misshapen reality, the participants in *Raise Your Voice* inject hope into a fraught time. And some of them, and of those they have inspired, are now of voting age.

These young musicians are meeting the growing horror of mass violence with a growing disruption of mass silence. There are voices at work, tirelessly calling out the interlocking racist, misogynist, homophobic, ableist structures that have fueled and enabled the deadly rage of men with guns. When lives are in danger and legislators send quiet, safe thoughts and prayers, students are responding with voices raised in impassioned speech, poetry, and song. They take to the streets and they take the mic and they *give* voice, to those erased from the world. They entreat each other, as survivors of the school shooting in Parkland did at the March for Our Lives, to "be the voice for those who don't have one," for those from whom all future singing, all poetry, was taken. Voices might waver in mourning. But then they rise.

***

This book has considered multivocality as the process of singing with many voices, as an actuation of the intersubjectivities of voice, and as a mode through which to navigate the borderscape of voice in the negotiation of identity. It has explored multivocality as both a result of and a form of resistance to neoliberal doctrine, a way to navigate both the promise of agency and its suppression. Informed by the manipulation of spaces inside and outside of the body, the possibilities of acoustic configuration are myriad. Likewise, the ways in which voices are perceived vary according to individual experience and cultural contexts; in this way, listening may function multivocally, as well. Vocality can mean choosing to sing and it can mean choosing silence; it may involve singing and listening within or without a framework of aurality; learning voices can occur through kinesthetic, mimetic listening, or through vibrational sensation, or through synesthetic processes. Vocalities can become layers of self—archaeological, temporally defined layers of a singers' vocal ways of being; or layers to be somehow fit together, like those of a cake, into a creative product.

Where the layers of multivocality press together, the seams become boundaries to be crossed, transgressed, reinforced, even erased in the borderscapes of voice. Singers consciously and unconsciously move between the cultural codes of different vocalities as they navigate, relying upon them in the dialogic construction of identities. Vocalities can serve as strategies of self, as well as strategies to sell, as despite the limitations imposed by corporeality voices can, to varying degrees, constitute choices. As vocal ontologies and vocal epistemologies, they are sites of vulnerability to external manipulation and control, and when they are lost, ways of being and knowing can be unmoored. When they are suppressed, it is felt as identity theft. Vocalities are sonic subjectivities, and are subject to hegemonic pressures and oppressive silencing. They also figure as crucial and effective instruments of disruption and resistance at a moment when intersections of neoliberal ideology, white supremacy, ableism, misogyny, homophobia, and transphobia have boiled to the surface of U.S. culture.

The embodiment and enactment of multiple vocalities reflect the inherently dialogic work of identity. Bakhtin's work cautions readers that individuals cannot be studied as isolated units; as Wayne Booth explains it in his introduction to *Problems of Dostoevsky's Poetics*, "everything that any scientist, of whatever persuasion, might say about 'me,' in isolation from the many voices that constitute me and with which I speak, will be *essentially* faulty" (Bakhtin 1984: xxv). And importantly, movement between vocalities can illustrate the intersection of ideologies about corporeal and agentive voice where stylistic choices are made because of the need for "cultural and psychic and political survival" (Butler 2000: 36). The present volume has been an effort undertaken with these thoughts in mind, with the goal to study the lived voices of singers in their internal and social interactions with identity, agency and power. I have learned, overall, to listen to the material, corporeal, metaphysical, political, polysemic ways in which singers liberate and withhold their vocal ways of being in the negotiation of self. I've learned to listen to lived experiences of voice, and to voices of lived experience.

Works Cited

Abitbol, Jean. 2006. *Odyssey of the Voice*. Translated by Patricia Crossley. San Diego, Oxford, and Brisbane: Plural Publishing.

Adelson, Betty M. 2005a. "Dwarfs: The Changing Lives of Archetypal 'Curiosities'—and Echoes of the Past." *Disability Studies Quarterly* 25(3): n.p.

Adelson, Betty M. 2005b. *The Lives of Dwarfs: Their Journey from Public Curiosity Toward Social Liberation*. Piscataway, NJ: Rutgers University Press.

Agha, Asif. 2006[2004]. "Registers of Language." In *A Companion to Linguistic Anthropology*, edited by Alessandro Duranti, 23–45. Malden and Oxford: Blackwell.

Ahlin, Lars. 2013. "Mutual Interests? Neoliberalism and the New Age During the 1980s." In *Religion in Consumer Society: Brands, Consumers and Markets*, edited by François Gauthier and Tuomas Martikainen. London and New York: Routledge.

Aizura, Aren Z. 2011. "The Persistence of Transgender Travel Narratives." In *Transgender Migrations: The Bodies, Borders, and Politics of Transition*, edited by Trystan Cotten, 139–156. New York and Abingdon: Routledge.

Andersen, Hans Christian. 1983[1837]. "The Little Mermaid." Translated by Jean Hersholt. The Hans Christian Andersen Centre, Denmark. http://www.andersen.sdu.dk/vaerk/hersholt/TheLittleMermaid_e.html.

Andersen, Peter, Janis F. Andersen, and Fohn P. Garrison. 1978. "Singing Apprehension and Talking Apprehension: The Development of Two Constructs." *Sign Language Studies* 19: 155–186.

Anderson, Laurie Halse. 1999. *Speak*. New York: Farrar, Straus, and Giroux.

Andrews, Helena. 2012. "Honey Boo Boo? Honey, Please." *The Root*, August 15. http://www.theroot.com/articles/culture/2012/08/honey_boo_boo_child_and_black_stereotypes.html.

Anzaldúa, Gloria. 1999[1987]. *Borderlands/La Frontera: The New Mestiza*, Second Edition. San Francisco, CA: Aunt Lute.

Apolloni, Alexandra. 2014. "Starstruck: On Gaga, Voice, and Disability." In *Lady Gaga and Popular Music: Performing Gender, Fashion and Culture*, edited by Martin Iddon and Melanie L. Marshall, 190–208. New York and Abingdon: Routledge.

Appadurai, Arjun. 1990. "Disjuncture and Difference in the Global Cultural Economy." *Theory Culture Society* 7: 295–310.

Ashby, Christine. 2011. "Whose 'Voice' Is It Anyway?: Giving Voice and Qualitative Research Involving Individuals that Type to Communicate." *Disability Studies Quarterly* 31(4). http://dsq-sds.org/article/view/1723/1771.

Ashley, Martin. 2006. "You Sing Like a Girl? An Exploration of "Boyness" Through the Treble Voice." *Sex Education: Sexuality, Society and Learning* 6(2): 193–205.

Audley, Brian. 2000. "The Provenance of the 'Londonderry Air.'" *Journal of the Royal Musical Association* 125(2): 205–247.

Austin, J. L. 1975. *How to Do Things with Words*. Cambridge, MA: Harvard University Press.

Bailey, B. 2007. "Heteroglossia and Boundaries." In *Bilingualism: A Social Approach*, edited by M. Heller, 257–274. London: Palgrave Macmillan.

Bairstow, Edward G., Edward J. Dent, Ernest Walker, Steuart Wilson, Paul England, H. Gregory Hast, and Owen Colyer. 1929. "Vocal and Unvocal." *Music & Letters* 10 (3): 235–255.

Bakhtin, Mikhail. 1984. *Problems of Dostoevsky's Poetics*. Minneapolis: University of Minnesota Press.

Bakhtin, Mikhail. 1981. *The Dialogic Imagination: Four Papers*. Translated by C. Emerson and M. Holquist. Austin: University of Texas Press.

Barad, Karen. 2007. *Meeting the Universe Halfway: Quantum Physics and the Entanglement of Matter and Meaning*. Durham, NC: Duke University Press.

Barbour-Payne, Yunina. 2016. "Carolina Chocolate Drops: Performative Expressions and Reception of Affrilachian Identity." In *Appalachia Revisited: New Perspectives on Place, Tradition, and Progress*, edited by William Schumann and Rebecca Adkins Fletcher, 43–58. Lexington: University Press of Kentucky.

Barlow, Eve. 2017. "How Milck's Women's March Anthem 'Quiet' Went Viral and Change Her Life." *LAWeekly.com*, May 17. http://www.laweekly.com/music/milcks-connie-lim-is-the-one-woman-riot-behind-the-womens-march-anthem-quiet-8236468.

Barthes, Roland. 1977. *Image, Music, Text*. Translated by Stephen Heath. New York: Hill and Wang.

Baudrillard, Jean. 1988. "Simulacra and Simulations." In *Jean Baudrillard: Selected Writings*, edited by Mark Poster, 166–184. Stanford, CA: Stanford University Press.

Bauman, H-Dirksen L. 2008a. "Introduction: Listening to Deaf Studies." In *Open Your Eyes: Deaf Studies Talking*, 1–34 (H-Dirksen L. Bauman, editor). Minneapolis: University of Minnesota Press.

Bauman, H-Dirksen L. 2008b. "Listening to Phonocentrism with Deaf Eyes: Derrida's Mute Philosophy of (Sign) Language." *Essays in Philosophy* 9(1): ??

Bauman, H-Dirksen L. 2006. "Toward a Poetics of Vision, Space, and the Body: Sign Language and Literary Theory." *The Disability Studies Reader*, 355–366 (Lennard J. Davis, editor). London and New York: Routledge.

Bauman, H-Dirksen L. 2004. "Audism: Exploring the Metaphysics of Opression." *Journal of Deaf Studies and Deaf Education* 9(2): 239–246.

Bauman, H-Dirksen L., and Jennifer Drake. 1995. "Silence Is Not Without Voice: Including Deaf Culture Within Multicultural Curricula." *Radical Teacher* 47: 22–28.

Bayton, Mavis. 1999. *Frock Rock*. Oxford and New York: Oxford University Press.

Belotel-Grenié, Agnès, and Michel Grenié. 2004. "The Creaky Voice Phonation and the Organisation of Chinese Discourse." *ISCA Archive*. International Symposium on Tonal Aspects of Languages: With Emphasis on Tone Languages, Beijing, China, March 28–31. http://www.isca-speech.org/archive_open/tal2004/tal4_005.pdf.

Belova, Olga, Ian King, and Martyna Sliwa. 2008. "Introduction: Polyphony and Organization Studies: Mikhail Bakhtin and Beyond." *Organization Studies* 29(4): 493–500.

Berberian, Cathy. 2014[1966]. "The New Vocality in Contemporary Music." Translated by Francesca Placanica. In *Cathy Berberian: Pioneer of Contemporary Vocality*, edited by Francesca Placanica, Pamela Karantonis, Pieter Verstraete, and Anne Sivuoja Kauppala, 47–50. Surrey: Ashgate.

Bernstein, Jonathan. 2017. "Inside the Americana Genre's Identity Crisis." *RollingStone.com*, September 13. https://www.rollingstone.com/music/music-country/inside-the-americana-genres-identity-crisis-202818/.

Bertau, Marie-Cécile. 2008a. "Voice: A Pathway to Consciousness as 'Social Contact to Oneself.'" *Journal of Integrative Psychological & Behavioral Science* 42(1): 92–113.

Bertau, Marie-Cécile. 2008b. "Voice as Materialistic Principle." *Journal of Integrative Psychological & Behavioral Science* 42(1): 121–127.

Bertau, Marie-Cécile. 2007. "On the Notion of Voice: An Exploration from a Psycholinguistic Perspective With Developmental Implications." *Journal of International Journal for Dialogical Science* 2(1): 133–161.

Bickford, J. Albert and Kathy Fraychineaud. "Mouth Morphemes in ASL: A Closer Look." *Sign Languages: Spinning and Unraveling the Past, Present, and Future*: TISLR9, Forty Five Papers and Three Posters from the 9th Theoretical Issues in Sign Language Research Conference, Florianopolis, Brazil, December 2006. (2008). R.M. de Quadros, editor. 32–47.

Bienvenu M. J. 1987. "The Third Culture: Working Together." Translated by Marina L. McIntire. *Journal of Interpretation* (RID) 4: 1–12.

Bigsby, Christopher. 1990. *Arthur Miller and Company: Arthur Miller Talks about his Work in the Company of Actors, Designers, Directors, and Writers*. (Christopher Bigsby, editor. London: Methuen Drama.

Blanco, Maria del Pilar, and Esther Peeren, editors. 2013. *The Spectralities Reader:Ghosts and Haunting in Contemporary Cultural Theory*. New York and London: Bloomsbury.

Blease, Charlotte, Havi Carel, and Keith Geraghty. 2016. "Epistemic Injustice in Healthcare Encounters: Evidence From Chronic Fatigue Syndrome." *Journal of Medical Ethics* 43(8): 1–9.

Bogdan, Robert C., and Sari Knopp Biklen. 1998. *Qualitative Research for Education: An Introduction to Theory and Method*. Boston, MA: Allyn & Bacon.

Bowden, Darsie. 1995. "The Rise of a Metaphor: 'Voice' In Composition Pedagogy." *Rhetoric Review* 14(1): 173–188.

Brambilla, Chiara. 2015. "Exploring the Critical Potential of the Borderscapes Concept." *Geopolitics* 20: 13–14.

Bravo, Tony. 2013. "First Openly Trans Opera Student at SF Conservatory." *KQED.org*, June 14. https://ww2.kqed.org/pop/2013/06/14/first-openly-trans-opera-student-at-sf-conservatory-breanna-sinclaire-lgbt/.

Brea, Jennifer. 2016. "What Happens When You Have a Disease Doctors Can't Diagnose." TED talk. https://www.ted.com/talks/jen_brea_what_happens_when_you_hav_a_disease_doctors_can_t_diagnose.

Brea, Jennifer. n.d. "Lessons From the AIDS Movement: ACT UP's Unique Resources." http://www.meaction.net/act-ups-unique-resources/).

Brewer, Diane. 2002. "West Side Silence: Producing *West Side Story* with Deaf and Hearing Actors." *Theatre Topics* 12(1): 17–34.

Brocklehurst, Steven. 2013. "Susan Boyle Is Part of Autism's 'Invisible Generation.'" *BBCNews.co.uk*, December 9. http://www.bbc.co.uk/news/uk-scotland- 25299300.

Brooks, Daphne A. 2008. "Amy Winehouse and the (Black) Art of Appropriation." *The Nation*. September 10. http://www.thenation.com/article/amy-winehouse-and-black-art-appropriation#.

Broos, Diane Austin. 2003. "The Anthropology of Conversion: An Introduction." In *The Anthropology of Religious Conversion*, edited by Andrew Buckser and Stephen D. Glazier, 1–4. Lanham, MD: Rowman & Littlefield.
Butler, Judith. 2005. *Giving an Account of Oneself.* New York: Fordham University Press.
Butler, Judith. 2000. "Agencies of Style For a Liminal Subject." In *Without Guarantees: In Honour of Stuart Hall*, edited by Paul Gilroy, Lawrence Grossberg, and Angela McRobbie, 33–37. London: Verson.
Butler, Judith. 1990. *Gender Trouble: Feminism and the Subversion of Identity.* New York: Routledge.
Cameron, Deborah. 2001. "Language: Designer Voices." *Critical Quarterly* 43(4): 81–85.
Carr, Revell. 2013. "Historical Authenticity and Gender Transgression in the Sea Music Revival." Unpublished paper, Society for Ethnomusicology Meeting. November 17. Indianapolis, Indiana.
Cavarero, Adriana. 2005. *For More than One Voice: Toward a Philosophy of Vocal Expression*. Palo Alto, CA: Stanford University Press.
Cavarero, Adriana. 2000. *Relating Narratives: Storytelling and Selfhood*. Translated by Paul A. Kottman. London: Routledge.
Cavarero, Adriana, Konstantinos Thomaidis, and Ilaria Pinna. 2018. "Towards a Hopeful Plurality of Democracy: An Interview on Vocal Ontology with Adriana Cavarero." *Journal of Interdisciplinary Voice Studies* 3(1): 81–93.
Chana, Nadia. 2013. "You Need Equal Measures of Extreme Joy and 'Don't Fuck with Me': An Embodied Approach to the Ethnography of Singing." Unpublished paper, delivered at the Society for Ethnomusicology Conference, November 17, Indianapolis, IN.
Chapman Dale. 2013. "The 'One-man Band' and Entrepreneurial Selfhood in Neoliberal Culture." *Popular Music* 32(3): 451–470.
Chenoweth, Erica, and Jeremy Pressman. 2017. "This Is What We Learned Counting the Women's Marches." *Washington Post*, February 7. https://www.washingtonpost.com/news/monkey-cage/wp/2017/02/07/this-is- what-we-learned-by-counting-the-womens-marches/?utm_term=.b35d7b9c4750.
Chesnoff, Richard Z. 2012. "Operatic Bass Anthony Russell: The New Voice of Yiddish Song." *Huffington Post*, August 8. http://www.huffingtonpost.com/richard-z chesnoff/anthony-russel-jewish-singer_b_1753047.html.
Cheung, Ingrid, and Peter Vadas. 2015. "A New Disease Cluster: Mast Cell Activation Syndrome, Postural Orthostatic Tachycardia Syndrome, and Ehlers-Danlos Syndrome." *Journal of Allergy and Cilnical Immunology* 135(2): AB65.
Chin, Terry W., and Michael R. Bye. 2014. "Congenital Central Hypoventilation." *Medscape.com*, June 9. http://emedicine.medscape.com/article/1002927-overview.
Chion, Michel. 1999. *The Voice in Cinema*. Translated by Claudia Gorbman. New York: Columbia University Press.
Choi, Juria (Julie). 2013. "Constructing a Multivocal Self: A Critical Autoethnography." Ph.D. thesis, University of Technology, Sydney.
Chrisman, Wendy L. 2011. "A Reflection on Inspiration: A Recuperative Call for Emotion in Disability Studies." *Journal of Literary & Cultural Disability Studies* 5(2): 173–184.
Chung, Christopher K., and Samson Cho. 2012. "Significance of "Jeong" in Korean Culture and Psychotherapy." Harbor-UCLA Medical Center. http://www. prcp. org/publications/sig.pdf.

Claburn, Thomas. 2017. "Lyrebird Steals Your Voice to Make You Say Things You Didn't— And We Hate This World." *TheRegister.com*, April 24. https://www.theregister.co.uk/2017/04/24/voice_stealing_lyrebird/.

Clarke, Kevin. 2015. "Gender-Explosion in der Oper." ??, August 21.M-Maenner.de. http://m-maenner.de/2015/08/15216/.

Cohane, Mary Ellen, and Kenneth S. Goldstein. 1996. "Folksongs and the Ethnography of Singing in Patrick Kennedy's *The Banks of the Boro*." *Journal of American Folklore* 109(434): 425–436.

Cohen, John. 1963. *The High Lonesome Sound*. http://www.folkstreams.net/filmdetail.php?id=417.

Cohen, Judah M. 2009. *The Making of A Reform Jewish Cantor: Musical Authority, Cultural Investment*. Bloomington: Indiana University Press.

Coll, Fiona. 2010. "'Just a Singing-Machine': The Making of an Automaton in George du Maurier's *Trilby*." *University of Toronto Quarterly* 79(2): 742–763.

Conley, Willy. 2001."In Search of the Perfect Sign-Language Script: Insights into the Diverse Writing Styles of Deaf Playwrights." In *Deaf World: A Historical Reader and Primary Sourcebook*, edited by Lois Bragg, 147–161. New York: New York University Press.

Connor, Steven. 2009. "The Chronopher." Talk given at the Rennselaer Polytechnic Institute, Troy, NY, April 2, 2009. Published at http://stevenconnor.com/chronopher.html (Accessed November 5, 2015).

Connor, Steven. 2000. *Dumbstruck: A Cultural History of Ventriloquism*. Oxford and New York: Oxford University Press.

Conrad, Peter. 2009. *The Sociology of Health and Illness*. Eighth Edition. New York: Worth.

Conrad, Peter, Julia Bandini, and Alexandria Vasquez. 2016. "Illness and the Internet From Private to Public Experience." *Health* 20(1): 22–32.

Constansis, A. N. 2013. "The Female-to-Male (FTM) Singing Voice and Its Interaction with Queer Theory: Roles and Interdependency." *Transposition. Musique et Sciences Sociales* 3. https://transposition.revues.org/353?lang=en.

Constansis, A. N. 2008. "The Changing Female-to-Male (FTM) Voice." *Radical Musicology* 3: 1–32. http://www.radicalmusicology.org.uk.

Couldry, Nick. 2010. *Why Voice Matters: Culture and Politics After Neoliberalism*. Thousand Oaks, CA: Sage.

Cowan, William. 1970. "The Vowels of Egyptian Arabic." *Word* 26(1): 94–100.

Crampton, Jeremy W. 2009. "Cartography: Performative, Participatory, Political." *Progress in Human Geography* 33(6): 840–848.

Cusick, Suzanne. 1999. "On Musical Performances of Gender and Sex." In *Audible Traces: Gender, Identity, and Music*, edited by Elaine Barkin and Lydia Hamessley, 25–49. Zürich: Carciofoli.

Danielson, Virginia. 1997. *The Voice of Egypt: Umm Kulthum, Arabic Song, and Egyptian Society in the Twentieth Century*. Chicago: The University of Chicago Press.

Danielson, Virginia. 1994. "Reviewed Work: Musique Arbe: Le Congrès du Caire de 1932, by Philippe Vigreux." *Yearbook for traditional Music* 26: 132–136.

Dargan, William T. 2006. *Lining out the Word: Dr. Watts Hymn Singing in the Music of Black Americans*. Berkeley and Los Angeles: University of California Press.

Darrow, Alice-Ann. 2006. "The Role of Music in Deaf Culture: Deaf Students' Perception of Emotion in Music." *Journal of Music Therapy* 43 (1): 2–15.

Darrow, Alice-Ann, and Diane Merchant Loomis. 1999. "Music and Deaf Culture: Images from the Media and Their Interpretation by Deaf and Hearing Students." *Journal of Music Therapy* 36 (2): 88–109.

Davenport, Tom. 2003. *Remembering the High Lonesome*. http://www.folkstreams.net/film-detail.php?id=42.

Davidson, Justin. 2017. "Rhiannon Giddens Lost Her Broadway Break But Gained Nashville." *Vulture.com*, February 27. http://www.vulture.com/2017/02/rhiannon-giddens-lost-broadway-but-gained-nashville.html.

Davies, Shelagh. 2016. "Training the Transgender Singer: Finding the Voice Inside." National Association of Teachers of Singing, April 14. https://www.nats.org/cgi/page.cgi/_article.html/What_s_New/Training_the_Transgender_Singer_Finding_the_Voice_Inside.

Dawson, Andrew. 2016[2007]. *New Era—New Religions: Religious Transformation in Contemporary Brazil*. London and New York: Routledge.

de Léry, Jean. 1578. "Excerpt from *History of a Voyage to the Land of Brazil*." In *Norton Anthology of English Literature*. Norton Topics Online. http://www.wwnorton.com/college/english/nael/16century/topic_2/delery.htm.

Derfner, Joel. 2009. *Swish: My Quest to Become the Gayest Person Ever and What Ended Up Happening Instead*. New York: Broadway Books.

Derrida, Jacques. 1997[1967]. *Of Grammatology*. Translated by Gayatri Spivak. Baltimore, MD: Johns Hopkins University Press.

Derrida, Jacques. 1994. *Specters of Marx: The State of the Debt, the Work of Mourning and the New International*. Translated by Peggy Kamuf. New York and London: Routledge.

Derrida, Jacques. 1973. *Speech and Phenomena and Other Essays on Husserl's Theory of Signs*. Translated by D. B. Allison. Chicago: Northwestern University Press.

DeVault, Marjorie. 1999. *Liberating Method: Feminism and Social Research*. Chicago: University of Chicago Press.

Dolar, Mladen. 2006. *A Voice and Nothing More*. Cambridge, MA: MIT Press.

Dolce, Kim. 2013. "A Portable History of MS." *MultipleSclerosis.net*, October 27. https://multiplesclerosis.net/living-with-ms/portable-history-ms/.

Driscoll, Catherine. 2008. "Girls Today: Girls, Girl Culture and Girl Studies." *Girlhood Studies* 1(1): 13–32.

Du Bois, W. E. B. 1903. *The Souls of Black Folk*. New York: Dover Publications.

Du Maurier, George. 1899. *Trilby*. New York: International Book.

Dunn, Leslie C., and Nancy Jones. 1994. "Introduction." In *Embodied Voices: Representing Female Vocality in Western Culture*, edited by Leslie C. Dunn and Nancy Jones, 1–13. Cambridge, UK: Cambridge University Press.

Eden, Vivian. 2015. "Poem of the Week: Let My People Go Again and Again and Again." *Haaretz.com*, March 31. http://www.haaretz.com/israel-news/culture/poem-of-the-week/1.649412.

Edwards, Gavin. 2014. "Laura Jane Grace's Fresh Start: Against Me!'s New 'Blues.'" *Rolling Stone*, January 21. http://www.rollingstone.com/music/news/laura-jane-graces-fresh-start-inside-against-me-s-new-blues-20140121.

Edwin, Robert. 2007. "Belt Is Legit." *Journal of Singing* 64(2): 213–215.

Eidsheim, Nina Sun. 2015. *Sensing Sound: Singing and Listening as Vibrational Practice*. Oxford: Oxford University Press.

Eidsheim, Nina Sun. 2011a. "Sensing Voice: Materiality and the Lived Body in Singing and Listening." *The Senses & Society* 6(2): 133–155.

Eidsheim, Nina Sun. 2011b. "Marian Anderson and 'Sonic Blackness' in American Opera." *American Quarterly* 6(3): 641–671.
Eidsheim, Nina Sun. 2009. "Synthesizing Race: Towards an Analysis of the Performativity of Vocal Timbre." *TRANS* 13. http://www.sibetrans.com/trans/articulo/57/synthesizing-race-towards-an- analysis-of-the-performativity-of-vocal-timbre.
Eidsheim, Nina Sun. 2008. "Voice as a Technology of Selfhood: Towards an Analysis of Racialized Timbre and Vocal Performance." Ph.D. dissertation, University of California at San Diego.
Eidsheim, Nina Sun, and Katherine Meizel, editors. 2019. *The Oxford Handbook of Voice Studies*. Oxford: Oxford University Press.
El Guindi, Fadwa. 2005. "The Veil Becomes a Movement." In *Women and Islam: Social Conditions, Obstacles and Prospects*, Vol. 2., edited by Haideh Moghisse, 70–91. Abingdon: Routledge.
Eskridge, J. T. 1900. "Some Points in the Diagnosis of Traumatic Injuries of the Central Nervous System." *Journal of the American Medical Association* 34(10): 579–584.
Esposito, Luigi, and Laura L. Finley. 2014. "Beyond Gun Control: Examining Neoliberalism, Pro-gun Politics and Gun Violence in the United States. *Theory in Action* 7(2): 74–103.
Eurich-Rascoe, Barbara L., and Hendrika Vande Kemp. 1997. *Femininity and Shame: Women, Men, and Giving Voice to the Feminine*. Lanham, MD: University Press of America.
Fairweather, DeLisa, and Noel R. Rose. 2004. "Women and Autoimmune Disease." *Emerging Infections Diseases* 10(11): 2005–2011.
Farrer, Martin. 2017. "Rhiannon Giddens Review—A Virtuoso Slice of Americana." *Guardian.com*, April 8. https://www.theguardian.com/music/2017/apr/09/rhiannon-giddens-review-a-virtuoso-slice-of-americana.
Feld, Steven, and Donald Brenneis. 2004. "Doing Anthropology in Sound." *American Ethnologist* 31(4): 461–474.
Feld, Steven, Aaron A. Fox, Thomas Porcello, and David Samuels. 2004. "Vocal Anthropology: From the Music of Language to the Language of Song." In *A Companion to Linguistic Anthropology*, edited by Alessandro Duranti, 321–346. Malden and Oxford: Blackwell.
Feldman, Martha. 2015. "The Interstitial Voice: An Opening." In "Colloquy: Why Voice Now?" *Journal of the American Musicological Society* 68(3): 653–685.
Filene, Benjamin. 2000. *Romancing the Folk: Public Memory and American Roots Music*. Chapel Hill and London: University of North Carolina Press.
Fleeger, Jennifer. 2014. *Mismatched Women: The Siren's Song Through the Machine*. Oxford: Oxford University Press.
Flores, Adolfo. 2017. "People Are Calling This Song the Anthem of the Women's March Movement." *Buzzfeed.com*, January 22. https://www.buzzfeed.com/adolfoflores/people-are-calling-this-song-the-anthem-of-the-womens-march?utm_term=.vvZ7RgdRB#.muymBlLBd.
Foucault, Michel. 1978. *The History of Sexuality: An Introduction*, vol. 1. New York: Vintage.
Freud, Sigmund. 2001[1901–1905]. "Fragments of an Analysis of a Case of Hysteria." In *The Standard Edition of the Complete Psychological Works of Sigmund Freud*, Vol. 7, edited by James Strachey, Anna Freud, Alix Strachey, and Alan Tyson, 1–122. London: Vintage.

Fricker, Miranda. 2007. *Epistemic Injustice: Power and the Ethics of Knowing*. Oxford: Oxford University Press.

Friedner, Michele. 2010. "Biopower, Biosociality, and Community Formation: How Biopower is Constitutive of the Deaf Community." *Sign Language Studies* 10(3): 336–347.

Frith, Simon. 1996. *Performing Rites: On the Value of Popular Music*. Cambridge, MA: Harvard University Press.

Fryer, Paul. 2005. *The Opera Singer and The Silent Film*. Jefferson, NC, and London: McFarland.

Fulford, Robert, Jane Ginsborg, and Juliet Goldbart. 2011. "Learning Not to Listen: The Experiences of Musicians with Hearing Impairments." *Music Education Research* 13(4): 447–464.

Garland-Thomson, Rosemarie. 2009. *Staring: How We Look*. London and New York: Oxford University Press.

Garland-Thomson, Rosemarie. 2005. "Dares to Stares: Disabled Women Performance Artists & the Dynamics of Staring." In *Bodies in Commotion: Disability and Performance*, edited by Carrie Sandahl and Philip Auslader, 30–41. Ann Arbor: University of Michigan Press.

Gates, J. Terry. 1989. "A Historical Comparison of Public Singing by American Men and Women." *Journal of Research in Music Education* 37(1): 32–47.

Geertz, Clifford. 1973. *The Interpretation of Cultures*. New York: Basic Books.

Gettell, Oliver. 2014. "Sofia Coppola in Talks to Direct Live-Action 'Little Mermaid' Film." *L.A. Times*, March 19. http://www.latimes.com/entertainment/movies/moviesnow/la-et-mn-sofia- coppola-to-direct-live-action-little-mermaid-film- 20140319,0,6529211.story#axzz2yAXop0Rx.

Gibb, G. Duncan. 1870. "The Character of the Voice in the Nations of Asia and Africa, Contrasted with That of the Nations of Europe." In *Memoirs Read Before the Anthropological Society of London*, Vol. 3, 1867–1869, 244–259. London: Longmans, Green.

Gibb, Duncan G., et al. 1869. "Comments on 'On the Character of the Voice in the Nations of Asia and Africa, Contrasted with That in the Nations of Europe.'" *Journal of the Anthropological Society of London* 7: lxii–lxvi.

Gibson, Corey. 2015. *The Voice of the People: Hamish Henderson and Scottish Cultural Politics*. Edinburgh: Edinburgh University Press.

Giddens, Rhiannon. 2017. Keynote Address at IBMA Conference Community and Connection. *Nonesuch.com*, October 3.http://www.nonesuch.com/journal/rhiannon-giddens-keynote-address-ibma-conference-community-connection-2017-10-03.

Giddins, Gary. 1986. "This Guy Wouldn't Give You the Parsley off His Fish." *Grand Street* 5(2): 202–217.

Gilchrist, Anne G. 1934. "A New Light on the Londonderry Air." *Journal of the English Folk Song and Dance Society* 1: 115–121.

Gilligan, Carol. 1997. "Remembering Iphigenia: Voice, Resonance, and the Talking Cure." In *The Handbook of Infant, Child, and Adolescent Psychotherapy. Vol. 2: New Directions in Integrative Treatment*, edited by Bonnie S. Mark and James A. Incorvaia, 69–194. Northvale, NJ: Jason Aronson.

Gloudeman, Nikki. 2014. "Connie Lim: Acclaimed Singer-Songwriter." *Ravishly.com*, October 6. http://www.ravishly.com/ladies-we-love/connie-lim-acclaimed-singer-songwriter.

Goldin-Perschbacher, Shana. 2015. "TransAmericana: Gender, Genre, and Journey." *New Literary History* 46(4): 775–803.

Goldin-Perschbacher, Shana. 2008. "Sexuality, Listening, and Intimacy: Gender Transgression in Popular Music, 1993–2008." Ph.D. dissertation, University of Virginia.

González, Emma. 2018. Full transcript of speech. In "Florida Student Emma Gonzalez to Lawmakers and Gun Advocates: 'We call BS.'" *CNN.com*, February 17. https://www.cnn.com/2018/02/17/us/florida-student-emma-gonzalez- speech/index.html.

Graham, Sandra Jean. 2018. *Spirituals and the Birth of a Black Entertainment Industry*. Urbana: University of Illinois Press.

Green, Emma. 2017. "Covert Nation." *The Atlantic*, August 12. https://www.theatlantic.com/politics/archive/2017/08/conversions-lincoln-mullen/536151/.

Grossberg, Lawrence. 1993. "The Media Economy of Rock Culture: Cinema, Post Modernity and Authenticity." In *Sound & Vision: The Music Video Reader*, edited by Simon Frith, Andrew Goodwin, and Lawrence Grossberg, 185–209. London: Routledge.

Grover-Friedlander, Michal. 2005. "The Afterlife of Maria Callas's Voice." *Musical Quarterly* 88(1): 35–62.

Grushkin, Donald. 2003. "The Dilemma of the Hard of Hearing Within the U.S. Deaf Community." In *Many Ways to Be Deaf: International Variation in Deaf Communities*, edited by Leila Frances Monaghan, 114–140. Washington, DC: Gallaudet University Press.

Haben, Michael C. 2018. "Voice Feminization." Professionalvoice.org. http://professionalvoice.org/feminization.aspx (Accessed February 3, 2019).

Hackley, Chris, Rungpaka Amy Hackley, and Stephen Brown. 2012. "The X-Factor Enigma: Simon Cowell and the Merketization of Existential Liminality." *Marketing Theory* 12(4): 451–469.

Haddad, Yvonne Yazbeck. 2007. "The Post-9/11 Hijab as Icon." *Sociology of Religion* 68(3): 253–267.

Hague, Seth, John Street, and Heather Savigny. 2008. "The Voice of the People? Musicians as Political Actors." *Cultural Politics* 4(1): 5–24.

Halavais, Alexander, and Maria Garrido. 2014. "Twitter as the People's Microphone: Emergence of Authorities During Protest Tweeting." In *Cyberactivism on the Participatory Web*, edited by Martha McCaughey, 117–139. New York and London: Routledge.

Hall, Stuart. 1992. "The Question of Cultural Identity." In *Modernity and Its Futures*, edited by Stuart Hall, David Held, and Anthony G. McGrew, 273–326. Cambridge: Polity Press.

Hammer, Juliane. 2012. *American Muslim Women, Religious Authority, and Activism: More Than a Prayer*. Austin: University of Texas Press.

Harkness, Nicholas. 2013. *Songs of Seoul: An Ethnography of Voice and Voicing in Christian South Korea*. Berkeley and Los Angeles: University of California Press.

Harris, Monica. 2012. "Mandy Harvey: Hope Pulls Us Out of Any Dark Situation." *LifeIsAwesome.net* (Life Is Awesome: Art and Music in Southern California), February 1. http://www.life-is-awesome.net/2012/02/01/1278/.

Harrison, Anthony. 2017. "You Don't Interrupt Rhiannon Giddens." *Triad City Beat*, February 1. https://triad-city-beat.com/dont-interrupt-rhiannon-giddens/.

Harvey, David. 2007. "Neoliberalism as Creative Destruction." *Annals of the American Academy of Political and Social Science* 610: 22–44.

Harvey, Mandy, and Mark Atteberry. 2017. *Sensing the Rhythm: Finding My Voice in a World Without Sound*. New York: Howard Books.

Hash, Phillip M. 2003. "Teaching Instrumental Music to Deaf and Hard of Hearing Students." *Research and Issues in Music Education* 1(1). http://files.eric.ed.gov/fulltext/EJ852403.pdf.

Haskell, John. 1987. "Vocal Self-Perception: The Other Side of the Equation." *Journal of Voice* 1(2): 172-179.

Hastrup, Kirsten. 1998. "Theatre as a Site of Passage: Some Reflections on the Magic of Acting." In *Ritual, Performance, Media*, edited by Felicia Hughes–Freeland, 29–46. London: Routledge.

Healy, Bernadine. 1991. "The Yentl Syndrome." *New England Journal of Medicine* 325: 274–276.

Heidegger, Martin. 1962. *Being and Time*. New York: Harper & Row.

Hermans, Hubert J. M. 1996. "Voicing the self: From information processing to dialogical interchange." *Psychological Bulletin* 119: 31–50.

Hicks, Taylor, with David Wild. 2007. *Heart Full of Soul: An Inspirational Memoir About Finding Your Voice and Finding Your Way*. New York: Crown.

Himes, Geoffrey. 2015. "Considering Diversity and Representation in Americana." *NashvilleScene.com*, September 7. https://www.nashvillescene.com/music/cover-story/article/20974636/considering-diversity-and-representation-in-americana.

Hirschkind, Charles. 2006. *The Ethical Soundscape: Cassette Sermons and Islamic Counterpublics*. New York: Columbia University Press.

Hoffman, Diane E., and Anita J. Tarzian. 2001. "The Girl Who Cried Pain: A Bias Against Women in the Treatment of Pain." *Journal of Law, Medicine & Ethics* 29: 13–27.

Hoffman, Kelly M., Sophie Trawalter, Jordan R. Axt, and M. Norman Oliver. 2016. "Racial Bias in Pain Assessment and Treatment Recommendations, and False Beliefs About Biological Differences between Blacks and Whites." *Proceedings of the National Academy of Sciences of the United States of America* 113(16): 4296–4301.

Hogan, Michael. 2013. "Simon Cowell Makes Surprise Appearance at *X Factor* Launch." *The Telegraph*, August 29. http://www.telegraph.co.uk/culture/tvandradio/x- actor/10274597/Simon-Cowell-makes-surprise-appearance-at-X-Factor- launch.html.

Holborow, Marnie. 2015. *Language and Neoliberalism*. Abingdon and New York: Routledge.

"How This Song Became the Anthem of the #WomensMarch Against Donald Trump." 2017. *BBC.co.uk*, January 24. http://www.bbc.co.uk/newsbeat/article/38717966/how-this-song-became-the- anthem-of-the-womensmarch-against-donald-trump.

Huron, David. 2002. "Listening Styles and Listening Strategies. Presentation handout, Society for Music Theory Conference, November 1, Columbus, OH. http://www.musiccog.ohio-state.edu/Huron/Talks/SMT.2002/handout.html.

Hymes, Dell. 1974. "Ways of Speaking." In *Explorations in the Ethnography of Speaking*, edited by Richard Bauman and Joel Sherzer, 433–452. London and New York: Cambridge University Press.

"Il Divo's David Miller Directs Opera Classic *A Hand of Bridge*." 2017. *BusinessWire.com*. http://www.businesswire.com/news/home/20170503006606/en/Il-Divo%E2%80%99s -David-Miller-Directs-Opera-Classic.

Infantry, Ashante. 2008. "Marion J. Caffey Promises You Mo' Opera for Your Money." *Thestar.com*, March 5. http://www.thestar.com/entertainment/article/309390.

Jane, Hollis. 2013. "On Being a Little Person." *A Bunch of Dumb Show*, October 9. http://holliseum.wordpress.com/2013/10/09/on-being-a-little-person/.

Janet, Pierre. 1907. *The Major Symptoms of Hysteria: Fifteen Lectures Given in the Medical School of Harvard University*. New York: Macmillan.

Jarman-Ivans, Freya. 2006. "Breaking Voices: Voice, Subjectivity and Fragmentation in Popular Music," 196–225. Ph.D. dissertation, University of Newcastle.

Jiang, Xinxin. 2018. "Whose Voice? A Critical Analysis of Identity, Media, and Popular Music in *The Voice Of China*." Ph.D. dissertation, Bowling Green State University.

John, Emma. 2018. "'White People Are So Fragile, Bless 'Em'... Meet Rhiannon Giddens, Banjo Warrior." *The Guardian*, July 23. https://www.theguardian.com/music/2018/jul/23/white-people-are-so-fragile-bless-em-rhiannon-giddens-banjo-warrior-cambridge-folk-festival.

Johnson, E. Patrick. 1995. "SNAP! Culture: A Different Kind of 'Reading.'" *Text and Performance Quarterly* 15: 122–142.

Johnson, Jason. 2018. "Yes, the March for Our Lives Was About Black People, Too—and It's About Time." TheRoot.com. March 26. https://www.theroot.com/yes-the-march-for-our-lives-was-about-black-people-too-1824082682 (Accessed March 22, 2019).

Jones, Alisha Lola. 2019. "Singing High: Black Countertenors and Gendered Sound in Gospel Performance." In *Oxford Handbook of Voice Studies*, edited by Nina Eidsheim and Katherine Meizel, 35–51. Oxford: Oxford University Press.

Jones, Jamila. 2014. Oral History Interview. The Civil Rights History Project PL111-19. Library of Congress and Smithsonian National Museum of African American History and Culture. Recorded April 27, 2011. https://www.youtube.com/watch?v=KJKPXsiR5m8.

Jones, Jeannette DiBernardo. 2016. "Imagined Hearing: Music-Making in Deaf Culture." In *The Oxford Handbook of Disability Studies*, edited by Blake Howe, Stephanie Jensen Moulton, Neil Lerner, and Joseph Straus, 54–72. Oxford: Oxford University Press.

Jones, Malcolm. 2015. "Patsy Cline, Alison Krauss, and Rhiannon Giddens." *TheDailyBeast.com*, March 8. https://www.thedailybeast.com/patsy-cline-alison-krauss-and-nowrhiannon-giddens.

"Juanes a la Ópera." 2009. *Semana.com*, March 26. http://www.semana.com/multimedia-cultura/juanes-opera/1802.aspx.

Juris, Jeffrey. 2008. *Networking Futures: The Movements Against Corporate Globalization*. Durham, NC: Duke University Press.

Karp, Jonathan. 2003. "Performing Black-Jewish Symbiosis: The 'Hassidic Chant' of Paul Robeson." *American Jewish History* 91(1): 53–81.

Keegan, Cael M. 2013. "Moving Bodies: Sympathetic Migrations in Transgender Narrativity." *Genders* 57: 1–29. https://go.galegroup.com/ps/i.do?p=AONE&sw=w&u =googlescholar&v=2.1& =r&id=GALE%7CA324981029&sid=classroomWidget&asi d=33497cb4.

Keightley, Keir. 2008. "Music for Middlebrows: Defining the Easy Listening Era, 1946-1966." *American Music* 26(3): 309–335.

Kennicott, Philip. 2005. "Il Divo: A Boy Band's Cheese, Aged." *WashingtonPost.com*. May 21. https://www.washingtonpost.com/archive/lifestyle/2005/05/21/il-divo-a-boy-bands-cheese-aged/51f4850a-2494-4419-8e4f-c0dad041221e/ (Accessed March 24, 2008).

Kieckhafer, Richard. 2004. *Theology in Stone: Church Architecture from Byzantium to Berkeley*. Oxford: Oxford University Press.

Kim, Minjeong, and Angie Y. Chung. 2008. "Consuming Orientalism: Images of Asian American Women in Multicultural Advertising." In *The Kaleidoscope of Gender: Prisms, Patterns, and Possibilities*, edited by Joan Z. Spade and Catherine G. Valentine, 256–268. Thousand Oaks, CA: SAGE Publications.

King, Danny. 2012. "Las Vegas Attracts Second-Highest Number of Visitors in 2011." *TravelWeekly.com*, February 10. http://www.travelweekly.com/North-America Travel/Las-Vegas-attracts-second-highest-number-of-visitors-since-2007.

King, Homay. 2012. "Antiphon: Notes on the People's Microphone." *Journal of Popular Music Studies* 24(2): 238–246.

Kisliuk, Michelle and Kelly Gross. 2004. What's the "It" That We Learn to Perform?: Teaching BaAka Music and Dance. In *Performing Ethnomusicology: Teaching and Representation in World Music Ensembles*. (Ted Solis, editor). Berkeley and Los Angeles: University of California Press. 249–260.

Kitamura, Tatsuya. 2008. "Acoustic Analysis of Imitated Voice Produced by a Professional Impersonator." *Interspeech* 813–816.

Klarreich, Erica. 2001. "Feel the Music: Deaf People Use 'Mind's Ear' to Process Vibrations." *Nature.com*, November 27. http://www.nature.com/news/2001/011127/full/news011129-10.html.

Klein, Jeff. 2014."Tom Waits and the Right of Pulicity: Protecting the Artist's Negative Voice." *Popular Music & Society* 37(5): 583–594.

Koestenbaum, Wayne. 1993. *The Queen's Throat: Opera, Homosexuality and theMystery of Desire*. New York: Poseidon Press.

Koplan, Jeffrey P. 2000. *Women and Smoking: A Report of the Surgeon General*. Washington, DC: U.S. Government, Department of Health and Human Services.

Koskoff, Ellen. 2000. *Music in Lubavitcher Life*. Urbana-Champaign: University of Illinois Press.

Krell, Elias. 2019. "Trans/forming White Noise: Gender, Race, and Dis/ability in the Music of Joe Stevens." In *The Oxford Handbook of Voice Studies*, edited by Nina Eidsheim and Katherine Meizel. Oxford: Oxford University Press. 143–164.

Krell, Elias. 2015. "'Who's the Crack Whore the End?' Performance, Violence, and Sonic Borderlands in the Music of Yva las Vegass." *Text and Performance Quarterly* 35(2-3): 95–118.

Krell, Elias. 2014. "Singing Strange: Transvocality in North American Music Performance." Ph.D. dissertation, Northwestern University.

Krell, Elias. 2013. "Contours Through Covers: Voice and Affect in the Music of Lucas Silveira." *Journal of Popular Music Studies* 25(4): 476–503.

Ladefoged, P. 2000. The sounds of speech. In *Sound* (P. Kruth and H. Stobart, editors).Cambridge: Cambridge University Press. 112–132.

Lang, Harry G. 2000. *A Phone of Our Own: The Deaf Insurrection Against Ma Bell*. Washington, DC: Gallaudet University Press.

Levänen, Sari, and Dorothea Hamdorf. 2001. "Feeling Vibrations: Enhanced Tactile Sensitivity in Congenitally Deaf Humans." *Neuroscience Letters* 301(1): 75–77.

Levin, David. 1985. *The Body's Recollection of Being*. London: Routledge & Kegan Paul.

Levine, Joseph. 2010. "From the Editor: The Issue of Yiddish Song: A Trade-Off for the Decline of Spoken Yiddish?" *Journal of Synagogue Music* 35: 4–5.

Levine, Lawrence W. 1988. *Highbrow/Lowbrow: The Emergence of Culutral Hierarchy in America*. Cambridge, MA: Harvard University Press.

Lifton, Robert Jay. 1999[1993]. *The Protean Self*. New York: Basic Books.

Lim, Connie. 2015. "How Music Can Save You: Connie Lim's Journey." *VoiceCouncil. com*, June 1. http://www.voicecouncil.com/how-music-can-save-you- connie-lims-journey/.

Lipsitz, George. 1991. "Review: *Highbrow/Lowbrow: The Emergence of Cultural Hierarchy in America* by Lawrence W. Levine." *American Quarterly* 43(3): 518–524.

Looby, Christopher. 1997. *Voicing America: Language, Literary Form, and the Origins of the United States*. Chicago: University of Chicago Press.

López, Sabrina, Pablo Riera, María Florencia Assaneo, Manuel Eguía, Mariano Sigman, and Marcos A. Trevisan. 2013. "Vocal Caricatures Reveal Signatures of Speaker Identtity." *Scientific Reports* 3(3407): 1–7.

Lorde, Audre. 1996[1976]. "Coal." In *Coal: Poems*. New York: W.W. Norton & Company. p. 6.

Lupton, Deborah. 1995. *The Imperative of Health: Public Health and the Regulated Body*. Thousand Oaks, CA: Sage.

Lyiscott, Jamila. 2017. "Your Pedagogy Might be More Aligned with Colonialism than You Realize." *Medium.com*, May 31. https://medium.com/@heinemann/your-pedagogy-might-be-more-aligned-with-colonialism-than-you-realize-1ae7ac6459ff.

Lynes, Russell. 1976[1949]. "Highbrow, Lowbrow, Middlebrow." *Wilson Quarterly* 1(1): 146–158.

Magowan, Fiona, and Louise Josepha Wrazen. 2013. "Introduction: Musical Intersections, Embodiments, and Emplacements." In *Performing Gender, Place, and Emotion in Music: Global Perspectives*, edited by Fiona Magowan and Louise Josepha Wrazen, 1–16. Rochester, NY: University of Rochester Press.

Makoni, S., and A. Pennycook. 2007. *Disinventing and Reconstituting Languages*. Clevedon: Multilingual Matters.

Maler, Anabel. 2013. "Songs for Hands: Analyzing Interactions of Sign Language and Music." *Music Theory Online* 19(1). http://www.mtosmt.org/issues/mto.13.19.1/mto.13.19.1.maler.pdf.

Marty, Martin E. 1993. "Where the Energies Go." *Annals of the American Academy of Political and Social Science* 527(May): 11–26.

Mathews, Gordon. 2000. *Global Culture/Individual Identity: Searching for Home in the Cultural Marketplace*. Abingdon and New York: Routledge.

Maurer, D., and Landis, T. 1990. "The Role of Bone Conduction in the Self-Perception of Speech." *Folia Phoniatrica et Logopaedica* 42(5): 226–229.

McChesney, Robert. 1999. "Introduction." In *Profit over People: Neoliberalism and Global Order*, by Noah Chomsky, 7–16. New York: Seven Stories.

McCormack, John. 1918. *John McCormack: His Own Life Story*. Transcribed by Pierre V. R. Key. Boston: Small, Maynard.

McCracken, Allison. 2015. *Real Men Don't Sing: Crooning in American Culture*. Durham, NC: Duke University Press.

McIlroy, Guy, and Claudine Storbeck. 2011. "Development of Deaf Identity: An Ethnographic Study." *Journal of Deaf Studies and Deaf Education* 16(4): 494–511.

McIlroy, Guy. 2010. *Discovering Deaf Identities: A Narrative Exploration of Educational Experiences on Deaf Identity*. Saarbrucken, Germany: Lambert Academic Publishers.

McKay, George. 2013. *Shakin' All Over: Popular Music and Disability*. Ann Arbor: University of Michigan Press.

McPherson, Eve. 2005. "The Turkish Call to Prayer: Correlating the AcousticDetails of Vocal Timbre with Cultural Phenomena." *Proceedings of the Conference of Interdisciplinary Musicology*, Montréal, March 10–12.

McPherson, Eve, Sandra McPherson, Roger Bouchard, and Robert Heath Meeks. 2015. "Some Meanings of the Islamic Call to Prayer: A Combined Qualitative and Quantitative Analysis of Some Turkish Narratives." *Narrative Matters 2014: Narrative Knowing/ Récit et Savoir.* https://hal.archives-ouvertes.fr/hal-01111087/document

McWilliams, A. T. 2018. "Sorry to Bother You, Black Americans and the Power and Peril of Code-Switching." *TheGuardian.com*, July 25. https://www.theguardian.com/film/2018/jul/25/sorry-to-bother-you-white-voice-code-switching.

Meizel, Katherine. 2019. "Finding a Voice: Narratives of Women's Voice Loss in American Popular Culture." In *The Singing Voice in Contemporary Cinema*, edited by Diane Hughes and Mark Evans. Sheffield, UK: Equinox.

Meizel, Katherine. 2018a. Liner notes for *Raise Your Voice: The Sound of Student Protest*. Little Village Foundation.

Meizel, Katherine. 2018b. Music and Protest, Hand in Hand: The Songs of the Student Walkouts. *NPR.org*, March 15. https://www.npr.org/sections/therecord/2018/03/15/593866152/music-and-protest-hand-in-hand-songs-of-the-student-walkouts.

Meizel, Katherine. 2016. "Belief Brings Relief—and Sadness—After Decades of Doubt." Stanford Medicine, *Scope*. February 16. https://scopeblog.stanford.edu/2016/02/16/belief-brings-relief-and-sadness-after-decades-of-doubt/

Meizel, Katherine. 2011a. "A Powerful Voice: Studying Vocality and Identity." *Voice and Speech Review: A World of Voice: Voice and Speech Across Cultures and Other Contemporary Issues in Professional Voice & Speech Training* 7(1): 267–273.

Meizel, Katherine. 2011b. *Idolized: Music, Media, and Identity in* American Idol. Bloomington: Indiana University Press.

Meizel, Katherine, and Ronald Scherer. 2019. "Fluid Voices: Processes and Practices in Singing Impersonation." In *Oxford Handbook of Voice Studies*, edited by Nina Eidsheim and Katherine Meizel. Oxford: Oxford University Press. 77–96.

Melamed, Jodi. 2006. "The Spirit of Neoliberalism: From Racial Liberalism to Neoliberal Multiculturalism." *Social Text* 24: 1–24.

Metzger, Melanie.1999. *Sign Language Interpreting: Deconstructing the Myth of Neutrality.* Washington, DC: Gallaudet University Press.

Mey, Jacob L. 1998. *When Voices Clash: A Study in Literary Pragmatics.* Berlin and New York: de Gruyter.

"MILCK—"Quiet." 2017. *PopMatters.com*, January 13. http://www.popmatters.com/post/milck-quiet-premiere/.

Edward Kerr Miller. 1981. *An Ethnography of Singing: The Use and Meaning of Song Within a Scottish Family.* Ph.D. Dissertation, University of Texas, Austin.

Mills, Mara. 2012. "Media and Prosthesis: The Vocoder, the Artificial Larynx, and the History of Signal Processing." *Qui Parle* 21(1): 107–149.

Minutaglio, Rose. 2018. "We Don't Talk about the Teen Victims Who Face Gun Violence Every Day." *Seventeen.com*, May 17. https://www.seventeen.com/life/a19496319/gun-violence-march-teens-everyday-shootings-everytown/.

Mitchell, David T., with Sharon L. Snyder. 2015. *The Biopolitics of Disability: Neoliberalism, Ablenationalism, and Peripheral Embodiment.* Ann Arbor: University of Michigan Press.

Modell, J. D., and G. J. Rich. 1915. "A Preliminary Study of Vowel Qualities." *American Journal of Psychology* 26(3): 453–456.

Mollow, Anna. 2006. "'When *Black* Women Start Going on Prozac . . . ': The Politics of Emotional Distress in Meri Nana-Ama Danquah's *Willow Weep for Me*." In *The*

Disability Studies Reader, second edition, edited by Lennard Davis. New York and London: Routledge.

Moloney, Mick. 2006. "Irish-American Popular Music." In *Making the Irish American: History and Heritage of the Irish in the United States*, edited by Joseph Lee and Marion R. Casey, 381–405. New York: New York University Press.

Moody, Nekesa Mumbi. 2001. "A 'People's Tenor' Shakes Up the Classical World." *The Record*. August 16. F-6.

Mosthof, Mariella. 2017. "If You're Not Talking About the Criticism Surrounding the Women's March, Then You're Part of the Problem." *Bustle.com*, January 30. https://www.bustle.com/p/if-youre-not-talking-about-the-criticism-surrounding-the-womens-march-then-youre-part-of-the-problem-33491.

Moye, David. 2012. "Florida Dwarf Tossing Ban Repeal Dropped by Bill Sponsor Ritch Workman." *HuffingtonPost.com*, April 12. http://www.huffingtonpost.com/2012/04/12/florida-dwarf-tossing-ban-repeal-ritch-workman_n_1421037.html.

Mundy, Barbara E. 2014. "Extirpation of Idolatry and Sensory Experience in Sixteenth Century Mexico." In *Sensational Religion: Sensory Cultures in Material Practice*, edited by Sally M. Promey, 515–536. New Haven, CT: Yale University Press.

Murg, Wilhelm. 2015. "Rhiannon Giddens: Pure Folk-Music Fire From 'A Good-Old Mixed-Race North Carolinian." Indian Country Media Network, March 10. https://indiancountrymedianetwork.com/culture/arts-entertainment/rhiannon-giddens-pure-folk-music-fire-from-a-good-ol-mixed-race-north-carolinian/.

Murphy, Caryle. 2015. "Interfaith Marriages Common in U.S., Particularly Among the Recently Wed." Pew Research Center, June 2. http://www.pewresearch.org/fact-tank/2015/06/02/interfaith-marriage/.

Newell, Christopher, and George Newell. 2014. "Opera Singers as Pop Stars: Opera Within the Popular Music Industry." In *Opera in the Media Age: Essays on Art, Technology, and Popular Culture*, edited by Paul Fryer, 116–148. Jefferson, NC: McFarland.

Newland, Marti. 2014. "Sounding "Black": An Ethnography of Racialized Vocality at Fisk University.: Ph.D. dissertation, Columbia University.

Newton, Benjamin J., Jane L. Southall, Jon H. Raphael, Robert L. Ashford, and Karen LeMarchand. 2013. "A Narrative Review of the Impact of Disbelief in Chronic Pain." *Pain Management in Nursing* 14(3): 161–171.

Nicholson, Timothy R. J., Jon Stone, and Richard A. A. Kanaan. 2011. "Conversion Disorder: A Problematic Diagnosis. *Neuropsychiatry* 82(11): 1267–1273. http://jnnp.bmj.com/content/82/11/1267.

Nilep, Chad. "'Code Switching' in Sociocultural Linguistics." *Colorado Research in Linguistics* 19(1): 1–22.

Norris, Rebecca Sachs. 2003. "Converting to What? Embodied Culture and the Adoption of New Beliefs." In *The Anthropology of Religious Conversion*, edited by Andrew Buckser and Stephen D. Glazier, 171–182. Lanham, MD: Rowman & Littlefield.

Oakes, Jason Lee. 2006. "Queering the Witch: Stevie Nicks and the Forging of Femininity at the Night of a Thousand Stevies." In *Queering the Popular Pitch*, edited by Sheila Whiteley and Jennifer Rycenga, 41–54. Abingdon: Routledge.

Ochoa Gautier, Ana María. 2014. *Aurality: Litening and Knowledge in Nineteenth Century Colombia*. Durham, NC: Duke University Press.

Ohna, Stein Erick. 2004. "Deaf-in-my-own-way: Identity, Learning, and Narratives." *Deafness & Education International* 6(1): 20–38.

Olssen, M. 2006. "Understanding the mechanisms of neoliberal control: Lifelong learning, flexibility and knowledge capitalism." *International Journal of Lifelong Education*, 25(3): 213–230.

Oppenheimer, Mark. 2014. "Examining the Growth of the 'Spiritual But Not Religious.'" *New York Times*, July 18. https://www.nytimes.com/2014/07/19/us/examining-the-growth-of-the-spiritual-but-not-religious.html.

O'Shea, Helen. 2009. "Defining the Nation and Confining the Musician: The Case of Irish Traditional Music." *Music & Politics* 3(2): 1–15.

Osseo-Asare, Afua. 2018. "Voicing the Possible: Technique, Vocal Sound, and Black Women on the Musical Stage." Ph.D. dissertation, New York University.

Ovid, *Metamorphoses*, Book. III. Translated by A. S. Kline. http://ovid.lib.virginia.edu/trans/Metamorph3.htm.

Patch, Holly, and Tomke König. 2018. "Trans* Vocality: Lived Experience, Singing Bodies, and Joyful Politics." *Freiburger Zeitschrift für Geschlechterstudien* 24: 31–53.

Park-Fuller, Linda M. 1986. "VOICES: Bakhtin's Heteroglossial and Polyphony, and the Performance of Narrative Literature." *Literature in Performance* 7: 1–12. http://www.csun.edu/~vcspc00g/604/voices-lpf.html.

Parsons, Talcott. 1951. *The Social System*. Glencoe, IL: Free Press.

Pennington, Stephan. Forthcoming. "Transgender Passing Guides and the Vocal Performance of Gender and Sexuality." In *The Oxford Handbook of Music and Queerness*, edited by Fred E. Maus and Sheila Whiteley. Oxford: Oxford University Press.

Perera, Suvendrini. 2007. "A Pacific Zone? (In)Security, Sovereignty, and Stories of the Pacific Borderscape." In *Borderscapes: Hidden Geographies and Politics at Territory's Edge*, edited by Prem Kumar Rajaram and Garl Grudy-Warr, 201–230.. Borderlines 29. Minneapolis: University of Minnesota Press.

Peterson, Richard A. 1996. "Changing Highbrow Taste: From Snob to Omnivore." *American Sociological Review* 61(5): 900–907.

Peterson, Richard A., and Roger M. Kern. 1996. "Changing Highbrow Taste: From Snob to Omnivore." *American Sociological Review* 61(5): 900–907.

Pfau, Roland, and Josep Quer. 2010. "Nonmanuals: Their Prosodic and Grammatical Roles." In *Sign languages*, edited by Diane Brentari, 381–402. Cambridge Language Surveys. Cambridge: Cambridge University Press.

Pisanski, Katarzyna, Anna Oleszkiewicz, and Agnieszka Sorokowska. 2016. "Can Blid \ Persons Accurately Assess Body Size From the Voice?" *Biology Letters* 12(4). http://rsbl.royalsocietypublishing.org/content/12/4/20160063.

Plasketes, George. 2010. "Introduction: Like a Version." In *Play It Again: Cover Songs in Popular Music*, edited by George Plasketes, 1–10. Surrey and Burlington, VT: Ashgate.

Potter, John. 2006[1998]. *Vocal Authority: Singing Style and Ideology*. Cambridge: Cambridge University Press.

Preston, Katherine. 2016. "Voicing the Real Self." *ASHA Leader*, February, pp. 42–48.

Principe, Walter. 1983. "Toward Defining Spirituality." *Studies in Religion/Sciences Religieuses* 12(2):127–141.

Publius, Xavia A. 2015. "Suggestions for Transgender Inclusion in Classical Music: A Mini-Cycle." Master of Arts thesis, University of Northern Iowa.

Rabinow, Paul. 1996 *Essays on the Anthropology of Reason*. Princeton, NJ: Princeton University Press.

Racy, Ali Jihad. 2003. *Making Music in the Arab World: The Culture and Artistry of Tarab*. Cambridge: Cambridge University Press.

Racy, Ali Jihad. 1982. "Musical Aesthetics in Present-Day Cairo." *Ethnomusicology* 26(3): 391–406.

Rafferty, Sean. 2012. Transcript of Interview with Sarah Grange, Stephen Bentley-Klein, and Janine Roebuck. *Wordpress.com*, August 5. http://aquietlifeopera.wordpress.com/.

Rahaim, Matt. 2012. *Musicking Bodies: Gesture and Voice in Hindustani Music*. Middletown, CT: Wesleyan University Press.

Rajaram, Prem Kumar, and Garl Grudy-Warr. 2007. *Borderscapes: Hidden Geographies and Politics at Territory's Edge*. Borderlines 29. Minneapolis: University of Minnesota Press.

Rampton, Ben. 2014[2005]. *Crossings: Language and Ethnicity Among Adolescents*. Second Edition. Abingdon: Routledge.

Rampton, Ben. 1995. "Language Crossing and the Problematisation of Ethnicity and Socialisation." *Pragmatics* 5(4): 485–513.

Rée, Jonathan. 1999. *I See A Voice: Deafness, Language, and the Senses—A Philosophical History*. New York: Metropolitan Books.

Resnicoff, Matt. 1990. "Dave Davies—One of the Survivors." *Guitar Player*, March. www.davedavies.com/articles/gp_0390.htm.

Roberts, Emmmert, Simon Wessely, Trudie Chalder, Chin-Kuo Chang, and Matthew Hotopf. 2016. "Mortality of People with Chronic Fatigue Syndrome: A Retrospective Cohort Study in England and Wales from the South London and Maudsley NHS Foundation Trust Biomedical Research Centre (SLaM BRC) Clinical Record Interactive Search (CRIS) Register. *The Lancet* 38(10028): 1638–1643.

Robinson, Michael. 1997. "Danny Boy, The Mystery Solved." *Folk Harp Journal* 95: 29–31.

Rodenburg, Patsy. 1992. *The Right to Speak*. New York: Routledge.

Roebuck, Janine. 2014. "I Know That Some Deaf People Are Against Cochlear Implants—But I Am Not One of Them.". *The Independent*, March 28. http://www.independent.co.uk/voices/comment/i-know-that-some-deaf-people-are-against-cochlear-implants--but-i-am-not-one-of-them-9221699.html.

Roebuck, Janine. 2007. "Experience: I Am a Deaf Opera Singer." *The Guardian*, September 29. http://www.theguardian.com/theguardian/2007/sep/29/weekend7.weekend2.

Roof, Wade Clarke. 1999. *Spiritual Marketplace: Baby Booomers and the Remaking of American Religion*. Princeton, NJ: Princeton University Press.

Rose, Beth. 2017. "The Singer Sent Death Threats From the 'Deaf Community.'" *BBCNews.com*, November 15. https://www.bbc.com/news/disability-41850498.

Rose, Nikolas. 1999. *The Powers of Freedom*. New York: Cambridge University Press.

Ross, Alex. 2005. "Applause. A *Rest Is Noise* Special Report." *The Rest Is Noise.com*, February 18. http://www.therestisnoise.com/2005/02/applause_a_rest.html.

Rossi, Allegra. 2005. *Romancing the World: A Biography of Il Divo*. London: Orion.

Rousseau, Jean-Jacques. 1975[1779]. *A Complete Dictionary of Music*. Second Edition. Translated by William Waring. New York: AMS Press.

Ruderman, Jay. 2018. "Episode 5: Interview with Deaf Singer Mandy Harvey." *All Inclusive with Jay Ruderman*, December 3. https://rudermanfoundation.org/podcast/episode-5-interview-with-deaf-singer-mandy-harvey/.

Russell, Anthony. 2015. "I'm Here to Perform Yiddish Music—Not Cater to Your Idea of Blackness." Forward.com. July 31. https://forward.com/culture/yiddish-culture/312390/tk-anthony-russell/ (Accessed July 31, 2015).

Russell, Joshua. 2006. "The Origin and Use of an Authentic Irish Folk Tune in American School Orchestra Arrangements." *Journal of Historical Research in Music Education* 28(1): 38–52.

Saḥḥāb, Ilyās. 1980. *Difaʿan ʿan al-Ughniyah al-ʿArabiyya*. Beirut: al-Muʾassasah al-ʿArabiyya li-al-Dirasat wa-al-Nashr.

St. John, Stevie. 2014. "Methodist Church That Fired Gay Choir Director is Closing." *Advocate.com*. December 18. < https://www.advocate.com/politics/religion/2014/12/18/methodist-church-fired-gay-choir-director-closing> (Accessed January 8, 2017).

Samuels, Ellen. 2014. *Fantasies of Identification: Disability, Gender, Race*. New York: New York University Press.

Sandahl, Carrie, and Philip Auslander, editors. 2005. *Bodies in Commotion: Disability and Performance*. Ann Arbor: University of Michigan Press.

Sanford, Sally. 1995. "A Comparison of French and Italian Singing in the Seventeenth Century." *Journal of Seventeenth-Century Music* 1: 1. http://sscm-jscm.press.uiuc.edu/jscm/v1/no1/sanford.html.

Sartre, Jean-Paul. 1984. *Being and Nothingness: An Essay on Phenomenological Ontology*, translated by Hazel Barnes. London: Methuen.

Saulny, Susan. 2011. "Black? White? Asian? More Young Americans Choose All of the Above." *New York Times*, January 29. https://www.nytimes.com/2011/01/30/us/30mixed.html.

Saville-Troike, Muriel. 2003. *The Ethnography of Communication: An Introduction*. Malden and Oxford: Blackwell.

Scarl, Hilari, producer. *See What I'm Saying: The Deaf Entertainers Documentary*. Film. Directed by Hilari Scarl. Worldplay. 2010.

Schaefer, Ursula. 1993. "Alterities: On Methodology in Medieval Literary Studies." *Oral Tradition* 8(1): 187–214.

Schaefer, Ursula. 1992. *Vokalität: Altenglische Dichtung zwischen Mundlichkeit und Schriftlichkeit*. Tubingen: Gunter Narr.

Schechner, Richard. 1985. *Between Theater and Anthropology*. Philadelphia: University of Pennsylvania Press.

Schürmann, Volker. 2008. "The Materiality of the Abstraction, Voice." *Journal of Integrative Psychological & Behavioral Science* 42(1):114–120.

Senior, Jennifer. 1994. "Language of the Deaf Evolves To Reflect New Sensibilities." *New York Times*, January 3. http://www.nytimes.com/1994/01/03/us/language-of-the-deaf-evolves-to-reflect-new-sensibilities.html.

Sharif, Samim. 1981. "Al-Qasabji wa Asmahan wa al-Aswat al-Jamila fi al-Marhala al Simimaʾiyya," In *Al-Ughniyya al-ʿArabiyya*, 221–222. Damascus: Wizarat al-Thaqafa wa al-Irshad.

Shattuc, Jane. 1997. *The Talking Cure: TV Talk Shows and Women*. London: Routledge.

Sheldon, Deborah. 1997. "The Illinois School for the Deaf Band: A Historical Perspective." *Journal of Research in Music Education* 45(4): 580–600.

Shields, Hugh. 1979. "New Dates for Old Songs—1766-1803." *Long Room* 18/19: 34–41.

Shubin, Sergei. 2012. Living on the Move: Mobility, Religion and Exclusion of Eastern European Migrants in Rural Scotland." *Population, Space and Place* 18 (5): 615–627.

Simon, Scott. 2012. "Carolina Chocolate Drops: Hooked on Old-Time Sounds." *NPR.org*, March 9. https://www.npr.org/templates/transcript/transcript.php?storyId=148300894.

"Simon Cowell on Il Divo: Classical Is So Snobby." 2008. *Telegraph.co.uk*, November 6. http://www.telegraph.co.uk/culture/music/3562914/Simon-Cowell-on-Il-Divo-classical-is-so-snobby.html.

Sims, Loraine. 2017. "Teaching Lucas: A Transgender Vocal Student's Journey from Soprano to Tenor." *Journal of Singing* 73(4): 367–375.

Sit, Ryan. 2018. "More than 2 Million in 90 Percent of voting Districts Joined March For Our Lives Protests." *Newsweek.com*. March 26. https://www.newsweek.com/march-our-lives-how-many-2-million-90-voting-district-860841.

Smith, Jacob. 2008. *Vocal Tracks: Performance and Sound Media*. Berkeley, Los Angeles, and London: University of California Press.

Spencer, Leland G. 2014. "Performing Transgender Identity in *The Little Mermaid*: From Andersen to Disney." *Communication Studies* 65(1): 112–127.

Spohr, Arne. 2009. "How Chances It They Travel?" In *Englische Musiker in Dänemark und Norddeutschland 1579–1630*, xlv. Wolfenbütteler Arbeiten zur Barockforschung. Wiesbaden: Harrassowitz.

Spoon, Rae. 2014. *Gender Failure*. Vancouver, BC: Arsenal Pulp Press.

Stahl, Matt. 2013. *Unfree Masters: Recording Artists and the Politics of Work*. Durham, NC: Duke University Press.

Steele, Scott. 1997. "Nude Angels and 'Creepy' People." *Maclean's* 110(5): 65.

Stewart, Donald. 1972. *The Authentic Voice: A Pre-Writing Approach to Student Writing*. Dubuque, IA: Brown.

Stirner, Max. 1907[1845]. *The Ego and His Own*. Translated by Steven T. Byington. Gutenberg.org. http://www.gutenberg.org/files/34580/34580-h/34580-h.htm.

Storey, John. 2002. "'Expecting Rain': Opera as Popular Culture?" In *High-Pop: Making Culture Into Popular Entertainment*, edited by Jim Collins, 32–55. Malden: Blackwell.

Stover, Cassandra. 2013. "Damsels and Heroines: The Conundrum of the Post-Feminist Disney Princess." *LUX: A Journal of Transdisciplinary Writing and Reearch from Claremont Graduate University* 2(1). http://scholarship.claremont.edu/lux/vol2/iss1/29.

Stras, Laurie. 2006. "The Organ of the Soul: Voice, Damage, and Affect." In *Theorizing Disability in Music*, edited by Neil Lerner and Joseph N. Straus, 173–184. New York and London: Routledge.

Straus, Joseph. 2011. *Extraordinary Measures: Disabilty in Music*. Oxford: Oxford University Press.

Strüver, Anke. 2005. *Stories of the "Boring Border": The Dutch-German Borderscape in People's Minds*. Berlin: LIT.

Summit, Jeffrey A. 2000. *The Lord's Song in a Strange Land: Music and Identity in Contemporary Jewish Worship*. Oxford: Oxford University Press.

Sundberg, Johan. 1987. *The Science of the Singing Voice*. Dekalb, IL: Northern Illinois University Press.

Sussman, Lance J. 1982. "'Toward Better Understanding'": The Rise the Interfaith Movement in America and the Role of Rabbi Isaac Landman." *American Jewish Archives* 34: 35–51.

Taste of Three Mo' Tenors: Live in Chicago. 2006. WMK Productions.

Taylor, Charles. 1989. *Sources of the Self*. Cambridge, MA: Harvard University Press.

Tillman, Adriane. 2017. "Musician with ME Produces EP from her Bed." *MEAction.net*, April 1. http://www.meaction.net/2017/04/01/musician-with-me-produces-ep-from-her-bed/.

Titze, Ingo. 2001. "Acoustic Interpretation of Resonant Voice." *Journal of Voice* 15 (4): 519–528.
Tomlinson, Gary. 1995. "Ideologies of Aztec Song." *Journal of the American Musicological Society* 48(3): 343–379.
Torrence, Stephen. 2014. "On the Ethics of 'My' Art." *Torrentsofthought.com*, September 20. http://www.torrentsofthought.com/on-the-ethics-of-my-art/.
Tunnell Kenneth D. "A Cultural Approach to Crime and Punishment, Buegrass Style." In *Cultural Criminology*, edited by Jeff Ferrell and Clinton Sanders, 80–105. Boston: Northeastern University Press.
Türken, Salman, Hilde Eileen Nafstad, Rolv Mikkel Blakar, and Katrina Roen. 2015. "Making Sense of Neoliberal Subjectivity: A Discourse Analysis of Media Language on Self-Development." *Globalizations* 13(1): 32–46.
Turner, Victor. 1982. *From Ritual to Theatre: The Human Seriousness of Play*. New York: PAJ Publications.
Tyson, Lee. 2016. "Transgender Vocalities and Sonic Glitches: Vocal Failure as Critical Practice." Unpublished manuscript, American Anthropological Association.
Utz, Christian, and Frederick Lau. 2013. "Introduction: Voice, Identities, and Reflexive Globalization in Contemporary Music Practices." In *Vocal Music and Contemporary Identities: Unlimited Voices in East Asia and the West*, 1–24. New York and London: Routledge.
Ventura, Dinah S. 2013. "Sonata Resonates with Feeling." *Daily Tribune*, September 11. http://www.tribune.net.ph/index.php/life-style/item/19018-sonata-resonates-with-feeling.
Ventura, Patricia. 2012. *Neoliberal Culture: Living with American Neoliberalism*. London and New York: Routledge.
"Video Premiere: Kaeley Pruitt-Hamm." 2017. *ImMusicMag.com*, March 17. http://www.immusicmag.com/2017/03/video-premier-kaeley-pruitt-hamm-believe-her/.
Vigreux, Philippe (editor). 1992. *Musique Arabe: Le Congrès du Caire de 1932*. Cairo: CEDEJ.
"Vocal Fry: The New Craze in Talking Inspired by Britney Spears, Ke$ha and Kim Kardashian." 2011. *Daily Mail*, December 13. http://www.dailymail.co.uk/news/article-2073800/Vocal-fry-The-new-craze-talking-inspired-Britney-Spears-Ke-ha.html.
Vygotsky, Lev S. 1998. *Child psychology: The Collected Works of L.S. Vygotsky*, Vol. 5. New York and London: Plenum.
Walker, Frank X. 2008. "Playing It Now: Carolina Chocolate Drops Upohold Traditional Folk Music but Make It New." *Pluck! The Journal for Affrilachian Aerts & Culture* 4: 38–40.
Wallach, Jeremy. 2008. *Modern Noise, Fluid Genres: Popular Music in Indonesia, 1997–2001*. New Perspectives in Southeast Asian Studies 3. Madison: University of Wisconsin Press.
Waterman, Jan. 2009. "Mandy Harvey: No Silent Songs." *Healing Path*, March.
Watson, Russell. 2008. *Finding My Voice: My Story*. London: Ebury Press.
Weber, Max. 2004[1930]. *The Protestant Ethic and the Spirit of Capitalism*. Translated by Talcott Parsons. London and New York: Routledge.
Weirich, N., and Simpson, A. 2013. "Investigating the Relationship Between Average Speaker Fundamental Frequency and Acoustic Vowel Space Size." *Journal of the Acoustical Society of America* 134(4): 2965–2974.

Weiss, A. P. 1920. "The Vowel Character of Fork Tones." *American Journal of Psychology* 31(2): 166–193.

Welch, Graham F., and David M. Howard. 2002. "Gendered Voice in the Cathedral Choir." *Psychology of Music* 30(1): 102–120.

Welkos, Robert W. 2006. "Rival Bands Clash Over Little-Person KISS Tribute." *Los Angeles Times*, April 11. http://articles.latimes.com/2006/apr/11/entertainment/et-minikiss11.

Wilson, Louise. 2012. "A Quiet Life—Not Your Usual Opera." *CactusLouise.com*, August 15. http://cactuslouise.com/2012/08/15/a-quiet-life-not-your-usual-opera/.

Winston, Kimberly. 2015. "African-American Opera Singer Revives the Songs of the Shtetl." *New York Jewish Week*, August 3. http://jewishweek.timesofisrael.com/african-american-opera-singer-revives-the-songs-of-the-shtetl/.

Wohlberg, Max. 2010. "The Music of the Synagogue as a Source of the Yiddish Folk Song." *Journal of Synagogue Music* 35: 6–34.

Wolk, Lesley, Nassima B. Abdelli-Beruh, and Dianne Slavin. 2012. "Habitual Use of Vocal Fry in Young Adult Female Speakers." *Journal of Voice* 26(3): 111–116.

Wong, Deborah. 2000. "The Asian American Body in Performance." In *Music and the Racial Imagination* (Ronald Radano and Philip V. Bohlman, editors). Chicago: University of Chicago Press. 57–94.

Woolard, Kathryn. 2004. "Codeswitching." In *A Companion to Linguistic Anthropology*, edited by Alessandro Duranti, 73–94. Malden and Oxford: Blackwell.

Wright, H. H. 1911. "Jubilee Songs at Chapel Exercises." *Fisk University News*, October.

"You know you're Trans* when..." 2014. http://youknowyouretrans.tumblr.com.

Young, Vershawn Ashanti. 2009. "'Nah, We Straight': An Argument Against Code Switching." *JAC: Journal of Rhetoric, Culture, & Politics* 29(1/2): 49–76.

Zink, James R. 2009. "The Language of Liberty and Law: James Wilson on America's Written Constitution." *American Political Science Review* 103(3): 442–455.

Žižek, Slavoj. 2001. *On Belief.* London: Routledge.

Zuhur, Sherifa. 2000. *Asmahan's Secrets: Woman, War, and Song.* Austin: University of Texas, Center for Middle Eastern Studies.

Zumthor, Paul. 1987. *La Lettre et la Voix: de la "Littérature" Médiévale.* Paris: Editions du Seuil.

Index

Page locators in italics refer to figures and photographs

Abitbol, Jean, 79
acousmatic voice, 72, 80–81, 159, 173
acoustemology, 6
acoustic formant, 36, 56, 63
acoustics, 99, 112, 124–125, 153;
    psychoacoustics, 7, 97
Adams, Sheila Kay, 32
advertising, 26–27, 119
Affrilachian music, 2, 35
Against Me! (band), 150
agency, 4–5, 20, 23, 26, 179; d/ Deaf identity
    and, 11, 91–92, 102, 105, 113–114;
    disability and, 82–83, 87, 89, 192, 195;
    global discourse of, 176; style and, 46–47
Ahlin, Lars, 117
Aizura, Aren Z., 141
Americana Music Association (AMA), 35
American Idol, 1, 5, 27, 32, 82, 170
American Sign Language (ASL), 92, 92n, 94, 95,
    96, 101, 103, 104, 108, 109, 110
American Songbook, 55, 150
Americans with Disabilities Act (ADA)
    anniversary, 91
America's Got Talent, 53, 60, 101–102
Andersen, Hans Christian, 137–138, 164, 171
Anderson, Laurie Halse, 170
Anderson, Marion, 154
André, Naomi, 67
Andrews, Helena, 107
Andy Hardy's Private Secretary (film), 43
Anzaldúa, Gloria, 14–15, 40, 140
Appadurai, Arjun, 15–16
Appalachian music, 1, 32–36
appropriation, 5–7, 32–37; of folk musics, 36–
    37; impersonation and, 75; interpretation,
    shift to, 39; nonverbal language, 107; sign-
    singing, 108–111; white, of Black musics,
    34–35, 66
Arab music, 42–45
Aristophanes, 162
"artivism", 212
Ashby, Christine, 20
Ashley, Martin, 143

"The Asian American Body in Performance"
    (Wong), 206
ASL. *See* American Sign Language
Asmahan (Syrian- Egyptian star), 42–45, *43*
al- Atrash, Farid, 42
audibility, 9
audience: code- switching and, 65; d/ Deaf, 103;
    female, 52–54; "middlebrow", 54–55; white
    nonparticipation, 67; YouTube viewers, 78
audiocentrism, 81, 100
audism, 94
Auditory Verbal UK, 112–113
aural gaze, 9
Auslander, Philip, 83
Austin, J. L., 199
Austin- Broos, Diane, 132
authenticity, 27–31, 132; disabled voices
    and, 82–83; microphones and, 64;
    transgender voices and, 145, 154
The Authentic Voice (Stewart), 26
authority, vocal, 8
autodidacticism, 58
autopathography, 83
Azrieli- Perez, Sharon, 126

BaAka ensemble, 39
bahha (hoarseness or break), 44
Bairstow, Edward G., 7
Bakhtin, Mikhail, 12–13, 20, 132, 206, 215
Bangerz (Cyrus, album), 87
bara and *asah* (creation in Genesis), 124
Barad, Karen, 11
Barbour- Payne, Yunina, 2, 35
Barthes, Roland, 10, 108
Baugher, Kristin Williams, 29, 31
Bauman, H. Dirksen L., 93–94, 95
Bayton, Mavis, 174
Beames, Finn, 151
becoming, politics of, 16–17, 137
"BedFest" virtual music festival, 189–190, 194–195
being- in- the- world, 6
Belarsky, Sidor, 130, 132
bel canto, 43–46, 52

"Believe Her" (Pruitt-Hamm), 189, 192, 194
Bell, Alexander Graham, 97
belonging, 16–17; of voice, 77, 81, 88
Bentley-Klein, Stephen, 111–112
Berberian, Cathy, 6, 7
Bernstein, Jonathan, 35
Bertau, Marie-Cécile, 11, 15
Beyoncé, 170
Bickford, J. Albert, 104
bi-culturality, 95–96
Bienvenu, M. J., 94–95, 110
Biklen, Sari Knopp, 20
Billboard "classical crossover" charts, 49
"Binary Optional" (show), 151
biocertification, 167, 192
biopolitics/biopower, 96, 178–179
The Birth of a Nation (film), 168
Bisserier, Lara, 30
Black Lives Matter movement, 3, 134, 189, 208–209
Black singers, 2–3, 32–35, 55; appropriation of, 65–66, 75–77; "Black voice," colonial concept of, 33, 76, 129, 130; popera/classical crossover as space for operatic, 65–69. *See also* Russell, Anthony Mordechai Zvi
Black student activists, 208–209
Blease, Charlotte, 190, 192–193
bluegrass style, 34
Bocelli, Andrea, 57
body: internal-external borders of, 14–15; racialized, 9, 54; scrutiny of, 81. *See also* embodiment
Bogdan, Robert C., 20
Booth, Wayne, 215
Borderlands/La Frontera: The New Mestiza (Anzaldúa), 40
borders: between belonging and nonbelonging, 16; code crossing, 13–14; crossings, 7; hearing/Deaf Borderlands, 95; internal-external, of body, 14–15; popera as, 51–52; as site of struggle, 17; transgression of, 49; websites, 52
borderscapes, 15–17, 21, 40, 73, 215; cultural bridging, 183–184; disability and, 195–196; geographical, 16; sonic borderlands, 15, 140; spirituality and, 120, 136; voice as, 46–47, 46–47, 15–17, 184; voice loss and, 178–179
Borderscapes: Hidden Geographies and Politics at Territory's Edge (Rajaram and Grundy-Warr), 16
Bowden, Darsie, 26
boy bands, 53, 58

Boyle, Susan, 31, 77, 82, 167
Brahms, Johannes, 130
Brambilla, Chiara, 16–17
Braxton, Toni, 56
Brea, Jennifer, 190
breathing, 10, 31, 43–44, 68, 164
Britain's Got Talent, 31, 57, 82, 167
British Empire, 9
British Sign Language (BSL), 112
Broadway, 64, 181
Brooks, Daphne, 76–77
Brown, Michael, 209
Bryan, Karen M., 67
Buckley, Jeff, 139
Buddhist chant, 122, 123
Bühler, Urs, 58
Bumbry, Grace, 154
Butler, Judith, 46, 138

Caffey, Marion, 31, 66–67, 68
Calvinism, 27
Cameron, Deborah, 25
Canaday, Melissa, 122
Cannon, Annie Jump, 111
Cantares Mexicanos, 14–15
cantors, 126–127, 130–134, *133*
Cantus (group), 31
Carel, Havi, 192–193
Carolina Chocolate Drops, 1, 35
Carr, Revell, 150–151
Carter, Nathan, 154
Casey, Karen, 32
Cavarero, Adriana, 4, 6, 30, 89
Celtic music, 2–3, 32
Central Conference of (Reform) American Rabbis (CCAR), 127–128
Chana, Nadia, 18, 121–122
Chapman, Dale, 5
chest voice, 19, 43
Cheung, Ingrid, 191
children's voices, 143–144
Chinese American musicians, 204–205
Chion, Michel, 167
Cho, Samson, 41
Choi, Julie, 13
choice, 9, 23, 89, 105, 119, 128, 215; consumer, 38–39, 52, 117, 120; Jews, importance to, 128; transgender/trans* singers and, 139, 145–146
Choir!Choir!Choir!, 202, 206
choral singing, 116, 121–123, 143, 160
Chronic Creatives Choir (virtual ensemble), 194–195

chronic fatigue syndrome (CFS)/ myalgica encephalomyelitis (ME), 190–192, 194
chronic illness, 186–195
"The Chronopher" (Connor), 186
Chung, Christopher, 41
Church of Santo Daime, 120–121
Cirque du Soleil, 85
Civil Rights movement, 26, 135, 208–209
classical crossover. *See* popera/ classical crossover
classical tradition, western: authenticity attributed to, 27; borderscapes traversed by, 28; singers trained in, 21, 27
class relations: folk song performance and, 7–8; "middlebrow," "lowbrow," and "highbrow," 54–55; "vox populi", 56–57
Closer (Groban, album), 58
Cloud, Khristopher, 147
code crossing, 13–14, 215
code- switching, 13, 21, 65
Cohane, Mary Ellen, 18
Cohen, John, 34
Cohen, Judah M., 127
collective voice, 12–13, 17, 198
colonialism, 7–9, 13; laryngoscope and racialized listening, 28; medical system and, 192
Columbian Exposition (Chicago, 1893), 117
Columbine High School (mass shooting), 208, 209
commodification of voice, 4–5, 163
communal singing, 121, 122, 125
Compañía Lírica Pópera, 65
Congrès de Musique Arabe du Caire (1932), 45
Connor, Steven, 81, 186
Conrad, Peter, 191, 195
Constansis, Alexandros, 139, 144, 146
consumer choice, 38–39, 52, 117, 120
control. *See* vocal control
"Convergence: Spirituals from the Shtetl. Davening from the Delta" (Russell), 132
conversion (religious), 25, 116, 129–136. *See also* spiritual multivocality
conversion disorder diagnosis, 187
Cooper, Jennifer Goode, 32
Cooper, Sean, 29, 64
Couldry, Nick, 3–5, 6, 50, 198–199
countertenor repertoire, 155
country music, trans and non- gender- conforming singers in, 139
"cover complex", 73
cover songs, 73
Cowell, Simon, 56, 58, 170

Coyote Grace (band), 147
Crane, Frank, 167
"creaky voice", 62
crisis of voice, 3–7, 50; adolescence as, 170
Crocker, Chris, 175–176
crooning, 51–53
crossover genres, 40–42; earlier eras, 55; finding a voice and, 30. *See also* popera/ classical crossover
Crow, Cheryl, 78
cultural construction, voice as site of, 184
cultural history of performer, 2–3
culture, as contested term, 37
Cummings, Sandy, 180, 195
Cusick, Suzanne, 15
Cyrus, Miley, 87

Dahir, Saida, 212, 213
Dailey, Patrick, 116
Damascus conservatory, 42, 43
dance, 28, 97, 103–104, 174
Dance of the Wind (film), 173
Danielson, Virginia, 43
"Danny Boy" (Weatherly), 59
Darro, Alice- Ann, 94
Davenport, Tom, 34
Davies, Dave, 26
Day, Andra, 209
d/ Deaf community, 11; agency and identity, 91–93, 102, 105; audism as discrimination against, 94; cochlear implants, 101, 113; institutionalized trauma, 93; interpreters, 106–111
Deaf culture, 91n, 92, 92n, 93, 94, 96, 101, 102, 110, 113
d/ Deaf singers, 22, 91–114, 178; d/ Deaf/ DeaF, 94–96; hearing/ deaf borderlands, 95; internal sensation, focus on, 100; singing and signing as dual vocalities, 93, 102. *See also* disability
"Deaf Can" discourse, 102
"deaf hearing", 112
Dechaine, Nichole, 159–165, 175
DeMille, Cecil B., 167
"Dem Milners Trern" (Yiddish song), 130
democracy, 3–6, 197
Dent, Edward J., 8, 10
Der Einzige sein Eigentum (The Unique One and Its Own) (Stirner), 148
Derfner, Joel, 123–124, 185, 195
Derrida, Jacques, 93–94, 148–149
De Voil, Simon, 138–139, 144, 146, 149–150, 178

DiCaire, Véronic, 74–80, *76*, 89
Dickinson, Emily, 195
Dickinson, Kandice, 195
Dictionnaire de Musique (Rousseau), 9
difference: within classical vocality, 29; embodied, 8, 82; theatrical transvestism and, 21; voice as site of, 9, 138
Diggs, Ramone, 66
Dinklage, Peter, 84
Dinnerstein, Norman, 124
Dion, Céline, 53, 57, 75, 88
"A Dio le Pido" (Juanes/ Compañía Lírica Pópera), 65
disability, 72–73; agency and, 82–83, 87, 89, 192, 195; biocertification requirement, 167, 192; borderscapes and, 195–196; "damaged" voices, study of, 179; Ehlers- Danlos Syndrome, 177–178, 186–187, 191, 194; epistemic injustice, 178, 192–193; Hard of Hearing (HOH) people, 95–96, 101, 108; impersonation and, 81–83; mast cell activation disorder, 186–187, 190; medical and social models of, 179; myalgica encephalomyelitis (ME)/chronic fatigue syndrome (CFS), 190–192, 194; non- speaking people, 20; resistance movement, 187; silencing and, 189, 192; voice loss and, 177–178, 181–182, 185–194; women and, 186–189, 192–195. *See also* d/Deaf singers; health, vocal
Disability March website, 188–189
disability studies, 82, 167, 192
disembodiment, vocal, 159–160, 163, 168
distributed voice, 198–199
Doctor Faustus (Mann), 164
Dolar, Mladen, 72, 118, 162
Doleman, Christopher, 210, 213
dominance, ideologies of, 4, 8
"Dora" case study (Freud), 171
Dostoevsky, Fyodor, 12, 215
double consciousness, 14
double- voicedness, 140
D-PAN (Deaf Performing Arts Network), 110
Dreamgirls (film), 170
dual vocalities, 40, 47, 93, 102, 105, 113–114, 150, 206
Du Bois, W. E. B., 14
du Maurier, George, 167–168, 170, 173
Dumbstruck: A Cultural History of Ventriloquism (Connor), 81
Dunn, Adrian, 67–69
Dunn, Leslie, 10, 164
Durbin, Deanna, 54, 167
Durbin, James, 82
dwarf- tossing, 86–87
dysautonomia, 186–187, 191

earplugs, 100
"easy listening", 54
echo, 163–164
Eden, Vivian, 135
Ehlers- Danlos Syndrome, 186, 191, 194
Eidsheim, Nina Sun, 9, 11, 17, 19, 27, 29, 112; ethical listening concept, 123; sensory aspect of voice, 120; vocal honesty concept, 32; on Vocaloid marketing, 160, 162
El Guindi, I Fadwa, 119
Elvis impersonators, 72, 84–88
"Embodied Approach to the Ethnography of Singing" (Chana), 18
Embodied Voices (Dunn and Jones), 10
embodiment, 8, 39, 75, 88, 102, 106, 168, 215; infant sounds as most authentic, 30; listener and, 10–11; in religious conversion, 129; transvocality and, 139. *See also* body
emotional connections, 183–184, 212, 214
entheogens, psychedelics as, 120
epistemic injustice, 178, 192–193
Ernman, Malena, 57
Esposito, Luigi, 4, 207
essentialism, 29, 75, 77, 84, 108
ethnography, 18–20
An Ethnography of Singing: The Use and Meaning of Song Within a Scottish Family (Miller), 18
Eurich- Rascoe, Barbara, 26
Eurovision Song Contest, 57, 59
Evanescence (band), 105
Everytown for Gun Safety, 208, 209, 214
"The Experiences of Musicians with Hearing Impairments" (Fulford et al.), 100
Extraordinary Measures: Disability in Music (Straus), 80

face/mouth, grammar in, 104
Fach (voice and character type), 56, 129–130, 142; gender transition and, 151–156
Fackrell, Kyle, 212
Fairweather, DeLisa, 187
family, silencing by, 180–181
Farrar, Geraldine, 167
Fathi, Ahmad, 44
Feld, Steven, 6, 8, 11
Feldman, Martha, 14, 15

INDEX

feminine taste, 53
femininity, 149–150, 152, 155–156, 168, 171, 174, 180
Femininity and Shame: Women, Men, and Giving Voice to the Feminine (Eurich-Rascoe and Vande Kemp), 26
feminist activisms, 188–189
feminist perspectives, 26
Fenwick, Ray, 78
Festival de la Medina (Tunisia), 46
film, 23, 40, 44, 55; acquired voicelessness in, 167–172; cinematization of opera, 167; global, voice loss in, 172–173; morality in, 168–173; New Wave of princess films, 170; women's voice loss in, 167–174
finding a voice, 25–47, 97; American musical styles and, 32–35; appropriative practices and, 32–37; crossing genre, geographical, and cultural borders, 40–42; imitation and, 105; liberating vocal thumbprint, 29–32; not singing like an opera singer, 35–40; as popular concept, 26–27; social suppression of voice, 27; transgender/trans* singers and, 140; "Ya Toyour," East-West qualities in, 42–47. *See also* voice
Finley, Laura L., 4, 207
Flamer, Ashlyn, 210, 213
flash-mob performances, 201, 206
Fleeger, Jennifer, 167, 168
Flood, David, 86
flow, 15–16
folk-revival movements, 39, 59
folk song, 8, 10
"Folksongs and the Enthography of Singing in Patrick Kennedy's *The Banks of the Boro*" (Cohane and Goldstein), 18
Forbes, Sean, 92
formants, 36, 56, 63
Forsberg, T. L., 100, 102–108, *107*, 112, 178
Forward, 134
forward voice, 99–100
Foster, Stephen, 51
Foucault, Michel, 96
Fraychineaud, Kathy, 104
freedom, 27, 31, 100, 204
Freedom Highway (Giddens), 3
Freud, Sigmund, 171, 188
Fricker, Miranda, 192–193
Friedman, Debbie, 127
Friedner, Michele, 96
Frock Rock (Bayton), 174
"Frühlingsstimmen" (Strauss), 44, 45
Fryer, Paul, 167

Fulford, Robert, 100
Full Frontal with Samantha Bee (television show), 202
Funny Kinda Guy (documentary), 138–139, 145

Garaghty, Keith, 192–193
Garcia, Manuel, II, 28, 29
Garland-Thomson, Rosemarie, 83, 84, 87
Garrido, Maria, 199–200
Gates, J. Terry, 174
Gawatz, Larry (Little E), 84–89
gay communities, 107
gay men, in African American churches, 116
Gazal (film), 172
gaze, 4, 9, 28, 143
Geertz, Clifford, 38
gender. *See* transgender/trans*; women
gendered performative prescriptions, 129–130
geno-song, 10
Genuine Negro Jig (album), 35
Geschlechtsreise, 152
"Ghost of a Boy" (Spoon), 147
ghosts/ghost selves, 146–149
Gibb, G. Duncan, 9
Giddens, Rhiannon, 1–3, 7, 17, 21, 32–35, 41
Giradoux, Jean, 164
The Girl of the Golden West (film), 167
A Girl of Yesterday (film), 168
"giving voice", 20
global capital crisis, 4
global cultural marketplace, 38–39
"Glory" (song), 209
"Go Down Moses (Let My People Go)" (spiritual), 135
Goldin-Perschbacher, Shana, 139
Goldstein, Kenneth S., 18
Gonzalez, Adrianne, 201
González, Emma, 207, 212
The Goose Woman (film), 169
Grace, Laura Jane, 150
Graham, Brendan, 57
"grain of the voice", 10
Grange, Sarah, 111
Grayson, Kathryn, 43
Great Compassion Repentance Ceremony (Buddhist), 123
Greendale Shapiro, Lilah, 125
Greenfield, Elizabeth Taylor, 65
Groban, Josh, 58
Gross, Kelly, 39
Grossberg, Lawrence, 83
Grover-Friedlander, Michal, 165
Grundy-Warr, Carl, 16
gun violence, 198, 207–214

Haddad, Yvonne Yazbeck, 119
Hague, Seth, 206
Halavais, Alexander, 199–200
Hall, Vera Ward, 32, 33
Hardly Strictly Bluegrass Festival (San Francisco), 213
Hard of Hearing (HOH) people, 95–96, 100–102, 108. *See also* d/ Deaf community; d/ Deaf singers
Harkness, Nicholas, 36, 41n5, 92, 123
Harvey, David, 4
Harvey, Mandy, 91, 98, 100–102, 104
Hasidic melody, 133–134
Haskell, John A., 98
Hastrup, Kirsten, 72
Hayward, Bill, 57
head voice, 19, 43
Healing Path Magazine, 100
health, vocal, 28–29, 31–32. *See also* disability
Healy, Bernadine, 188
Heart Full of Soul: An Inspirational Memoir About Finding Your Voice and Finding Your Way (Hicks), 27
Heidegger, Martin, 6
Herder, Johann Gottfried, 197
Hermans, Hubert J. M., 15
hermeneutical injustice, 192–193
heteroglossia, 12
Hicks, Taylor, 27
hierarchy of realities, 72
Hi From Pillows (Pruitt-Hamm), 188–189
"highbrow", 54
High Lonesome (album), 34
High Lonesome (film), 34
"high lonesome" timbre, 1, 32–39
hijab movement, 119
Hindustani music, 96–97
hip hop, 67–69
Hirschkind, Charles, 123
HIV/AIDS epidemic, 190
"Hof un Gloyb" ("Hope and Believe," Yiddish labor song), 134
Hogg, David, 212
Holbcomb, Roscoe, 34
honesty, 29, 32, 130, 145
Hood, Mantle, 37
"HOPERA", 67–69
Hounddog (film), 171
Houston, Whitney, 108–109
human capital, 25, 159–160
Huron, David, 74
Husserl, Edmund, 93
hybridity, 54–55, 139
Hymes, Dell, 18

#ICan'tKeepQuiet, 201–206, *203*
identity: 21st-century, 6–7; crisis of, 30, 181; d/ Deaf agency and, 91–93, 102, 105; as fabrication, 138; negotiation of, 7, 15–17, 21–23; popera and, 57; separation between personal and theatrical life, 152; sociovocal strategies, 73; spirituality and, 132; vocal negotiation of, 7, 17, 26, 184; voice loss and, 23, 164
identity theft, 163
Il Divo (popera group), 49, 51, *51*, 69; Anglophone pop ballads in romance languages, 55, 56–58; gendered demographic of audience, 52–54; technique and technology used by, 61–65, *62*, *63*
Image, Music, Text (Barthes), 10
"I'm Here to Perform Yiddish Music--Not Cater to Your Idea of Blackness" (Russell), 134
imitation, 1–2, 32–33, 36; singing along with stars, 102–103, 105
immigration, 14, 40–47, 50, 54, 59, 92, 120, 121, 198, 214
imperialism, vocal, 8
impersonation, 21–22, 71–89, 156; 50 voices, 74–77, *76*; acousmatic voice, 72; blind auditions, 79–81; disabled singers and, 81–83; of Elvis Presley, 72, 80; as hyper-representational, 88–89; lip-synching, 83, 87–88; "mini" impersonators, 83–87; oculo-centric techniques, 74; "own" voice of impersonator, 77–79; representation and, 73, 88; spoken, 77; visual/ aural incongruities, 72–73
individualism, 4, 6, 20, 23, 27, 117; hyperindividualism, 207; of voice, in neoliberalism, 25–26
infant sounds, 30
In Living Color (television show), 107
"inner voice", 27
intent, 125–128, 132
International Women's Day, 202
interpretation, sign, 106–111; melisma/ runs, 108–109; nonverbal language, 107; sign-gestures, 107
intersectionality, 15, 128, 203–206; voice as sonic negotiation of, 17; voice intertwined with, 27; (en)voicing, 129–136
interstitiality of voice, 7, 14
intersubjectivity, 7, 10–12, 26, 198, 215
Iraq, 173
Irish Americans, 59
Irish music, *sean-nós* tradition, 181

Irish nationalist folk-culture movement, 58
Irish tenor crossover music, 58–61
I See a Voice: Deafness, Language, and the Senses (Rée) 93
Islam, 118–119, 123, 129; Quranic recitation, 43
"isochronic tones", 122
Italian language, 9–10, 56–58
Izambard, Sébastien, 56, 57–58, 69

James, Branden, 53, 60
Jane, Hollis, 87
Janet, Pierre, 188
Jarman-Ivens, Freya, 72
Jean-Baptiste, Jerramiah, 212, 213
Jenkins, Tyler, 212
jeong (Korean concept), 40–41
Jewish musical traditions, 125–128; choice, importance of, 128; davening (praying), 122–123, 129; integrated theology, 127–128; *kavanah* and, 126; *krekhts* (moaning), 131–132; *nusach* (melodic modes), 126–127
Jewish refugees, 168
Jobin, Sara, 182
Johnson, E. Patrick, 107
Jones, Alisha, 116
Jones, Jamila, 208
Jones, Jeannette DiBernardo, 92
Jones, Nancy, 10, 164
Jones, Sissieretta, 65
Journal of American Sign Language, 94
Journal of Medical Ethics, 192
Journal of the American Medical Association, 187
Journal of the American Musicological Society, 15
Journal of Voice, 62
journey, notion of, 141, 152
Juanes (musician), 65
Jubilee Singers (Fisk University), 65
Judaism, 124–128; conversion to, 128–136. *See also* Jewish musical traditions
Juris, Jeffrey, 198

Kamakawiwo'ole, Israel, 80
Kansau, Jimmy, 30
Keegan, Cael M., 141
Keightley, Keir, 54
Kelly, Emmanuel, 82
Kennicott, Philip, 64
Kern, Roger M., 55
Killen, Louisa Jo, 150
Kim, Charlene Chi, 21, 36, 39–40
kinesthetic experience, 32, 74, 80, 112, 120, 129, 215

King, David, 60
King, Homay, 199
Kisliuk, Michelle, 39
Klein, Jeff, 119
Kline, A. S., 163
Klipp, Joshua, 132, 143, 146–147, 149–150, 178
Klipptones (band), 150
Koestenbaum, Wayne, 25
"Kol Nidrei" (Jewish recitation), 130
König, Tomke, 11, 139
Korean concept (*jeong*), 40–41
Korean folk music, 36
Korean Protestant Christianity, 123
Krell, Elías, 15, 139–140, 147–148
Kristeva, Julia, 30
Kriya (band), 103

La Bohème, 64
Ladefoged, 36
Landers, Ann, 26
language: French, 9–10; gestural vs. spoken, 103–104; Náhuatl, 14–15; nonmanual markers, 104; romance languages, 55, 56–58; sonic characteristics of, 9–10
Lanza, Mario, 54, 55
laryngoscope, 28, 29
larynx, 9, 79
Las Vegas, 21–22, 71; "mini" impersonators, 83–87
Lau, Frederick, 27
Lavelle Preparatory Charter School, 212–213
lawn khāss (special color), 45–46
Lawrence, Martin, 107
Legend, John, 209
Le May, Alan, 34
Léry, Jean de, 8
Levin, David, 129
Lewandowski, Louis, 123
"Lift Every Voice and Sing" (Johnson), 134
Lifton, Robert Jay, 38
Lim, Connie (MILCK), 201–206
linguistic modes, 18
lining out, 34, 134
lip-synching, 83, 87–88, 97, 155–156, 174
listeners: aurality and, 9; blind, 79–81; d/Deaf, 80; Egyptian, 43; embodiment and, 10–11; Korean, 41
listening, 17; ethical, 123; by impersonators, 74; kinesthetic, 74; to one's own voice, 98–99; spiritual, 123; synaesthetic, 80; transvocality and, 139
listening gaze, 9
literacy, 10
literary theory, 12

literary voice, 26
A Little Bit of Heaven (film), 169, 172
Little E (Larry Gawatz), 84–89
"Little Girl" (Klipp), 143, 147, 150
"Little Legends" show Planet Hollywood Casino and Resort, Las Vegas), 83–87
"The Little Mermaid" (Andersen/ Disney film), 137–138, *166*, 170, 172, 174; competition, 165–166; critiques of, 175–176; singing careers launched by, 186
Little People, as impersonators, 83–87. *See also* short- statured performers
Little People of America (LPA), 86
Little Village Foundation, 209
"Londonderry Air" (song), 58–59
Loomis, Diane Merchant, 94
López, Sabrina, 77
The Lord's Song in a Strange Land: Music and Identity in Contemporary Jewish Worship (Summit), 126
lost voices, 177–196; difference and, 185; due to disability, 177–178, 181–182, 185–194; due to family and relationships, 180–181; epistemic injustice, 178, 192–193; neoliberalism and, 178–179; refugee status and border crossing, 182–184. *See also* voice loss
The Lost Voice (film), 173
Loving v. Virginia, 2
Løvland, Rolf, 58
"lowbrow", 54
Lucas, Lucia, 150–154
Lupton, Deborah, 28
The L Word (television show), 143
Lyiscott, Jamila, 176
Lyme disease, 186, 190, 194
Lynes, Russell, 54, 58
Lyrebird software, 163, 166

MacNamara, 60
Magowan, Fiona, 214
"make- it- your- own" phenomenon, 73
Making Music in the Arab World: The Culture and Artistry of Tarab (Racy), 45
Makoni, S., 13
Maler, Anabel, 111
"Mama" (Il Divo), 52–53
mammy character, 53
Mann, Chris, 106
Mann, Thomas, 164
Many Voices (Giddens), 1
maqam virtuosity, 42n, 43, 46
March For Our Lives (2018), 207–214

marginalization, 198; medical, 187–189, 193; neoliberalism reinforces, 4–5, 50, 198
Marín, Carlos, 58, 62–63, *62*, *63*
Marjory Stoneman Douglas High School (mass shooting), 207, 209, 213, 214
marketing strategies: advertising, 26–27, 119; popera, 52–55
Marshall, Chris, 162
Marty, Martin E., 117
Marx, Karl, 148
masculinity, 130, 142, 150–151, 152, 154, 156, 178
mashups, 132, 150
mask, resonance in singing, 25
mass shootings. *See* gun violence
materiality of vocality, 7, 11, 19
Mathews, Gordon, 37–38
"Maybe This Time" (Kander and Ebbs), 109
McCormack, John, 59
McCracken, Allison, 51, 53–54, 61
McIlroy, Guy, 96
McKay, George, 82–83
McNeal, Jeff, 73–74, 78
McPherson, Eve, 129
ME Action, 190
medical gaze, 28
medical system, disbelief of patients, 187–188, 191–193
Meizel, Katherine, 19
Melamed, Jodi, 5
Melba, Nellie, 51
melisma/ runs, 108–109, 134
Metamorphoses (Ovid), 163
methodology, 18–20
Mey, Jacob, 12
microphone- based singing styles, 39, 153; popera, 51, 61–64, 68
"middlebrow", 54–55, 58, 61
"Mideast X Midwest: A Dialogue of Music, Food, and Fun at America's Crossroads", 42
migration, transnational, 119–120
"Mikdash Melech" (Yiddish song), 132–134, *133*
MILCK (Connie Lim). *See* Lim, Connie (MILCK)
Miller, David, 56, 58, 61, 63, 64, 69
Miller, Edward Kerr, 18
Miller, Kathryn, 116, 125
Miller, Robert, 28
"mini" impersonators, 83–87
Minnelli, Liza, 109
minstrel repertoire, 34, 51, 53, 59, 65, 67
Mitchell, David T., 178

modes: *Ahava Rabbah*, *133*, 133–134; linguistic, 18; *nusach* (melodic modes), 126–127; Ukrainian Dorian, *133*, 133–134
Mollow, Anna, 191
monolinguality, 13
Monroe, Bill, 34
Montenegro, Daniel, 64
moral discourses: of disability, 82; of health, 28; mismatch between body and voice, 82; neoliberal control of voice, 175–176; silenced voices in film, 167–173; voice loss as punishment, 137
Morgan, Arwel Treharne, 99
morphemes, 104
Mortgage on Life (novel), 170
mothers, singing and, 180
mother songs, 53
muezzin, 129
multiculturalism, neoliberal, 5–6; "ethnic" timbres championed, 29; omnivory of, 38, 55
multilinguality, 13
multiple sclerosis (MS), 187
multivocality, 12–14; dialogic, 128; disability-induced, 177–178; dual vocality, 40, 47, 93, 102, 105, 113–114, 150; as resistance, 6, 17; temporal distortion of, 165; unwanted, 177–178; Western classical trained singers and, 21. *See also* popera/classical crossover; transvocality; vocality
multi-voicedness, 12
Mundy, Barbara, 120
Murdock, Lane, 208
Music and Letters, 7
musical theater, 31, 36, 36n, 37, 54, 60, 66, 69, 74, 108
music industry, 1, 5, 39, 50, 105; neoliberal global, 50. *See also* singing competitions
Musicking Bodies (Rahaim), 96–97
music videos, 97, 110
myalgica encephalomyelitis (ME)/chronic fatigue syndrome (CFS), 190–192, 194

Najarian, Lois, 52, 56
narrative voice, 26
nasality, 19–20, 34
Nashville (television show), 1
National Arab Orchestra, 42, 182
National School Walkouts (2018), 208
naturalist philosophy, 27
negative voice, 119
neoliberalism, 4–5; biosociality, 96; consumer choice, 38–39, 52, 117, 120; gun-control discourse and, 207; health and wellness discourse, 28, 178–179; hyperindividualism, 207; journey, notion of, 141; in Las Vegas imagery, 71; marginalization by, 4, 50, 198; marketability of voice, 25–26, 50, 58, 159–160; market system, 4–5; multiculturalism, 5–6; neoliberal subject, 5, 13, 25, 28, 159, 179; religion and, 117; as self-entrepreneur, 25, 159–160; voice control and, 174–175; voice loss and, 178–179
New Age movement, 117
Newell, Christopher, 61, 65
Newell, George, 61, 65
Newland, Marti, 65
New Lost City Ramblers, 34
New Vocality, 6
nigun (wordless Hasidic tune), 134
nodes (nodules on vocal folds), 37
non-auditory attending, 100
non-binarian vocality, 139
nonmanual markers, 104
non-verbal meanings, 10
nonviolence, performance of, 66
non-vocal/nonverbal communication, 11
Norris, Rebecca Sachs, 129
North Carolina heritage, 2, 3

Occupy Wall Street, 199
Ochoa Gautier, Ana Maria, 8–9
ocular-centrism, 74, 87
O'Dell, Adam, 121
The Odyssey of the Voice (Abitbol), 79
Of Grammatology (Derrida), 93
old-time music, 1–3, 32–39; folk-revival movements, 39
omnivory, shift from snobbery to, 38, 55
Ondine (Giradoux), 164
"On the Ethics of 'My' Art" (Torrence), 110–111
opera, 25, 35–37; Black singers, 65–69; bodies stilled, 97; as both democratic and elite, 57; Delsarte method of expression, 167; in film, 167; made unpopular, 50, 64; multi-sensory, 111–112; parlor songs and, 51; stealth-operatic singing, 63; transgender singers and, 151–152. *See also* popera/classical crossover
oppressive systems, 20, 27–28, 39, 94, 128, 132
orality, 10
ornithological imitation, 44
O'Shea, Helen, 59
Osseo-Asare, Afua, 28

INDEX

Otherness, 20, 79, 122, 160, 164
Ouatu, Cesar "The Voice", 57
Ovid, 163
The Oxford Handbook of Voice Studies, 147

Parkland, Florida (mass shooting), 198, 207, 208, 209, 210, 211, 212, 214
parlor songs, 51
Parsifal (Wagner), 97
Parsons, Talcott, 192
"Part of Your World" (song), 166
passing (transgender, vocal), 156–157
Patch, Holly, 11, 139
Pavarotti, Luciano, 64
Peaslee, Mike, 162
Pennington, Stephan, 156
Pennycook, A., 13
"people's microphone", 199–200, 213
performativity, 7, 25; disabled singers and, 83; raced body and, 205–206; in religion, 129
Performing Ethnomusicology: Teaching and Representation in World Music Ensembles (Kisliuk and Gross), 39
Perlman, Itzhak, 195
permeative experience, 74
"Peter Pan" (de Voil), 138–139
Peterson, Richard A., 38, 55
Pew Religion and Public Life Project, 117
pheno-song, 10
phoneme, 93
phonocentrism, 93–94
phonograph, 168
phrenology, 54
The Pirate Queen, 181
placement of voice, 99–100
Plasketes, George, 73
Plato, 162
Play It Again: Cover Songs in Popular Music, 73
plurality of voice, 2–3, 5–6
pluriphony, 6
"Poem for the Fallen" (Dahir), 212–213
political climate, multivocality and, 23
political vocality, 15–17, 23, 26–28, 198, 206–216
polyphony, 12
polyvocality, 12, 127–128
"Poor Mourner" (spiritual), 132–134, *133*
popera/ classical crossover, 21, 49–69; Anglophone pop ballads in romance languages, 55, 56–58; Black opera singers, space for, 65–69; as both democratic and elite, 57; defining, 50–52; diasporic history and repertoire, 58–61; marketing strategies, 52–55; "middlebrow" characteristics, 54, 61; mothers, homages to, 53; 19th-century songs in, 50, 55; racialized/ ethnic songs, 55; repertoire, 55–61; technique and technology, 61–65, *62, 63*; "vox populi" concept, 56–57. See also opera
PopMatters.com, 205
portmanteau culture, 49
postfeminist cultural studies, 170
postural orthostatic tachycardia syndrome (POTS), 186–187, 191, 194
Potter, John, 8
presence, 93
Presley, Elvis, 81; impersonations of, 72, 80, 84–87
Preston, Katherine, 25
Principe, Walter, 117
Problems of Dostoevsky's Poetics (Booth), 215
process, voice as, 4
protest culture, 175
Proutskova, Polina, 122
Pruitt-Hamm, Kaeley, 186–189, 192–194
Publius, Xavia, 142, 152, 155
Puccini arias, 55
Pulliam, Limmie, 31
Pure Country (film), 172
Pure Country 2: The Gift (film), 171
Pussy Hat Project, 202

al-Qasabji, Muhammad, 43–44
Quaker Society of Friends, 118
Queen Elisabeth competition (2000), 46
"Quiet" (MILCK and AG), 201–206, *203*
Al-Quntar, Lubana, 42–44, 46–47, 182, 195

Rabinow, Paul, 96
racialized body and voice, 9, 129; bone structure, colonial beliefs about, 76; disability and, 190; early 20th-century constructions, 51; "highbrow" and "lowbrow", 54; medical racial bias, 188; miscegenation fears, 65; politicization of, 204–205
racialized genres, 33–34
Racy, Ali, 44, 45
Radio From Hell show, 213
radio programming, 54
Rahaim, Matt, 96–97
Rainey, Ma, 32, 33
Raise Your Voice (film), 171
Raise Your Voice: The Sound of Student Protest (album), 210–214

Rajaram, Prem Kumar, 16
Rampton, Ben, 13–14
The Realm of Singing (Searing), 91
Rée, Jonathan, 88, 92, 93, 103–104
refugees, 42–46, 168, 173, 178, 182–184, 212, 213
regional differences, 33
register, 13, 41–42, 106
"Regresa a Mi" (Braxton/ Il Divo), 56, 62–63, *62, 63*
religion, 116–117; and silence, 118–119; religious conversion, 129–136. *See also* spiritual multivocality
Remembering the High Lonesome (documentary), 34
Rent (television show), 109
representations, 16–17, 73, 109; in scholarship, 20, 37, 39
resistance: borderscapes and, 15–16; Deaf culture and, 96; disability movement, 187; multivocality as, 6, 17; not singing as, 119; popera and, 50; singing, role in, 198–199; vocal, 198; voice as in need of liberation, 27
"Rise Up" (Day), 209
ritual, 12, 129
Riverdance, 59, 64, 181
Robert, Kati, 29
Robeson, Paul, 130, 135–136
rock and roll, 54, 58
Rodenburg, Patsy, 8
Roebuck, Janine, 99–100, 102, 111–114
role shifting, 109
Roloff family, 84
romance languages, 55, 56–58
Romantic nationalism, 197
Roof, Wade Clarke, 117, 120
Rose, Nikolas, 96
Rose, Noel R., 187
Rosenblatt, Yossele, 131–132
Ross, Alex, 97
Rossi, Allegra, 57, 63
Rousseau, Jean- Jacques, 9, 11
Ruderman, Jay, 102
Ruschman, Gary, 30–31
Russell, Anthony Mordechai Zvi, 22, 126, 128–129

Sachs, Curt, 45n10
Sakamoto, Kyu, 78
sampling library, 159–165
Samuels, Ellen, 192
Sandahl, Carrie, 83
Sanders, Bernie, 189

Sandy Hook Elementary School (mass shooting), 207, 210, 211, 214
Sanford, Sally, 9–10
San Francisco Boys Choir, 30
San Francisco Conservatory of Music, 156
Santo Daime religion, 120–121
Sataloff, Robert, 28
Saville- Troike, Muriel, 18
Saylor, Eric, 67
-scape suffix, 15–16
Schaefer, Ursula, 10
Schechner, Richard, 72
Scherer, Ronald, 79
school shootings, 198, 207–214
Schumann- Heink, Ernestine, 59
Schürmann, Volker, 11
sea- music community, 150–151
"Seasons of Love" (song), 109
Seattle World Trade Organization protests (1999), 199
Secret Garden (duo), 58
See Hear (television program) 99
See What I'm Saying? (documentary) 102–105, *107*
self: construction of, 11; as consumer choice, 38–39; digitally mediated, 37–38; discrete voices within, 41–42; ghost selves, 146–149; neoliberal subject, 25; postmodern, 38; spatialization of, 15; strategies of, 3, 73, 215; voice and sense of, 17
self- development, 25–28, 159–160, 178–179
self- narration, 4, 6, 13
Selfness, 140
self- presence, 93
Selma (film), 209
Semana.com (online magazine), 65
Sensing Sound: Singing and Listening as Vibrational Practice (Eidsheim), 120
Sensing the Rhythm: Finding My Voice in a World Without Sound (Harvey), 98
sensory experience of singing, 119–121, 124–125, 136, 139
"The Separation" (Flamer and Doleman), 210, 213
A Serious Man (film), 130
Shakin' All Over: Popular Music and Disability, 82–83
Shannon, James Royce, 60
shared traditions, 1–3, 34
al- Sharif, Samim, 43
Sherry, Fionnuala, 58
"Shine" (Garrity and Peña), 210. 211, 213

short- statured performers, 83–87. *See also* Little People as impersonators
Shubin, Sergei, 119–120
sign- gestures, 107
Signing Exact English (SEE II), 101
sign language, 22, 91–94, 109
Signmark (rapper), 92
sign- singing, 108–111
silence, 20, 91, 119
silencing, 3, 6, 40, 92; of disabled people, 189, 192; by family, 180–181
simcom, 101, 104
Sinclairé, Breanna, 142, 154–157
singing competitions, 1, 5–6, 50, 204; blind auditions, 31, 79–81; Corn Uí Riada, 181; disabled singers, 82; Eurovision Song Contest, 57, 59; "Find Your Voice" (Disney), 165–166; Tenor Competition, 59
"Singing Strange: Transvocality in North American Music Performance" (Krell), 139–140
Sing unto God (Friedman), 127
slave narratives, songs from, 3
Smith, Bessie, 32, 33
Smith, Jacob, 39
Smith, Mark, 111
snapping gesture, 107
Snyder, Sharon, 178
social justice activism, 186, 197–216
social media, 189–190, 194–195, 199–200; tweets and retweets, 199, 200
social movements of 1970s, 26
Solas, 32
Soler, Aeva, 212, 213
solo multi- instrumentalist, 5
solo voices, in religious settings, 122–123
Sonata (film), 173
song context, 18
"The Song Is You", 91, 98
"song leading", 127
sonic borderlands, 15, 140
Sontag, Susan, 191
soul, voice intertwined with, 117–118, 163–165, 171
sound, as multisensory phenomenon, 112
Soundiron, 159–162
soundtracks, cinematic, 55
spatialization of self, 15
Speak (Anderson), 170
speech, 18; privileging of, 93–94
Speech and Phenomena (Derrida), 93
Spencer, Leland G., 138
spiritual but not religious (SBNR), 117, 121

spirituality, 144; baby boomers and, 117; borderscapes and, 120, 136; voice as agent of the sacred, 117–118. *See also* spiritual multivocality
Spiritual Marketplace: Baby Boomers and the Remaking of American Religion (Roof), 117, 120
spiritual multivocality, 22, 115; acoustics in, 124–125; cantors, 126–127, 130–134, *133*; chanting, 122–123; communal singing, 121, 122, 125; creation, sense of, 124; decision not to sing, 118–119; faith- based sensations, 119–120; intent and, 125–128, 131; outsider participation in worship, 116; polyvocality, 127–128; sensory experience of singing, 119–121, 124–125, 136, 139; solo voices in religious settings, 122–123; spiritual mobility, 119–128; transcendence, experience of, 117–118, 121–122, 124; (en)voicing intersectionality, 129–136. *See also* religion; spirituality
spirituals, 65–66
Spivak, Gayatri, 93
Spohr, Arne, 116
Spoon, Rae, 147
Spurlock, Michelle, 104, 108
stadium venues, 52, 59, 64
Staley, Peter, 190
Standard English, 13
staring, 83, 87
state aurality, 9
Stephens, Gregg, 162
Stevens, Joe, 147
Stewart, Donald, 26
Stirner, Max, 148
Stockley, Miriam, 160
The Stolen Voice (Crane/ film), 167, 168
Storbeck, Claudine, 96
Storey, John, 50
Stover, Cassandra, 170
Stras, Laurie, 179
Straus, Joseph, 80, 112
Strauss, Johann, 43
Streisand, Barbra, 53, 188
Strüver, Anke, 15–16, 73
student activists, 198, 207–214
Students Demand Action, 211
Suarez, Tyler, 211–212
subject, neoliberal, 5, 13, 25, 28, 159, 179
subjectivities, vocal, 3
subject positions, 15
subjugation, liberation from, 27

Suggs, Karl, 88
Sumi Jo (Jo Sumi), 41
Summit, Jeffrey A., 126
Sundberg, Johan, 36
Sung, Heather, 123
Supreme Court, 197
Svengali (character), 168, 170, 174
Swish: My Quest to Become the Gayest Person Ever and What Ended Up Happening Instead (Derfner), 124, 185
Symposium (Plato), 162
synaesthesia, 80, 110, 112
"syndrome," association with controversy, 191
Syria, 182–183

"Taghrid al-Balabil" ("The Warbling of the Nightingales") (al-Qasabji). *See* "Ya Toyour" ("Oh, Birds") (al-Qasabji)
"taking the mic," as expression, 199
tarab music, 42–47
taste-making journalism, 54
Taylor, Charles, 27
technology: 20th-century recordings and, 39; digital, 37–38; digital sampling, 23, 159; gendered, 174; popera and, 61–65, 62, 63; social media, 189–190, 194–195; voice as technology of self-development, 25–26
Tee Set (band), 78
telephone, as isolating, 97
television, 52, 107, 170
temporal displacement, 29
Tenor Competition, 59
tenors, 50; The American Tenors, 60, 64; Black tenors, 66; Forte (tenor trio), 61; Irish tenor crossover music, 58–61; The Irish Tenors, 59–60; "the people's tenor", 57; "Three Mo' Tenors", 66–67; Three Tenors, 55, 59, 66; Twelve Irish Tenors, 53, 60
Terry, Jon, 85
tessitura, 153
testimonial injustice, 192–193
Tête à Tête Festival, 111
Tetteroo, Peter, 78
theater, musical, 36
"The Truth: We Need Change" video, 212
third culture, 95, 102, 110
This is Not the End (album), 207
Thompson, Joe, 2
"Three Mo' Divas: A Celebration of Class, Sass, and Style", 66
"Three Mo' Tenors, That's Us" (song), 67
throat modeling, 74
thumbprint, vocal, 29–32, 79

timbre, 12–13, 18, 29, 31, 32–39, 45, 62, 65, 89, 154–155, 160
Titze, Ingo, 19–20, 28
Toledo Symphony Orchestra, 42, 182
Tomorrow Is My Turn (Giddens), 2
Torrence, Stephen, 110–111
Tourneur, Maurice, 167, 168
"Toward an Ethnology of Speaking" (Hymes), 18
trans, defining, 140–142
transgender/ trans* people, 214; deception attributed to, 156, 193; vocal passing, 156–157
transgender/ trans* singers, 11, 22–23, 137, 178; non-binarian vocality, 139; singing guides for, 146; transfeminine singers, 142, 150–158, 178; transmasculine singers, 141–150; transvocality, 138–140, 146, 150; unchanged singing voices, 150–154
transition, 23, 140–141
transmasculinity, 139, 141, 144, 147
transparency, 137
transvestism, theatrical, 21
transvocality, 138–140, 146, 150
tribute bands, 73, 78
Trilby (du Maurier/ film), 167–168, 170, 173
Trump, Donald, 188–189, 198, 207, 214
truth-bearers, 206
tuning fork, 7
Tunnell, Keith, 34
Türken, Salman, 25, 159
Turner, Brock, 189
Turner, Tina, impersonation of, 74–75, 155
Turner, Victor, 12, 72
Tyson, Lee, 141, 144

Uí Cheallaigh, Áine, 181–182, 184, 195
Umm Kulthum, 42, 43
"Unbreak My Heart"/ "Regresa a Mi" (Braxton/ Il Divo), 56, 62–63, 62, 63
"Unchained Melody", 55, 56
unhealth, 28, 177–178
United States: presidential election of 2016, 188; religious fluidity in, 116–117, 120
unvocality, 7
Utz, Christian, 27

Vadas, Peter, 191
value, voice as, 4–6
Vande Kemp, Hendrika, 26
Vanderhoef, Susanne, 122, 123
vaudeville, 51–54, 59
Vaughan, Sarah, 152

Vegas. *See* Las Vegas
ventriloquism, 72, 81
Ventura, Patricia, 71
Very Special Arts (VSA), 91
Victims of Immigration Crime Engagement (VOICE), 198
Victoria, Adia, 35
Victorian cult of motherhood, 53
violence, vocal resistance to, 198–199
Virginia Slims, 27
visual/aural incongruities, 31, 72–73, 167; blind auditions, 31, 79–81; impersonation and, 75
visual phonics, 103–104
viva voce (live voice), 199
"vocal authority", 8
"vocal fry", 61–62, 65
vocal timbre. *See* timbre
vocality: contested spaces, 15–16; definitions of, 7–11, 13; dual, 40, 47, 93, 102, 105, 113–114, 150, 206; as embodied process, 11; as epistemology, 6, 8, 17, 215; hybrid, 139; imitation as essential for acquiring, 36; as intermediate between orality and literacy, 10; materiality of, 7, 11, 19; multiple, 6–7; negative, 174; as ontology, 6, 8, 17, 215; political, 15–17, 23, 26–28, 198, 205–216; racializations of, 9, 76; relationship between singer and listener, 10–11; as vowel-ness, 7, 45. *See also* multivocality
Vocaloid systems, 160
Vocal Tracks: Performance and Sound Media (Smith), 39
La Voce (Watson, album), 57
voice: acousmatic, 72, 80; agency intertwined with, 179; as borderscape, 15–17, 46–47, 184; collective, 12–13; distributed, 198–199; inclusive model of, 198; liberation from hegemony, 27; material, 138, 179; as metaphor for difference, 8–9, 138; metaphorical, 179, 192; neoliberal "offer" of, 4–5, 29; as process, 4; as secret, 74; sense of self and, 17; soul intertwined with, 117–118, 163–165, 171; spectral autonomy of, 88; as static possession, 2; as technology of self-development, 25–26; uniqueness of, 31; as value, 4; vocality distinguished from, 10. *See also* finding a voice
voice actors, 73
A Voice and Nothing More (Dolar), 162
voice-body divorce, 97

voice control, 144, 159–176; acquired voicelessness in film history, 167–172; disability-induced loss of, 178; global voice loss, 172–173; loss of physical voice, 178; non-singing sounds as "human", 162; reasons for voice loss, 173–174; *Voices of Rapture* software, 159–162; women's voices in film, 167–172. *See also* lost voices; voice loss
voice feminization surgery, 142
voice loss, 123–124, 215; in film, 167–172; gender and agency as factors, 174–175; identity and, 23, 164; morality and, 168–173; as punishment, 137; as strategy, 169; in "The Little Mermaid", 164–165; trauma and, 23, 178–179. *See also* disability; lost voices; voice control
The Voice of China, 204
"voice of the people", 199, 201
Voices of Rapture software, 159–162
The Voice (album), 57
"The Voice" (Graham), 57
The Voice singing competition, 31, 106, 204
The Voice Thief (film), 173
Vokalität, 10
vote, as term, 197
vowel-ness, 7, 45–46
vowels, 36–37, 43, 56
vox populi, 197; in popera, 49, 56–57
Vygotsky, Lev, 11, 73

Wagner, Richard, 97
Wallach, Jeremy, 54
Walt Disney Company, 165
Watson, Russell, 57
ways of speaking, 18
Weatherly, Fred, 59
websites, 52
"We Can" (High School for Recording Arts), 213
Wells-Jensen, Sheri, 79–81
"We Shall Overcome", 208
Western classical terminology, privileging of, 20
Westlife (Irish boy band), 58
"What Happens When You Have a Disease Doctors Can't Diagnose" (Brea), 190
"When David Heard" (Dinnerstein), 124–125
white supremacy, 4
"Why Voice Now?" colloquy, 15
Wilbourne, Emily, 15
will, 25

"Will There Really Be a Morning?" (Dickinson), 195
Wilson, James, 197
Winehouse, Amy, 76–77
Wohlberg, Max, 130
Wolf, Ellen, 29, 31
Wolof communities (Senegal), 18
A Woman's Secret (film), 169–170
women: as audience, 52–54; disability and, 186–9, 192–195; female voice sexualized, 119, 164, 166–168; public singing, rise in, 174; singing as feminine, 174; as symbols of classed and racialized aesthetic, 54; voice loss in film, 167–174
Women's March on Washington, D.C. (2017), 200–203
Women's March organization, 208
Women's March rallies, 175, 188–189
Wong, Deborah, 206
Woolard, Kathryn A., 13
Workman, Ritch, 86
world music ensembles, 39
Wrazen, Louise Josepha, 214

X Factor, 82, 170

Yassin, Bavi, 173
"Ya Toyour" ("Oh, Birds") (al-Qasabji), 44–47
Yearsley, Madison, 210–211
Yentl (musical film), 188
Yiddish repertoire, 128–135
Young, Vershawn Ashanti, 13–14
"You Raise Me Up" (Graham), 57, 58 106
YouTube, 78, 82, 110, 202
yuppies (young socioeconomically mobile white people), 190

Zero-G, 160
Zigeunerlieder (Brahms), 130
Žižek, Slavoj, 88
Zuhur, Sherifa, 44, 45
Zumthor, Paul, 10